Why Do You Need This New Edition?

If you're wondering why you should buy this new edition of *Fifty Great Essays*, here are four great reasons:

1 One quarter of the essays are new to this edition ranging from beloved classics to new contemporary works.

2 New essays include selections from such esteemed writers as Herman Melville and G. K. Chesterton to dynamic contemporary voices like Mark Doty.

3 You'll also find new essays from such widely admired writers as James Baldwin, Barbara Kingsolver, and Lewis Thomas.

4 A new thematic Table of Contents invites you to explore the essays by theme including: Identity, Gender, Families, Education, Nature and Environment, Language and Thought, Ethics and Values, and Work and Play.

W9-CLN-652

PEARSON

ROBERT DIYANNI is a professor of Humanities at New York University. Dr. DiYanni, who holds a B.A. from Rutgers University and a Ph.D. from the City University of New York, has taught English and Humanities at a variety of institutions, including NYU, CUNY, and Harvard. He has written and edited many books for college students of writing, literature, and humanities.

PENGUIN ACADEMICS

FIFTY GREAT ESSAYS

FIFTH EDITION

Edited by

Robert DiYanni

New York University

Boston   Columbus   Indianapolis   New York   San Francisco   Upper Saddle River
Amsterdam   Cape Town   Dubai   London   Madrid   Milan   Munich   Paris   Montréal   Toronto
Delhi   Mexico City   São Paulo   Sydney   Hong Kong   Seoul   Singapore   Taipei   Tokyo

Senior Sponsoring Editor: Katharine Glynn
Assistant Editor: Rebecca Gilpin
Senior Marketing Manager: Sandra McGuire
Senior Supplements Editor: Donna Campion
Production Manager: Frances Russello

Full Service Project Management: Hema Latha/Integra
Cover Design Manager: Jayne Conte
Cover Designer: Suzanne Behnke
Cover Art: Trail in a Bamboo Forest © maida
Printer/Binder: Edwards Brothers Malloy
Cover Printer: Lehigh Phoenix

Credits and acknowledgments borrowed from other sources and reproduced, with permission, in this textbook appear on the appropriate page within text on pages 315–318.

For more information about the Penguin Academics series, please contact us by mail at Pearson Education, attn. Marketing Department, 51 Madison Avenue, 28th Floor, New York, NY 10010, or visit us online at www.pearsonhighered.com/english.

Library of Congress Cataloging-in-Publication Data

Fifty great essays/edited by Robert DiYanni.—5th ed.
    p. cm.—(Penguin academics)
  Includes bibliographical references and index.
  ISBN-13: 978-0-321-84849-9
  ISBN-10: 0-321-84849-7
  1. College readers.   2. English language—Rhetoric—Problems, exercises, etc.   I. DiYanni, Robert.   II. Title: 50 great essays.
  PE1417.F49 2013
  808'.0427—dc23

                                        2012023576

10 9 8 7 6 5 4 3—EBM—16 15 14 13

PEARSON

ISBN 10:   0-321-84849-7
ISBN 13: 978-0-321-84849-9

For Eric Wimmers
Cherished Friend and Colleague

contents

preface

Fifty Great Essays is one volume of a two-book series designed to provide college students and teachers with an outstanding collection of essays for use in university writing courses. These volumes are based upon the conviction that reading and writing are reciprocal acts that should be married rather than divorced. Because reading and writing stimulate and reinforce one another, it is best that they be allied rather than separated. In learning to read and respond critically both to their own writing and to the writing of others, students mature as writers themselves.

Fifty Great Essays offers a compendium of the best essays written during the past four hundred years. Readers will find here essays by the great early practitioners of the genre, Montaigne and Bacon, as well as numerous examples from the centuries that follow, both classic and contemporary. Taken together, the essayists whose work is anthologized here offer an abundance of nonfiction that takes the form of autobiographical and polemical essays, observations and speculations, reminiscences and sketches, meditations and expostulations, celebrations and attacks. Overall, the selections balance and blend the flamboyant and innovative with the restrained and classically lucid.

Each of the essays in *Fifty Great Essays* can be considered "great," but is not necessarily great in the same way. Montaigne's greatness as an essayist is not Franklin's, nor is Hazlitt's essay writing matched equivalently by Swift's. And Orwell's greatness, inspired by a political animus, differs dramatically from that of E. B. White, whose inspiration and emphasis derive less from grand social issues than from personal observation and experience. Yet however much these essayists and essays differ, two aspects of greatness they share are readability and teachability. Whether classic, modern, or contemporary, and whatever their styles, subjects, and rhetorical strategies, these fifty essays are worth reading and teaching. They have served students and teachers of reading and writing well for many years.

What's New in the Fifth Edition

1. One quarter of the essays are new to this edition ranging from beloved classics to new contemporary works.
2. New essays include selections from such esteemed writers as Herman Melville and G. K. Chesterton to dynamic contemporary voices like Mark Doty.
3. You'll also find new essays from such widely admired writers as James Baldwin, Barbara Kingsolver, and Lewis Thomas.
4. A new thematic Table of Contents and a new Rhetorical Table of Contents have been added to offer ways of teaching the essays found in the anthology.
5. In response to instructors' requests, headnotes have been sharpened and tightened.

This collection should be of great value to university instructors who are teaching writing courses both introductory and advanced. They will find here an abundance of outstanding writing to serve as models for their students—models of style and structure, models of thought and feeling expressed in, with, and through carefully wrought language.

Students will find in this collection a source of ideas and models for their own writing. They will also discover here writers who will serve as inspiration and influence as they develop their own styles and voices. In studying these essays as models of good writing, students will profit from analyzing not so much what these writers say, but as how they say what they do.

Writers, too, can benefit from reading the essays collected here and studying the craftsmanship they embody. Montaigne's ease and elegance, and his quirky individuality, while not easily imitated, provide an example of how the familiar material of everyday life can be artfully blended with the exploration of ideas. Bacon's pithy prose exemplifies ideas expressed with aphoristic acuteness. And while these early stars of the constellation of essayists may shine more brightly than others, writers who read with care the contemporary pieces collected here will learn new tricks of the trade and discover unexpected surprises and pleasures.

The heart and soul of *Fifty Great Essays* are fifty outstanding essays. The essays provide a rich sampling of styles and voices across a wide spectrum of topics. They range in length and complexity—some more accessible, others more challenging—all worth reading. These fifty essays provide excellent opportunities for readers to meet new writers and to become reacquainted with writers and essays they already know. General readers—both those who have completed their formal education and those still in college—will find in these excellent essays promises and provocations, ideas to respond to and wrestle with, and sometimes argue against.

The Introduction to *Fifty Great Essays* provides an historical overview of the essay from antiquity to the present. It traces developments in the ways writers used essays to entertain readers as well as to inform and persuade them, and it describes the wide range of interests that writers of essays have pursued over the centuries. The Introduction also includes discussion of various types of essays and the pleasures that readers find in them.

Guidelines for reading essays are identified and exemplified with a close reading of a contemporary essay—Annie Dillard's "Living Like Weasels." Readers are provided with a series of guiding questions, commentary about the essay's style and voice, as well as its structure and ideas. The guidelines for reading essays are supplemented by guidelines for writing them. A discussion of the qualities of good writing is supplemented by an approach to the writing process, which includes consideration of three major phases or stages—planning, drafting, and revising.

In addition to a set of general essay-writing guidelines, the Introduction provides an approach to writing about reading, with sample text from Susan Sontag's essay "A Woman's Beauty: Put-Down or Power Source?" The approach to writing about Sontag's essay takes the form of strategies for blending critical reading and writing, including annotating, freewriting, using a double-column notebook, and writing a summary. A further set of guidelines linking reading with writing focuses on observing details, making connections, drawing inferences, and formulating an interpretation. Throughout the discussion of writing and the sample demonstration, the emphasis is on analysis, reflection, and deliberation—on considering what the essayist is saying, what the reader thinks of it, and why.

Students should be interested in the Introduction's advice about how to read essays critically and thoughtfully. Other readers may be interested in the historical overview of the essay's development. And all readers can practice their reading skills by reading Susan Sontag's essay "A Woman's Beauty: Put-Down or Power Source?" along with the commentary that explains and explores the writer's ideas.

Each essay in *Fifty Great Essays* is preceded by a biographical sketch and headnote. The biographical information provides context, while the commentary provides a starting point for consideration of the writer's ideas and values. Three questions for thinking and writing follow each essay. All in all, *Fifty Great Essays* should provide readers with many hours of reading pleasure and numerous ideas and models for writing.

Patient and persistent work with *Fifty Great Essays* in the classroom and out will help users understand the qualities of good writing and discover ways to emulate it. With the guided practice in critical reading and essay writing that *Fifty Great Essays* provides, students will increase both their competence and their confidence as perceptive readers and as cogent and able writers. Through repeated acts of attention to their own writing and to the writing of others, students can be expected to acquire a sense of the original meaning of "essay": a foray into thought, an attempt to discover an idea, work out its implications, and express it with distinctiveness. Readers and users of *Fifty Great Essays* should come to see the essay as a way of enriching their experience and their thinking while discovering effective ways to share them with others.

Robert DiYanni
New York University

Introduction: Reading and Writing Essays

History and Context

The essay has a long and distinguished history. Its roots go back to Greco-Roman antiquity. Forerunners of the essay include the Greek writer Plutarch (46–120), whose *Parallel Lives* of noble Greeks and Romans influenced the art of biography, and who also wrote essays in his *Moralia*. The early Roman writer Seneca, a philosopher, dramatist, and orator, also wrote essays in the grand manner of classical oratory, on topics that include "Asthma" and "Noise." These two early western writers of essays are complemented by a pair of Japanese writers: Sei Shonagon, a court lady who lived and wrote in the tenth century, and Yoshida Kenko (1283–1350), a poet and Buddhist monk, whose brief, fragmentary essays echo the quick brushstrokes of Zen painting.

In one sense, the modern essay begins with Michel de Montaigne in France and with Francis Bacon in England. Both writers published books of essays at the end of the sixteenth century. Montaigne's first two books of essays came out together in 1580 and Bacon's first collection in 1597. Each followed with additional volumes—Montaigne in 1588, and Bacon in 1612 and 1625. With each later volume, both writers revised and expanded essays previously published in the earlier volumes as well as added new ones. They also wrote longer and more elaborate essays from one collection to the next.

Generally recognized as the father of the essay, Michel de Montaigne called his works *essais*, French for attempts. In his essays, Montaigne explored his thinking on a wide variety of subjects, including virtue and vice, customs and behavior, children and cannibals. Although Montaigne's first essays began as reflections about his reading and made liberal use of quoted passages, his later essays relied much less on external sources for impetus and inspiration.

The power of Montaigne's essays derives largely from their personal tone, their improvisatory nature, and their display of an energetic and inquiring mind. In his essays, Montaigne talks about himself and the world as he experienced it. He repeatedly tests his opinions and presents an encyclopedia of information that sets him thinking. Amid an essay's varied details, Montaigne reveals himself, telling us what he likes, thinks, and believes. The openness and flexibility of his essay form make its direction unpredictable, its argument arranged less as a logical structure than as a meandering exploration of its subject. But what may be most impressive about Montaigne's essays is that they reveal his mind in the act of thinking. The self-revelatory circling around his subject constitutes the essential subject of the essays. Ironically, in reading him we learn not only about Montaigne but about ourselves.

Another Renaissance writer credited with an influential role in the development of the essay is Francis Bacon—statesman, philosopher, scientist, and essayist. Unlike Montaigne, who retired from active political life early to read, reflect, and write in his private library tower, Bacon remained politically active and intellectually prominent until the last few years of his life. His life and work exhibit a curious interplay between ancient and modern forms of thought. Coupled with a modernity that valued experiment and individual experience was a respect for the authority of tradition. Bacon's scientific and literary writings both display this uneasy alliance of tradition and innovation.

Bacon's essays differ from Montaigne's in striking ways. First, most of Bacon's essays are short. Second, his essays are much less personal than Montaigne's. And third, many of Bacon's essays offer advice on how to live. Their admonitory intent differs from Montaigne's more exploratory temper.

Eighteenth-century America included a profusion of essayists writing in a variety of nonfictional forms. Thomas Paine wrote essays of political persuasion in the periodical *The Crisis.* J. Hector St. John de Crèvecoeur wrote his essayistic *Letters from an American Farmer.* And Benjamin Franklin compiled his *Autobiography* and his *Poor Richard's Almanack,* which is a loosely stitched collection of aphorisms, including "haste makes waste," "a stitch in time saves nine," and "Fish and visitors stink after three days."

During the eighteenth century, more and more writers produced essays, along with their work in other genres. Among them are Samuel Johnson (1709–1784), whose philosophical and moral periodical essays appeared regularly in his own *Rambler, Idler,* and *Adventurer.* The gravity and sobriety of Johnson's essays were complemented by the more lighthearted and satirical vein mined by Joseph Addison (1672–1719) and Richard Steele (1672–1729), whose essays in their *Tatler* and *Spectator* periodicals, which they jointly wrote and published, were avidly awaited when they appeared, as often as three times a week. Jonathan Swift (1667–1745), best known for his satire *Gulliver's Travels,* also wrote a number of essays, including what is perhaps the most famous satirical essay ever written (and the essay with one of the longest titles): "A Modest Proposal for Preventing the Children of the Poor People in Ireland from being a Burden to their Parents or Country; and for making them beneficial to their Publick."

The nineteenth century saw the rise of the essay less as moralistic and satirical than as entertaining and even a bit eccentric. Among the most notable practitioners were Charles Lamb (1775–1834), whose *Essays of Elia* and *More Essays of Elia* are constructed to read less like random assortments than as books centered on characters, and whose stories form a loose plot. Among these essays is his "A Bachelor's Complaint," in which Lamb, himself a lifelong bachelor, takes up a list of grievances he holds against his married friends and acquaintances. Complementing the playful essays of Charles Lamb during this time are the passionate and highly opinionated essays of William Hazlitt (1778–1830), a friend of the English Romantic poets William Wordsworth and Samuel Taylor Coleridge. Hazlitt's "On the Pleasure of Hating" is written with his customary "gusto," a characteristic he brought to his writing from his life and one in synch with the Romantic poets' emphasis on the importance of feeling.

Nineteenth-century American essayists include the powerful twosome of Ralph Waldo Emerson and Henry David Thoreau. Emerson's essays grew out of his public lectures. He was at home in the form and wrote a large number of essays in a highly aphoristic style that contained nuggets of wisdom served up in striking images and memorably pithy expressions. A few quotable examples include "hitch your wagon to a star," "trust thyself," and "give all to love." Much of Emerson's writing focused on nature, which he envisioned as a divine moral guide to life.

Thoreau, a friend and protégé of Emerson, was another New Englander who limned the natural world in prose. Like Emerson, Thoreau wrote essays on a variety of topics, but mostly about nature. Thoreau's most famous essay, however, is political—his "On the Duty of Civil Disobedience"—in which he argues that each individual human being has not only the right but the obligation to break the law when the law is unjust or immoral. Thoreau's "Civil Disobedience," a much-cited essay, has also been an influential one, affecting the stances of peaceful nonviolent political resistance taken up by both Mahatma Gandhi and Martin Luther King, Jr. But it is Thoreau's *Walden* that contains his most beautifully crafted essays in his most artfully composed book. Who can forget the matchless prose of sentences such as, "If a man cannot keep pace with his companions, perhaps he hears the sound of a different drummer. Let him step to the music which he hears, however measured or far away."

If in one sense the Renaissance can be considered the beginnings of the modern essay, in another, the modern essay is synonymous with the twentieth-century essay, a period in which the essay developed into a literary genre that began to rival fiction and poetry in importance. George Orwell (1903–1950), best known for his satirical *Animal Farm* and *1984,* is equally eminent for the four thick volumes of essays and letters he produced. Orwell's "A Hanging" and "Shooting an Elephant" are modern classics of the genre, as is his "Politics and the English Language," perhaps the best-known essay on language in English. Another English writer better known for her work as a novelist, Virginia Woolf (1882–1941), like Orwell, left a splendid set of essay volumes, including her "Common Reader" series, in which she presents her views on a wide range of authors and works of literature in a relaxed, casual style. "The Death of the Moth" is deservedly among her most highly regarded essays.

On the twentieth-century American scene, E. B. White (1899–1985) stands out as a modern master of the genre. White, too, is best known for his fiction, in his case the books he wrote for children, all gems with the diamond among them the ever-popular *Charlotte's Web.* White published many of his essays in the *New Yorker* and a number of others in *Harper's* magazine. "Once More to the Lake," his best known and oft-reprinted essay, is also among his most beautifully written, and some would argue, among his most enduring contributions to literature.

Along with White, who rarely wrote about social issues per se, there is James Baldwin (1924–1987), who wrote almost exclusively about race, particularly about race relations in America and about his place in society as a black man and a writer. In fact, Baldwin's consistent theme is identity, his identity as a black writer, who became an expatriate, living in Paris, in part to discover what it meant for him to be an American. A third modern American essayist is James Thurber, a humorist who published satirical cartoons, humorous stories, and parables, as well as journalism. His "The Secret Life of Walter Mitty" and "The Catbird Seat" are two comic story masterpieces. His *My Life and Hard Times* is a classic of American autobiography, and his *Is Sex Necessary?* a spoof on pop psychology.

At the beginning of the twenty-first century, the essay is continuing to thrive. Essayists of all stripes and persuasions continue to publish in magazines and anthologies and in books of collected essays. The annual series, *The Best American Essays,* has recently celebrated its twenty-fifth anniversary. Other annual series of essays have joined it, notably *The Anchor Essay Annual.* These essay volumes are joined by others that are not part of any annual series, but which, nevertheless, come out with great frequency and regularity. The essay, in short, is alive and well in the new millennium.

Pleasures of the Essay

But why has the essay been so well regarded for such a long time? What attracts readers to essays? And what attracts writers to the form? Why has the essay endured?

One answer lies in the wide variety the genre affords. There are essays for everybody, essay voices and visions and styles to suit every taste, to satisfy every kind of intellectual craving. There is variety of subject—of topic—from matters of immediate and practical concern to those of apparently purely theoretical interest; from essays of somber gravity to those in a lighter more playful vein; from easy essays on familiar topics to complex and challenging ones on subjects outside the bounds of most readers' knowledge and experience.

An essay can be about anything. And essayists have written about every topic under the sun, from their own lives and experience to what they have read and observed in the world, to their speculations and imaginings. All of these are available, for example, in Montaigne's little essay, "Of Smells." In fact, to list just a handful of the more than one hundred essays Montaigne alone wrote is to convey a sense of the essay's bewildering variety. In addition to "Of Smells," Montaigne wrote "Of Friendship," "Of Sadness," "Of Idleness," "Of Liars," "Of Constancy," "Of Solitude," "Of Sleep," "Of Fear," "Of Age," "Of Prayers," "Of Conscience," "How We Cry and Laugh for the Same Thing," "Of Moderation," "Of Thumbs," "Of Cannibals," "Of Names," "Of Virtue," "Of Anger," "Of Vanity," "Of Cruelty," "Of Cripples," "Of Glory," "Of Presumption," "Of Books," "How Our Mind Hinders Itself," "That Our Desire Is Increased By Difficulty," "Of the Inconsistency of Our Actions," "Of the Love of Fathers for Their Children," and "That to Philosophize Is to Learn to Die." A similarly wide-ranging list of topics could be culled from Bacon's essays, expressing an equally strong interest in the human condition.

For all his essayistic variety, Montaigne did not write much about nature. Many others, however, have written about the natural world, including Ralph Waldo Emerson in "Nature," N. Scott Momaday in "The Way to Rainy Mountain," Annie Dillard in "Living Like Weasels," Mark Twain in "Reading the River," and Virginia Woolf in "The Death of the Moth." In each of these essays the writer describes an encounter with nature and explores his or her relationship to it.

When not writing about themselves or about nature, and when not speculating on one or another aspect of the human condition, essayists often write about the social world. Joan Didion's "Marrying Absurd" is about Las Vegas weddings; James Thurber's "University Days" about college; and Pico Iyer's "Nowhere Man" about living in multiple places and being a member of no single social group.

Identity, in fact, is a frequent topic among contemporary essayists, with writers exploring their roots and their relationships in essays that touch on race and gender, and on broad social and cultural values. James Baldwin explores what it means to be a black man in a white world; Frederick Douglass writes about his struggle for literacy as a black slave; Judith Ortiz Cofer writes about her dual cultural and linguistic identity; Martin Luther King, Jr., writes about racial prejudice and injustice, and what must be done to establish and ensure racial equality, and why; and Jamaica Kincaid writes about finding and valuing her Caribbean Antiguan identity under the seductive influence of British colonial culture.

Issues of gender are equally important for essayists. Gretel Ehrlich writes about what it means to be a cowboy who cares for animals as an integral part of his life, and of how cowboys, if they are to be good at what they do, need as much maternalism as machismo, if not a good deal more. Maxine Hong Kingston writes about the power and place of gender in traditional China by telling the story of a man, Tang Ao, who visits the land of women, is captured, and is transformed into a woman. Another strong woman who appears in an essay is N. Scott Momaday's Kiowa Indian grandmother, who reflects the cultural values of her tribe and its Native American tradition.

Besides a wide variety of topics and a broad spectrum of human concerns, including gender, race, culture, and identity, essays appeal, too, because of their style, the craftsmanship and beauty with which they are written. And just as there are many essay subjects, so also are there many styles. There are as many styles, in fact, as essayists, for each essayist of distinction develops his or her own style, finding a voice and tone appropriate to the topic, audience, and situation that occasioned the writing of each essay.

E. B. White's "Once More to the Lake" is written in a style at once easy and elegant, familiar and formal, in a splendid blend of language that is as easy on the ear as it is on the eye. For the sheer beauty of language, it begs to be read aloud. George Orwell's "Shooting an Elephant" is less lyrical but no less memorable, written in a style that seems to be no style at all—as clear as a windowpane. Amy Tan's "Mother Tongue" is written in a mixture of styles, an indication that she speaks more than one brand of English, as she describes the worlds of English both she and her Chinese mother inhabit. Langston Hughes uses a simple and direct style in his "Salvation," which tells the story of his religious "anti-conversion." Martin Luther King, Jr., writes in a style that appeals to thinking people, as he develops his own arguments and rebuts the arguments of others about the right of African Americans to protest against racial injustice.

Types of Essays

The word "essay" comes from the French *essai* (essay), which derives from the French verb *essayer*—to try or attempt. The word "essay" suggests less a formal and systematic approach to a topic than a casual, even random one. In this sense, an essay differs from other prose forms such as the magazine article, whose purpose is usually to inform or persuade, and the review, which evaluates a book or performance. Essays, to be sure, may also evaluate, and they often inform as well as persuade. But their manner of going about offering information, making a case, and providing an evaluation differs from those less variable genres.

The essay can be compared with the short story in that some essays, like short stories, include narrative. But the short story is fiction, the essay fact. And fiction works largely by implication, the essay mostly by expository discursiveness. Essays explain what stories imply. This is not to say that essayists don't make use of fictional techniques and strategies. They do so often, particularly in personal or familiar essays, which include narration and description.

The essay can also be linked with poetry, particularly with the more discursive poems that explain as well as image ideas that tell straightforwardly rather than hint or suggest in a more oblique manner. Essayists, on the other hand, typically say what's on their mind fairly directly. They explain what they are thinking. Poets more often write about one thing in terms of another (they write about love, for example, in terms of war). And they prefer implication to explication, which is more characteristic of the essay writer.

Kinds of essays include, broadly, personal essays and formal essays. Personal essays are those in which the writer is amply evident—front and center. Employing the personal pronoun "I," personal essays include opinions and perspectives explicitly presented as the writer's own in a personal, even idiosyncratic, manner. Formal essays, by contrast, typically avoid the pronoun "I," and they omit personal details. Formal essays include expository essays, analytical essays, and argumentative, or persuasive, essays. Expository essays explain ideas and scenarios using standard patterns of organization, including comparison and contrast, classification, and cause and effect. Analytical essays offer an analysis and interpretation of a text or performance, typically breaking that text or performance into parts or aspects, and presenting both an evaluative judgment and the evidence on which it is based. Argumentative, or persuasive, essays advance a thesis or claim and present evidence that is organized as part of a logical demonstration, utilizing the modes of deductive and inductive reasoning and including support for the argumentative claim in the form of reasons, examples, and data as evidence.

Most essays, even the most personal ones, are composites and blends. They may tell personal stories rich in descriptive detail to provide evidence to support an idea or claim to persuasion. They may use traditional patterns of expository organization such as comparison and contrast in the cause of developing a logical argument. And they may include information and explanation along with personal experience and argumentation. More often than not, the most interesting and memorable of essays mix and match what are typically thought of as distinct essay types and the conventions associated with them. Contemporary essayists, in particular, cross borders and mix modes, as they write essays that break the rules in a quest to be engaging, persuasive, and interesting.

Reading Essays

Reading essays is a lot like reading other forms of literature. It requires careful attention to language—to the words on the page and to what's "written between the lines." Reading essays involves essentially five interrelated mental acts: observing, connecting, inferring, questioning, and concluding. Good readers attend to the details of language and structure of the essays they read. They note not only the information that writers of essays provide, but also how that information is presented, how any stories are told, how arguments are made, and how evidence is presented. Good readers of essays look for connections among the details they observe—details of image and structure, argument and evidence. And good readers draw inferences based on those connected observations, inferences that prepare them to make an interpretive conclusion from their inferences.

Good readers are also engaged by what they read. They respond with questions that echo in their minds as they read. They make their reading an active engagement with the essay text, an involvement that continues after their actual reading of the words on the page has been completed.

Reading in this manner—observing, connecting, inferring, questioning, and concluding—alerts readers to nuances, to things rendered but not explained or elaborated by the writer. Active, deliberative reading of this sort involves both intellectual comprehension and emotional apprehension, a consideration of the feelings essays generate as well as the thinking they stimulate. This reading process requires that readers make sense of gaps in texts; that they recognize linguistic, literary, and cultural conventions; that they generalize on the basis of textual details; that they bring their values to bear on the essays they read; and that they do all these things concurrently and simultaneously.

Reading Annie Dillard's "Living Like Weasels"

We can illustrate this kind of active, engaged reading by looking at the opening paragraphs of Annie Dillard's "Living Like Weasels," an essay printed in full on pages 118–122.

> A weasel is wild. Who knows what he thinks? He sleeps in his underground den, his tail draped over his nose. Sometimes he lives in his den for two days without leaving. Outside, he stalks rabbits, mice, muskrats, and birds, killing more bodies than he can eat warm, and often dragging the carcasses home. Obedient to instinct, he bites his prey at the neck, either splitting the jugular vein at the throat or crunching the brain at the base of the skull, and he does not let go. One naturalist refused to kill a weasel who was socketed into his hand deeply as a rattlesnake. The man could in no way pry the tiny weasel off, and he had to walk half a mile to water, the weasel dangling from his palm, and soak him off like a stubborn label.

First, a few questions. What strikes us most about this passage? What do we notice on first reading it? What observations would we most like to make about it? What questions do we have? What feelings does the text inspire? What expectations do we have about where the essayist is taking us?

Next, some observations. The first sentence is abrupt. It announces forcefully the key point that a weasel is wild. But what does it imply? What do we understand by the word "wild"? How wild? In what way is the weasel wild? The second sentence is a question, one that invites us to consider what a weasel thinks about. (Or perhaps it suggests that we shouldn't bother because we simply cannot know.) "Who knows what he thinks?" How we take this sentence depends on how we hear it, which in turn, affects how we say it. Here's one way: Who knows what he *thinks*? Here's another: Who knows *what* he thinks? And still another: Who *knows* what he thinks? Whichever way we prefer, we recognize the possibility of alternative emphases and thus, alternative ways of understanding what the writer is saying and suggesting about weasels.

Dillard's next two sentences provide information—that weasels sleep in dens where they can remain for up to two days at a time. There's nothing really surprising here. But what about that other little bit of information—*how* the weasel sleeps: with his tail draped over his nose. Whether factual or fanciful, that draped tail is a lovely surprise, a gratuitous image offered to engage and entertain as well as inform.

The fifth and sixth sentences of the opening paragraph reveal the weasel as hunter—stalking prey, killing it, dragging it to his den, where he eats it and then, presumably, sleeps. When we are told that the weasel is obedient to instinct and are shown exactly how he kills—by splitting the jugular vein or by crunching his victim's brain—we remember the opening sentence: "A weasel is wild." And we begin to understand in a new way just what this means. Although we "understood" before, on first encountering the sentence, that vague and general knowledge is now particularized. We have since acquired specific information that we can understand intellectually and respond to emotionally. Now, we know more fully what it means to say that a weasel is "wild."

It is here, in the middle of the paragraph, that we perhaps register our strongest emotional response. How do we respond to Dillard's details about the weasel's method of killing its victims? Are we amazed? Engaged? Appalled? Or what? That question about response is directed at our experience of the essay. We can also ask a technical question: Does Dillard need that degree of detail? Suppose she had diluted it or perhaps even omitted such concrete details entirely. Or conversely, suppose that she had provided an even fuller rendition of the killing. How would such alternatives have affected our response?

Dillard's opening paragraph concludes with an anecdote about a naturalist bitten by the tenacious weasel. The anecdote makes a point, to be sure. But it does more. The image impresses itself on our minds in language worth noting: the verb "socketed"; the comparison with the rattlesnake; the image of the stubborn label. To make sense of Dillard's opening paragraph, even a preliminary kind of sense, is to make such observations and to wonder about their significance. And it is to wonder, too, where the essay is heading, where the writer is taking us. What *do* we expect at this point? Why?

Once we read the second paragraph of Dillard's essay, we can consider how it affects our understanding of and response to the first. How does it follow from the opening paragraph? What does it do rhetorically? That is, what effect does it have on us, and how does it advance Dillard's point about the wildness of the weasel?

Here is Dillard's next paragraph:

> And once, says Ernest Thompson Seton—once, a man shot an eagle
> out of the sky. He examined the eagle and found the dry skull of a
> weasel fixed by the jaws to his throat. The supposition is that the eagle
> had pounced on the weasel and the weasel swiveled and bit as instinct

taught him, tooth to neck, and nearly won. I would like to have seen
that eagle from the air a few weeks or months before he was shot: was
the whole weasel still attached to his feathered throat, a fur pendant?
Or did the eagle eat what he could reach, gutting the living weasel with
his talons before his breast, bending his beak, cleaning the beautiful
airborne bones?

Our questions at the beginning of this second paragraph of
Dillard's essay necessarily invite our responses, both intellectual and
emotional. In asking what strikes us about the details or the language
of this paragraph, we move from subjective responses to objective considerations. On the basis of the details we notice and relate, we form
inferences. We move backward, in a way, from our initial response to
a set of observations about the essay's rhetoric. We might observe, for
example, that the second paragraph begins with an image very much
like the one at the end of the opening paragraph. The tenacious weasel
holds on fiercely, in one instance to a man's hand, and in another,
to an eagle's throat. And we might register the justness of this pair of
images, the more striking image of the eagle following and intensify-
ing the first image of the weasel socketed to a man's hand. We might
also observe that the second paragraph begins with statements—with
declarative sentences—and ends with questions. We might notice, further, that it includes a reference to another written text (did we notice
that this occurs in the opening paragraph as well?). And, finally, that
the writer speaks personally, using the personal pronoun "I," revealing
her desire to have seen the amazing thing she had only read about.

In addition, we should note Dillard's profusion of precise, vivid,
strong verbs, which contribute to the power of her prose. We should
note, too, the image of the eagle gutting the living weasel, bending his
beak and cleaning the weasel's bones of its flesh—an image brought
forward and elaborated from the previous sentence, where it exists as
a pair of adjectives and corresponding nouns: "his feathered throat, a
fur pendant." Dillard actually brings the dormant image to life in that
string of participles: *gutting, living, bending, cleaning.*

The repeated words in this second paragraph create a litany of
eagle and weasel, their rhyming sound echoed again in "*eat,*" "*reach,*"
"*beak,*" and "*cleaning.*" We should notice, as well, the alliterative b's of
the final sentence: "his talons *before* his *breast, bending* his *beak*, cleaning the *beautiful* airborne *bones.*" And further, we might see how the
paragraph's monosyllabic diction is counterpointed against both the

polysyllabic name of the naturalist, Ernest Thompson Seton, and the continual yoking and re-yoking of the animals, eagle and weasel always coming together. To hear the remarkable sound play of Dillard's prose, including its subtle yet muscular rhythms, we must read it aloud.

We can make some observations about the overall structure of Dillard's complete essay. We have described how the first two paragraphs present facts about weasels, especially about their wildness and their tenaciousness. This introductory section of the essay is followed by a section, paragraphs 3–7, that depicts Dillard's encounter with a weasel and their exchange of glances. The middle paragraphs of that section—4 through 6—set the scene, while paragraphs 3 and 7 frame this section, with an emphasis on Dillard's and the weasel's repeated locked glances. Paragraph 5 is of particular interest in its mix of details that contrast wilderness and civilization. They exist, surprisingly, side by side, one within the other: beer cans coexist with muskrat holes; turtle eggs sit in motorcycle tracks; a highway runs alongside a duck pond.

Dillard's next large section of the essay, paragraphs 8–13, provides a crescendo and a climax. Dillard describes the weasel in detail, emphasizing the shock of their locked looks and the shattering of the spell. She also laments her unsuccessful attempt to re-forge the link with the weasel after the spell had been broken. The section ends with Dillard and her readers pondering the mysterious encounter she experienced.

In her concluding section, paragraphs 14–17, Dillard speculates about the meaning of her encounter with the weasel. She contemplates living like a weasel—what it means, why it appeals to her. She explores the implications of what a weasel's life is like, and how its life relates to the life of human beings like her own. She concludes with an image from the opening: an eagle carrying something that is clinging fiercely to it, not letting go, holding on into and beyond death. The image brings the essay full circle—but with the important difference that we, Dillard's readers, have taken the weasel's place.

We are now poised to consider the ideas, the meaning, of "Living Like Weasels," though, clearly, it is necessary to read the essay in its entirety at least once for the following remarks to be completely comprehensible.

What begins as an expository essay that outlines facts about the wildness and tenacity of weasels turns into a meditation on the value of wildness and the necessity of tenacity in human life. By the end of the essay, Dillard has made the weasel a symbol and a model of how human beings might, even should, live. And her tone changes from the factual declaration of the essay's introductory section to speculative wonder, and finally to admonition. Dillard encourages her readers to identify their one necessity, and then, like the weasel, to latch on to it and never let it go.

Dillard also suggests that there is between human and animal the possibility of communication, of understanding. She opts for a mystical communion between woman and weasel, by necessity a brief communion, one beyond the power of words to describe. The experience for Dillard stuns her into stillness and momentarily stops time. In linking her mind even briefly with the weasel, Dillard undergoes an extraordinary transforming experience. But it's an experience that, as much as she wishes it to continue, she cannot prolong because her own consciousness, the distinctive human quality of her thinking mind, which enables her to appreciate the experience in the first place, prevents her, finally, from staying at one with an animal.

There seems to be, thus, in Dillard's essay, a pull in two directions. On one hand, there is the suggestion that human beings can link themselves with the animal world, and like the weasel, live in necessity instinctively. On the other hand sits an opposing idea: that human beings cannot stay linked with the weasel or any animal, primarily because our minds prohibit it. We are creatures for whom remembering is necessary, vital. The mindlessness of the weasel, thus, can never be ours, for we are mindful creatures, not mindless ones. Our living as we should is necessarily different from the weasel's living as it should. And although we can certainly learn from the weasel's tenacity and purity of living, we can follow it only so far on the way to wildness.

Writing Essays

Reading actively and with critical judgment is a necessary adjunct to writing well. In reading carefully and critically, we learn about suggestiveness, about allusion, about economy, about richness. We learn about rhetorical and stylistic possibilities for our own essay writing.

The Qualities of Good Writing

But what constitutes good writing, the kind of writing expected of students in college courses, the kind expected of professional employees on the job? Writing, essentially, is characterized by the following qualities: (1) clarity; (2) coherence; (3) logical organization; (4) accuracy and correctness; (5) sufficiency; and (6) style.

Good writing is *clear* writing. Readers can follow and understand it easily. This is harder to accomplish than it sounds because what is clear to the writer may not be clear to the reader. Writers need to remember that the entire context of their thinking is not readily apparent to their readers. Readers can determine what a writer is saying only from the words on the page.

Good writing is *coherent* writing. Coherence refers to how a writer's sentences "hang together," how those sentences relate to one another sensibly and logically. We can think of coherence, first, though not exclusively, as a quality of paragraphs. Good writing allows readers to determine the focus and point of every paragraph, and to determine, further, the relation of one paragraph to another. This aspect of coherence reveals a writer's inescapable concern with essay organization overall.

Good writing is carefully *organized* writing. A well-written essay has a discernible beginning, middle, and ending (a clearly identifiable introduction, body, and conclusion). Each of these three main parts of an essay need not be baldly announced, but each should be readily discernible by a careful reader. But the organization of an essay requires more than including these three broad aspects. Of particular importance is how the essay unfolds, how its information and evidence are deployed, how each aspect of the writer's idea leads into the next, how the paragraphs that make up the middle, or body, of an essay exhibit a logical structure.

Good writing is also *accurate* and *correct* both in terms of information included and in terms of its language. Grammatical accuracy is essential. So are accurate spelling and punctuation. These elements of good writing can be assisted through the use of grammar and spell-check features of word processing programs, through the use of a college dictionary, and through keeping a reliable handbook, such as *The Scribner Handbook for Writers,* nearby.

Good writing is also *sufficient* to the scope of its subject and the limits of its topic. Short essays may be adequate to discussing highly focused aspects of a topic, while broader and more inclusive topics require longer, more detailed writing. Sufficiency, of course, is a relative concept. But it is important for a writer to include enough evidence to support an idea persuasively, enough examples to illustrate a concept clearly, a sufficient number of reasons to support a claim in developing an argument.

Good writing, finally, has a sense of *style.* Every writer needs to develop his or her own way with words. Paradoxically, one of the best ways to do this is to observe and imitate the style of other writers.

Good writers attend to how other successful writers structure their essays, shape their sentences, and select their words. One of the reasons to develop skillful habits of reading is to glean, from that attentiveness, strategies and techniques for good writing.

An Overview of the Writing Process

These six qualities of good writing require patience, persistence, and practice. Good writing can't be rushed. It requires planning, drafting, and revising.

Planning

In the planning stage of the writing process, it is important to take notes and to make notes. Taking notes involves mostly marking or copying passages, which you might use in your essay. It also involves summarizing and paraphrasing what you read—putting it into your own words. Making notes refers to the act of thinking about what you have marked, copied, summarized, or paraphrased. Writing out notes about what you think about your reading, beginning to formulate your own thinking about it, is an active and reflective process that provides an important step toward drafting your essay.

Planning your essay requires making notes to yourself in other ways as well. You can make lists of observations from your reading or lists of aspects or elements of your topic to consider in your essay draft. You can jot down questions, and you can do some freewriting to jump-start your thinking. These and other preliminary planning strategies are necessary for all but the most informal of writing projects. Time spent on them pays off later during the drafting stage.

Drafting

A draft is a first take, one that provides an overview of your essay, including some kind of beginning and ending, and much of the body or middle, with its examples and evidence to support and develop your ideas. First drafts of essays are often called "rough" drafts, and for good reason. The preliminary draft is not meant to be worried into final form. The first draft is not intended to be a finished product, fit for public display. It is, rather, an attempt the writer makes to see where the topic is going, and whether there are sufficient examples and evidence to support the idea. The idea too, may very well require adjustment and revision, more often than not.

In drafting an essay, it is important to consider your purpose. Are you writing to provide information? To convey an experience? To amuse and entertain? To present an idea for your readers' consideration? To persuade your readers to see something your way? Being clear about your purpose will help with decisions about other aspects of writing your essay, including how to begin and end, as well as choices of language and tone.

Your draft should also make a good start toward providing the supporting evidence necessary for making your ideas persuasive. In marshalling evidence for your ideas from your reading of primary sources, such as works of literature (including the essays in this book), and from secondary sources written about the primary sources, keep the following guidelines in mind:

1. Be fair-minded. Be careful not to oversimplify or distort either a primary or secondary source.
2. Be cautious. Qualify your claims. Limit your assertions to what you can comfortably demonstrate.
3. Be logical. See that the various elements of your argument fit together and that you don't contradict yourself.
4. Be accurate. Present facts, details, and quotations with care.
5. Be confident. Believe in your ideas and present them with conviction.

After writing a draft of an essay, put it aside for a while—ideally for at least a day or two. When you return to it, assess whether what you are saying still makes sense, whether you have provided enough examples to clarify your ideas and presented sufficient evidence to make them persuasive. Read the draft critically, asking yourself what is convincing and what is not, what makes sense and what doesn't. Consider whether the draft centers on a single idea and stays on track.

If the first draft accomplishes these things, you can begin thinking about how to tighten its organization and refine its style. If, on the other hand, the draft contains frequent changes of direction, confusions of thought, multiple unrelated ideas, incoherent paragraphs, and more, you will need to decide what to salvage and what to discard. You will need to return to the planning stage—though now with a clearer sense of your essay's possibilities, and begin the process of drafting your essay again—a second attempt in a second draft. This scenario, by the way, is not uncommon. It simply represents the way first efforts often begin: in some degree of confusion that is eventually dispelled. This common scenario, moreover, argues for leaving enough time to do a second (and, if necessary, a third) draft.

Revising

Revision is not something that occurs only once, at the end of the writing process. Redrafting your essay to consider the ordering of paragraphs and the use of examples is itself a significant act of revision. So, too, is doing additional reading and even rereading some materials to reconsider your original idea. Revision occurs throughout the entire arc of the writing process. It requires you to reconsider your writing and your thinking not once, but several times. This reconsideration is made on three levels: conceptual, organizational, and stylistic.

Conceptual revision involves reconsidering your ideas. As you write your first and subsequent drafts, your understanding of the topic may change. While accumulating evidence in support of your idea, you may find evidence that subverts or challenges it. And you might decide, if not to change your idea dramatically, at least to qualify it to account for this contradictory or complicating evidence. On the other hand, as you write your various drafts, you might find yourself thinking of additional ways to develop and strengthen your idea, to support it with additional evidence, examples, and reasons.

Organizational or structural revision involves asking yourself whether your essay's arrangement best presents your line of thinking. You might ask yourself questions such as these: Is the organizational framework readily discernible? Does it make sense? Have you written an introduction that identifies your topic and clarifies your intent? Have you organized your supporting details in a sensible and logical manner? Does your conclusion follow from your discussion, and does it bring your essay to a satisfying close? However you choose to end your essay, your conclusion should answer the question "So what?" for the reader. Even though you may have presented details, reasons, and examples to support your idea, your readers will still expect you to explain their significance, and in ways that they themselves will want to see as interesting and valuable.

Stylistic revision concerns smaller-scale details, such as matters of syntax or word order, of diction or word choice, of tone, imagery, and rhythm. Even though you may think about some of these things a bit in early drafts, it is better to defer critical attention to them until your final draft, largely because such microscopic stylistic considerations may undergo significant alteration as you rethink and reorganize your essay. You might find, for example, that a paragraph you worked on carefully for style in a first draft is no longer important or relevant, and thus disappears from the final draft.

Focus on aspects of style that may require revision with the following questions:

1. Are your sentences concise and clear?
2. Can you eliminate words that are not doing their job?
3. Is your tone consistent? (i.e., You need to avoid shifts from a formal to an informal or colloquial tone.)
4. Is your level of language appropriate for the subject of your essay?
5. Are there any grammatical errors? Any mistakes in spelling or punctuation? And, finally, before letting an essay go public, be sure to proofread it to check for typos and other unintended mistakes.

Writing from Reading—An Example

In order to write essays about what you read, it is always useful to work through some preliminary, informal writing en route to preparing a more formal piece, whether a short summary or a longer, full-fledged essay.

Earlier, some types of preliminary writing were mentioned. Here they will be illustrated with a short excerpt from Susan Sontag's essay, "A Woman's Beauty" (pp. 507–510).

We begin with annotation.

Annotations are brief notes you write about a text while reading it. You can underline and circle words and phrases that strike you as important. You can highlight passages. You can make marginal comments that reflect your understanding of and attitude toward the text. Your annotations might also include arrows that link related points, question marks that indicate possible confusion, and exclamation marks to express surprise or agreement.

Annotations can be single words or brief phrases; they can be written as statements or as questions. And depending on how extensively you annotate a text, your annotations may form a secondary text that reminds you of the one you are reading and analyzing. Annotations used this way serve as an abbreviated guide to what the text says and what you think about it.

As you read the following passage, notice the various types of annotations, and, if you like, add additional annotations of your own.

Here, first, for convenience, is an excerpt from Sontag's essay.

Excerpt from Susan Sontag's

A Woman's Beauty: Put-Down or Power Source?

Is beauty really essential? Seems exaggerated. Society defines names of beauty. Women are pushed into overconcern with their appearance. Contrast: men do well; women look good.

To be called beautiful is thought to name something essential to women's character and concerns. (In contrast to men—whose essence is to be strong, or effective, or competent.) It does not take someone in the throes of advanced feminist awareness to perceive that the way women are taught to be involved with beauty encourages narcissism, reinforces dependence and immaturity. Everybody (women and men) knows that. For it is "everybody," a whole society, that has identified being feminine with caring about how one looks. (In contrast to being masculine—which is identified with caring about what one is and does and only secondarily, if at all, about how one looks.) [...]

Contrast: desire for beauty versus obligation to be beautiful. Sontag politicizes the issue—beauty as means of oppression. Women + beauty = body parts.

It is not, of course, the desire to be beautiful that is wrong but the obligation to be—or to try. What is accepted by most women as a flattering idealization of their sex is a way of making women feel inferior to what they actually are—or normally grow to be. For the ideal of beauty is administered as a form of self-oppression. Women are taught to see their bodies in parts, and to evaluate each part separately. Breasts, feet, hips, waistline, neck, eyes, nose, complexion, hair, and so on—each in turn is submitted to an anxious, fretful, often despairing scrutiny. Even if some pass muster, some will always be found wanting. [...]

In <u>men, good looks is a whole</u>, something taken in at a glance. It does not need to be confirmed by giving measurements of different regions of the body; nobody encourages a man to dissect his appearance, feature by feature. As for <u>perfection</u>, that is considered trivial— almost unmanly.

Doesn't author exaggerate here about perfection? Nice distinction here on beauty and the sexes.

Freewriting

Your initial impressions of a text, which you can record with annotations, will often lead you to further thoughts about it. You can begin developing these thoughts with freewriting. As with annotating, in freewriting you record ideas, reactions, or feelings about a text without arranging them in any special order. Freewriting is free-form writing. You simply write down what you think about the passage, without worrying about logical organization. The point is to get your ideas down on paper and not to censor or judge them prematurely. Freewriting, in fact, provides a way to pursue an idea and develop your thinking to see where it may lead.

Both annotation and freewriting precede the more intricate and deliberative work of analysis, interpretation, and evaluation. Annotation and freewriting also provide a convenient way to prepare for writing essays and reports. These two informal techniques work well together; the brief, quickly noted annotations complement the more leisurely paced, longer elaborations of freewriting.

Here is an example of freewriting about the Susan Sontag essay excerpt annotated earlier. Notice how the freewriting includes questions that stimulate reflection on the passage.

Example of Freewriting

Interesting questions. Women do seem to think more about their looks than men do. But since it's men women wish to please by looking good, men may be responsible (some? much?) for women's obsession with appearance. How far have women bought into the beauty myth? How much are they responsible for obsessing about beauty? How about money and profit? And at whose expense?

Why don't men *need* to be beautiful? To please parents—employers? To attract a mate? To be considered "normal"? Sontag says beauty is irrelevant for men—men judged by different standards—strength, competence, effectiveness. She doesn't mention power, money, status—leaves out intelligence and moral qualities—kindness, decency, generosity? How important?

Distinction between *desiring* to be beautiful (perhaps to be desired or admired) and *needing* to be. Nothing wrong with women wanting to be attractive, to look good. Problem is when desire becomes *obligation*—a waste of women's talents—minimizes them, keeps them subservient.

Parts and whole—are women concerned with *parts* of their bodies—certain parts? Their overall appearance? Their sense of self? Silicone breast implants? Face lifts? (But men have nose jobs, pec implants.) Men are concerned with *some* parts of their bodies more than others—like women? Or not?

What about the words for good-looking women—and men? Beautiful women, but handsome men. Foxy lady—gorgeous woman (guy?), attractive girl. And what of men? Handsome, good-looking. Pretty boy? Hunk—derogatory for men. A real "he-man."

Double-Column Notebook

Still another way to develop your thinking about what you read is to make entries in a double-column notebook. To create a double-column notebook, simply divide a page in half. One half is for summarizing and interpreting what you read. Use this side to record your understanding of the text. Use the other side to respond to what you read, to think about implications, and to relate it to knowledge gleaned elsewhere.

The advantage of a double-column notebook is that it encourages you to be an active reader, to think about your reading, and to make connections with your other reading and with your experience. You can use the double-column notebook to think further about your earlier reactions and thoughts recorded in your annotations and freewriting.

Here is, first, a generic look at how a double-column notebook page appears, and then an example based on the Sontag essay excerpt.

Double-Column Notebook Page

Summary	Comments
Summarize the text.	Respond to your summary.
Interpret the author's ideas.	Reflect on the author's ideas.
Explain the ideas succinctly.	Consider your agreement or disagreement.
Identify important details.	Raise questions about those details.
Relate details to central idea.	Relate main idea to reading & experience.

The following sample page details how a double-column notebook page might look based on Sontag's essay excerpt. But it's not an attempt to comment on every aspect of her essay.

Double-Column Notebook
for Sontag Essay Excerpt

Summary	Comments
Sontag argues that women's beauty is more dangerous than beneficial. Their beauty and their concern with it hurt women by distracting them from more important things, such as intellectual pursuits and political opportunities.	Sontag's agenda here seems genuine. She values women as intelligent people with a contribution to make to society. She seems genuinely angry by their being forced to be overly concerned with their appearance.
Sontag claims that women are seen as superficial and frivolous because they occupy much of their time with attempting to improve their appearance.	Sontag implies that women are damned if they do and damned if they don't. Women have to look their best in a world that expects

Summary	Comments
She criticizes a society that relegates women to a form of second-class citizenship in which beauty counts less than brains, and in which obsessing about appearance, instead of devoting time and energy to power and status, allows women to be dismissed as superficial and decorative.	nothing less of them. If women neglect their looks, they are criticized for it; if they labor to be beautiful, they are equally criticized. It's a no-win situation for them.
She sets the standards and ideals for women's beauty over and against those for men, and she finds the standards for men's appearance more sensible, reasonable, and meaningful.	In blaming society for women's beauty dilemma, is she really blaming men? Isn't it men who continue to rule the world and set the standards and expectations? Or is she blaming the consumerism and commercialism that dominate contemporary culture?

Writing a Summary

A summary is a compressed version of a text in which you explain the author's meaning in your own words. You summarize a text when you need to give your readers the gist of what it says. A summary should present the author's text accurately and represent his or her views fairly. You build your summary on the observations, connections, and inferences you make while reading. Although there is no rule for how long or short a summary should be, a summary of a text is always shorter than the text itself.

Writing a summary requires careful reading, in part to ensure that you thoroughly understand what you are reading. Writing a summary helps you respond to what you read by requiring careful analysis and consideration of its details.

Writing a summary requires essentially two kinds of skills: identifying the idea of the text you are summarizing and recognizing the evidence that supports that idea. One strategy for writing a summary is to find the key points that support the main idea. You can do this by looking for clusters of sentences or groups of paragraphs that convey the writer's meaning. Because paragraphs work together, you cannot simply summarize each paragraph independently. You may need to summarize a cluster of paragraphs to convey the idea of a text effectively. It all depends on the length and complexity of the text you are summarizing and on how it is organized.

Here is an example of the process applied to the essay excerpt by Sontag.

Sample Notes toward Summary

General idea of passage: Women are seen as superficial and trivial, concerned with surface beauty rather than with deeper qualities of character. Women are viewed as beautiful objects, valued for how they look rather than for who they are and what they have achieved.
Key supporting points:

■ Women's preoccupation with their beauty is a sign of their self-absorption.
■ Women's concern for beauty is a form of enslavement to appearances.
■ Men are less concerned with appearances, especially with perfecting their appearance.
■ Women are objectified in connection with parts of their bodies.
■ Women are deemed inconsequential and frivolous.

To create a smooth summary from these key-supporting points, it is necessary to expand and elaborate on them a bit. It is also necessary to put them in a logical order, and to create introductory and concluding sentences for the summary paragraph. Transitions also need to be provided.

Here is an example of such a summary. This one avoids direct quotation from Sontag's text, though quoting her essay is certainly permissible in a summary. Opinions and judgmental words and phrases are avoided, and the writer and text are identified in the opening sentence.

Sample Summary
Sontag Essay Excerpt

In her essay "A Woman's Beauty: Put-Down or Power Source?" Susan Sontag explains how women's need to appear beautiful trivializes them, making them sound superficial and identifying them as creatures preoccupied with how they look rather than with who they are and what they have achieved. Sontag suggests that women's preoccupation with physical beauty is a sign of their self-absorption and triviality. Through being taught to see themselves as mere body parts, women become both objectified and ridden with anxiety that their parts may not measure up. Unlike women, men are viewed as a whole rather than for their parts. Their looks are considered as part of an overall package, one that includes not only the appearance they present, but their knowledge, intelligence, and status. Unlike women, who lack power, men are perceived as more serious, more confident, and more powerful than the women who anxiously labor to be beautiful in order to please them.

Going Further

Once you have gotten far enough to be comfortable with the writer's idea so that you can summarize it accurately, you are ready to return to the text to look for additional evidence to develop and expand your summary into a full-fledged essay. Earlier a process for accomplishing this revisionary reading was described. Now we will add some notes which, coupled with the summary, can prepare for the writing of a more elaborate essay about Sontag's perspective on women's beauty. The notes can help you expand your summary.

There are four basic steps in this process: observing details of the text, connecting or relating them, making inferences based on those connections, and drawing a conclusion, or interpretation, about the text's meaning and significance. This four-stage process allows for the accumulation of the evidence needed to support a textual interpretation that could be formulated in an essay about it.

Observing Details

The kinds of observations you make about a text depend on the kind of text you are reading. Here are some observations about Sontag's essay excerpt:

- Sontag focuses throughout on surface beauty—on appearance.
- She distinguishes between beauty in women and in men.
- She sees women's obsession with beauty as dangerous.

- She describes men as strong and competent.
- She italicizes certain key words.
- She places certain sentences in parentheses.
- She puts some words in quotation marks.
- She punctuates heavily with dashes.

Look back at the passage. Make your own observations about the ideas in Sontag's comments; select one sentence in each paragraph that crystallizes her thought. Make a few observations about Sontag's sentences: their type, length, and form. Notice how she begins and ends her paragraphs. Observe what evidence she provides to support her views.

Connecting Details

It is not enough, however, simply to observe details about a text. You must also connect them; relate them to one another. To make a connection is to see one thing in relation to another. You may notice that some details reinforce others, or that the writer repeats certain words or ideas. Perhaps she sets up a contrast, as Sontag does between men's and women's attitudes toward beauty.

While you are noticing aspects of a text, you can also begin making connections among its details. Your goal is to see how the connected details help you make sense of the text as a whole. One way to do this is to group information in lists or in outline form. This involves setting up categories or headings for related kinds of details. In the Sontag passage, for example, you could create heads for details about men and about women. Or you could group observations about style under one head and observations about ideas under another. Notice, for example, how the list of observations made earlier can be divided exactly in this manner, with the first four items concerning Sontag's ideas and the last four her style.

Making observations about a text and establishing connections among them form the basis of analysis. From that basis you begin to consider the significance of what you observe and proceed to develop an interpretation of the text overall. Breaking the interpretive process down in this manner enables you to understand what it involves and should prepare you to practice it on other occasions.

Making Inferences

An inference is a statement based on what has been observed. You infer a writer's idea or point of view, for instance, from the examples and evidence he or she provides. Inferences drive the interpretive process. They push readers beyond making observations and toward explaining their significance. Without inferences there can be no interpretation based on textual evidence.

There is nothing mysterious about the process of making inferences. We do it all the time in our everyday lives, from inferring what someone feels when they complain about something we have done (or failed to do) to inferring the significance of a situation based upon visual observation, as when we see someone with a large ring of keys opening rooms in an academic building early in the morning.

The same is true of making inferences about a text. The inferences we make in reading represent our way of "reading between the lines" by discovering what is implied rather than explicitly stated. The freewriting sample about the Sontag essay excerpt contains inferences. Here are a few additional inferences a reader could draw from the Sontag passage:

- Sontag thinks that the double standard by which women are judged for their beauty and men for other qualities is wrong (paragraph 1).
- She implies that few women can meet the high standards for beauty that society imposes (paragraph 2).
- She seems to approve of the way masculine beauty is considered as a sum of each feature of a man's overall appearance (paragraph 3).
- She implies that women would be better off regarded as whole beings as well.

Sontag does not say any of these things outright. But readers can infer them based on what she does say explicitly. Remember that an inference can be right or wrong, and thus different readers might debate the reliability of these or other inferences we might make about Sontag's essay excerpt. The important thing is not to be afraid to make inferences because of uncertainty about their accuracy. Critical reading and writing involve thinking, and thinking involves making inferences. It is this kind of inferential thinking, moreover, that is essential to good reading and good writing.

Arriving at an Interpretation

The step from making inferences to arriving at an interpretation is not an overly large one. An interpretation is a way of explaining the meaning of a text; it represents your way of understanding the text expressed as an idea. In formulating an interpretation of the Sontag essay, you might write something like the following:

> *Sontag examines the meaning of beauty in the lives of women, seeing women's beauty, to echo her title, as more of a "put-down" than a source of power. Although she recognizes that beautiful women can use their attractive appearance to their advantage, she argues that the very beauty that gives beautiful women a social advantage, simultaneously detracts from the overall estimation and regard which others have of them.*

This interpretation can be debated, and it can be, indeed needs to be, further elaborated and explained. But the interpretation is based on the inferences made while reading the text, and upon the observations and connections among them that provided the foundation for those inferences. In arriving at this or any interpretation, it is necessary to look back at the text's details to reconsider your initial observations, as well as to review the connections and inferences based upon them. Your inferences must be defensible, that is supportable, either by textual evidence or by logical reasoning.

In looking back at the Sontag passage, you might notice something you overlooked earlier. You might notice, for example, that Sontag mentions society's responsibility for foisting certain ideals of beauty upon women. In thinking about the implications of that observation, you might make other inferences, which may lead you to an interpretive emphasis that differs from your previous understanding of her text. You might decide that the central issue for Sontag is society's role and responsibility in forcing such an ideal of beauty upon women. In that case, you would probably select your evidence from the essay differently to support this new focus of your interpretation.

In writing a full-fledged interpretive essay based on Sontag's piece, or in writing your own essay on the subject of beauty—whether or not you restrict it to "women's beauty"—you would go through the same process described here. The only difference is that the essay you develop would be long enough to provide a full explanation of your ideas and sufficient evidence to make your ideas worthy of a reader's consideration, and that it be long and detailed enough either to fulfill the demands of an assignment to which it might be a response or to satisfy you as its writer that you have said what you wanted to with enough evidence to make it convincing to others.

Gloria Anzaldúa (1942–2004) grew up in the Rio Grande Valley of south Texas, a rural area near the Mexican border that was home to many Chicanos. She graduated from Pan American University in Austin, taught high school, and later found her way to San Francisco, where she became an outspoken member of the feminist movement. A lesbian and a woman of mixed cultural heritage, she has described herself as the "new mestiza," straddling many personal and cultural influences. In addition to several children's stories, Anzaldúa has published two highly influential books in the field of cultural studies: Borderlands/La Frontera: The New Mestiza *(1987), which mixes prose and poetry, narrative and polemic, and* Making Face, Making Soul/Haciendo Caras: Creative and Critical Perspectives by Women of Color, *co-edited with Cherie Moraga.*

GLORIA ANZALDÚA

How to Tame a Wild Tongue

In "How to Tame a Wild Tongue," Gloria Anzaldúa addresses intertwined issues of language, culture, identity, and power. Her essay is radical in idea, organization, and style. Anzaldúa's idea includes suggestions about the need for a broader view of what constitutes both "English" and "Spanish." She argues for the usefulness of a Chicano Spanish, which deviates in many ways from the Spanish brought from Europe to Mexico and to Central and South America. She also argues for the value of a border-crossing Tex-Mex blend of Spanish and English in a kind of "Spanglish."

"We're going to have to control your tongue," the dentist says, pulling out all the metal from my mouth. Silver bits plop and tinkle into the basin. My mouth is a motherlode.

The dentist is cleaning out my roots. I get a whiff of the stench when I gasp. "I can't cap that tooth yet, you're still draining," he says.

"We're going to have to do something about your tongue," I hear the anger rising in his voice. My tongue keeps pushing out the wads of cotton, pushing back the drills, the long thin needles. "I've never seen anything as strong or as stubborn," he says. And I think, how do you tame a wild tongue, train it to be quiet, how do you bridle and saddle it? How do you make it lie down?

Who is to say that robbing a people of its language is less violent than war?

—RAY GWYN SMITH[1]

---

[1]Ray Gwyn Smith, *Moorland Is Cold Country*, unpublished book.

I remember being caught speaking Spanish at recess—that was good for three licks on the knuckles with a sharp ruler. I remember being sent to the corner of the classroom for "talking back" to the Anglo teacher when all I was trying to do was tell her how to pronounce my name. "If you want to be American, speak 'American.' If you don't like it, go back to Mexico where you belong."

"I want you to speak English. *Pa'hallar buen trabajo tienes que saber hablar el inglés bien. Qué vale toda tu educación si todavía hablas inglés con un 'accent'*," my mother would say, mortified that I spoke English like a Mexican. At Pan American University, I and all Chicano students were required to take two speech classes. Their purpose: to get rid of our accents.

Attacks on one's form of expression with the intent to censor are a violation of the First Amendment. *El Anglo con cara de inocente nos arrancó la lengua.* Wild tongues can't be tamed, they can only be cut out.

Overcoming the Tradition of Silence

> *Ahogadas, escupimos el oscuro.*
> *Peleando con nuestra propia sombra*
> *el silencio nos sepulta.*

En boca cerrada no entran moscas. "Flies don't enter a closed mouth" is a saying I kept hearing when I was a child. *Ser habladora* was to be a gossip and a liar, to talk too much. *Muchachitas bien criadas,* well-bred girls don't answer back. *Es una falta de respeto* to talk back to one's mother or father. I remember one of the sins I'd recite to the priest in the confession box the few times I went to confession: talking back to my mother, *hablar pa' 'tras, repelar. Hocicona, repelona, chismosa,* having a big mouth, questioning, carrying tales are all signs of being *mal criada.* In my culture they are all words that are derogatory if applied to women—I've never heard them applied to men.

The first time I heard two women, a Puerto Rican and a Cuban, say the word "*nosotras*," I was shocked. I had not known the word existed. Chicanas use *nosotros* whether we're male or female. We are robbed of our female being by the masculine plural. Language is a male discourse.

> And our tongues have become
> dry   the wilderness has

dried out our tongues   and
we have forgotten speech.

—Irena Klepfisz[2]

Even our own people, other Spanish speakers *nos quieren poner canda-
dos en la boca.* They would hold us back with their bag of *reglas de academia.*

Oyé como ladra: el lenguaje de la frontera

Quien tiene boca se equivoca.

—Mexican Saying

"*Pocho,* cultural traitor, you're speaking the oppressor's language
by speaking English, you're ruining the Spanish language," I have been
accused by various Latinos and Latinas. Chicano Spanish is considered
by the purist and by most Latinos deficient, a mutilation of Spanish.

But Chicano Spanish is a border tongue which developed naturally. Change, *evolución, enriquecimiento de palabras nuevas por invención
o adopción* have created variants of Chicano Spanish, *un nuevo lenguaje.
Un lenguaje que corresponde a un modo de vivir.* Chicano Spanish is not
incorrect, it is a living language.

For a people who are neither Spanish nor live in a country in which
Spanish is the first language; for a people who live in a country in which
English is the reigning tongue but who are not Anglo; for a people who
cannot entirely identify with either standard (formal, Castilian) Spanish
nor standard English, what recourse is left to them but to create their
own language? A language which they can connect their identity to, one
capable of communicating the realities and values true to themselves—
a language with terms that are neither *español ni inglés,* but both. We
speak a patois, a forked tongue, a variation of two languages.

Chicano Spanish sprang out of the Chicanos' need to identify
ourselves as a distinct people. We needed a language with which
we could communicate with ourselves, a secret language. For some
of us, language is a homeland closer than the Southwest—for many
Chicanos today live in the Midwest and the East. And because we are
a complex, heterogeneous people, we speak many languages. Some of
the languages we speak are

1. Standard English
2. Working class and slang English

[2]Irena Klepfisz, "*Di rayze aheym*/The Journey Home," in *The Tribe of Dina: A Jewish Women's
Anthology,* Melanie Kaye/Kantrowitz and Irena Klepfisz, eds. (Montpelier, VT: Sinister Wisdom
Books, 1986), 49.

3. Standard Spanish
4. Standard Mexican Spanish
5. North Mexican Spanish dialect
6. Chicano Spanish (Texas, New Mexico, Arizona, and California have regional variations)
7. Tex-Mex
8. *Pachuco* (called *caló*)

My "home" tongues are the languages I speak with my sister and brothers, with my friends. They are the last five listed, with 6 and 7 being closest to my heart. From school, the media, and job situations, I've picked up standard and working-class English. From Mamagrande Locha and from reading Spanish and Mexican literature, I've picked up Standard Spanish and Standard Mexican Spanish. From *los recién llegados,* Mexican immigrants, and *braceros,* I learned the North Mexican dialect. With Mexicans I'll try to speak either Standard Mexican Spanish or the North Mexican dialect. From my parents and Chicanos living in the Valley, I picked up Chicano Texas Spanish, and I speak it with my mom, younger brother (who married a Mexican and who rarely mixes Spanish with English), aunts, and older relatives.

With Chicanas from *Nuevo México* or *Arizona* I will speak Chicano Spanish a little, but often they don't understand what I'm saying. With most California Chicanas I speak entirely in English (unless I forget). When I first moved to San Francisco, I'd rattle off something in Spanish, unintentionally embarrassing them. Often it is only with another Chicana *tejano* that I can talk freely.

Words distorted by English are known as anglicisms or *pochismos.* The *pocho* is an anglicized Mexican or American of Mexican origin who speaks Spanish with an accent characteristic of North Americans and who distorts and reconstructs the language according to the influence of English.[3] Tex-Mex, or Spanglish, comes most naturally to me. I may switch back and forth from English to Spanish in the same sentence or in the same word. With my sister and my brother Nune and with Chicano *tejano* contemporaries I speak in Tex-Mex.

From kids and people my own age I picked up *Pachuco. Pachuco* (the language of the zoot suiters) is a language of rebellion, both against Standard Spanish and Standard English. It is a secret language. Adults of the culture and outsiders cannot understand it. It is made

[3]R. C. Ortega, *Dialectología Del Barrio*, trans. Hortencia S. Alwan (Los Angeles, CA: R. C. Ortega Publisher & Bookseller, 1977), 132.

up of slang words from both English and Spanish. *Ruca* means girl or woman, *vato* means guy or dude, *chale* means no, *simón* means yes, *churro* is sure, talk is *periquiar, pigionear* means petting, *que gacho* means how nerdy, *ponte águila* means watch out, death is called *la pelona.* Through lack of practice and not having others who can speak it, I've lost most of the *Pachuco* tongue.

Chicano Spanish

Chicanos, after 250 years of Spanish/Anglo colonization, have developed significant differences in the Spanish we speak. We collapse two adjacent vowels into a single syllable and sometimes shift the stress in certain words such as *maíz/maiz, cohete/cuete.* We leave out certain consonants when they appear between vowels: *lado/lao, mojado/mojao.* Chicanos from South Texas pronounce *f* as *j* as in *jue (fue).* Chicanos use "archaisms," words that are no longer in the Spanish language, words that have been evolved out. We say *semos, truje, haiga, ansina,* and *naiden.* We retain the "archaic" *j,* as in *jalar,* that derives from an earlier *h* (the French *halar* or the Germanic *halon,* which was lost to standard Spanish in the sixteenth century), but which is still found in several regional dialects such as the one spoken in South Texas. (Due to geography, Chicanos from the Valley of South Texas were cut off linguistically from other Spanish speakers. We tend to use words that the Spaniards brought over from Medieval Spain. The majority of the Spanish colonizers in Mexico and the Southwest came from Extremadura—Hernán Cortés was one of them—and Andalucía. Andalucians pronounce *ll* like a *y,* and their *d*'s tend to be absorbed by adjacent vowels: *tirado* becomes *tirao.* They brought *el lenguaje popular, dialectos y regionalismos.*[4])

Chicanos and other Spanish speakers also shift *ll* to *y* and *z* to *s.*[5] We leave out initial syllables, saying *tar* for *estar, toy* for *estoy, hora* for *ahora* (*cubanos* and *puertorriqueños* also leave out initial letters of some words). We also leave out the final syllable such as *pa* for *para.* The intervocalic *y,* the *ll* as in *tortilla, ella, botella,* gets replaced by *tortia* or *tortiya, ea, botea.* We add an additional syllable at the beginning of certain words: *atocar* for *tocar, agastar* for *gastar.* Sometimes we'll say *lavaste las vacijas,* other times *lavates* (substituting the *ates* verb endings for the *aste*).

[4]Eduardo Hernandéz-Chávez, Andrew D. Cohen, and Anthony F. Beltramo, El Lenguaje de los Chicanos: *Regional and Social Characteristics of Language Used by Mexican Americans* (Arlington, VA: Center for Applied Linguistics, 1975), 39.
[5]Hernandéz-Chávez, xvii.

We used anglicisms, words borrowed from English: *bola* from ball, *carpeta* from carpet, *máchina de lavar* (instead of *lavadora*) from washing machine. Tex-Mex argot, created by adding a Spanish sound at the beginning or end of an English word, such as *cookiar* for cook, *watchar* for watch, *parkiar* for park, and *rapiar* for rape, is the result of the pressures on Spanish speakers to adapt to English.

We don't use the word *vosotros/as* or its accompanying verb form. We don't say *claro* (to mean *yes*), *imaginate*, or *me emociona*, unless we picked up Spanish from Latinas, out of a book, or in a classroom. Other Spanish-speaking groups are going through the same, or similar, development in their Spanish.

Linguistic Terrorism

Deslenguadas. Somos los del español deficiente. We are your linguistic nightmare, your linguistic aberration, your linguistic mestisaje, the subject of your burla. Because we speak with tongues of fire we are culturally crucified. Racially, culturally, and linguistically somos huérfanos—we speak an orphan tongue.

Chicanas who grew up speaking Chicano Spanish have internalized the belief that we speak poor Spanish. It is illegitimate, a bastard language. And because we internalize how our language has been used against us by the dominant culture, we use our language differences against each other.

Chicana feminists often skirt around each other with suspicion and hesitation. For the longest time I couldn't figure it out. Then it dawned on me. To be close to another Chicana is like looking into the mirror. We are afraid of what we'll see there. *Pena.* Shame. Low estimation of self. In childhood we are told that our language is wrong. Repeated attacks on our native tongue diminish our sense of self. The attacks continue throughout our lives.

Chicanas feel uncomfortable talking in Spanish to Latinas, afraid of their censure. Their language was not outlawed in their countries. They had a whole lifetime of being immersed in their native tongue; generations, centuries in which Spanish was a first language, taught in school, heard on radio and TV, and read in the newspaper.

If a person, Chicana or Latina, has a low estimation of my native tongue, she also has a low estimation of me. Often with *mexicanas y latinas* we'll speak English as a neutral language. Even among

Chicanas we tend to speak English at parties or conferences. Yet, at the same time, we're afraid the other will think we're *agringadas* because we don't speak Chicano Spanish. We oppress each other trying to out-Chicano each other, vying to be the "real" Chicanas, to speak like Chicanos. There is no one Chicano language just as there is no one Chicano experience. A monolingual Chicana whose first language is English or Spanish is just as much a Chicana as one who speaks several variants of Spanish. A Chicana from Michigan or Chicago or Detroit is just as much a Chicana as one from the Southwest. Chicano Spanish is as diverse linguistically as it is regionally.

By the end of this century, Spanish speakers will comprise the biggest minority group in the United States, a country where students in high schools and colleges are encouraged to take French classes because French is considered more "cultured." But for a language to remain alive it must be used.[6] By the end of this century English, and not Spanish, will be the mother tongue of most Chicanos and Latinos.

So, if you want to really hurt me, talk badly about my language. Ethnic identity is twin skin to linguistic identity—I am my language. Until I can take pride in my language, I cannot take pride in myself. Until I can accept as legitimate Chicano Texas Spanish, Tex-Mex, and all the other languages I speak, I cannot accept the legitimacy of myself. Until I am free to write bilingually and to switch codes without having always to translate, while I still have to speak English or Spanish when I would rather speak Spanglish, and as long as I have to accommodate the English speakers rather than having them accommodate me, my tongue will be illegitimate.

I will no longer be made to feel ashamed of existing. I will have my voice: Indian, Spanish, white. I will have my serpent's tongue—my woman's voice, my sexual voice, my poet's voice. I will overcome the tradition of silence.

> My fingers
> move sly against your palm
> Like women everywhere, we speak in code.
> —MELANIE KAYE/KANTROWITZ[7]

[6]Irena Klepfisz, "Secular Jewish Identity: Yidishkayt in America," in *The Tribe of Dina*, Kaye/Kantrowitz and Klepfisz, eds., 43.
[7]Melanie Kaye/Kantrowitz, "Sign," in *We Speak in Code: Poems and Other Writings* (Pittsburgh, PA: Motheroot Publications, Inc., 1980), 85.

"Vistas," corridos, y comida: My Native Tongue

In the 1960s, I read my first Chicano novel. It was *City of Night* by John Rechy, a gay Texan, son of a Scottish father and a Mexican mother. For days I walked around in stunned amazement that a Chicano could write and could get published. When I read *I Am Joaquín*[8] I was surprised to see a bilingual book by a Chicano in print. When I saw poetry written in Tex-Mex for the first time, a feeling of pure joy flashed through me. I felt like we really existed as a people. In 1971, when I started teaching High School English to Chicano students, I tried to supplement the required texts with works by Chicanos, only to be reprimanded and forbidden to do so by the principal. He claimed that I was supposed to teach "American" and English literature. At the risk of being fired, I swore my students to secrecy and slipped in Chicano short stories, poems, a play. In graduate school, while working toward a Ph.D., I had to "argue" with one adviser after the other, semester after semester, before I was allowed to make Chicano literature an area of focus.

Even before I read books by Chicanos or Mexicans, it was the Mexican movies I saw at the drive-in—the Thursday night special of $1.00 a carload—that gave me a sense of belonging. "*Vámonos a las vistas,*" my mother would call out and we'd all—grandmother, brothers, sister, and cousins—squeeze into the car. We'd wolf down cheese and bologna white bread sandwiches while watching Pedro Infante in melodramatic tearjerkers like *Nosotros los pobres,* the first "real" Mexican movie (that was not an imitation of European movies). I remember seeing *Cuando los hijos se van* and surmising that all Mexican movies played up the love a mother has for her children and what ungrateful sons and daughters suffer when they are not devoted to their mothers. I remember the singing-type "westerns" of Jorge Negrete and Miquel Aceves Mejía. When watching Mexican movies, I felt a sense of homecoming as well as alienation. People who were to amount to something didn't go to Mexican movies, or *bailes,* or tune their radios to *bolero, rancherita,* and *corrido* music.

The whole time I was growing up, there was *norteño* music sometimes called North Mexican border music, or Tex-Mex music, or Chicano music, or *cantina* (bar) music. I grew up listening to *conjuntos,* three- or four-piece bands made up of folk musicians playing guitar, *bajo sexto,* drums, and button accordion, which Chicanos had

[8]Rodolfo Gonzales, *I Am Joaquín/Yo Soy Joaquín* (New York, NY: Bantam Books, 1972). It was first published in 1967.

borrowed from the German immigrants who had come to Central Texas and Mexico to farm and build breweries. In the Rio Grande Valley, Steve Jordan and Little Joe Hernández were popular, and Flaco Jiménez was the accordion king. The rhythms of Tex-Mex music are those of the polka, also adapted from the Germans, who in turn had borrowed the polka from the Czechs and Bohemians.

I remember the hot, sultry evenings when *corridos*—songs of love and death on the Texas-Mexican borderlands—reverberated out of cheap amplifiers from the local *cantinas* and wafted in through my bedroom window.

Corridos first became widely used along the South Texas/Mexican border during the early conflict between Chicanos and Anglos. The *corridos* are usually about Mexican heroes who do valiant deeds against the Anglo oppressors. Pancho Villa's song, "*La cucaracha*," is the most famous one. *Corridos* of John F. Kennedy and his death are still very popular in the Valley. Older Chicanos remember Lydia Mendoza, one of the great border *corrido* singers who was called *la Gloria de Tejas*. Her "*El tango negro*," sung during the Great Depression, made her a singer of the people. The ever-present *corridos* narrated one hundred years of border history, bringing news of events as well as entertaining. These folk musicians and folk songs are our chief cultural mythmakers, and they made our hard lives seem bearable.

I grew up feeling ambivalent about our music. Country-western and rock-and-roll had more status. In the fifties and sixties, for the slightly educated and *agringado* Chicanos, there existed a sense of shame at being caught listening to our music. Yet I couldn't stop my feet from thumping to the music, could not stop humming the words, nor hide from myself the exhilaration I felt when I heard it.

There are more subtle ways that we internalize identification, especially in the forms of images and emotions. For me food and certain smells are tied to my identity, to my homeland. Woodsmoke curling up to an immense blue sky; woodsmoke perfuming my grandmother's clothes, her skin. The stench of cow manure and the yellow patches on the ground; the crack of a .22 rifle and the reek of cordite. Homemade white cheese sizzling in a pan, melting inside a folded *tortilla*. My sister Hilda's hot, spicy *menudo, chile colorado* making it deep red, pieces of *panza* and hominy floating on top. My brother Carito barbequing *fajitas* in the backyard. Even now and 3,000 miles away, I can see my mother spicing the ground beef, pork, and venison with *chile*. My mouth salivates at the thought of the hot steaming *tamales* I would be eating if I were home.

Si le preguntas a mi mamá, "¿Qué eres?"

> Identity is the essential core of who
> we are as individuals, the conscious
> experience of the self inside.
>
> —GERSHEN KAUFMAN[9]

Nosotros los Chicanos straddle the borderlands. On one side of us, we are constantly exposed to the Spanish of the Mexicans, on the other side we hear the Anglos' incessant clamoring so that we forget our language. Among ourselves we don't say *nosotros los americanos, o nosotros los españoles, o nosotros los hispanos.* We say *nosotros los mexicanos* (by *mexicanos* we do not mean citizens of Mexico; we do not mean a national identity, but a racial one). We distinguish between *mexicanos del otro lado* and *mexicanos de este lado.* Deep in our hearts we believe that being Mexican has nothing to do with which country one lives in. Being Mexican is a state of soul—not one of mind, not one of citizenship. Neither eagle nor serpent, but both. And like the ocean, neither animal respects borders.

> *Dime con quien andas y te diré quien eres.*
> (Tell me who your friends are and I'll tell you who you are.)
>
> —MEXICAN SAYING

Si le preguntas a mi mamá, "¿Qué eres?" te dirá, "Soy mexicana." My brothers and sister say the same. I sometimes will answer "*soy mexicana*" and at others will say "*soy Chicana*" *o* "*soy tejana.*" But I identified as "*Raza*" before I ever identified as "*mexicana*" or "*Chicana.*"

As a culture, we call ourselves Spanish when referring to ourselves as a linguistic group and when copping out. It is then that we forget our predominant Indian genes. We are 70–80 percent Indian.[10] We call ourselves Hispanic[11] or Spanish-American or Latin American or Latin when linking ourselves to other Spanish-speaking peoples of the Western hemisphere and when copping out. We call ourselves Mexican-American[12] to signify we are neither Mexican nor American, but more the noun "American" than the adjective "Mexican" (and when copping out).

[9]Gershen Kaufman, *Shame: The Power of Caring* (Cambridge, MA: Schenken Books, Inc., 1980), 68.
[10]John R. Chavez, *The Lost Land: The Chicano Images of the Southwest* (Albuquerque NM: The University of New Mexico Press, 1984), 88–90
[11]"Hispanic" is derived from *Hispanis* (*España*, a name given to the Iberian Peninsula in ancient times when it was part of the Roman Empire) and is a term designated by the U.S. government to make it easier to handle us on paper.
[12]The Treaty of Guadalupe Hidalgo created the Mexican-American in 1848.

Chicanos and other people of color suffer economically for not acculturating. This voluntary (yet forced) alienation makes for psychological conflict, a kind of dual identity—we don't identify with the Anglo-American cultural values and we don't totally identify with the Mexican cultural values. We are a synergy of two cultures with various degrees of Mexicanness or Angloness. I have so internalized the borderland conflict that sometimes I feel like one cancels out the other and we are zero, nothing, no one. *A veces no soy nada ni nadie. Pero hasta cuando no lo soy, lo soy.*

When not copping out, when we know we are more than nothing, we call ourselves Mexican, referring to race and ancestry; *mestizo* when affirming both our Indian and Spanish (but we hardly ever own our Black) ancestry; Chicano when referring to a politically aware people born and/or raised in the United States; *Raza* when referring to Chicanos; *tejanos* when we are Chicanos from Texas.

Chicanos did not know we were a people until 1965 when Cesar Chavez and the farmworkers united and *I Am Joaquín* was published and *la Raza Unida* party was formed in Texas. With that recognition, we became a distinct people. Something momentous happened to the Chicano soul—we became aware of our reality and acquired a name and a language (Chicano Spanish) that reflected that reality. Now that we had a name, some of the fragmented pieces began to fall together—who we were, what we were, how we had evolved. We began to get glimpses of what we might eventually become.

Yet the struggle of identities continues, the struggle of borders is our reality still. One day the inner struggle will cease and a true integration take place. In the meantime, *tenémos que hacer la lucha. ¿Quién está protegiendo los ranchos de mi gente? ¿Quién está tratando de cerrar la fisura entre la india y el blanco en nuestra sangre? El Chicano, si, el Chicano que anda como un landrón en su propia casa.*

Los Chicanos, how patient we seem, how very patient. There is the quiet of the Indian about us.[13] We know how to survive. When other races have given up their tongue, we've kept ours. We know what it is to live under the hammer blow of the dominant *norteamericano* culture. But more than we count the blows, we count the days the weeks the years the centuries the aeons until the white laws and commerce and

[13]Anglos, in order to alleviate their guilt for dispossessing the Chicano, stressed the Spanish part of us and perpetrated the myth of the Spanish Southwest. We have accepted the fiction that we are Hispanic, that is Spanish, in order to accommodate ourselves to the dominant culture and its abhorrence of Indians. Chávez, 88–91.

customs will rot in the deserts they've created, lie bleached. *Humildes* yet proud, *quietos* yet wild, *nosotros los mexicanos-Chicanos* will walk by the crumbling ashes as we go about our business. Stubborn, persevering, impenetrable as stone, yet possessing a malleability that renders us unbreakable, we, the *mestizas* and *mestizos,* will remain.

POSSIBILITIES FOR WRITING

1. Anzaldúa focuses here not only on language but on other aspects of culture as well, including music and movies. How do these various examples contribute to her overall argument?
2. After the introductory paragraphs, the essay is divided into four separately headed sections. What points does Anzaldúa make in each section? What links can you find among the sections? For you, does she succeed in making a coherent argument?
3. Think about your own use of language—at home, at school, at work, among friends, with strangers, in formal and informal situations. When do you feel most comfortable and when least comfortable? How do you account for your feelings? Are they in any way related to the point Anzaldúa is making?

Francis Bacon (1561–1626) *was born in London to parents who were members of the court of Queen Elizabeth I. He attended Trinity College, entered the practice of law in his late teens, and became a member of the House of Commons at the age of 23. His career flourished under King James I, but later scandals ended his life as a politician. A philosopher/scientist by nature and one of the most admired thinkers of his day, Bacon was a founder of the modern empirical tradition based on closely observing the physical world, conducting controlled experiments, and interpreting results rationally to discover the workings of the universe. Of his many published works, he is best remembered today for his* Essays *(collected from 1597 until after his death), brief meditations noted for their wit and insight.*

FRANCIS BACON

Of Studies

In "Of Studies," Bacon lays out the value of knowledge in practical terms. Bacon considers to what use studies might be put. He is less interested in their theoretical promise than in their practical utility. From his opening sentence Bacon gets directly to the point: "Studies serve for delight, for ornament, and for ability." He then elaborates on how studies are useful in these three ways. And he wastes no words in detailing the uses of "studies" for a Renaissance gentleman.

Studies serve for delight, for ornament, and for ability. Their chief use for delight is in privateness and retiring; for ornament, is in discourse; and for ability, is in the judgment and disposition of business. For expert men can execute, and perhaps judge of particulars, one by one; but the general counsels, and the plots and marshaling of affairs, come best from those that are learned. To spend too much time in studies is sloth; to use them too much for ornament is affectation; to make judgment wholly by their rules is the humor of a scholar. They perfect nature, and are perfected by experience; for natural abilities are like natural plants, that need pruning by study; and studies themselves do give forth directions too much at large, except they be bounded in by experience. Crafty men contemn studies, simple men admire them, and wise men use them, for they teach not their own use; but that is a wisdom without them, and above them, won by observation. Read not to contradict and confute, nor to believe and take for granted, nor to find talk and discourse, but to weigh and consider. Some books are to be tasted, others to be swallowed, and some few to be chewed and digested; that is, some books are to be read only in parts; others to be read, but not curiously; and some few to be read wholly, and with diligence and attention. Some books also may be read by deputy and extracts made of them by others, but that would be only in the less important arguments and the meaner sort of books; else distilled books are like common distilled waters, flashy things. Reading maketh a full man, conference a ready man, and writing an exact man. And therefore, if a man write little, he had need have a great memory; if he confer little, he had need have a present wit; and if he read little, he had need have much cunning, to seem to know that he doth not. Histories make men wise; poets, witty; the mathematics, subtle; natural philosophy, deep; moral, grave; logic and rhetoric, able to contend. *Abeunt studia in mores.* Nay, there is no stond or impediment in the wit but may be wrought out by fit studies, like as diseases of the body may have appropriate exercises. Bowling is good for the stone and reins, shooting for the lungs and breast, gentle walking for the stomach, riding for the head, and the like. So if a man's wit be wandering, let him study the mathematics; for in demonstrations, if his wit be called away never so little, he must begin again. If his wit be not apt to distinguish or find differences, let him study the schoolmen, for they are *cumini sectores.* If he be not apt to beat over matters and to call up one thing to prove and illustrate another, let him study the lawyer's cases. So every defect of the mind may have a special receipt.

POSSIBILITIES FOR WRITING

1. Bacon's essay was composed some four hundred years ago in a society that was in many ways very different from ours today. Write an analysis of "Of Studies" in which you summarize the main points Bacon makes and then go on to explore the extent to which his remarks continue to seem relevant. As you reread "Of Studies" and make preliminary notes, you will need to find ways to "translate" much of his vocabulary into its modern equivalent.

2. Bacon's brief essay contains many aphorisms, concise statements of a general principle or truth—for example, "Read not to contradict and confute, nor to believe and take for granted, nor to find talk and discourse, but to weigh and consider." Take one of these, put it in your own words, and use it as the starting point for an essay of your own. Elaborate on the statement with examples and further details that come from your own experience or imagination.

3. Changing Bacon's focus a bit, write an essay for modern audiences titled "On Reading." In it consider different types of reading, purposes for reading, benefits of reading, difficulties involved in reading, and so forth. Your essay may be quite personal, focusing on your own experiences as a reader, or, like Bacon's, more formal.

James Baldwin (1924–1987) *is widely considered one of the premiere stylists of modern American letters and among its most impassioned chroniclers of the African American experience. Born in Harlem, Baldwin became interested in literature as a child, and he began publishing essays and reviews in his early twenties. He used the proceeds of a 1948 fellowship to relocate to Paris, where he lived for much of the rest of his life. There he worked on the novel* Go Tell It on the Mountain, *which was published in 1953 to great praise. This was followed by* Giovanni's Room *(1956) and* Another Country *(1962), both of which dealt openly with issues of homosexuality as well as race. A major figure in the civil rights movement, Baldwin also published a number of acclaimed essay collections, mostly based on the experiences of blacks grappling with prejudice and social injustice.*

JAMES BALDWIN

If Black English Isn't a Language, Then Tell Me What Is

In his essay on black English, Baldwin argues that black English provides a distinctive view of experience that could not be expressed in any other language or dialect. Baldwin makes his argument in part by comparing different black and white Englishes with the different French language dialects spoken by inhabitants of Paris, Quebec, Guadeloupe, and Senegal.

St. Paul De Vence, France—The argument concerning the use, or the status, or the reality, of black English is rooted in American history and has absolutely nothing to do with the question the argument supposes itself to be posing. The argument has nothing to do with language itself but with the *role* of language. Language, incontestably, reveals the speaker. Language, also, far more dubiously, is meant to define the other—and, in this case, the other is refusing to be defined by a language that has never been able to recognize him.

People evolve a language in order to describe and thus control their circumstances, or in order not to be submerged by a reality that they cannot articulate. (And, if they cannot articulate it, they *are* submerged.) A Frenchman living in Paris speaks a subtly and crucially different language from that of the man living in Marseilles; neither sounds very much like a man living in Quebec; and they would all have great difficulty in apprehending what the man from Guadeloupe, or Martinique, is saying, to say nothing of the man from Senegal—although the "common" language of all these areas is French. But each has paid, and is paying, a different price for this "common" language, in which, as it turns out, they are not saying, and cannot be saying, the same things: They each have very different realities to articulate, or control.

What joins all languages, and all men, is the necessity to confront life, in order, not inconceivably, to outwit death: The price for this is the acceptance, and achievement, of one's temporal identity. So that, for example, though it is not taught in the schools (and this has the potential of becoming a political issue) the south of France still clings to its ancient and musical Provençal, which resists being described as a "dialect." And much of the tension in the Basque countries, and in Wales, is due to the Basque and Welsh determination not to allow their languages to be destroyed. This determination also feeds the flames in Ireland, for among the many indignities the Irish have been forced to undergo at English hands is the English contempt for their language.

It goes without saying, then, that language is also a political instrument, means, and proof of power. It is the most vivid and crucial key to identity: It reveals the private identity, and connects one with, or divorces one from, the larger, public, or communal identity. There have been, and are, times, and places, when to speak a certain language could be dangerous, even fatal. Or, one may speak the same language, but in such a way that one's antecedents are revealed, or (one hopes) hidden. This is true in France, and is absolutely true in England: The range (and reign) of accents on that damp little island make England coherent for the English and totally incomprehensible for everyone else. To open your mouth in England is (if I may use black English) to "put your business in the street": You have confessed your parents, your youth, your school, your salary, your self-esteem, and, alas, your future.

Now, I do not know what white Americans would sound like if there had never been any black people in the United States, but they would not sound the way they sound. *Jazz*, for example, is a very specific sexual term, as in *jazz me, baby*, but white people purified it into the Jazz Age. *Sock it to me*, which means, roughly, the same thing, has been adopted by Nathaniel Hawthorne's descendants with no qualms or hesitations at all, along with *let it all hang out* and *right on! Beat to his socks*, which was once the black's most total and despairing image of poverty, was transformed into a thing called the Beat Generation, which phenomenon was, largely, composed of *uptight*, middle-class white people, imitating poverty, trying to *get down*, to get *with it*, doing their *thing*, doing their despairing best to be *funky*, which we, the blacks, never dreamed of doing—we *were* funky, baby, like *funk* was going out of style.

Now, no one can eat his cake, and have it, too, and it is late in the day to attempt to penalize black people for having created a language that permits the nation its only glimpse of reality, a language without which the nation would be even more *whipped* than it is.

I say that this present skirmish is rooted in American history, and it is. Black English is the creation of the black diaspora. Blacks came to the United States chained to each other, but from different tribes: Neither could speak the other's language. If two black people, at that bitter hour of the world's history, had been able to speak to each other, the institution of chattel slavery could never have lasted as long as it did. Subsequently, the slave was given, under the eye, and the gun, of his master, Congo Square, and the Bible—or, in other words, and under these conditions, the slave began the formation of the black church, and it is within this unprecedented tabernacle that black English began to be formed. This was not, merely, as in the European example, the adoption of a foreign tongue, but an alchemy that trans-formed ancient elements into a new language: *A language comes into existence by means of brutal necessity, and the rules of the language are dictated by what the language must convey.*

There was a moment, in time, and in this place, when my brother, or my mother, or my father, or my sister, had to convey to me, for example, the danger in which I was standing from the white man standing just behind me, and to convey this with a speed, and in a language, that the white man could not possibly understand, and that, indeed, he cannot understand, until today. He cannot afford to understand it. This understanding would reveal to him too much about himself, and smash that mirror before which he has been frozen for so long.

Now, if this passion, this skill, this (to quote Toni Morrison) "sheer intelligence," this incredible music, the mighty achievement of having brought a people utterly unknown to, or despised by "history"—to have brought this people to their present, troubled, troubling, and un-assailable and unanswerable place—if this absolutely unprecedented journey does not indicate that black English is a language, I am curi-ous to know what definition of language is to be trusted.

A people at the center of the Western world, and in the midst of so hostile a population, has not endured and transcended by means of what is patronizingly called a "dialect." We, the blacks, are in trouble, certainly, but we are not doomed, and we are not inarticulate because we are not compelled to defend a morality that we know to be a lie.

The brutal truth is that the bulk of the white people in America never had any interest in educating black people, except as this could serve white purposes. It is not the black child's language that is in question, it is not his language that is despised: It is his experience. A child cannot be taught by anyone who despises him, and a child cannot afford to be fooled. A child cannot be taught by anyone whose demand, essentially, is that the child repudiate his experience, and all that gives him sustenance, and enter a limbo in which he will no longer be black, and in which he knows that he can never become white. Black people have lost too many black children that way.

And, after all, finally, in a country with standards so untrustworthy, a country that makes heroes of so many criminal mediocrities, a country unable to face why so many of the non-white are in prison, or on the needle, or standing, futureless, in the streets—it may very well be that both the child, and his elder, have concluded that they have nothing whatever to learn from the people of a country that has managed to learn so little.

POSSIBILITIES FOR WRITING

1. Write a couple of paragraphs explaining how Baldwin articulates and supports his position. Consider the evidence he brings to bear. And consider whether you agree with his argument.
2. Discuss Baldwin's idea that language is a key to identity—both personal identity and social identity.
3. Agree or disagree with Baldwin's comment that to open your mouth and speak is to confess "your parents, your youth, your school, your salary, your self-esteem, and, alas, your future."

Dave Barry (b. 1947), a native of Armonk, New York, graduated from Haverford College. After ten years of working as a newspaper reporter and later as a business writing consultant, he began turning out a freelance humor column in 1980. He is now on the staff of the Miami Herald, *and his popular column is syndicated in more than one hundred fifty papers around the country. Barry has published many collections of these columns, which often find irony and humor in the everyday circumstances of middle-class Americans; among his collections is* Dave Barry Is Not Taking This Sitting Down (2000). *His recent book of nonfiction is* I'll Mature When I'm Dead (2010).

DAVE BARRY

Road Warrior

In "Road Warrior," the humor columnist Dave Barry writes about the recently diagnosed quality of "road rage" that is said to afflict America's motorists. "Road rage" refers to the pent-up and explosively released anger and hostility that drivers feel and express in an era of increasing automobile traffic congestion and ever-increasing delays. Social analysts attribute driver "road rage" not only to all the additional cars and drivers clogging the roads, but also to a decline in civility that seems to many to afflict American society today.

If you do much driving on our nation's highways, you've probably noticed that, more and more often, bullets are coming through your windshield. This is a common sign of Road Rage, which the opinion-makers in the news media have decided is a serious problem, currently ranking just behind global warming and several points ahead of Asia.

How widespread is Road Rage? To answer that question, researchers for the National Institute of Traffic Safety recently did a study in which they drove on the interstate highway system in a specially equipped observation van. By the third day, they were deliberately running other motorists off the road.

"These people are MORONS!" was their official report.

That is the main cause of Road Rage: the realization that many of your fellow motorists have the same brain structure as a cashew. The most common example, of course, is the motorists who feel a need to drive in the left-hand, or "passing," lane, even though they are going slower than everybody else. Nobody knows why these motorists do this. Maybe they belong to some kind of religious cult that believes the right lane is sacred and must never come in direct contact with tires. Maybe one time, years ago, these motorists happened to be driving in the left lane when their favorite song came on the radio, so they've driven over there ever since, in hopes that the radio will play that song again.

But whatever makes these people drive this way, there's nothing you can do about it. You can honk at them, but it will have no effect. People have been honking at them for years: It's a normal part of their environment. They've decided that, for some mysterious reason, wherever they drive, there is honking. They choose not to ponder this mystery any further, lest they overburden their cashews.

I am very familiar with this problem, because I live and drive in Miami, which proudly bills itself as The Inappropriate-Lane-Driving Capital Of The World, a place where the left lane is thought of not so much as a thoroughfare as a public recreational area, where motorists feel free to stop, hold family reunions, barbecue pigs, play volleyball, etc. Compounding this problem is another common type of Miami motorist, the aggressive young male whose car has a sound system so powerful that the driver must go faster than the speed of sound at all times, because otherwise the nuclear bass notes emanating from his rear speakers will catch up to him and cause his head to explode.

So the tiny minority of us Miami drivers who actually qualify as normal find ourselves constantly being trapped behind people drifting along on the interstate at the speed of diseased livestock, while at the same time we are being tailgated and occasionally bumped from behind by testosterone-deranged youths who got their driver training from watching the space-fighter battle scenes in *Star Wars*. And of course nobody EVER signals or yields, and people are CONSTANTLY cutting us off, and AFTER A WHILE WE START TO FEEL SOME RAGE, OK? YOU GOT A PROBLEM WITH THAT, MISTER NEWS MEDIA OPINION-MAKER??

In addition to Road Rage, I frequently experience Parking Lot Rage, which occurs when I pull into a crowded supermarket parking lot, and I see people get into their car, clearly ready to leave, so I stop my car and wait for them to vacate the spot, and…nothing happens! They just stay there! WHAT THE HELL ARE THEY DOING IN THERE??!! COOKING DINNER???

When I finally get into the supermarket, I often experience Shopping Cart Rage. This is caused by the people—and you just KNOW these are the same people who always drive in the left-hand lane—who routinely manage, by careful placement, to block the entire aisle with a single shopping cart. If we really want to keep illegal immigrants from entering the United States, we should employ Miami residents armed with shopping carts; we'd only need about two dozen to block the entire Mexican border.

What makes the supermarket congestion even worse is that shoppers are taking longer and longer to decide what to buy, because every product in America now comes in an insane number of styles and sizes. For example, I recently went to the supermarket to get orange juice. For just *one brand* of orange juice, Tropicana, I had to decide whether I wanted Original, HomeStyle, Pulp Plus, Double Vitamin C, Grovestand, Calcium, or Old-Fashioned; I also had to decide whether I wanted the 16-ounce, 32-ounce, 64-ounce, 96-ounce, or six-pack size. This is WAY too many product choices. It caused me to experience Way Too Many Product Choices Rage. I would have called Tropicana and complained, but I probably would have wound up experiencing Automated Phone Answering System Rage. ("...For questions about Pulp Plus in the 32-ounce size, press 23. For questions about Pulp Plus in the 64-ounce size, press 24. For questions about....")

My point is that there are many causes for rage in our modern world, and if we're going to avoid unnecessary violence, we all need to "keep our cool." So let's try to be more considerate, OK? Otherwise I will kill you.

DAVE BARRY

50

POSSIBILITIES FOR WRITING

1. Barry's point, he writes, is that "there are many causes for rage in our modern world, and if we're going to avoid unnecessary violence, we all need to 'keep our cool'." Use this idea as the basis for a more serious essay on the topic of controlling conflict and violence.
2. Write a comic essay about other sorts of behavior that can spark irritation or "rage." Don't be afraid to use exaggeration, as Barry does, but do so in ways that readers will find amusing rather than offensive.
3. Scan some newspapers or magazines for another recent social trend being reported in the media. Examine this trend from your own perspective and using your own examples—either comically, as Barry does, or more seriously.

Roland Barthes (1915–1980) was born in France and studied French literature and classics at the University of Paris. After teaching in universities in Bucharest, Romania, and Alexandria, Egypt, he joined the National Center for Scientific Research, where he pursued research studies in sociology and language. As a leader of France's new critics, Barthes drew on the insights of Karl Marx and Sigmund Freud as well as on the work of the influential linguist Ferdinand de Saussure to expand the science of semiology, the study of signs and symbols underlying all aspects of human culture. His many works include Elements of Semiology, Empire of Signs, A Lover's Discourse, The Pleasure of the Text, *and* Mythologies, *from which "Toys" has been taken.*

ROLAND BARTHES

Toys

In "Toys," Barthes meditates on the cultural significance of French toys, seeing them as a "microcosm" of the adult world. Barthes analyzes the social implications of French toys, arguing that it is no accident that toys reflect the "myths and techniques" of modern life. Toys, according to Barthes, epitomize what is socially important and culturally validated by the country in which they are produced and purchased. A second area Barthes investigates concerns the forms and materials from which French toys are made. He considers the extent to which certain kinds of toys are imitative of actual life—girl dolls that take in and eliminate water being one example. He contrasts such imitative toys with simple toys such as wooden blocks, which allow children to be more creative in their play.

French toys: one could not find a better illustration of the fact that the adult Frenchman sees the child as another self. All the toys one commonly sees are essentially a microcosm of the adult world; they are all reduced copies of human objects, as if in the eyes of the public the child was, all told, nothing but a smaller man, a homunculus to whom must be supplied objects of his own size.

Invented forms are very rare: a few sets of blocks, which appeal to the spirit of do-it-yourself, are the only ones which offer dynamic forms. As for the others, French toys *always mean something*, and this something is always entirely socialized, constituted by the myths or the techniques of modern adult life: the Army, Broadcasting, the Post Office, Medicine (miniature instrument-cases, operating theatres for dolls), School, Hair-Styling (driers for permanent-waving), the Air Force (Parachutists), Transport (trains, Citroëns, Vedettes, Vespas, petrol-stations), Science (Martian toys).

The fact that French toys *literally* prefigure the world of adult functions obviously cannot but prepare the child to accept them all, by constituting for him, even before he can think about it, the alibi of a Nature which has at all times created soldiers, postmen, and Vespas. Toys here reveal the list of all the things the adult does not find unusual: war, bureaucracy, ugliness, Martians, etc. It is not so much, in fact, the imitation which is the sign of an abdication, as its literalness: French toys are like a Jivaro head, in which one recognizes, shrunken to the size of an apple, the wrinkles and hair of an adult. There exist, for instance, dolls which urinate; they have an oesophagus, one gives them a bottle, they wet their nappies; soon, no doubt, milk will turn to water in their stomachs. This is meant to prepare the little girl for the causality of house-keeping, to "condition" her to her future role as mother. However, faced with this world of faithful and complicated objects, the child can only identify himself as owner, as user, never as creator; he does not invent the world, he uses it: there are, prepared for him, actions without adventure, without wonder, without joy. He is turned into a little stay-at-home householder who does not even have to invent the mainsprings of adult causality; they are supplied to him ready-made: he has only to help himself, he is never allowed to discover anything from start to finish. The merest set of blocks, provided it is not too refined, implies a very different learning of the world: then, the child does not in any way create meaningful objects, it matters little to him whether they have an adult name; the actions he performs are not those of a user but those of a demiurge. He creates forms which walk, which roll, he creates life, not property: objects now act by themselves, they are no longer an inert and complicated material in the palm of his hand. But such toys are rather rare: French toys are usually based on imitation, they are meant to produce children who are users, not creators.

The bourgeois status of toys can be recognized not only in their forms, which are all functional, but also in their substances. Current toys are made of a graceless material, the product of chemistry, not of nature. Many are now molded from complicated mixtures; the plastic material of which they are made has an appearance at once gross and hygienic, it destroys all the pleasure, the sweetness, the humanity of touch. A sign which fills one with consternation is the gradual disappearance of wood, in spite of its being an ideal material because of its firmness and its softness, and the natural warmth of its touch. Wood removes, from all the forms which it supports, the wounding quality of angles which are too sharp, the chemical coldness of metal. When the child handles it and knocks it, it neither vibrates nor grates, it has a sound at once muffled and sharp. It is a familiar and poetic substance, which does not sever the child from close contact with the tree, the table, the floor. Wood does not wound or break down; it does not shatter, it wears out, it can last a long time, live with the child, alter little by little the relations between the object and the hand. If it dies, it is in dwindling, not in swelling out like those mechanical toys which disappear behind the hernia of a broken spring. Wood makes essential objects, objects for all time. Yet there hardly remain any of these wooden toys from the Vosges, these fretwork farms with their animals, which were only possible, it is true, in the days of the craftsman. Henceforth, toys are chemical in substance and color; their very material introduces one to a coenaesthesis of use, not pleasure. These toys die in fact very quickly, and once dead, they have no posthumous life for the child.

POSSIBILITIES FOR WRITING

1. Barthes suggests that French toys "always mean something." Consider the examples he provides and identify just how and what they signify about French society and culture at the time the essay was written.
2. To what extent do you agree with Barthes that toys can stifle as well as stimulate creativity? What sorts of toys limit the imagination of children, and what kinds of toys help them develop their imaginative capacity? Why?
3. Write an essay in which you explore and analyze contemporary American toys and the extent to which they convey implications about American cultural and social life today. Or write an essay in which you analyze another aspect of American popular culture, such as fast food, wrestling, casino gambling, or video games, to explain how and what they reveal about American social and cultural life.

Sven Birkerts (b. 1951) is a literary critic and writing teacher. Birkerts has taught at Emerson and Bennington Colleges, at Mount Holyoke, Amherst, and Harvard. His essays and reviews have appeared in many journals, including the New York Times Book Review, Harper's, the Atlantic, the New Republic, and the New York Review of Books. He has published collections of essays on twentieth-century literature; a book of essays, Readings (1999); a memoir, My Sky Blue Trades (2002); and college textbooks on writing and studying literature. Currently editor of the journal Agni, Birkerts is best known for his 1994 book The Gutenberg Elegies: The Fate of Reading in an Electronic Age. Birkerts has written a recent memoir: The Other Walk (2011) and a book about memoir, Then Again (2008).

SVEN BIRKERTS

Into the Electronic Millennium

In "Into the Electronic Millennium," Sven Birkerts takes aim at what were then, in 1994, recent developments in electronic culture. As Birkerts notes, the move toward electronic forms of information was well under way at that time and no longer, even then, the imaginings of an avant-garde. It's clear from the anecdotes he includes that Birkerts is both concerned with and upset about the developments and consequences of a rapidly rising electronic culture.

Some years ago, a friend and I comanaged a used and rare book shop in Ann Arbor, Michigan. We were often asked to appraise and purchase libraries—by retiring academics, widows, and disgruntled graduate students. One day we took a call from a professor of English at one of the community colleges outside Detroit. When he answered the buzzer I did a double take—he looked to be only a year or two older than we were. "I'm selling everything," he said, leading the way through a large apartment. As he opened the door of his study I felt a nudge from my partner. The room was wall-to-wall books and as neat as a chapel.

The professor had a remarkable collection. It reflected not only the needs of his vocation—he taught nineteenth- and twentieth-century literature—but a book lover's sensibility as well. The shelves were strictly arranged, and the books themselves were in superb condition. When he left the room we set to work inspecting, counting, and es- timating. This is always a delicate procedure, for the buyer is at once anxious to avoid insult to the seller and eager to get the goods for the best price. We adopted our usual strategy, working out a lower offer and a more generous fallback price. But there was no need to worry. The professor took our first offer without batting an eye.

As we boxed up the books, we chatted. My partner asked the man if he was moving. "No," he said, "but I am getting out." We both looked up. "Out of the teaching business, I mean. Out of books." He then said that he wanted to show us something. And indeed, as soon as the books were packed and loaded, he led us back through the apartment and down a set of stairs. When we reached the basement, he flicked on the light. There, on a long table, displayed like an exhibit in the Space Museum, was a computer. I didn't know what kind it was then, nor could I tell you now, fifteen years later. But the professor was keen to explain and demonstrate.

While he and my partner hunched over the terminal, I roamed to and fro, inspecting the shelves. It was purely a reflex gesture, for they held nothing but thick binders and paperbound manuals. "I'm changing my life," the ex-professor was saying. "This is definitely where it's all going to happen." He told us that he already had several good job offers. And the books? I asked. Why was he selling them all? He paused for a few beats. "The whole profession represents a lot of pain to me," he said. "I don't want to see any of these books again."

The scene has stuck with me. It is now a kind of marker in my mental life. That afternoon I got my first serious inkling that all was not well in the world of print and letters. All sorts of corroborations followed. Our professor was by no means an isolated case. Over a period of two years we met with several others like him. New men and new women who had glimpsed the future and had decided to get out while the getting was good. The selling off of books was sometimes done for financial reasons, but the need to burn bridges was usually there as well. It was as if heading to the future also required the destruction of tokens from the past.

A change is upon us—nothing could be clearer. The printed word is part of a vestigial order that we are moving away from—by choice and by societal compulsion. I'm not just talking about disaffected academics, either. This shift is happening throughout our culture, away from the patterns and habits of the printed page and toward a new world distinguished by its reliance on electronic communications.

This is not, of course, the first such shift in our long history. In Greece, in the time of Socrates, several centuries after Homer, the dominant oral culture was overtaken by the writing technology. And in Europe another epochal transition was effected in the late fifteenth century after Gutenberg invented movable type. In both cases the long-term societal effects were overwhelming, as they will be for us in the years to come.

The evidence of the change is all around us, though possibly in the manner of the forest that we cannot see for the trees. The electronic media, while conspicuous in gadgetry, are very nearly invisible in their functioning. They have slipped deeply and irrevocably into our midst, creating sluices and circulating through them. I'm not referring to any one product or function in isolation, such as television or fax machines or the networks that make them possible. I mean the interdependent totality that has arisen from the conjoining of parts—the disk drives hooked to modems, transmissions linked to technologies of reception, recording, duplication, and storage. Numbers and codes and frequencies. Buttons and signals. And this is no longer "the future," except for the poor or the self-consciously atavistic—it is now. . . .

To get a sense of the enormity of the change, you must force yourself to imagine—deeply and in nontelevisual terms—what the world was like a hundred, even fifty, years ago. If the feat is too difficult, spend some time with a novel from the period. Read between the lines and reconstruct. Move through the sequence of a character's day and then juxtapose the images and sensations you find with those in the life of the average urban or suburban dweller today.

Inevitably, one of the first realizations is that a communications net, a soft and pliable mesh woven from invisible threads, has fallen over everything. The so-called natural world, the place we used to live, which served us so long as the yardstick for all measurements, can now only be perceived through a scrim. Nature was then; this is now. Trees and rocks have receded. And the great geographical Other, the faraway rest of the world, has been transformed by the pure possibility of access. The numbers of distance and time no longer mean what they used to. Every place, once unique, itself, is strangely shot through with radiations from every other place. "There" was then; "here" is now. . . .

To underscore my point, I have been making it sound as if we were all abruptly walking out of one room and into another, leaving our books to the moths while we settle ourselves in front of our state-of-the-art terminals. The truth is that we are living through a period of overlap; one way of being is pushed athwart another. Antonio Gramsci's often-cited sentence comes inevitably to mind: "The crisis consists precisely in the fact that the old is dying and the new cannot be born; in this interregnum a great variety of morbid symptoms appears." The old surely is dying, but I'm not so sure that the new is having any great difficulty being born. As for the morbid symptoms, these we have in abundance.

The overlap in communications modes, and the ways of living that they are associated with, invites comparison with the transitional epoch in ancient Greek society, certainly in terms of the relative degree of disturbance. Historian Eric Havelock designated that period as one of "protoliteracy," of which his fellow scholar Oswyn Murray has written:

> To him [Havelock] the basic shift from oral to literate culture was a slow process; for centuries, despite the existence of writing, Greece remained essentially an oral culture. This culture was one which depended heavily on the encoding of information in poetic texts, to be learned by rote and to provide a cultural encyclopedia of conduct. It was not until the age of Plato in the fourth century that the dominance of poetry in an oral culture was challenged in the final triumph of literacy.

That challenge came in the form of philosophy, among other things, and poetry has never recovered its cultural primacy. What oral poetry was for the Greeks, printed books in general are for us. But our historical moment, which we might call "proto-electronic," will not require a transition period of two centuries. The very essence of electronic transmissions is to surmount impedances and to hasten transitions. Fifty years, I'm sure, will suffice. As for what the conversion will bring—and *mean*—to us, we might glean a few clues by looking to some of the "morbid symptoms" of the change. But to understand what these portend, we need to remark a few of the more obvious ways in which our various technologies condition our senses and sensibilities.

I won't tire my reader with an extended rehash of the differences between the print orientation and that of electronic systems. Media theorists from Marshall McLuhan to Walter Ong to Neil Postman have discoursed upon these at length. What's more, they are reasonably commonsensical. I therefore will abbreviate.

The order of print is linear, and is bound to logic by the imperatives of syntax. Syntax is the substructure of discourse, a mapping of the ways that the mind makes sense through language. Print communication requires the active engagement of the reader's attention, for reading is fundamentally an act of translation. Symbols are turned into their verbal referents and these are in turn interpreted. The print engagement is essentially private. While it does represent an act of communication, the contents pass from the privacy of the sender to the privacy of the receiver. Print also posits a time axis; the turning of pages, not to mention the vertical descent down the page, is a forward-moving succession, with earlier contents at every point serving as a ground for what follows. Moreover, the printed material is static—it is the reader, not the book, that moves forward. The physical arrangements of print are in accord with our traditional sense of history. Materials are layered; they lend themselves to rereading and to sustained attention. The pace of reading is variable, with progress determined by the reader's focus and comprehension.

The electronic order is in most ways opposite. Information and contents do not simply move from one private space to another, but they travel along a network. Engagement is intrinsically public, taking place within a circuit of larger connectedness. The vast resources of the network are always there, potential, even if they do not impinge on the immediate communication. Electronic communication can be passive, as with television watching, or interactive, as with computers. Contents, unless they are printed out (at which point they become part of the static order of print) are felt to be evanescent. They can be changed or deleted with the stroke of a key. With visual media (television, projected graphs, highlighted "bullets"), impression and image take precedence over logic and concept, and detail and linear sequentiality are sacrificed. The pace is rapid, driven by jump-cut increments, and the basic movement is laterally associative rather than vertically cumulative. The presentation structures the reception and, in time, the expectation about how information is organized.

Further, the visual and nonvisual technology in every way encourages in the user a heightened and ever-changing awareness of the present. It works against historical perception, which must depend on the inimical notions of logic and sequential succession. If the print medium exalts the word, fixing it into permanence, the electronic counterpart reduces it to a signal, a means to an end.

Transitions like the one from print to electronic media do not take place without rippling or, more likely, *reweaving* the entire social and cultural web. The tendencies outlined above are already at work. We don't need to look far to find their effects. We can begin with the newspaper headlines and the millennial lamentations sounded in the op-ed pages: that our educational systems are in decline; that our students are less and less able to read and comprehend their required texts, and that their aptitude scores have leveled off well below those of previous generations. Tag-line communication, called "bite-speak" by some, is destroying the last remnants of political discourse; spin doctors and media consultants are our new shamans. As communications empires fight for control of all information outlets, including publishers, the latter have succumbed to the tyranny of the bottom line; they are less and less willing to publish work, however worthy, that will not make a tidy profit. And, on every front, funding for the arts is being cut while the arts themselves appear to be suffering a deep crisis of relevance. And so on.

Every one of these developments is, of course, overdetermined, but there can be no doubt that they are connected, perhaps profoundly, to the transition that is underway.

Certain other trends bear watching. One could argue, for instance, that the entire movement of postmodernism in the arts is a consequence of this same macroscopic shift. For what is postmodernism at root but an aesthetic that rebukes the idea of an historical time line, as well as previously uncontested assumptions of cultural hierarchy. The postmodern artifact manipulates its stylistic signatures like Lego blocks and makes free with combinations from the formerly sequestered spheres of high and popular art. Its combinatory momentum and relentless referencing of the surrounding culture mirror perfectly the associative dynamics of electronic media.

One might argue likewise, that the virulent debate within academia over the canon and multiculturalism may not be a simple struggle between the entrenched ideologies of white male elites and the forces of formerly disenfranchised gender, racial, and cultural groups. Many of those who would revise the canon (or end it altogether) are trying to outflank the assumption of historical tradition itself. The underlying question, avoided by many, may be not only whether the tradition is relevant, but whether it might not be too taxing a system for students to comprehend. Both the traditionalists and the progressives have valid arguments, and we must certainly have sympathy for those who would try to expose and eradicate the hidden assumptions of bias in the Western tradition. But it also seems clear that this debate could only have taken the form it has in a society that has begun to come loose from its textual moorings. To challenge repression is salutary. To challenge history itself, proclaiming it to be simply an archive of repressions and justifications, is idiotic.[1] . . .

---

[1] The outcry against the modification of the canon can be seen as a plea for old reflexes and routines. And the cry for multicultural representation may be a last-ditch bid for connection to the fading legacy of print. The logic is simple. When a resource is threatened—made scarce—people fight over it. In this case the struggle is over textual power in an increasingly nontextual age. The future of books and reading is what is at stake, and a dim intuition of this drives the contending factions.

As Katha Pollitt argued so shrewdly in her much-cited article in *The Nation:* If we were a nation of readers, there would be no issue. No one would be arguing about whether to put Toni Morrison on the syllabus because her work would be a staple of the reader's regular diet anyway. These lists are suddenly so important because they represent, very often, the only serious works that the student is ever likely to be exposed to. Whoever controls the lists comes out ahead in the struggle for the hearts and minds of the young.

INTO THE ELECTRONIC MILLENNIUM

A collective change of sensibility may already be upon us. We need to take seriously the possibility that the young truly "know no other way," that they are not made of the same stuff that their elders are. In her *Harper's* magazine debate with Neil Postman, Camille Paglia observed:

> *Some people have more developed sensoriums than others. I've found that most people born before World War II are turned off by the modern media. They can't understand how we who were born after the war can read and watch TV at the same time. But we can. When I wrote my book, I had earphones on, blasting rock music or Puccini and Brahms. The soap operas—with the sound turned down—flickered on my TV. I'd be talking on the phone at the same time. Baby boomers have a multilayered, multitrack ability to deal with the world.*

I don't know whether to be impressed or depressed by Paglia's ability to disperse her focus in so many directions. Nor can I say, not having read her book, in what ways her multitrack sensibility has informed her prose. But I'm baffled by what she means when she talks about an ability to "deal with the world." From the context, "dealing" sounds more like a matter of incessantly repositioning the self within a barrage of on-rushing stimuli....

My final exhibit—I don't know if it qualifies as a morbid symptom as such—is drawn from a *Washington Post Magazine* essay on the future of the Library of Congress, our national shrine to the printed word. One of the individuals interviewed in the piece is Robert Zich, so-called "special projects czar" of the institution. Zich, too, has seen the future, and he is surprisingly candid with his interlocutor. Before long, Zich maintains, people will be able to get what information they want directly off their terminals. The function of the Library of Congress (and perhaps libraries in general) will change. He envisions his library becoming more like a museum: "Just as you go to the National Gallery to see its Leonardo or go to the Smithsonian to see the Spirit of St. Louis and so on, you will want to go to libraries to see the Gutenberg or the original printing of Shakespeare's plays or to see Lincoln's handwritten version of the Gettysburg Address."

Zich is outspoken, voicing what other administrators must be thinking privately. The big research libraries, he says, "and the great national libraries and their buildings will go the way of the railroad stations and the movie palaces of an earlier era which were really vital institutions in their time.... Somehow folks moved away from that when the technology changed."

And books? Zich expresses excitement about Sony's hand-held electronic book, and a miniature encyclopedia coming from Franklin Electronic Publishers. "Slip it in your pocket," he says. "Little keyboard, punch in your words and it will do the full text searching and all the rest of it. Its limitation, of course, is that it's devoted just to that one book." Zich is likewise interested in the possibility of memory cards. What he likes about the Sony product is the portability: one machine, a screen that will display the contents of whatever electronic card you feed it.

I cite Zich's views at some length here because he is not some Silicon Valley research and development visionary, but a highly placed executive at what might be called, in a very literal sense, our most conservative public institution. When men like Zich embrace the electronic future, we can be sure it's well on its way.

Others might argue that the technologies cited by Zich merely represent a modification in the "form" of reading, and that reading itself will be unaffected, as there is little difference between following words on a pocket screen or a printed page. Here I have to hold my line. The context cannot but condition the process. Screen and book may exhibit the same string of words, but the assumptions that underlie their significance are entirely different depending on whether we are staring at a book or a circuit-generated text. As the nature of looking—at the natural world, at paintings—changed with the arrival of photography and mechanical reproduction, so will the collective relation to language alter as new modes of dissemination prevail.

Whether all of this sounds dire or merely "different" will depend upon the reader's own values and priorities. I find these portents of change depressing, but also exhilarating—at least to speculate about. On the one hand, I have a great feeling of loss and a fear about what habitations will exist for self and soul in the future. But there is also a quickening, a sense that important things are on the line. As Heraclitus once observed, "The mixture that is not shaken soon stagnates." Well, the mixture is being shaken, no doubt about it. And here are some of the kinds of developments we might watch for as our "proto-electronic" era yields to an all-electronic future:

1. *Language erosion*. There is no question but that the transition from the culture of the book to the culture of electronic communication will radically alter the ways in which we use language on every societal level. The complexity and distinctiveness of spoken and written expression, which are deeply bound to traditions of print literacy,

will gradually be replaced by a more telegraphic sort of "plainspeak." Syntactic masonry is already a dying art. Neil Postman and others have already suggested what losses have been incurred by the advent of telegraphy and television—how the complex discourse patterns of the nineteenth century were flattened by the requirements of communication over distances. That tendency runs riot as the layers of mediation thicken. Simple linguistic prefab is now the norm, while ambiguity, paradox, irony, subtlety, and wit are fast disappearing. In their place, the simple "vision thing" and myriad other "things." Verbal intelligence, which has long been viewed as suspect as the act of reading, will come to seem positively conspiratorial. The greater part of any articulate person's energy will be deployed in dumbing-down her discourse.

Language will grow increasingly impoverished through a series of vicious cycles. For, of course, the usages of literature and scholarship are connected in fundamental ways to the general speech of the tribe. We can expect that curricula will be further streamlined, and difficult texts in the humanities will be pruned and glossed. One need only compare a college textbook from twenty years ago to its contemporary version. A poem by Milton, a play by Shakespeare—one can hardly find the text among the explanatory notes nowadays. Fewer and fewer people will be able to contend with the so-called masterworks of literature or ideas. Joyce, Woolf, Soyinka, not to mention the masters who preceded them, will go unread, and the civilizing energies of their prose will circulate aimlessly between closed covers.

2. *Flattening of historical perspectives.* As the circuit supplants the printed page, and as more and more of our communications involve us in network processes—which of their nature plant us in a perpetual present—our perception of history will inevitably alter. Changes in information storage and access are bound to impinge on our historical memory. The depth of field that is our sense of the past is not only a linguistic construct, but is in some essential way represented by the book and the physical accumulation of books in library spaces. In the contemplation of the single volume, or mass of volumes, we form a picture of time past as a growing deposit of sediment; we capture a sense of its depth and dimensionality. Moreover, we meet the past as much in the presentation of words in books of specific vintage as we do in any isolated fact or statistic. The database, useful as it is, expunges this context, this sense of chronology, and admits us to a weightless order in which all information is equally accessible....

3. *The waning of the private self.* We may even now be in the first stages of a process of social collectivization that will over time all but vanquish the ideal of the isolated individual. For some decades now we have been edging away from the perception of private life as something opaque, closed off to the world; we increasingly accept the transparency of a life lived within a set of systems, electronic or otherwise. Our technologies are not bound by season or light—it's always the same time in the circuit. And so long as time is money and money matters, those circuits will keep humming. The doors and walls of our habitations matter less and less—the world sweeps through the wires as it needs to, or as we need it to. The monitor light is always blinking; we are always potentially on-line.

I am not suggesting that we are all about to become mindless, soulless robots, or that personality will disappear altogether into an oceanic homogeneity. But certainly the idea of what it means to be a person living a life will be much changed. The figure-ground model, which has always featured a solitary self before a background that is the society of other selves, is romantic in the extreme. It is ever less tenable in the world as it is becoming. There are no more wildernesses, no more lonely homesteads, and, outside of cinema, no more emblems of the exalted individual.

The self must change as the nature of subjective space changes. And one of the many incremental transformations of our age has been the slow but steady destruction of subjective space. The physical and psychological distance between individuals has been shrinking for at least a century. In the process, the figure-ground image has begun to blur its boundary distinctions. One day we will conduct our public and private lives within networks so dense, among so many channels of instantaneous information, that it will make almost no sense to speak of the differentiations of subjective individualism.

We are already captive in our webs. Our slight solitudes are transected by codes, wires, and pulsations. We punch a number to check in with the answering machine, another to tape a show that we are too busy to watch. The strands of the web grow finer and finer—this is obvious. What is no less obvious is the fact that they will continue to proliferate, gaining in sophistication, merging functions so that one can bank by phone, shop via television, and so on. The natural tendency is toward streamlining: The smart dollar keeps finding ways to shorten the path, double-up the function. We might think in terms of a circuit-board model, picturing ourselves as the contact points. The expansion of electronic options is always at the cost of contractions in the private sphere. We will soon be navigating with ease among cataracts of organized pulsations, putting out and taking in signals. We will bring our terminals, our modems, and menus further and further into our former privacies; we will implicate ourselves by degrees in the unitary life, and there may come a day when we no longer remember that there was any other life....

Trafficking with tendencies—extrapolating and projecting as I have been doing—must finally remain a kind of gambling. One bets high on the validity of a notion and low on the human capacity for resistance and for unpredictable initiatives. No one can really predict how we will adapt to the transformations taking place all around us. We may discover, too, that language is a hardier thing than I have allowed. It may flourish among the beep and the click and the monitor as readily as it ever did on the printed page. I hope so, for language is the soul's ozone layer and we thin it at our peril.

POSSIBILITIES FOR WRITING

1. Identify the anecdotes that Birkerts includes as part of his essay, and explain his purpose in using each. Consider the extent to which they are useful to Birkerts in making his point about the development of electronic culture.

2. Summarize the three main consequences that Birkerts foresees as outcomes of the rise of an electronic culture and its dominance of print. Consider the extent to which you agree with his assessment.

3. Reflect on your own use of computer technology and your reliance on print culture. Write an essay in which you explore Birkerts's ideas in light of your personal experience, your observation of others, and your reading.

Judy Brady (b. 1937) *was born in San Francisco and attended the University of Iowa, graduating with a B.A. in 1962. A feminist and political activist, she edited* Women and Cancer (1990) *and* 1 in 3: Women with Cancer Confront an Epidemic (1991). *Her essays and articles have appeared in* Greenpeace *magazine and in the* Women's Review of Books. *Her best-known essay is "I Want a Wife."*

JUDY BRADY

I Want a Wife

"I Want a Wife" first appeared in the feminist magazine Ms., in its preview issue in 1972, under the name Judy Syfers, Brady's married name. The essay was twice reprinted in the magazine, in 1979 and in 1990. And it has been a popular and frequently anthologized piece for three decades. A large part of the essay's appeal and power derives from its wit and irony. Part derives from its humor and part from its style, particularly its use of repetition. But its biggest draw for many readers is the truths it tells in characterizing the endless work of a wife as she provides every imaginable service for her husband and children.

I belong to that classification of people known as wives. I am a Wife. And, not altogether incidentally, I am a mother.

Not too long ago a male friend of mine appeared on the scene fresh from a recent divorce. He had one child, who is, of course, with his ex-wife. He is obviously looking for another wife. As I thought about him while I was ironing one evening, it suddenly occurred to me that I, too, would like to have a wife. Why do I want a wife?

I would like to go back to school so that I can become economically independent, support myself, and, if need be, support those dependent upon me. I want a wife who will work and send me to school. And while I am going to school I want a wife to take care of my children. I want a wife to keep track of the children's doctor and dentist appointments. And to keep track of mine, too. I want a wife to make sure my children eat properly and are kept clean. I want a wife who will wash the children's clothes and keep them mended. I want a wife who is a good nurturant attendant to my children, who arranges for their schooling, makes sure that they have an adequate social life with their peers, takes them to the park, the zoo, etc. I want a wife who takes care of the children when they are sick, a wife who arranges to be around when the children need special care, because, of course, I cannot miss classes at school. My wife must arrange to lose time at work and not lose the job. It may mean a small cut in my wife's income from time to time, but I guess I can tolerate that. Needless to say, my wife will arrange and pay for the care of the children while my wife is working.

I want a wife who will take care of *my* physical needs. I want a wife who will keep my house clean. A wife who will pick up after me. I want a wife who will keep my clothes clean, ironed, mended, replaced when need be, and who will see to it that my personal things are kept in their proper place so that I can find what I need the minute I need it. I want a wife who cooks the meals, a wife who is a *good* cook. I want a wife who will plan the menus, do the necessary grocery shopping, prepare the meals, serve them pleasantly, and then do the cleaning up while I do my studying. I want a wife who will care for me when I am sick and sympathize with my pain and loss of time from school. I want a wife to go along when our family takes a vacation so that someone can continue to care for me and my children when I need a rest and change of scene.

I want a wife who will not bother me with rambling complaints about a wife's duties. But I want a wife who will listen to me when I feel the need to explain a rather difficult point I have come across in my course of studies. And I want a wife who will type my papers for me when I have written them.

I want a wife who will take care of the details of my social life. When my wife and I are invited out by my friends, I want a wife who will take care of the babysitting arrangements. When I meet people at school that I like and want to entertain, I want a wife who will have the house clean, will prepare a special meal, serve it to me and my friends, and not interrupt when I talk about the things that interest me and my friends. I want a wife who will have arranged that the children are fed and ready for bed before my guests arrive so that the children do not bother us. I want a wife who takes care of the needs of my guests so that they feel comfortable, who makes sure that they have an ashtray, that they are passed the hors d'oeuvres, that they are offered a second helping of the food, that their wine glasses are replenished when necessary, that their coffee is served to them as they like it. And I want a wife who knows that sometimes I need a night out by myself.

I want a wife who is sensitive to my sexual needs, a wife who makes love passionately and eagerly when I feel like it, a wife who makes sure that I am satisfied. And, of course, I want a wife who will not demand sexual attention when I am not in the mood for it. I want a wife who assumes the complete responsibility for birth control, because I do not want more children. I want a wife who will remain sexually faithful to me so that I do not have to clutter up my intellectual life with jealousies. And I want a wife who understands that *my* sexual needs may entail more than strict adherence to monogamy. I must, after all, be able to relate to people as fully as possible.

If, by chance, I find another person more suitable as a wife than the wife I already have, I want the liberty to replace my present wife with another one. Naturally, I will expect a fresh, new life; my wife will take the children and be solely responsible for them so that I am left free.

When I am through with school and have a job, I want my wife to quit working and remain at home so that my wife can more fully and completely take care of a wife's duties.

My God, who *wouldn't* want a wife?

POSSIBILITIES FOR WRITING

1. How does Brady define what it means to be a "wife"? How does she organize the many services a wife provides her husband and family? What do you think of Brady's characterization of a wife and her responsibilities? How do you think she wants her readers to respond to this characterization? Why?
2. Write a letter to Brady responding to "I Want a Wife." Let her know what you admire or don't admire about the essay and the extent to which you consider it effective and/or persuasive.
3. Write your own piece entitled "I Want a/an X." You can use Brady's essay as a model, and in the process, imitate some of her stylistic techniques. Or, alternatively, write an essay about the role of a "wife" in the early twenty-first century, explaining how a wife's responsibilities complement and are complemented by those of a spouse.

G(ilbert) K(eith) Chesterton (1874–1936) *was a prolific English critic and author of verse, essays, biographies, novels, and short stories. Author of more than one hundred books, Chesterton was born in London into a middle-class family on May 29, 1874. He studied at University College and the Slade School of Art* (1893–1896). *In 1922, Chesterton was converted from Anglicanism to Roman Catholicism, and thereafter he wrote several theologically oriented works, including lives of Francis of Assisi and Thomas Aquinas. He received honorary degrees from Edinburgh, Dublin, and Notre Dame universities.*

G. K. CHESTERTON

The Fallacy of Success

In "The Fallacy of Success," G. K. Chesterton takes a contrarian view about the usually positive value people put on success. He goes so far as to insist that "success" doesn't exist, that the concept of success is both empty and meaningless. His essay makes use of a number of literary devices, including allusion, irony, and hyperbole, in order to convey his critical attitude toward the fallacy of success.

There has appeared in our time a particular class of books and articles which I sincerely and solemnly think may be called the silliest ever known among men. They are much more wild than the wildest romances of chivalry and much more dull than the dullest religious tract. Moreover, the romances of chivalry were at least about chivalry; the religious tracts are about religion. But these things are about nothing; they are about what is called Success. On every bookstall, in every magazine, you may find works telling people how to succeed. They are books showing men how to succeed in everything; they are written by men who cannot even succeed in writing books. To begin with, of course, there is no such thing as Success. Or, if you like to put it so, there is nothing that is not successful. That a thing is successful merely means that it is; a millionaire is successful in being a millionaire and a donkey in being a donkey. Any live man has succeeded in living; any dead man may have succeeded in committing suicide. But, passing over the bad logic and bad philosophy in the phrase, we may take it, as these writers do, in the ordinary sense of success in obtaining money or worldly position. These writers profess to tell the ordinary man how he may succeed in his trade or speculation— how, if he is a builder, he may succeed as a builder; how, if he is a stockbroker, he may succeed as a stockbroker. They profess to show him how, if he is a grocer, he may become a sporting yachtsman;

how, if he is a tenth-rate journalist, he may become a peer; and how, if he is a German Jew, he may become an Anglo-Saxon. This is a definite and business-like proposal, and I really think that the people who buy these books (if any people do buy them) have a moral, if not a legal, right to ask for their money back. Nobody would dare to publish a book about electricity which literally told one nothing about electricity; no one would dare publish an article on botany which showed that the writer did not know which end of a plant grew in the earth. Yet our modern world is full of books about Success and successful people which literally contain no kind of idea, and scarcely any kind of verbal sense.

It is perfectly obvious that in any decent occupation (such as bricklaying or writing books) there are only two ways (in any special sense) of succeeding. One is by doing very good work, the other is by cheating. Both are much too simple to require any literary explanation. If you are in for the high jump, either jump higher than any one else, or manage somehow to pretend that you have done so. If you want to succeed at whist, either be a good whist-player, or play with marked cards. You may want a book about jumping; you may want a book about whist; you may want a book about cheating at whist. But you cannot want a book about Success. Especially you cannot want a book about Success such as those which you can now find scattered by the hundred about the book-market. You may want to jump or to play cards; but you do not want to read wandering statements to the effect that jumping is jumping, or that games are won by winners. If these writers, for instance, said anything about success in jumping it would be something like this: "The jumper must have a clear aim before him. He must desire definitely to jump higher than the other men who are in for the same competition. He must let no feeble feelings of mercy (sneaked from the sickening Little Englanders and Pro-Boers) prevent him from trying to *do his best*. He must remember that a competition in jumping is distinctly competitive, and that, as Darwin has gloriously demonstrated, THE WEAKEST GO TO THE WALL." That is the kind of thing the book would say, and very useful it would be, no doubt, if read out in a low and tense voice to a young man just about to take the high jump. Or suppose that in the course of his intellectual rambles the philosopher of Success dropped upon our other case, that of playing cards, his bracing advice would run—"In playing cards it is very necessary to avoid the mistake (commonly made by maudlin humanitarians and Free Traders) of permitting your opponent to win the game. You must have grit and snap and *go in to win*. The days of idealism and superstition are over. We live in a time of science and hard common sense, and it has now been definitely proved that in any game where two are playing IF ONE DOES NOT WIN, THE OTHER WILL." It is all very stirring, of course; but I confess that if I were playing cards I would rather have some decent little book which told me the rules of the game. Beyond the rules of the game it is all a question either of talent or dishonesty; and I will undertake to provide either one or the other—which, it is not for me to say.

Turning over a popular magazine, I find a queer and amusing example. There is an article called "The Instinct that Makes People Rich." It is decorated in front with a formidable portrait of Lord Rothschild. There are many definite methods, honest and dishonest, which make people rich; the only "instinct" I know of which does it is that instinct which theological Christianity crudely describes as "the sin of avarice." That, however, is beside the present point. I wish to quote the following exquisite paragraphs as a piece of typical advice as to how to succeed. It is so practical; it leaves so little doubt about what should be our next step—

> The name of Vanderbilt is synonymous with wealth gained by modern enterprise. 'Cornelius,' the founder of the family, was the first of the great American magnates of commerce. He started as the son of a poor farmer; he ended as a millionaire twenty times over.
>
> He had the money-making instinct. He seized his opportunities, the opportunities that were given by the application of the steam-engine to ocean traffic, and by the birth of railway locomotion in the wealthy but underdeveloped United States of America, and consequently he amassed an immense fortune.
>
> Now it is, of course, obvious that we cannot all follow exactly in the footsteps of this great railway monarch. The precise opportunities that fell to him do not occur to us. Circumstances have changed. But, although this is so, still, in our own sphere and in our own circumstances, we can follow his general methods; we can seize those opportunities that are given us, and give ourselves a very fair chance of attaining riches.

In such strange utterances we see quite clearly what is really at the bottom of all these articles and books. It is not mere business; it is not even mere cynicism. It is mysticism; the horrible mysticism of money. The writer of that passage did not really have the remotest notion of how Vanderbilt made his money, or of how anybody else is to make his. He does, indeed, conclude his remarks by advocating some scheme; but it has nothing in the world to do with Vanderbilt. He merely wished to prostrate himself before the mystery of a millionaire. For when we really worship anything, we love not only its clearness but its obscurity. We exult in its very invisibility. Thus, for instance, when a man is in love with a woman he takes special pleasure in the fact that a woman is unreasonable. Thus, again, the very pious poet, celebrating his Creator, takes pleasure in saying that God moves in a mysterious way. Now, the writer of the paragraph which I have quoted does not seem to have had anything to do with a god and I should not think (judging by his extreme unpracticality) that he had ever been really in love with a woman. But the thing he does worship—Vanderbilt—he treats in exactly this mystical manner. He really revels in the fact his deity Vanderbilt is keeping a secret from him. And it fills his soul with a sort of transport of cunning, an ecstasy of priestcraft, that he should pretend to be telling to the multitude that terrible secret which he does not know.

Speaking about the instinct that makes people rich, the same writer remarks—

> In the olden days, its existence was fully understood. The Greeks enshrined it in the story of Midas, of the 'Golden Touch.' Here was a man who turned everything he laid his hands upon into gold. His life was a progress amidst riches. Out of everything that came in his way he created the precious metal. 'A foolish legend,' said the wiseacres of the Victorian age. 'A truth,' say we of to-day. We all know of such men. We are ever meeting or reading about such persons who turn everything they touch into gold. Success dogs their very footsteps. Their life's pathway leads unerringly upwards. They cannot fail.

Unfortunately, however, Midas could fail; he did. His path did not lead unerringly upward. He starved because whenever he touched a biscuit or a ham sandwich it turned to gold. That was the whole point of the story, though the writer has to suppress it delicately, writing so near to a portrait of Lord Rothschild. The old fables of mankind are, indeed, unfathomably wise; but we must not have them expurgated in the interests of Mr. Vanderbilt. We must not have King Midas represented as an example of success; he was a failure of an unusually painful kind. Also, he had the ears of an ass. Also (like most other prominent and wealthy persons) he endeavoured to conceal the fact. It was his barber (if I remember right) who had to be treated on a confidential footing with regard to this peculiarity; and his barber, instead of behaving like a go-ahead person of the Succeed-at-all-costs school and trying to blackmail King Midas, went away and whispered this splendid piece of society scandal to the reeds, who enjoyed it enormously. It is said that they also whispered it as the winds swayed them to and fro. I look reverently at the portrait of Lord Rothschild; I read reverently about the exploits of Mr. Vanderbilt. I know that I cannot turn everything I touch to gold; but then I also know that I have never tried, having a preference for other substances, such as grass, and good wine. I know that these people have certainly succeeded in something; that they have certainly overcome somebody; I know that they are kings in a sense that no men were ever kings before; that they create markets and bestride continents. Yet it always seems to me that there is some small domestic fact that they are hiding, and I have sometimes thought I heard upon the wind the laughter and whisper of the reeds.

At least, let us hope that we shall all live to see these absurd books about Success covered with a proper derision and neglect. They do not teach people to be successful, but they do teach people to be snobbish; they do spread a sort of evil poetry of worldliness. The Puritans are always denouncing books that inflame lust; what shall we say of books that inflame the viler passions of avarice and pride? A hundred years ago we had the ideal of the Industrious Apprentice; boys were told that by thrift and work they would all become Lord Mayors. This was fallacious, but it was manly, and had a minimum of moral truth. In our society, temperance will not help a poor man to enrich himself, but it may help him to respect himself. Good work will not make him a rich man, but good work may make him a good workman. The Industrious Apprentice rose by virtues few and narrow indeed, but still virtues. But what shall we say of the gospel preached to the new Industrious Apprentice; the Apprentice who rises not by his virtues, but avowedly by his vices?

POSSIBILITIES FOR WRITING

1. Summarize the argument Chesterton makes about why books claiming to help others achieve success are not worth buying and reading. Consider the evidence Chesterton cites, and the degree to which you are or are not persuaded by his argument.
2. Analyze the strategies and techniques Chesterton uses to convey his attitude toward success. Identify specific uses of language and detail that show how Chesterton establishes a critical attitude and a sarcastic tone toward his subject.
3. Write an essay in which you explain whether you believe there is such a thing as success. If you believe there is, explain where and how you disagree with Chesterton. In the process, explain what you believe success involves and how it might be achieved.

Judith Ortiz Cofer (b. 1952) spent her childhood in the small Puerto Rican town where she was born and in Paterson, New Jersey, where her family lived for most of each year, from the time she was three. She attended Catholic schools in Paterson and she holds degrees from the University of Georgia and Florida Atlantic University. She has published several volumes of poetry, including Reaching for the Mainland *(1996), and her 1989 novel* The Line of the Sun *was nominated for a Pulitzer Prize. Cofer has also published two autobiographical works:* Silent Dancing: A Partial Remembrance of a Puerto Rican Childhood *(1990) and* The Latin Deli: Prose and Poetry *(1993). More recent books are* Woman in Front of the Sun: On Becoming a Writer *(2000),* The Meaning of Consuelo *(2003), and* Lessons from a Writer's Life *(2011).*

JUDITH ORTIZ COFER

Casa: A Partial Remembrance of a Puerto Rican Childhood

In "Casa: A Partial Remembrance of a Puerto Rican Childhood," Judith Ortiz Cofer describes the bonds among a community of women— three generations of a family headed by the matriarch, Mamá, the author's grandmother. In celebrating the intertwined lives of these women of her family, Cofer simultaneously celebrates the power of storytelling. Weaving these two strands of her essay together—family and stories— Cofer conveys some important ideas about women and their relations with men, along with important ideas about culture and its significance for identity.

At three or four o'clock in the afternoon, the hour of *café con leche*, the women of my family gathered in Mamá's living room to speak of important things and retell familiar stories meant to be overheard by us young girls, their daughters. In Mamá's house (everyone called my grandmother Mamá) was a large parlor built by my grandfather to his wife's exact specifications so that it was always cool, facing away from the sun. The doorway was on the side of the house so no one could walk directly into her living room. First they had to take a little stroll through and around her beautiful garden where prize-winning orchids grew in the trunk of an ancient tree she had hollowed out for that purpose. This room was furnished with several mahogany rocking chairs, acquired at the births of her children, and one intricately carved rocker that had passed down to Mamá at the death of her own mother.

It was on these rockers that my mother, her sisters, and my grandmother sat on these afternoons of my childhood to tell their stories, teaching each other, and my cousin and me, what it was like to be a woman, more specifically, a Puerto Rican woman. They talked about life on the island, and life in *Los Nueva Yores,* their way of referring to the United States from New York City to California: the other place, not home, all the same. They told real-life stories, though as I later learned, always embellishing them with a little or a lot of dramatic detail. And they told *cuentos,* the morality and cautionary tales told by the women in our family for generations: stories that became a part of my subconscious as I grew up in two worlds, the tropical island and the cold city, and that would later surface in my dreams and in my poetry.

One of these tales was about the woman who was left at the altar. Mamá liked to tell that one with histrionic intensity. I remember the rise and fall of her voice, the sighs, and her constantly gesturing hands, like two birds swooping through her words. This particular story usually would come up in a conversation as a result of someone mentioning a forthcoming engagement or wedding. The first time I remember hearing it, I was sitting on the floor at Mamá's feet, pretending to read a comic book. I may have been eleven or twelve years old, at that difficult age when a girl was no longer a child who could be ordered to leave the room if the women wanted freedom to take their talk into forbidden zones, nor really old enough to be considered a part of their conclave. I could only sit quietly, pretending to be in another world, while absorbing it all in a sort of unspoken agreement of my status as silent auditor. On this day, Mamá had taken my long, tangled mane of hair into her ever-busy hands. Without looking down at me and with no interruption of her flow of words, she began braiding my hair, working at it with the quickness and determination that characterized all her actions. My mother was watching us impassively from her rocker across the room. On her lips played a little ironic smile. I would never sit still for *her* ministrations, but even then, I instinctively knew that she did not possess Mamá's matriarchal power to command and keep everyone's attention. This was never more evident than in the spell she cast when telling a story.

"It is not like it used to be when I was a girl," Mamá announced. "Then, a man could leave a girl standing at the church altar with a bouquet of fresh flowers in her hands and disappear off the face of the earth. No way to track him down if he was from another town.

He could be a married man, with maybe even two or three families all over the island. There was no way to know. And there were men who did this. Hombres with the devil in their flesh who would come to a pueblo, like this one, take a job at one of the haciendas, never meaning to stay, only to have a good time and to seduce the women."

The whole time she was speaking, Mamá would be weaving my hair into a flat plait that required pulling apart the two sections of hair with little jerks that made my eyes water; but knowing how grandmother detested whining and *boba* (sissy) tears, as she called them, I just sat up as straight and stiff as I did at La Escuela San José, where the nuns enforced good posture with a flexible plastic ruler they bounced off of slumped shoulders and heads. As Mamá's story progressed, I noticed how my young Aunt Laura lowered her eyes, refusing to meet Mamá's meaningful gaze. Laura was seventeen, in her last year of high school, and already engaged to a boy from another town who had staked his claim with a tiny diamond ring, then left for Los Nueva Yores to make his fortune. They were planning to get married in a year. Mamá had expressed serious doubts that the wedding would ever take place. In Mamá's eyes, a man set free without a legal contract was a man lost. She believed that marriage was not something men desired, but simply the price they had to pay for the privilege of children and, of course, for what no decent (synonymous with "smart") woman would give away for free.

"María La Loca was only seventeen when *it* happened to her." I listened closely at the mention of this name. María was a town character, a fat middle-aged woman who lived with her old mother on the outskirts of town. She was to be seen around the pueblo delivering the meat pies the two women made for a living. The most peculiar thing about María, in my eyes, was that she walked and moved like a little girl though she had the thick body and wrinkled face of an old woman. She would swing her hips in an exaggerated, clownish way, and sometimes even hop and skip up to someone's house. She spoke to no one. Even if you asked her a question, she would just look at you and smile, showing her yellow teeth. But I had heard that if you got close enough, you could hear her humming a tune without words. The kids yelled out nasty things at her, calling her *La Loca,* and the men who hang out at the bodega playing dominoes sometimes whistled mockingly as she passed by with her funny, outlandish walk. But María seemed impervious to it all, carrying her basket of *pasteles* like a grotesque Little Red Riding Hood through the forest.

María La Loca interested me, as did all the eccentrics and crazies of our pueblo. Their weirdness was a measuring stick I used in my serious quest for a definition of normal. As a Navy brat shuttling between New Jersey and the pueblo, I was constantly made to feel like an oddball by my peers, who made fun of my two-way accent: a Spanish accent when I spoke English, and when I spoke Spanish I was told that I sounded like a *Gringa*. Being the outsider had already turned my brother and me into cultural chameleons. We developed early on the ability to blend into a crowd, to sit and read quietly in a fifth story apartment building for days and days when it was too bitterly cold to play outside, or, set free, to run wild in Mamá's realm, where she took charge of our lives, releasing Mother for a while from the intense fear for our safety that our father's absences instilled in her. In order to keep us from harm when Father was away, Mother kept us under strict surveillance. She even walked us to and from Public School No. 11, which we attended during the months we lived in Paterson, New Jersey, our home base in the states. Mamá freed all three of us like pigeons from a cage. I saw her as my liberator and my model. Her stories were parables from which to glean the *Truth*.

"María La Loca was once a beautiful girl. Everyone thought she would marry the Méndez boy." As everyone knew, Rogelio Méndez was the richest man in town. "But," Mamá continued, knitting my hair with the same intensity she was putting into her story, "this *macho* made a fool out of her and ruined her life." She paused for the effect of her use of the word "macho," which at that time had not yet become a popular epithet for an unliberated man. This word had for us the crude and comical connotation of "male of the species," stud; a *macho* was what you put in a pen to increase your stock.

I peeked over my comic book at my mother. She too was under Mamá's spell, smiling conspiratorially at this little swipe at men. She was safe from Mamá's contempt in this area. Married at an early age, an unspotted lamb, she had been accepted by a good family of strict Spaniards whose name was old and respected, though their fortune had been lost long before my birth. In a rocker Papá had painted sky blue sat Mamá's oldest child, Aunt Nena. Mother of three children, stepmother of two more, she was a quiet woman who liked books but had married an ignorant and abusive widower whose main interest in life was accumulating wealth. He too was in the mainland working on his dream of returning home rich and triumphant to buy the *finca* of his dreams. She was waiting for him to send for her. She would leave her children with Mamá for several years while the two of them slaved away in factories. He would one day be a rich man, and she a sadder woman. Even now her life-light was dimming. She spoke little, an aberration in Mamá's house, and she read avidly, as if storing up spiritual food for the long winters that awaited her in Los Nueva Yores without her family. But even Aunt Nena came alive to Mamá's words, rocking gently, her hands over a thick book in her lap.

Her daughter, my cousin Sara, played jacks by herself on the tile porch outside the room where we sat. She was a year older than I. We shared a bed and all our family's secrets. Collaborators in search of answers, Sara and I discussed everything we heard the women say, trying to fit it all together like a puzzle that, once assembled, would reveal life's mysteries to us. Though she and I still enjoyed taking part in boys' games—chase, volleyball, and even *vaqueros,* the island version of cowboys and Indians involving cap-gun battles and violent shoot-outs under the mango tree in Mamá's backyard—we loved best the quiet hours in the afternoon when the men were still at work, and the boys had gone to play serious baseball at the park. Then Mamá's house belonged only to us women. The aroma of coffee perking in the kitchen, the mesmerizing creaks and groans of the rockers, and the women telling their lives in *cuentos* are forever woven into the fabric of my imagination, braided like my hair that day I felt my grandmother's hands teaching me about strength, her voice convincing me of the power of storytelling.

That day Mamá told how the beautiful María had fallen prey to a man whose name was never the same in subsequent versions of the story; it was Juan one time, José, Rafael, Diego, another. We understood that neither the name nor any of the *facts* were important, only that a woman had allowed love to defeat her. Mamá put each of us in María's place by describing her wedding dress in loving detail: how she looked like a princess in her lace as she waited at the altar. Then, as Mamá approached the tragic denouement of her story, I was distracted by the sound of my aunt Laura's violent rocking. She seemed on the verge of tears. She knew the fable was intended for her. That week she was going to have her wedding gown fitted, though no firm date had been set for the marriage. Mamá ignored Laura's obvious discomfort, digging out a ribbon from the sewing basket she kept by her rocker while describing María's long illness, "a fever that would not break for days." She spoke of a mother's despair: "that woman climbed the church steps on her knees every morning, wore only black as a *promesa* to the Holy Virgin in exchange for her daughter's health." By the time María returned from her honeymoon with death, she was ravished, no longer young or sane. "As you can see, she is almost as old as her mother already," Mamá lamented while tying the ribbon to the ends of my hair, pulling it back with such force that I just knew I would never be able to close my eyes completely again.

"That María's getting crazier every day." Mamá's voice would take a lighter tone now, expressing satisfaction, either for the perfection of my braid, or for a story well told—it was hard to tell. "You know that tune María is always humming?" Carried away by her enthusiasm, I tried to nod, but Mamá still had me pinned between her knees.

"Well, that's the wedding march." Surprising us all, Mamá sang out, "Da, da, dara...da, da, dara." Then lifting me off the floor by my skinny shoulders, she would lead me around the room in an impromptu waltz—another session ending with the laughter of women, all of us caught up in the infectious joke of our lives.

POSSIBILITIES FOR WRITING

1. The longest and most elaborate example Cofer uses is that of María La Loca. Explain the significance of this example, and identify and explain the significance of another example that Cofer includes.

2. Cofer uses a number of Spanish words and phrases in "Casa," some of which she translates and others of which she leaves untranslated. What is the effect of these Spanish words and phrases? What would be gained or lost if they were omitted?

3. Use the following quotation as a springboard to write about identity as a theme in "Casa": "It was on these rockers that my mother, her sisters, and my grandmother sat on these afternoons of my childhood to tell their stories, teaching each other, and my cousin and me, what it was like to be a woman, more specifically, a Puerto Rican woman."

Bernard Cooper (b.1951) *grew up in Hollywood, California, and received a BFA and an MFA from the California Institute of the Arts. Winner of the PEN/Ernest Hemingway award and the O. Henry Prize, Cooper has published two highly praised collections of short stories,* A Year of Rhymes (1993) *and* Guess Again (2000). *He is also the author of two volumes of autobiographical essays,* Maps to Anywhere (1990) *and* Truth Serum (1996), *in he which focuses on coming to terms with his homosexuality and with the onset of AIDS. More recently, he has published* The Bill from My Father: A Memoir (2007). *He currently teaches creative writing at Antioch College in Los Angeles and is an art critic for the* Los Angeles Times.

BERNARD COOPER

Labyrinthine

In "Labyrinthine," Bernard Cooper employs the images of the labyrinth, or maze, to explore ideas about aging, learning, and complexity. His childhood love of solving and creating mazes serves as a starting point for his reflections about the way mazes come to symbolize the labyrinthine complications that emerge in later life.

When I discovered my first maze among the pages of a coloring book, I dutifully guided the mouse in the margins toward his wedge of cheese at the center. I dragged my crayon through narrow alleys and around corners, backing out of dead ends, trying this direction instead of that. Often I had to stop and rethink my strategy, squinting until some unobstructed path became clear and I could start to move the crayon again.

I kept my sights on the small chamber in the middle of the page and knew that being lost would not be in vain; wrong turns only improved my chances, showed me that one true path toward my reward. Even when trapped in the hallways of the maze, I felt an embracing safety, as if I'd been zipped in a sleeping bag.

Reaching the cheese had about it a triumph and finality I'd never experienced after coloring a picture or connecting the dots. If only I'd known a word like "inevitable," since that's how it felt to finally slip into the innermost room. I gripped the crayon, savored the place.

The lines on the next maze in the coloring book curved and rippled like waves on water. The object of this maze was to lead a hungry dog to his bone. Mouse to cheese, dog to bone—the premise quickly ceased to matter. It was the tricky, halting travel I was after, forging a passage, finding my way.

Later that day, as I walked through our living room, a maze revealed itself to me in the mahogany coffee table. I sat on the floor, fingered the wood grain, and found a winding avenue through it. The fabric of my parents' blanket was a pattern of climbing ivy and, from one end of the bed to the other, I traced the air between the tendrils. Soon I didn't need to use a finger, mapping my path by sight. I moved through the veins of the marble heart, through the space between the paisleys on my mother's blouse. At the age of seven I changed forever, like the faithful who see Christ on the side of a barn or peering up from a corn tortilla. Everywhere I looked, a labyrinth meandered.

Soon the mazes in the coloring books, in the comic-strip section of the Sunday paper, or on the placemats of coffee shops that served "children's meals" became too easy. And so I began to make my own. I drew them on the cardboard rectangles that my father's dress shirts were folded around when they came back from the cleaner's. My frugal mother, hoarder of jelly jars and rubber bands, had saved a stack of them. She was happy to put the cardboard to use, if a bit mystified by my new obsession.

The best method was to start from the center and work outward with a sharpened pencil, creating layers of complication. I left a few gaps in every line, and after I'd gotten a feel for the architecture of the whole, I'd close off openings, reinforce walls, a slave sealing the pharaoh's tomb. My blind alleys were especially treacherous; I constructed them so that, by the time one realized he'd gotten stuck, turning back would be an exquisite ordeal.

My hobby required a twofold concentration: carefully planning a maze while allowing myself the fresh pleasure of moving through it. Alone in my bedroom, sitting at my desk, I sometimes spent the better part of an afternoon on a single maze. I worked with the patience of a redwood growing rings. Drawing myself into corners, erasing a wall if all else failed, I fooled and baffled and freed myself.

Eventually I used shelf paper, tearing off larger and larger sheets to accommodate my burgeoning ambition. Once I brought a huge maze to my mother, who was drinking a cup of coffee in the kitchen. It wafted behind me like an ostentatious cape. I draped it over the table and challenged her to try it. She hadn't looked at it for more than a second before she refused. "You've got to be kidding," she said, blotting her lips with a paper napkin. "I'm lost enough as it is." When my father returned from work that night, he hefted his briefcase into the closet, his hat wet and drooping from the rain. "Later," he said (his code word for "never") when I waved the banner of my labyrinth before him.

It was inconceivable to me that someone wouldn't want to enter a maze, wouldn't lapse into the trance it required, wouldn't sacrifice the time to find a solution. But mazes had a strange effect on my parents: they took one look at those tangled paths and seemed to wilt.

I was a late child, a "big surprise" as my mother liked to say; by the time I'd turned seven, my parents were trying to cut a swath through the forest of middle age. Their mortgage ballooned. The plumbing rusted. Old friends grew sick or moved away. The creases in their skin deepened, so complex a network of lines, my mazes paled by comparison. Father's hair receded, Mother's grayed. "When you've lived as long as we have...," they'd say, which meant no surprises loomed in their future; it was repetition from here on out. The endless succession of burdens and concerns was enough to make anyone forgetful. Eggs were boiled until they turned brown, sprinklers left on till the lawn grew soggy, keys and glasses and watches misplaced. When I asked my parents about their past, they cocked their heads, stared into the distance, and often couldn't recall the details.

Thirty years later, I understand my parents' refusal. Why would anyone choose to get mired in a maze when the days encase us, loopy and confusing? Remembered events merge together or fade away. Places and dates grow dubious, a jumble of guesswork and speculation. *What's-his-name* and *thingama-jig* replace the bright particular. Recollecting the past becomes as unreliable as forecasting the future; you consult yourself with a certain trepidation and take your answer with a grain of salt. The friends you turn to for confirmation are just as muddled; they furrow their brows and look at you blankly. Of course, once in a while you find the tiny, pungent details poised on your tongue like caviar. But more often than not, you settle for sloppy approximations—"I was visiting Texas or Colorado, in 1971 or '72"— and the anecdote rambles on regardless. When the face of a friend from childhood suddenly comes back to me, it's sad to think that if a certain synapse hadn't fired just then, I may never have recalled that friend again. Sometimes I'm not sure if I've overheard a story in conversation, read it in a book, or if I'm the person to whom it happened; whose adventures, besides my own, are wedged in my memory? Then there are the things I've dreamed and mistaken as fact. When you've lived as long as I have, uncertainty is virtually indistinguishable from the truth, which as far as I know is never naked, but always wearing some disguise.

Mother, Father: I'm growing middle-aged, lost in the folds and bones of my body. It gets harder to remember the days when you were here. I suppose it was inevitable that, gazing down at this piece of paper, I'd feel your weary expressions on my face. What have things been like since you've been gone? Labyrinthine. The very sound of that word sums it up—as slippery as thought, as perplexing as the truth, as long and convoluted as a life.

POSSIBILITIES FOR WRITING

1. Analyze the structure of Cooper's essay. Explain how its parts are related and how its central idea is developed. What is Cooper's central idea, and how does your analysis of the essay's structure help you to understand it?
2. Besides the image of the maze, or labyrinth, what other images does Cooper use to convey his thinking? Explain the role his parents play in this essay and in Cooper's thinking, including any images associated with them.
3. Write a paragraph or two about what Cooper says and suggests about "truth." Explain what Cooper means by saying, "uncertainty is virtually indistinguishable from truth" and that truth is "never naked," but is always "wearing some disguise."

Joan Didion (b. 1934) grew up in central California, where her family had lived for many generations. After graduating from the University of California at Berkeley in 1956, she joined the staff of Vogue *magazine, where she worked until the publication of her first novel,* Run River, *in 1963. Other novels followed—including* Play It As It Lays *(1970),* A Book of Common Prayer *(1977), and* The Last Thing He Wanted *(1996)—but it is her essays, particularly those collected in* Slouching Towards Bethlehem *(1968) and* The White Album *(1979), that established Didion as one of the most admired voices of her generation. A meticulous stylist who combines sharply observed detail with wry— even bracing—irony, she has examined subjects that range from life in Southern California to the Washington political scene to the war in El Salvador to Las Vegas weddings. More recently, Didion has published a pair of memoirs:* The Year of Magical Thinking *(2006) and* Blue Nights *(2011), "about the loss of her husband and her daughter, respectively."*

JOAN DIDION

On Self-Respect

The title of Didion's essay promises an exploration of the meaning of self-respect, and, not surprisingly, it delivers on that promise. Along the way it also says what self-respect is not: a technique of "negative definition" writers often use when explaining an abstract concept. Besides using negative definition, Didion provides examples to clarify what she means by self-respect. Didion's essay is loosely structured. Its form, like its title, owes something to Montaigne, who envisioned the essay as an exploration of a topic, without a strictly logical structure and a clearly defined thesis. Didion asserts the importance of self-respect, and she identifies a number of key qualities it comprises, including honesty, integrity, and discipline.

Once, in a dry season, I wrote in large letters across two pages of a notebook that innocence ends when one is stripped of the delusion that one likes oneself. Although now, some years later, I marvel that a mind on the outs with itself should have nonetheless made painstaking record of its every tremor, I recall with embarrassing clarity the flavor of those particular ashes. It was a matter of misplaced self-respect.

I had not been elected to Phi Beta Kappa. This failure could scarcely have been more predictable or less ambiguous (I simply did not have the grades), but I was unnerved by it; I had somehow thought myself a kind of academic Raskolnikov, curiously exempt from the cause-effect relationships which hampered others. Although even the humorless nineteen-year-old that I was must have recognized that the situation lacked real tragic stature, the day that I did not make Phi Beta Kappa nonetheless marked the end of something, and innocence may well be the word for it. I lost the conviction that lights would always turn green for me, the pleasant certainty that those rather passive virtues which had won me approval as a child automatically guaranteed me not only Phi Beta Kappa keys but happiness, honor, and the love of a good man; lost a certain touching faith in the totem power of good manners, clean hair, and proven competence on the Stanford-Binet scale. To such doubtful amulets had my self-respect been pinned, and I faced myself that day with the nonplused apprehension of someone who has come across a vampire and has no crucifix at hand.

Although to be driven back upon oneself is an uneasy affair at best, rather like trying to cross a border with borrowed credentials, it seems to me now the one condition necessary to the beginnings of real self-respect. Most of our platitudes notwithstanding, self-deception remains the most difficult deception. The tricks that work on others count for nothing in that very well-lit back alley where one keeps assignations with oneself: no winning smiles will do here, no prettily drawn lists of good intentions. One shuffles flashily but in vain through one's marked cards—the kindness done for the wrong reason, the apparent triumph which involved no real effort, the seemingly heroic act into which one had been shamed. The dismal fact is that self-respect has nothing to do with the approval of others—who are, after all, deceived easily enough; has nothing to do with reputation, which, as Rhett Butler told Scarlett O'Hara, is something people with courage can do without.

To do without self-respect, on the other hand, is to be an unwilling audience of one to an interminable documentary that details one's failings, both real and imagined, with fresh footage spliced in for every screening. *There's the glass you broke in anger, there's the hurt on X's face; watch now, this next scene, the night Y came back from Houston, see how you muff this one.* To live without self-respect is to lie awake some night, beyond the reach of warm milk, phenobarbital, and the sleeping hand on the coverlet, counting up the sins of commission and omission, the trusts betrayed, the promises subtly broken, the gifts irrevocably wasted through sloth or cowardice or carelessness. However long we postpone it, we eventually lie down alone in that notoriously uncomfortable bed, the one we make ourselves. Whether or not we sleep in it depends, of course, on whether or not we respect ourselves.

To protest that some fairly improbable people, some people who *could not possibly respect themselves* seem to sleep easily enough is to miss the point entirely, as surely as those people miss it who think that self-respect has necessarily to do with not having safety pins in one's underwear. There is a common superstition that "self-respect" is a kind of charm against snakes, something that keeps those who have it locked in some unblighted Eden, out of strange beds, ambivalent conversations, and trouble in general. It does not at all. It has nothing to do with the face of things, but concerns instead a separate peace, a private reconciliation. Although the careless, suicidal Julian English in *Appointment in Samarra* and the careless, incurably dishonest Jordan Baker in *The Great Gatsby* seem equally improbable candidates for self-respect, Jordan Baker had it, Julian English did not. With that genius for accommodation more often seen in women than in men, Jordan took her own measure, made her own peace, avoided threats to that peace: "I hate careless people," she told Nick Carraway. "It takes two to make an accident."

Like Jordan Baker, people with self-respect have the courage of their mistakes. They know the price of things. If they choose to commit adultery, they do not then go running, in an access of bad conscience, to receive absolution from the wronged parties; nor do they complain unduly of the unfairness, the undeserved embarrass-ment, of being named co-respondent. In brief, people with self-respect exhibit a certain toughness, a kind of moral nerve; they display what was once called *character,* a quality which, although approved in the abstract, sometimes loses ground to other, more instantly negotiable virtues. The measure of its slipping prestige is that one tends to think of it only in connection with homely children and United States sena-tors who have been defeated, preferably in the primary, for reelection. Nonetheless, character—the willingness to accept responsibility for one's own life—is the source from which self-respect springs.

Self-respect is something that our grandparents, whether or not they had it, knew all about. They had instilled in them, young, a certain discipline, the sense that one lives by doing things one does not particularly want to do, by putting fears and doubts to one side, by weighing immediate comforts against the possibility of larger, even in-tangible, comforts. It seemed to the nineteenth century admirable, but not remarkable, that Chinese Gordon put on a clean white suit and held Khartoum against the Mahdi; it did not seem unjust that the way to free land in California involved death and difficulty and dirt. In a diary kept during the winter of 1846, an emigrating twelve-year-old named

Narcissa Cornwall noted coolly: "Father was busy reading and did not notice that the house was being filled with strange Indians until Mother spoke about it." Even lacking any clue as to what Mother said, one can scarcely fail to be impressed by the entire incident: the father reading, the Indians filing in, the mother choosing the words that would not alarm, the child duly recording the event and noting further that those particular Indians were not, "fortunately for us," hostile. Indians were simply part of the *donnée*.

In one guise or another, Indians always are. Again, it is a question of recognizing that anything worth having has its price. People who respect themselves are willing to accept the risk that the Indians will be hostile, that the venture will go bankrupt, that the liaison may not turn out to be one in which *every day is a holiday because you're married to me*. They are willing to invest something of themselves; they may not play at all, but when they do play, they know the odds.

That kind of self-respect is a discipline, a habit of mind that can never be faked but can be developed, trained, coaxed forth. It was once suggested to me that, as an antidote to crying, I put my head in a paper bag. As it happens, there is a sound physiological reason, something to do with oxygen, for doing exactly that, but the psychological effect alone is incalculable: it is difficult in the extreme to continue fancying oneself Cathy in *Wuthering Heights* with one's head in a Food Fair bag. There is a similar case for all the small disciplines, unimportant in themselves; imagine maintaining any kind of swoon, commiserative or carnal, in a cold shower.

But those small disciplines are valuable only insofar as they represent larger ones. To say that Waterloo was won on the playing fields of Eton is not to say that Napoleon might have been saved by a crash program in cricket; to give formal dinners in the rain forest would be pointless did not the candlelight flickering on the liana call forth deeper, stronger disciplines, values instilled long before. It is a kind of ritual, helping us to remember who and what we are. In order to remember it, one must have known it.

To have that sense of one's intrinsic worth which constitutes self-respect is potentially to have everything: the ability to discriminate, to love and to remain indifferent. To lack it is to be locked within oneself, paradoxically incapable of either love or indifference. If we do not respect ourselves, we are on the one hand forced to despise those who have so few resources as to consort with us, so little perception as to remain blind to our fatal weaknesses. On the other, we are peculiarly in thrall to everyone we see, curiously determined to live out—since our self-image is untenable—their false notions of us. We flatter ourselves by thinking this compulsion to please others an attractive trait: a gist for imaginative empathy, evidence of our willingness to give. *Of course* I will play Francesca to your Paolo, Helen Keller to anyone's Annie Sullivan: no expectation is too misplaced, no role too ludicrous. At the mercy of those we cannot but hold in contempt, we play roles doomed to failure before they are begun, each defeat generating fresh despair at the urgency of divining and meeting the next demand made upon us.

It is the phenomenon sometimes called "alienation from self." In its advanced stages, we no longer answer the telephone, because someone might want something; that we could say *no* without drowning in self-reproach is an idea alien to this game. Every encounter demands too much, tears the nerves, drains the will, and the specter of something as small as an unanswered letter arouses such disproportionate guilt that answering it becomes out of the question. To assign unanswered letters their proper weight, to free us from the expectations of others, to give us back to ourselves—there lies the great, the singular power of self-respect. Without it, one eventually discovers the final turn of the screw: one runs away to find oneself, and finds no one at home.

POSSIBILITIES FOR WRITING

1. Didion's definition of "self-respect" is based primarily on examples. Analyze her use of these, making sure to look up any references or allusions with which you are unfamiliar.
2. Didion uses a variety of closely related words in defining "self-respect," among them "character," "courage," "discipline," and "private reconciliation." Using these and others you find in the essay, consider how the nuances of these terms help contribute to the overall definition.
3. Define "self-respect" from your own perspective, offering examples to suggest people you believe do and do not possess it.

ANNIE DILLARD

Living Like Weasels

In "Living Like Weasels," Annie Dillard describes an encounter with a weasel she had one day while resting on a log in a patch of woods near a housing development in Virginia. Dillard begins in the expository mode, detailing facts about weasels, especially their tenacity and wildness. But she shifts, before long, into a meditation on the value and necessity of instinct and tenacity in human life. Dillard's tone changes from the factual declaration of the opening into speculative wonder at the weasel's virtues and, finally, into urgent admonition. By the end of the essay, Dillard has made the weasel a symbol of how human beings might live.

I

A weasel is wild. Who knows what he thinks? He sleeps in his underground den, his tail draped over his nose. Sometimes he lives in his den for two days without leaving. Outside, he stalks rabbits, mice, muskrats, and birds, killing more bodies than he can eat warm, and often dragging the carcasses home. Obedient to instinct, he bites his prey at the neck, either splitting the jugular vein at the throat or crunching the brain at the base of the skull, and he does not let go. One naturalist refused to kill a weasel who was socketed into his hand deeply as a rattlesnake. The man could in no way pry the tiny weasel off, and he had to walk half a mile to water, the weasel dangling from his palm, and soak him off like a stubborn label.

And once, says Ernest Thompson Seton—once, a man shot an eagle out of the sky. He examined the eagle and found the dry skull of a weasel fixed by the jaws to his throat. The supposition is that the eagle had pounced on the weasel and the weasel swiveled and bit as instinct taught him, tooth to neck, and nearly won. I would like to have seen that eagle from the air a few weeks or months before he was shot: was the whole weasel still attached to his feathered throat, a fur pendant? Or did the eagle eat what he could reach, gutting the living weasel with his talons before his breast, bending his beak, cleaning the beautiful airborne bones?

II

I have been reading about weasels because I saw one last week. I startled a weasel who startled me, and we exchanged a long glance.

Twenty minutes from my house, through the woods by the quarry and across the highway, is Hollins Pond, a remarkable piece of shallowness, where I like to go at sunset and sit on a tree trunk. Hollins Pond is also called Murray's Pond; it covers two acres of bottomland near Tinker Creek with six inches of water and six thousand lily pads. In winter, brown-and-white steers stand in the middle of it, merely dampening their hooves; from the distant shore they look like miracle itself, complete with miracle's nonchalance. Now, in summer, the steers are gone. The water lilies have blossomed and spread to a green horizontal plane that is terra firma to plodding blackbirds, and tremulous ceiling to black leeches, cray fish, and carp.

This is, mind you, suburbia. It is a five-minute walk in three directions to rows of houses, though none is visible here. There's a 55 mph highway at one end of the pond, and a nesting pair of wood ducks at the other. Under every bush is a muskrat hole or a beer can. The far end is an alternating series of fields and woods, fields and woods, threaded everywhere with motorcycle tracks—in whose bare clay wild turtles lay eggs.

So, I had crossed the highway, stepped over two low barbed-wire fences, and traced the motorcycle path in all gratitude through the wild rose and poison ivy of the pond's shoreline up into high grassy fields. Then I cut down through the woods to the mossy fallen tree where I sit. This tree is excellent. It makes a dry, upholstered bench at the upper, marshy end of the pond, a plush jetty raised from the thorn shore between a shallow blue body of water and a deep blue body of sky.

The sun had just set. I was relaxed on the tree trunk, ensconced in the lap of lichen, watching the lily pads at my feet tremble and part dreamily over the thrusting path of a carp. A yellow bird appeared to my right and flew behind me. It caught my eye; I swiveled around—and the next instant, inexplicably, I was looking down at a weasel, who was looking up at me.

III

Weasel! I'd never seen one wild before. He was ten inches long, thin as a curve, a muscled ribbon, brown as fruitwood, soft-furred, alert. His face was fierce, small and pointed as a lizard's; he would have made a good arrowhead. There was just a dot of chin, maybe two brown hairs' worth, and then the pure white fur began that spread down his underside. He had two black eyes I didn't see, any more than you see a window.

The weasel was stunned into stillness as he was emerging from beneath an enormous shaggy wild rose bush four feet away. I was stunned into stillness twisted backward on the tree trunk. Our eyes locked, and someone threw away the key.

Our look was as if two lovers, or deadly enemies, met unexpectedly on an overgrown path when each had been thinking of something else: a clearing blow to the gut. It was also a bright blow to the brain, or a sudden beating of brains with all the charge and intimate grate of rubbed balloons. It emptied our lungs. It felled the forest, moved the fields, and drained the pond; the world dismantled and tumbled into that black hole of eyes. If you and I looked at each other that way, our skulls would split and drop to our shoulders. But we don't. We keep our skulls. So.

He disappeared. This was only last week, and already I don't remember what shattered the enchantment. I think I blinked, I think I retrieved my brain from the weasel's brain, and tried to memorize what I was seeing, and the weasel felt the yank of separation, the careening splashdown into real life and the urgent current of instinct. He vanished under the wild rose. I waited motionless, my mind suddenly full of data and my spirit with pleadings, but he didn't return.

Please do not tell me about "approach-avoidance conflicts." I tell you I've been in that weasel's brain for sixty seconds, and he was in mine. Brains are private places, muttering through unique and secret tapes—but the weasel and I both plugged into another tape simultaneously, for a sweet and shocking time. Can I help it if it was a blank?

What goes on in his brain the rest of the time? What does a weasel think about? He won't say. His journal is tracks in clay, a spray of feathers, mouse blood and bone: uncollected, unconnected, loose-leaf, and blown.

IV

I would like to learn, or remember, how to live. I come to Hollins Pond not so much to learn how to live as, frankly, to forget about it. That is, I don't think I can learn from a wild animal how to live in particular—shall I suck warm blood, hold my tail high, walk with my footprints precisely over the prints of my hands?—but I might learn something of mindlessness, something of the purity of living in the physical senses and the dignity of living without bias or motive. The weasel lives in necessity and we live in choice, hating necessity and dying at the last ignobly in its talons. I would like to live as I should, as the weasel lives as he should. And I suspect that for me the way is like the weasel's: open to time and death painlessly, noticing everything, remembering nothing, choosing the given with a fierce and pointed will.

V

I missed my chance. I should have gone for the throat. I should have lunged for that streak of white under the weasel's chin and held on, held on through mud and into the wild rose, held on for a dearer life. We could live under the wild rose wild as weasels, mute and uncomprehending. I could very calmly go wild. I could live two days in the den, curled, leaning on mouse fur, sniffing bird bones, blinking, licking, breathing musk, my hair tangled in the roots of grasses. Down is a good place to go, where the mind is single. Down is out, out of your ever-loving mind and back to your careless senses. I remember muteness as a prolonged and giddy fast, where every moment is a feast of utterance received. Time and events are merely poured, unremarked, and ingested directly, like blood pulsed into my gut through a jugular vein. Could two live that way? Could two live under the wild rose, and explore by the pond, so that the smooth mind of each is as everywhere present to the other, and as received and as unchallenged, as falling snow?

We could, you know. We can live any way we want. People take vows of poverty, chastity, and obedience—even of silence—by choice. The thing is to stalk your calling in a certain skilled and supple way, to locate the most tender and live spot and plug into that pulse. This is yielding, not fighting. A weasel doesn't "attack" anything; a weasel lives as he's meant to, yielding at every moment to the perfect freedom of single necessity.

VI

I think it would be well, and proper, and obedient, and pure, to grasp your one necessity and not let it go, to dangle from it limp wherever it takes you. Then even death, where you're going no matter how you live, cannot you part. Seize it and let it seize you up aloft even, till your eyes burn out and drop; let your musky flesh fall off in shreds, and let your very bones unhinge and scatter, loosened over fields, over fields and woods, lightly, thoughtless, from any height at all, from as high as eagles.

POSSIBILITIES FOR WRITING

1. Central to Dillard's idea here are the concepts of "mindlessness" and "necessity" as opposed to consciousness and choice. In an essay, explore what Dillard means by these terms and what value she apparently finds in giving oneself over to mindlessness and necessity.
2. Dillard's essay is divided into six parts, all linked by repeated images and words. Analyze the essay to note as many of these linkages as you can. Then explore how several of these threads function meaningfully in the essay.
3. Dillard's encounter with the weasel provides her with a profound insight about humans and the natural world. Recall a time when an encounter or experience led you to see some aspect of life in a new light. In an essay explore the circumstances of this sudden insight.

Mark Doty (b. 1953) is the author of twelve volumes of poetry and five books of nonfiction. Doty was born in Maryville, Tennessee. He earned a B.A. from Drake University and an MFA from Goddard College in Vermont. Among the awards Doty has won for his books are the T. S. Eliot Prize, the National Books Critics' Circle Award, the Los Angeles Times Book Prize for Poetry, and a Whiting Writing Award. His Fire to Fire: New and Selected Poems (2008) won the National Book Award for poetry. Doty lives on Fire Island, New York City, and teaches at Rutgers University.

MARK DOTY

Souls on Ice

In "Souls on Ice," Mark Doty reveals how he made an extraordinary poem from an everyday experience. In the essay, he describes his composing process, focusing in particular on how his imagination integrates image, metaphor, and idea in the creative act. The poem, "A Display of Mackerel," is included at the essay's conclusion.

In the Stop 'n Shop in Orleans, Massachusetts, I was struck by the elegance of the mackerel in the fresh-fish display. They were rowed and stacked, brilliant against the white of the crushed ice; I loved how black and glistening the bands of dark scales were, and the prismed sheen of the patches between, and their shining fish eyes. I stood and looked at them for a while, just paying attention while I leaned on my cart—before I remembered where I was and realized that I was standing in someone's way.

Our metaphors go on ahead of us, they know before we do. And thank goodness for that, for if I were dependent on other ways of coming to knowledge, I think I'd be a very slow study. I need something to serve as a container for emotion and idea, a vessel that can hold what's too slippery or charged or difficult to touch. Will doesn't have much to do with this; I can't choose what's going to serve as a compelling image for me. But I've learned to trust that part of my imagination that gropes forward, feeling its way toward what it needs; to watch for the signs of fascination, the sense of compelled attention (*Look at me,* something seems to say, *closely)* that indicates that there's something I need to attend to. Sometimes it seems to me as if metaphor were the advance guard of the mind; something in us reaches out, into the landscape in front of us, looking for the right vessel, the right vehicle, for whatever will serve.

Driving home from the grocery, I found myself thinking again about the fish, and even scribbled some phrases on an envelope in the car, something about stained glass, soapbubbles, while I was driving. It wasn't long—that same day? the next?—before I was at my desk, trying simply to describe what I had seen. I almost always begin with description, as a way of focusing on that compelling image, the poem's "given." I know that what I can see is just the proverbial tip of the iceberg; if I do my work of study and examination, and if I am lucky, the image which I've been intrigued by will become a metaphor, will yield depth and meaning, will lead me to insight. The goal here is inquiry, the attempt to get at what it is that's so interesting about what's struck me. Because it isn't just beauty; the world is full of lovely things and that in itself wouldn't compel me to write. There's something else, some gravity or charge to this image that makes me need to investigate it.

Exploratory description, then; I'm a scientist trying to measure and record what's seen. The first two sentences of the poem attempt sheer observation, but by the second's list of tropes (abalone, soapbubble skin, oil on a puddle) it's clear to me that these descriptive terms aren't merely there to chronicle the physical reality of the object. Like all descriptions, they reflect the psychic state of the observer; they aren't "neutral," though they might pretend to be, but instead suggest a point of view, a stance toward what is being seen. In this case one of the things suggested by these tropes is interchangeability; if you've seen one abalone shell or prismy soapbubble or psychedelic puddle, you've seen them all.

And thus my image began to unfold for me, in the evidence these terms provided, and I had a clue toward the focus my poem would take. Another day, another time in my life, the mackerel might have been metaphor for something else; they might have served as the crux for an entirely different examination. But now I began to see why they mattered for *this* poem; and the sentence that follows commences the poem's investigative process:

> Splendor, and splendor,
> and not a one in any way
>
> distinguished from the other
> —nothing about them
> of individuality.

There's a terrific kind of exhilaration for me at this point in the unfolding of a poem, when a line of questioning has been launched, and the work has moved from evocation to meditation. A direction is coming clear, and it bears within it the energy that the image contained for me in the first place. Now, I think, we're getting down to it. This plan carried me along through two more sentences, one that considers the fish as replications of the ideal, Platonic Mackerel, and one that likewise imagines them as the intricate creations of an obsessively repetitive jeweler.

Of course my process of unfolding the poem wasn't quite this neat. There were false starts, wrong turnings that I wound up throwing out when they didn't seem to lead anywhere. I can't remember now, because the poem has worked the charm of its craft on my memory; it convinces me that it is an artifact of a process of inquiry. The drama of the poem is its action of thinking through a question. Mimicking a sequence of perceptions and meditation, it tries to make us think that this feeling and thinking and knowing is taking place even as the poem is being written. Which, in a way, it *is*—just not this neatly or seamlessly! A poem is always a *made* version of experience.

Also, needless to say, my poem was full of repetitions, weak lines, unfinished phrases and extra descriptions, later trimmed. I like to work on a computer, because I can type quickly, put everything in, and still read the results later on, which isn't always true of my handwriting. I *did* feel early on that the poem seemed to want to be a short-lined one; I liked breaking the movement of these extended sentences over the clipped line, and the spotlight-bright focus the short line puts on individual terms felt right. "Iridescent, watery," for instance, pleased me as a line-unit, as did this stanza:

> prismatics: think abalone,
> the wildly rainbowed
> mirror of a soapbubble sphere,

Short lines underline sonic textures, heightening tension. The short a's of *prismatics* and *abalone* ring more firmly, as do the o's of *abalone, rainbowed* and *soapbubble*. The rhyme of mirror and sphere at beginning and end of line engages me, and I'm also pleased by the way in which these short lines slow the poem down, parceling it out as it were to the reader, with the frequent pauses introduced by the stanza breaks between tercets adding lots of white space, a meditative pacing.

And there, on the jeweler's bench, my poem seemed to come to rest, though it was clear there was more to be done. Some further pressure needed to be placed on the poem's material to force it to yield its depths. I waited a while, I read it over. Again, in what I had already written, the clues contained in image pushed the poem forward.

Soul, heaven... The poem had already moved into the realm of theology, but the question that arose ("Suppose we could iridesce...") startled me nonetheless, because the notion of losing oneself "entirely in the universe/of shimmer" referred both to these fish and to something quite other, something overwhelmingly close to home. The poem was written some six months after my partner of a dozen years had died of AIDS, and of course everything I wrote—everything I *saw*—was informed by that loss, by the overpowering emotional force of it. Epidemic was the central fact of the community in which I lived. Naively, I hadn't realized that my mackerel were already of a piece with the work I'd been writing for the previous couple of years—poems that wrestled, in one way or another, with the notion of limit, with the line between being someone and no one. What did it mean to be a self, when that self would be lost? To praise the collectivity of the fish, their common identity as "flashing participants," is to make a sort of anti-elegy, to suggest that what matters is perhaps not our individual selves but our brief soldiering in the broad streaming school of humanity—which is composed of us, yes, but also goes on without us.

> The one of a kind, the singular, like
> my dear lover, cannot last.
> And yet the collective life, which is
> also us, shimmers on.

Once I realized the poem's subject-beneath-the-subject, the final stanzas of the poem opened swiftly out from there. The collective momentum of the fish is such that even death doesn't seem to still rob its forward movement; the singularity of each fish more or less doesn't really exist, it's "all for all," like the Three Musketeers. I could not have considered these ideas "nakedly," without the vehicle of mackerel to help me think about human identity. Nor, I think, could I have addressed these things without a certain playfulness of tone, which appeared first in the archness of "oily fabulation" and the neologism of "iridesce." It's the blessed permission distance gives that allows me to speak of such things at all; a little comedy can also help to hold terrific anxiety at bay. Thus the "rainbowed school/and its acres of brilliant classrooms" is a joke, but one that's already collapsing on itself, since what is taught there—the limits of "me"—is our hardest lesson. No verb is singular because it is the school that acts, or the tribe, the group, the species; or every verb is singular because the only I there *is* is a we.

The poem held one more surprise for me, which was the final statement—it came as a bit of a shock, actually, and when I'd written it I knew I was done. It's a formulation of the theory that the poem has been moving toward all along: that our glory is not our individuality (much as we long for the Romantic self and its private golden heights) but our commonness. I do not like this idea. I would rather be one fish, sparkling in my own pond, but experience does not bear this out. And so I have tried to convince myself, here, that beauty lies in the whole and that therefore death, the loss of the part, is not so bad—is, in fact, almost nothing. What does our individual disappearance mean—or our love, or our desire—when, as the Marvelettes put it, "There's too many fish in the sea..."?

I find this consoling, strangely, and maybe that's the best way to think of this poem—an attempt at cheering oneself up about the mystery of being both an individual and part of a group, an attempt on the part of the speaker in the poem (me) to convince himself that losing individuality, slipping into the life of the world, could be a good thing. All attempts to console ourselves, I believe, are doomed, because the world is more complicated than we are. Our explanations will fail, but it is our human work to make them. And my beautiful fish, limited though they may be as parable, do help me; they are an image I return to in order to remember, in the face of individual erasures, the burgeoning, good, common life. Even after my work of inquiry, my metaphor may still know more than I do; the bright eyes of those fish gleam on, in memory, brighter than what I've made of them.

A Display of Mackerel

They lie in parallel rows,
on ice, head to tail,
each a foot of luminosity

barred with black bands,
which divide the scales'
radiant sections

like seams of lead
in a Tiffany window.
Iridescent, watery

prismatics: think abalone,
the wildly rainbowed
mirror of a soapbubble sphere,

think sun on gasoline. Splendor,
and splendor,
and not a one in any way

distinguished from the other
—nothing about them
of individuality. Instead

they're *all* exact expressions
of one soul,
each a perfect fulfillment

of heaven's template,
mackerel essence. As if,
after a lifetime arriving

at this enameling, the jeweler's
made uncountable examples,
each as intricate

in its oily fabulation
as the one before.
Suppose we could iridesce,

like these, and lose ourselves
entirely in the universe
of shimmer—would you want

to be yourself only,
unduplicatable, doomed
to be lost? They'd prefer,

plainly, to be flashing participants,
multitudinous. Even now
they seem to be bolting

forward, heedless of stasis.
They don't care they're dead
and nearly frozen,

just as, presumably,
they didn't care that they were living:
all, all for all,

the rainbowed school
and its acres of brilliant classrooms,
in which no verb is singular,

or every one is. How happy they seem,
even on ice, to be together, selfless,
which is the price of gleaming.

POSSIBILITIES FOR WRITING

1. Explain in a paragraph the central idea of Doty's essay. To what extent is the essay about identity and community? To what extent is it about loss and mourning?

2. Analyze the images and metaphors in "A Display of Mackerel." Consider how Doty's explanation in the essay "Souls on Ice" illuminates the poem for you.

3. Write a short essay in which you explore the relationship between something that you have written (or otherwise created) and the process you used to compose or create it.

Brian Doyle (b. 1956) is the editor of Portland magazine at the University of Portland, Oregon. His essays have appeared in the American Scholar, the Atlantic Monthly, Harper's, Orion, Commonweal, and the Georgia Review. A number of his essays have been selected to appear in the annual Best American Essays series. Among his books are an edited collection of spiritual writing, God Is Love (2003), and two of his own five collections of essays, Leaping: Revelations & Epiphanies (2004), and The Wet Engine (2005), in which "Joyas Voladoras" appears. More recently, Doyle has published Grace Notes (2011), a collection of essays, and Mink River (2011), his first novel.

BRIAN DOYLE

Joyas Voladoras

In "Joyas Voladoras," Brian Doyle's characteristic wit, grace, and writerly elegance are in evidence as he explores one of life's mysteries—the beautiful jewel-like hummingbird. The essay blends scientific information with spiritual appreciation of this miniature marvel of creation. Doyle celebrates the wonders of the hummingbird, cataloging its myriad species and highlighting the intensity of its life force. Beyond describing and celebrating the life of the hummingbird, Doyle branches out to mention other marvels of creation, especially the largest of all creatures, the blue whale. It is the heart of this great beast that interests Doyle, as well as the heart of the hummingbird, and then beyond these hearts great and small, the heart of that other marvel of creation—the human species.

Consider the hummingbird for a long moment. A hummingbird's heart beats ten times a second. A hummingbird's heart is the size of a pencil eraser. A hummingbird's heart is a lot of the hummingbird. *Joyas voladoras,* flying jewels, the first white explorers in the Americas called them, and the white men had never seen such creatures, for hummingbirds came into the world only in the Americas, nowhere else in the universe, more than three hundred species of them whirring and zooming and nectaring in hummer time zones nine times removed from ours, their hearts hammering faster than we could clearly hear if we pressed our elephantine ears to their infinitesimal chests.

Each one visits a thousand flowers a day. They can dive at sixty miles an hour. They can fly backward. They can fly more than five hundred miles without pausing to rest. But when they rest they come close to death: on frigid nights, or when they are starving, they retreat into torpor, their metabolic rate slowing to a fifteenth of their normal sleep rate, their hearts sludging nearly to a halt, barely beating, and if they are not soon warmed, if they do not soon find that which is sweet, their hearts grow cold, and they cease to be. Consider for a moment those hummingbirds who did not open their eyes again today, this very day, in the Americas: bearded helmetcrests and booted racket-tails, violet-tailed sylphs and violet-capped woodnymphs, crimson topazes and purple-crowned fairies, red-tailed comets and amethyst woodstars, rainbow-bearded thornbills and glittering-bellied emeralds, velvet-purple coronets and golden-bellied star-frontlets, fiery-tailed awlbills and Andean hillstars, spatuletails and pufflegs, each the most amazing thing you have never seen, each thunderous wild heart the size of an infant's fingernail, each mad heart silent, a brilliant music stilled.

Hummingbirds, like all flying birds but more so, have incredible enormous immense ferocious metabolisms. To drive those metabolisms they have racecar hearts that eat oxygen at an eye-popping rate. Their hearts are built of thinner, leaner fibers than ours. Their arteries are stiffer and more taut. They have more mitochondria in their heart muscles—anything to gulp more oxygen. Their hearts are stripped to the skin for the war against gravity and inertia, the mad search for food, the insane idea of flight. The price of their ambition is a life closer to death; they suffer more heart attacks and aneurysms and ruptures than any other living creature. It's expensive to fly. You burn out. You fry the machine. You melt the engine. Every creature on earth has approximately two billion heartbeats to spend in a lifetime. You can spend them slowly, like a tortoise, and live to be two hundred years old, or you can spend them fast, like a hummingbird, and live to be two years old.

The biggest heart in the world is inside the blue whale. It weighs more than seven tons. It's as big as a room. It *is* a room, with four chambers. A child could walk around in it, head high, bending only to step through the valves. The valves are as big as the swinging doors in a saloon. This house of a heart drives a creature a hundred feet long. When this creature is born it is twenty feet long and weighs four tons. It is waaaaay bigger than your car. It drinks a hundred gallons of milk from its mama every day and gains two hundred pounds a day, and when it is seven or eight years old it endures an unimaginable puberty and then it essentially disappears from human ken, for next to nothing is known of the mating habits, travel patterns, diet, social life, language, social structure, diseases, spirituality, wars, stories, despairs, and arts of the blue whale. There are perhaps ten thousand blue whales in the world, living in every ocean on earth, and of the largest mammal who ever lived we know nearly nothing. But we know this: the animals with the largest hearts in the world generally travel in pairs, and their penetrating moaning cries, their piercing yearning tongue, can be heard underwater for miles and miles.

Mammals and birds have hearts with four chambers. Reptiles and turtles have hearts with three chambers. Fish have hearts with two chambers. Insects and mollusks have hearts with one chamber. Worms have hearts with one chamber, although they may have as many as eleven single-chambered hearts. Unicellular bacteria have no hearts at all; but even they have fluid eternally in motion, washing from one side of the cell to the other, swirling and whirling. No living being is without interior liquid motion. We all churn inside.

So much held in a heart in a lifetime. So much held in a heart in a day, an hour, a moment. We are utterly open with no one, in the end—not mother and father, not wife or husband, not lover, not child, not friend. We open windows to each but we live alone in the house of the heart. Perhaps we must. Perhaps we could not bear to be so naked, for fear of a constantly harrowed heart. When young we think there will come one person who will savor and sustain us always; when we are older we know this is the dream of a child, that all hearts finally are bruised and scarred, scored and torn, repaired by time and will, patched by force of character, yet fragile and rickety forevermore, no matter how ferocious the defense and how many bricks you bring to the wall. You can brick up your heart as stout and tight and hard and cold and impregnable as you possibly can and down it comes in an instant, felled by a woman's second glance, a child's apple breath, the shatter of glass in the road, the words "I have something to tell you," a cat with a broken spine dragging itself into the forest to die, the brush of your mother's papery ancient hand in the thicket of your hair, the memory of your father's voice early in the morning echoing from the kitchen where he is making pancakes for his children.

POSSIBILITIES FOR WRITING

1. Why do you think Doyle wrote this little essay? What is his main idea? How does his discussion of the hummingbird contribute to the development of this idea? What is the purpose of his including the description of the heart of the blue whale?

2. Take an inventory of Doyle's essay, identifying the places where his writing anchors itself in scientific detail and description, where it verges on spiritual celebration rather than the factual, and where it seems to blend or shift rapidly between the two modes of writing.

3. Write an essay in which you celebrate one of the marvels of creation. You may wish to choose something very large or very small to write about—and you may wish, like Doyle, to work in a contrast to whatever you choose to describe. You should do some research so you can present a number of factual details; and you should do some reflecting so you can provide a perspective that transcends the factual information you include.

Gretel Ehrlich (b. 1946), a native Californian, attended Bennington College and later the film school at New York University. Her work as a documentary filmmaker took her to Wyoming in 1979, and she found herself drawn to the state's sweeping open countryside and to the people who inhabit it. During her seventeen years working as a rancher there, she produced several books of reflections on her experiences, including The Solace of Open Spaces (1985) and A Match to the Heart (1994), as well as a novel and other works. Currently dividing her time between California and Wyoming, she has most recently published Questions from Heaven (1997), an account of her pilgrimage as a Buddhist to shrines in China, and John Muir: Nature's Visionary (2000), a biography of the great American naturalist and conservationist. More recently, Ehrlich published In the Empire of Ice: Encounters in a Changing Landscape (2010).

GRETEL EHRLICH

About Men

Ehrlich's brief essay, "About Men," originally appeared in *Time* magazine and was included in her first essay collection, *The Solace of Open Spaces*. Ehrlich's primary purpose in the essay is to reconsider some basic stereotypes about men—particularly western men, including, of course, "cowboys." Ehrlich encourages readers to consider how manliness is a quality which, for cowboys, also requires a balancing of more conventionally typical feminine qualities, such as caring and compassion. The cowboys Ehrlich knows and describes are, as she writes, "androgynous at the core."

When I'm in New York but feeling lonely for Wyoming I look for the Marlboro ads in the subway. What I'm aching to see is horseflesh, the glint of a spur, a line of distant mountains, brimming creeks, and a reminder of the ranchers and cowboys I've ridden with for the last eight years. But the men I see in those posters with their stern, humorless looks remind me of no one I know here. In our hellbent earnestness to romanticize the cowboy we've ironically disesteemed his true character. If he's "strong and silent," it's because there's probably no one to talk to. If he "rides away into the sunset," it's because he's been on horseback since four in the morning moving cattle and he's trying, fifteen hours later, to get home to his family. If he's "a rugged individualist," he's also part of a team: ranch work is teamwork, and even the glorified open-range cowboys of the 1880s rode up and down the Chisholm Trail in the company of twenty or thirty other riders. Instead of the macho, trigger-happy man our culture has perversely wanted him to be, the cowboy is more apt to be convivial, quirky, and softhearted. To be "tough" on a ranch has nothing to do with conquests and displays of power. More often than not, circumstances—like the colt he's riding or an unexpected blizzard—are overpowering him. It's not toughness but "toughing it out" that counts. In other words, this macho, cultural artifact the cowboy has become is simply a man who possesses resilience, patience, and an instinct for survival. "Cowboys are just like a pile of rocks—everything happens to them. They get climbed on, kicked, rained and snowed on, scuffed up by wind. Their job is 'just to take it,'" one old-timer told me.

A cowboy is someone who loves his work. Since the hours are long—ten to fifteen hours a day—and the pay is $30, he has to. What's required of him is an odd mixture of physical vigor and maternalism. His part of the beef-raising industry is to birth and nurture calves and take care of their mothers. For the most part his work is done on horseback, and in a lifetime he sees and comes to know more animals than people. The iconic myth surrounding him is built on American notions of heroism: the index of a man's value as measured in physical courage. Such ideas have perverted manliness into a self-absorbed race for cheap thrills. In a rancher's world, courage has less to do with facing danger than with acting spontaneously—usually on behalf of an animal or another rider. If a cow is stuck in a boghole, he throws a loop around her neck, takes his dally (a half hitch around the saddle horn), and pulls her out with horsepower. If a calf is born sick, he may take her home, warm her in front of the kitchen fire, and massage her legs until dawn. One friend, whose favorite horse was trying to swim a lake with hobbles on, dove under water and cut her legs loose with a knife, then swam her to shore, his arm around her neck lifeguard-style, and saved her from drowning. Because these incidents are usually linked to someone or something outside himself, the westerner's courage is selfless, a form of compassion.

The physical punishment that goes with cowboying is greatly underplayed. Once fear is dispensed with, the threshold of pain rises to meet the demands of the job. When Jane Fonda asked Robert Redford (in the film *The Electric Horseman*) if he was sick as he struggled to his feet one morning, he replied, "No, just bent." For once the movies had it right. The cowboys I was sitting with laughed in agreement. Cowboys are rarely complainers; they show their stoicism by laughing at themselves.

If a rancher or cowboy has been thought of as a "man's man"—laconic, hard-drinking, inscrutable—there's almost no place in which the balancing act between male and female, manliness and femininity, can be more natural. If he's gruff, handsome, and physically fit on the outside, he's androgynous at the core. Ranchers are midwives, hunters, nurturers, providers, and conservationists all at once. What we've interpreted as toughness—weathered skin, calloused hands, a squint in the eye and a growl in the voice—only masks the tenderness inside. "Now don't go telling me these lambs are cute," one rancher warned me the first day I walked into the football-field-sized lambing sheds. The next thing I knew he was holding a black lamb. "Ain't this little rat good-lookin'?"

So many of the men who came to the West were southerners—men looking for work and a new life after the Civil War—that chivalrousness and strict codes of honor were soon thought of as western traits. There were very few women in Wyoming during territorial days, so when they did arrive (some as mail-order brides from places like Philadelphia) there was a stand-offishness between the sexes and a formality that persists now. Ranchers still tip their hats and say, "Howdy, ma'am" instead of shaking hands with me.

Even young cowboys are often evasive with women. It's not that they're Jekyll and Hyde creatures—gentle with animals and rough on women—but rather, that they don't know how to bring their tenderness into the house and lack the vocabulary to express the complexity of what they feel. Dancing wildly all night becomes a metaphor for the explosive emotions pent up inside, and when these are, on occasion, released, they're so battery-charged and potent that one caress of the face or one "I love you" will peal for a long while.

The geographical vastness and the social isolation here make emotional evolution seem impossible. Those contradictions of the heart between respectability, logic, and convention on the one hand, and impulse, passion, and intuition on the other, played out wordlessly against the paradisiacal beauty of the West, give cowboys a wide-eyed but drawn look. Their lips pucker up, not with kisses but with immutability. They may want to break out, staying up all night with a lover just to talk, but they don't know how and can't imagine what the consequences will be. Those rare occasions when they do bare themselves result in confusion. "I feel as if I'd sprained my heart," one friend told me a month after such a meeting.

My friend Ted Hoagland wrote, "No one is as fragile as a woman but no one is as fragile as a man." For all the women here who use "fragileness" to avoid work or as a sexual ploy, there are men who try to hide theirs, all the while clinging to an adolescent dependency on women to cook their meals, wash their clothes, and keep the ranch house warm in winter. But there is true vulnerability in evidence here. Because these men work with animals, not machines or numbers, because they live outside in landscapes of torrential beauty, because they are confined to a place and a routine embellished with awesome variables, because calves die in the arms that pulled others into life, because they go to the mountains as if on a pilgrimage to find out what makes a herd of elk tick, their strength is also a softness, their toughness, a rare delicacy.

POSSIBILITIES FOR WRITING

1. What does Ehrlich find so admirable and so sympathetic about the cowboys and ranchers she encounters in Wyoming? What does this suggest about her view of male roles more generally in our culture? Using specific examples from her essay, explore her central themes.
2. Cowboys, as Ehrlich describes them, seem to have trouble communicating with and relating to women, yet cling to an "adolescent dependency" on women to take care of them. How does Ehrlich square this with her positive image of cowboys? Do you think she does so effectively, or does this point diminish her image of cowboys in your eyes?
3. The media depict many different stereotypes in terms of gender, ethnicity, and so on. Choose a particular stereotype you have encountered, describe it and how it is exemplified in the media, and then, as Ehrlich does, question the stereotype based on your own experiences.

RALPH ELLISON

Living with Music

In "Living with Music," Ellison describes himself as a young man living between two musical worlds—the world of classical music and the world of jazz. As a young writer struggling to find his voice and hone his art, Ellison lived amid the sounds of musicians practicing and performing music in these diverse styles and forms. As a lover of music, Ellison was, by turns, distracted and inspired by what he heard from these musicians, who themselves were perfecting their own art through intense practice and inspired performance.

In those days it was either live with music or die with noise, and we chose rather desperately to live. In the process our apartment—what with its booby-trappings of audio equipment, wires, discs and tapes—came to resemble the Collyer mansion, but that was later. First there was the neighborhood, assorted drunks and a singer.

We were living at the time in a tiny ground-floor-rear apartment in which I was also trying to write. I say "trying" advisedly. To our right, separated by a thin wall, was a small restaurant with a juke box the size of the Roxy. To our left, a night-employed swing enthusiast who took his lullaby music so loud that every morning promptly at nine Basie's brasses started blasting my typewriter off its stand. Our living room looked out across a small back yard to a rough stone wall to an apartment building which, towering above, caught every passing thoroughfare sound and rifled it straight down to me. There were also howling cats and barking dogs, none capable of music worth living with, so we'll pass them by.

But the court behind the wall, which on the far side came knee-high to a short Iroquois, was a forum for various singing and/or preaching

drunks who wandered back from the corner bar. From these you sometimes heard a fair barbershop style "Bill Bailey," free-wheeling versions
of "The Bastard King of England," the saga of Uncle Bud, or a deeply
felt rendition of Leroy Carr's "How Long Blues." The preaching drunks
took on any topic that came to mind: current events, the fate of the
long-sunk *Titanic* or the relative merits of the Giants and the Dodgers.
Naturally there was great argument and occasional fighting—none of
it fatal but all of it loud.

I shouldn't complain, however, for these were rather entertaining
drunks, who, like the birds, appeared in the spring and left with the
first fall cold. A more dedicated fellow was there all the time, day
and night, come rain, come shine. Up on the corner lived a drunk
of legend, a true phenomenon, who could surely have qualified as
the king of all the world's winos—not excluding the French. He was
neither poetic like the others nor ambitious like the singer (to whom
we'll presently come) but his drinking bouts were truly awe-inspiring
and he was not without his sensitivity. In the throes of his passion he
would shout to the whole wide world one concise command, "Shut
up!" Which was disconcerting enough to all who heard (except,
perhaps, the singer), but such were the labyrinthine acoustics of
courtyards and areaways that he seemed to direct his command at
me. The writer's block which this produced is indescribable. On one
heroic occasion he yelled his obsessive command without one interruption longer than necessary to take another drink (and with no
appreciable loss of volume, penetration or authority) for three long
summer days and nights, and shortly afterwards he died. Just how
many lines of agitated prose he cost me I'll never know, but in all
that chaos of sound I sympathized with his obsession, for I, too,
hungered and thirsted for quiet. Nor did he inspire me to a painful
identification, and for that I was thankful. Identification, after all,
involves feelings of guilt and responsibility, and since I could hardly
hear my own typewriter keys I felt in no way accountable for his
condition. We were simply fellow victims of the madding crowd.
May he rest in peace.

No, these more involved feelings were aroused by a more intimate
source of noise, one that got beneath the skin and worked into the very
structure of one's consciousness—like the "fate" motif in Beethoven's
Fifth or the knocking-at-the-gates scene in *Macbeth*. For at the top of
our pyramid of noise there was a singer who lived directly above us,
you might say we had a singer on our ceiling.

Now, I had learned from the jazz musicians I had known as a boy in Oklahoma City something of the discipline and devotion to his art required of the artist. Hence I knew something of what the singer faced. These jazzmen, many of them now world-famous, lived for and with music intensely. Their driving motivation was neither money nor fame, but the will to achieve the most eloquent expression of idea-emotions through the technical mastery of their instruments (which, incidentally, some of them wore as a priest wears the cross) and the give and take, the subtle rhythmical shaping and blending of idea, tone and imagination demanded of group improvisation. The delicate balance struck between strong individual personality and the group during those early jam sessions was a marvel of social organization. I had learned too that the end of all this discipline and technical mastery was the desire to express an affirmative way of life through its musical tradition, and that this tradition insisted that each artist achieve his creativity within its frame. He must learn the best of the past, and add to it his personal vision. Life could be harsh, loud and wrong if it wished, but they lived it fully, and when they expressed their attitude toward the world it was with a fluid style that reduced the chaos of living to form.

The objectives of these jazzmen were not at all those of the singer on our ceiling, but though a purist committed to the mastery of the *bel canto* style, German *lieder,* modern French art songs and a few American slave songs sung as if *bel canto,* she was intensely devoted to her art. From morning to night she vocalized, regardless of the condition of her voice, the weather or my screaming nerves. There were times when her notes, sifting through her floor and my ceiling, bouncing down the walls and ricocheting off the building in the rear, whistled like tenpenny nails, buzzed like a saw, wheezed like the asthma of a Hercules, trumpeted like an enraged African elephant— and the squeaky pedal of her piano rested plumb center above my typing chair. After a year of non-cooperation from the neighbor on my left I became desperate enough to cool down the hot blast of his phonograph by calling the cops, but the singer presented a serious ethical problem: Could I, an aspiring artist, complain against the hard work and devotion to craft of another aspiring artist?

Then there was my sense of guilt. Each time I prepared to shatter the ceiling in protest I was restrained by the knowledge that I, too, during my boyhood, had tried to master a musical instrument and to the great distress of my neighbors—perhaps even greater than that which I now suffered. For while our singer was concerned basically with a single tradition and style, I had been caught actively between two: that of the Negro folk music, both sacred and profane, slave song and jazz, and that of Western classical music. It was most confusing; the folk tradition demanded that I play what I heard and felt around me, while those who were seeking to teach the classical tradition in the schools insisted that I play strictly according to the book and express that which I was *supposed* to feel. This sometimes led to heated clashes of wills. Once during a third-grade music appreciation class a friend of mine insisted that it was a large green snake he saw swimming down a quiet brook instead of the snowy bird the teacher felt that Saint-Saëns' *Carnival of the Animals* should evoke. The rest of us sat there and lied like little black, brown and yellow Trojans about that swan, but our stalwart classmate held firm to his snake. In the end he got himself spanked and reduced the teacher to tears, but truth, reality and our environment were redeemed. For we were all familiar with snakes, while a swan was simply something the Ugly Duckling of the story grew up to be. Fortunately some of us grew up with a genuine appreciation of classical music *despite* such teaching methods. But as an inspiring trumpeter I was to wallow in sin for years before being awakened to guilt by our singer.

Caught mid-range between my two traditions, where one attitude often clashed with the other and one technique of playing was by the other opposed, I caused whole blocks of people to suffer.

Indeed, I terrorized a good part of an entire city section. During summer vacation I blew sustained tones out of the window for hours, usually starting—especially on Sunday mornings—before breakfast. I sputtered whole days through M. Arban's (he's the great authority on the instrument) double- and triple-tonguing exercises—with an effect like that of a jackass hiccupping off a big meal of briars. During school-term mornings I practiced a truly exhibitionist "Reveille" before leaving for school, and in the evening I generously gave the ever-listening world a long, slow version of "Taps," ineptly played but throbbing with what I in my adolescent vagueness felt was a romantic sadness. For it was farewell to day and a love song to life and a peace-be-with-you to all the dead and dying.

On hot summer afternoons I tormented the ears of all not blessedly deaf with imitations of the latest hot solos of Hot Lips Paige (then a local hero), the leaping right hand of Earl "Fatha" Hines, or the rowdy poetic flights of Louis Armstrong. Naturally I rehearsed also such school-band standbys as the *Light Cavalry* Overture, Sousa's "Stars and Stripes Forever," the *William Tell* Overture, and "Tiger Rag." (Not even an after-school job as office boy to a dentist could stop my efforts. Frequently, by way of encouraging my development in the proper cultural direction, the dentist asked me proudly to render Schubert's *Serenade* for some poor devil with his jaw propped open in the dental chair. When the drill got going, or the forceps bit deep, I blew real strong.)

Sometimes, inspired by the even then considerable virtuosity of the late Charlie Christian (who during our school days played marvelous riffs on a cigar box banjo), I'd give whole summer afternoons and the evening hours after heavy suppers of black-eyed peas and turnip greens, cracklin' bread and buttermilk, lemonade and sweet potato cobbler, to practicing hard-driving blues. Such food oversupplied me with bursting energy, and from listening to Ma Rainey, Ida Cox and Clara Smith, who made regular appearances in our town, I knew exactly how I wanted my horn to sound. But in the effort to make it do so (I was no embryo Joe Smith or Tricky Sam Nanton) I sustained the curses of both Christian and infidel—along with the encouragement of those more sympathetic citizens who understood the profound satisfaction to be found in expressing oneself in the blues.

Despite those who complained and cried to heaven for Gabriel to blow a chorus so heavenly sweet and so hellishly hot that I'd forever put down my horn, there were more tolerant ones who were willing to pay in present pain for future pride.

For who knew what skinny kid with his chops wrapped around a trumpet mouthpiece and a faraway look in his eyes might become the next Armstrong? Yes, and send you, at some big dance a few years hence, into an ecstasy of rhythm and memory and brassy affirmation of the goodness of being alive and part of the community? Someone had to; for it was part of the group tradition—though that was not how they said it.

"Let that boy blow," they'd say to the protesting ones. "He's got to talk baby talk on that thing before he can preach on it. Next thing you know he's liable to be up there with Duke Ellington. Sure, plenty Oklahoma boys are up there with the big bands. Son, let's hear you try those 'Trouble in Mind Blues.' Now try and make it sound like ole Ida Cox sings it."

And I'd draw in my breath and do Miss Cox great violence.

Thus the crimes and aspirations of my youth. It had been years since I had played the trumpet or irritated a single ear with other than the spoken or written word, but as far as my singing neighbor was concerned I had to hold my peace. I was forced to listen, and in listening I soon became involved to the point of identification. If she sang badly I'd hear my own futility in the windy sound; if well, I'd stare at my typewriter and despair that I should ever make my prose so sing. She left me neither night nor day, this singer on our ceiling, and as my writing languished I became more and more upset. Thus one desperate morning I decided that since I seemed doomed to live within a shrieking chaos I might as well contribute my share; perhaps if I fought noise with noise I'd attain some small peace. Then a miracle: I turned on my radio (an old Philco AM set connected to a small Pilot FM tuner) and I heard the words

> Art thou troubled?
> Music will calm thee...

I stopped as though struck by the voice of an angel. It was Kathleen Ferrier, that loveliest of singers, giving voice to the aria from Handel's *Rodelinda*. The voice was so completely expressive of words and music that I accepted it without question—what lover of the vocal art could resist her?

Yet it was ironic, for after giving up my trumpet for the typewriter I had avoided too close a contact with the very art which she recommended as balm. For I had started music early and lived with it daily, and when I broke I tried to break clean. Now in this magical moment all the old love, the old fascination with music superbly rendered, flooded back. When she finished I realized that with such music in my own apartment, the chaotic sounds from without and above had sunk, if not into silence, then well below the level where they mattered. Here was a way out. If I was to live and write in that apartment, it would be only through the grace of music. I had tuned in a Ferrier recital, and when it ended I rushed out for several of her records, certain that now deliverance was mine.

But not yet. Between the hi-fi record and the ear, I learned, there was a new electronic world. In that realization our apartment was well on its way toward becoming an audio booby trap. It was 1949, and I rushed to the Audio Fair. I have, I confess, as much gadget-resistance as the next American of my age, weight and slight income; but little did I dream of the test to which it would be put. I had hardly entered the fair before I heard David Sarser's and Mel Sprinkle's Musician's Amplifier, took a look at its schematic and, recalling a boyhood acquaintance with such matters, decided that I could build one. I did—several times—before it measured within specifications. And still our system was lacking. Fortunately my wife shared my passion for music, so we went on to buy, piece by piece, a fine speaker system, a first-rate AM-FM tuner, a transcription turntable and a speaker cabinet. I built half a dozen or more preamplifiers and record compensators before finding a commercial one that satisfied my ear, and, finally, we acquired an arm, a magnetic cartridge and—glory of the house—a tape recorder. All this plunge into electronics, mind you, had as its simple end the enjoyment of recorded music as it was intended to be heard. I was obsessed with the idea of reproducing sound with such fidelity that even when using music as a defense behind which I could write, it would reach the unconscious levels of the mind with the least distortion. And it didn't come easily. There were wires and pieces of equipment all over the tiny apartment (I became a compulsive experimenter) and it was worth your life to move about without first taking careful bearings. Once we were almost crushed in our sleep by the tape machine, for which there was space only on a shelf at the head of our bed. But it was worth it.

For now when we played a recording on our system even the drunks on the wall could recognize its quality. I'm ashamed to admit, however, that I did not always restrict its use to the demands of pleasure or defense. Indeed, with such marvels of science at my control I lost my humility. My ethical consideration for the singer up above shriveled like a plant in too much sunlight. For instead of soothing, music seemed to release the beast in me. Now when jarred from my writer's reveries by some especially enthusiastic flourish of our singer, I'd rush to my music system with blood in my eyes and burst a few decibels in her direction. If she defied me with a few more pounds of pressure against her diaphragm, then a war of decibels was declared.

If, let us say, she were singing *"Depuis le Jour"* from *Louise,* I'd put on a tape of Bidu Sayão performing the same aria, and let the rafters ring. If it was some song by Mahler, I'd match her spitefully with Marian Anderson or Kathleen Ferrier; if she offended with something from *Der Rosenkavalier,* I'd attack her flank with Lotte Lehmann. If she brought me up from my desk with art songs by Ravel or Rachmaninoff, I'd defend myself with Maggie Teyte or Jennie Tourel. If she polished a spiritual to a meaningless artiness, I'd play Bessie Smith to remind her of the earth out of which we came. Once in a while I'd forget completely that I was supposed to be a gentleman and blast her with Strauss' *Zarathustra*, Bartók's *Concerto for Orchestra*, Ellington's "Flaming Sword," the famous crescendo from *The Pines of Rome*, or Satchmo scatting, "I'll be Glad When You're Dead" (you rascal you!). Oh, I was living with music with a sweet vengeance.

One might think that all this would have made me her most hated enemy, but not at all. When I met her on the stoop a few weeks after my rebellion, expecting her fully to slap my face, she astonished me by complimenting our music system. She even questioned me concerning the artists I had used against her. After that, on days when the acoustics were right, she'd stop singing until the piece was finished and then applaud—not always, I guessed, without a justifiable touch of sarcasm. And although I was now getting on with my writing, the unfairness of this business bore in upon me. Aware that I could not have withstood a similar comparison with literary artists of like caliber, I grew remorseful. I also came to admire the singer's courage and control, for she was neither intimidated into silence nor goaded into undisciplined screaming; she persevered, she marked the phrasing of the great singers I sent her way, she improved her style.

Better still, she vocalized more softly, and I, in turn, used music less and less as a weapon and more for its magic with mood and memory. After a while a simple twirl of the volume control up a few decibels and down again would bring a live-and-let-live reduction of her volume. We have long since moved from that apartment and that most interesting neighborhood, and now the floors and walls of our present apartment are adequately thick, and there is even a closet large enough to house the audio system; the only wire visible is that leading from the closet to the corner speaker system. Still, we are indebted to the singer and the old environment for forcing us to discover one of the most deeply satisfying aspects of our living. Perhaps the enjoyment of music is always suffused with past experience; for me, at least, this is true.

It seems a long way and a long time from the glorious days of Oklahoma jazz dances, the jam sessions at Halley Richardson's place on Deep Second, from the phonographs shouting the blues in the back alleys I knew as a delivery boy and from the days when watermelon men with voices like mellow bugles shouted their wares in time with the rhythm of their horses' hoofs, and farther still from the washerwomen singing slave songs as they stirred sooty tubs in sunny yards; and a long time, too, from those intense, conflicting days when the school music program of Oklahoma City was tuning our earthy young ears to classical accents—with music appreciation classes and free musical instruments and basic instruction for any child who cared to learn and uniforms for all who made the band. There was a mistaken notion on the part of some of the teachers that classical music had nothing to do with the rhythms, relaxed or hectic, of daily living, and that one should crook the little finger when listening to such refined strains. And the blues and the spirituals—jazz—? they would have destroyed them and scattered the pieces. Nevertheless, we learned some of it all, for in the United States when traditions are juxtaposed they tend, regardless of what we do to prevent it, irresistibly to merge. Thus, musically at least, each child in our town was an heir of all the ages. One learns by moving from the familiar to the unfamiliar, and while it might sound incongruous at first, the step from the spirituality of the spirituals to that of the Beethoven of the symphonies or the Bach of the chorales is not as vast as it seems. Nor is the romanticism of a Brahms or Chopin completely unrelated to that of Louis Armstrong. Those who know their native culture and love it unchauvinistically are never lost when encountering the unfamiliar.

Living with music today we find Mozart and Ellington, Kirsten Flagstad and Chippie Hill, William L. Dawson and Carl Orff all forming part of our regular fare. For all exalt life in rhythm and melody; all add to its significance. Perhaps in the swift change of American society in which the meanings of one's origin are so quickly lost, one of the chief values of living with music lies in its power to give us an orientation in time. In doing so, it gives significance to all those indefinable aspects of experience which nevertheless help to make us what we are. In the swift whirl of time music is a constant, reminding us of what we were and of that toward which we aspired. Art thou troubled? Music will not only calm, it will ennoble thee.

POSSIBILITIES FOR WRITING

1. Ellison suggests that music has meant many things to him over the course of his life, from the days of his childhood to the years in the apartment he describes here to the time when he was writing this essay. Focusing on each of these stages in his life, analyze his various feelings about music.

2. Ellison's tone in this essay ranges from serious to light, from outraged to self-deprecating, from "classical" to "jazzy." Analyze these various elements of his voice and how they work together to help make his larger point.

3. Write an essay of your own about "living with music," focusing on the music you grew up with, were taught in school, learned to play yourself, listen to now, and so forth. Try to draw some larger conclusions, as Ellison does, about your relationship with music.

Malcolm Gladwell (b. 1963) was born in England and graduated with a
degree in history from the University of Toronto. A former business and science
writer at the Washington Post, *he was named the newspaper's New York City
bureau chief. Gladwell is currently a staff writer for the* New Yorker *magazine.
Gladwell has written two best-selling books:* The Tipping Point *(2002) and*
Blink *(2007). More recently, he has published* What the Dog Saw *(2009)
and* Outliers *(2008).*

MALCOLM GLADWELL

The Tipping Point

In "The Tipping Point," excerpted from his 2002 book of the same title,
Gladwell describes the phenomenon of "tipping," or the process by which
a sequence of events proceeds beyond human control and becomes an
epidemic. His main idea is that there is a point at which a situation "tips"
into epidemic and that there are a number of identifiable factors that lead
up to this tipping point.

In the mid-1990s, the city of Baltimore was attacked by an epidemic
of syphilis. In the space of a year, from 1995 to 1996, the number of
children born with the disease increased by 500 percent. If you look
at Baltimore's syphilis rates on a graph, the line runs straight for years
and then, when it hits 1995, rises almost at a right angle.

What caused Baltimore's syphilis problem to tip? According to the
Centers for Disease Control, the problem was crack cocaine. Crack is
known to cause a dramatic increase in the kind of risky sexual behavior that leads to the spread of things like HIV and syphilis. It brings
far more people into poor areas to buy drugs, which then increases
the likelihood that they will take an infection home with them to their
own neighborhood. It changes the patterns of social connections between neighborhoods. Crack, the CDC said, was the little push that
the syphilis problem needed to turn into a raging epidemic.

John Zenilman of Johns Hopkins University in Baltimore, an expert on sexually transmitted diseases, has another explanation: the
breakdown of medical services in the city's poorest neighborhoods. "In
1990–91, we had thirty-six thousand patient visits at the city's sexually transmitted disease clinics," Zenilman says. "Then the city decided
to gradually cut back because of budgetary problems. The number of
clinicians [medical personnel] went from seventeen to ten. The number of physicians went from three to essentially nobody. Patient visits

dropped to twenty-one thousand. There also was a similar drop in the amount of field outreach staff. There was a lot of politics—things that used to happen, like computer upgrades, didn't happen. It was a worst-case scenario of city bureaucracy not functioning. They would run out of drugs."

When there were 36,000 patient visits a year in the STD clinics of Baltimore's inner city, in other words, the disease was kept in equilibrium. At some point between 36,000 and 21,000 patient visits a year, according to Zenilman, the disease erupted. It began spilling out of the inner city, up the streets and highways that connect those neighborhoods to the rest of the city. Suddenly, people who might have been infectious for a week before getting treated were now going around infecting others for two or three or four weeks before they got cured. The breakdown in treatment made syphilis a much bigger issue than it had been before.

There is a third theory, which belongs to John Potterat, one of the country's leading epidemiologists. His culprits are the physical changes in those years affecting East and West Baltimore, the heavily depressed neighborhoods on either side of Baltimore's downtown, where the syphilis problem was centered. In the mid-1990s, he points out, the city of Baltimore embarked on a highly publicized policy of dynamiting the old 1960s-style public housing high-rises in East and West Baltimore. Two of the most publicized demolitions—Lexington Terrace in West Baltimore and Lafayette Courts in East Baltimore—were huge projects, housing hundreds of families, that served as centers for crime and infectious disease. At the same time, people began to move out of the old row houses in East and West Baltimore, as those began to deteriorate as well.

"It was absolutely striking," Potterat says, of the first time he toured East and West Baltimore. "Fifty percent of the row houses were boarded up, and there was also a process where they destroyed the projects. What happened was a kind of hollowing out. This fueled the diaspora. For years syphilis had been confined to a specific region of Baltimore, within highly confined sociosexual networks. The housing dislocation process served to move these people to other parts of Baltimore, and they took their syphilis and other behaviors with them."

What is interesting about these three explanations is that none of them is at all dramatic. The CDC thought that crack was the problem. But it wasn't as if crack came to Baltimore for the first time in 1995. It had been there for years. What they were saying is that there was a subtle increase in the severity of the crack problem in the mid-1990s, and that change was enough to set off the syphilis epidemic. Zenilman, likewise, wasn't saying that the STD clinics in Baltimore were shut down. They were simply scaled back, the number of clinicians cut from seventeen to ten. Nor was Potterat saying that all Baltimore was hollowed out. All it took, he said, was the demolition of a handful of housing projects and the abandonment of homes in key downtown neighborhoods to send syphilis over the top. It takes only the smallest of changes to shatter an epidemic's equilibrium.

The second, and perhaps more interesting, fact about these explanations is that all of them are describing a very different way of tipping an epidemic. The CDC is talking about the overall context for the disease—how the introduction and growth of an addictive drug can so change the environment of a city that it can cause a disease to tip. Zenilman is talking about the disease itself. When the clinics were cut back, syphilis was given a second life. It had been an acute infection. It was now a chronic infection. It had become a lingering problem that stayed around for weeks. Potterat, for his part, was focused on the people who were carrying syphilis. Syphilis, he was saying, was a disease carried by a certain kind of person in Baltimore—a very poor, probably drug-using, sexually active individual. If that kind of person was suddenly transported from his or her old neighborhood to a new one—to a new part of town, where syphilis had never been a problem before—the disease would have an opportunity to tip.

There is more than one way to tip an epidemic, in other words. Epidemics are a function of the people who transmit infectious agents, the infectious agent itself, and the environment in which the infectious agent is operating. And when an epidemic tips, when it is jolted out of equilibrium, it tips because something has happened, some change has occurred in one (or two or three) of those areas. These three agents of change I call the Law of the Few, the Stickiness Factor, and the Power of Context.

1.

When we say that a handful of East Village kids started the Hush Puppies epidemic, or that the scattering of the residents of a few housing projects was sufficient to start Baltimore's syphilis epidemic, what we are really saying is that in a given process or system some people matter more than others. This is not, on the face of it, a particularly radical notion. Economists often talk about the 80/20 Principle, which is the idea that in any situation roughly 80 percent of the "work" will be done by 20 percent of the participants. In most societies, 20 percent of criminals commit 80 percent of crimes. Twenty percent of motorists cause 80 percent of all accidents. Twenty percent of beer drinkers drink 80 percent of all beer. When it comes to epidemics, though, this disproportionality becomes even more extreme: a tiny percentage of people do the majority of the work.

Potterat, for example, once did an analysis of a gonorrhea epidemic in Colorado Springs, Colorado, looking at everyone who came to a public health clinic for treatment of the disease over the space of six months. He found that about half of the cases came, essentially, from four neighborhoods representing about 6 percent of the geographic area of the city. Half of those in that 6 percent, in turn, were socializing in the same six bars. Potterat then interviewed 768 people in that tiny subgroup and found that 600 of them either didn't give gonorrhea to anyone else or gave it to only one other person. These people he called nontransmitters. The ones causing the epidemic to grow—the ones who were infecting two and three and four and five others with their disease—were the remaining 168. In other words, in all of the city of Colorado Springs— a town of well in excess of 100,000 people—the epidemic of gonorrhea tipped because of the activities of 168 people living in four small neighborhoods and basically frequenting the same six bars.

Who were those 168 people? They aren't like you or me. They are people who go out every night, people who have vastly more sexual partners than the norm, people whose lives and behavior are well outside of the ordinary. In the mid-1990s, for example, in the pool halls and roller-skating rinks of East St. Louis, Missouri, there was a man named Darnell "Boss Man" McGee. He was big—over six feet— and charming, a talented skater who wowed young girls with his exploits on the rink. His specialty was thirteen- and fourteen-year-olds. He bought them jewelry, took them for rides in his Cadillac, got them high on crack, and had sex with them. Between 1995 and 1997, when he was shot dead by an unknown assailant, he slept with at least 100 women and—it turned out later—infected at least 30 of them with HIV.

In the same two-year period, fifteen hundred miles away, near Buffalo, New York, another man—a kind of Boss Man clone— worked the distressed downtown streets of Jamestown. His name was Nushawn Williams, although he also went by the names "Face," "Sly," and "Shyteek." Williams juggled dozens of girls, maintaining three or four different apartments around the city, and all the while supporting himself by smuggling drugs up from the Bronx. (As one epidemiologist familiar with the case told me flatly, "The man was a genius. If I could get away with what Williams did, I'd never have to work a day again in my life.") Williams, like Boss Man, was a charmer. He would buy his girlfriends roses, let them braid his long hair, and host all-night marijuana and malt liquor–fueled orgies at his apartments. "I slept with him three or four times in one night," one of his partners remembered. "Me and him, we used to party together all the time . . . . After Face had sex, his friends would do it too. One would walk out, the other would walk in." Williams is now in jail. He is known to have infected at least sixteen of his former girlfriends with the AIDS virus. And most famously, in the book *And the Band Played On* Randy Shilts discusses at length the so-called Patient Zero of AIDS, the French-Canadian flight attendant Gaetan Dugas, who claimed to have 2,500 sexual partners all over North America, and who was linked to at least 40 of the earliest cases of AIDS in California and New York. These are the kinds of people who make epidemics of disease tip.

Social epidemics work in exactly the same way. They are also driven by the efforts of a handful of exceptional people. In this case, it's not sexual appetites that set them apart. It's things like how sociable they are, or how energetic or knowledgeable or influential among their peers. In the case of Hush Puppies, the great mystery is how those shoes went from something worn by a few fashion-forward downtown Manhattan hipsters to being sold in malls across the country. What was the connection between the East Village and Middle America? The Law of the Few says the answer is that one of these exceptional people found out about the trend, and through social connections and energy and enthusiasm and personality spread the word about Hush Puppies just as people like Gaetan Dugas and Nushawn Williams were able to spread HIV.

2.

In Baltimore, when the city's public clinics suffered cutbacks, the nature of the syphilis affecting the city's poor neighborhoods changed. It used to be an acute infection, something that most people could get treated fairly quickly before they had a chance to infect many others.

But with the cutbacks, syphilis increasingly became a chronic disease, and the disease's *carriers* had three or four or five times longer to pass on their infection. Epidemics tip because of the extraordinary efforts of a few select carriers. But they also sometimes tip when something happens to transform the epidemic agent itself.

This is a well-known principle in virology. The strains of flu that circulate at the beginning of each winter's flu epidemic are quite different from the strains of flu that circulate at the end. The most famous flu epidemic of all—the pandemic of 1918—was first spotted in the spring of that year and was, relatively speaking, quite tame. But over the summer the virus underwent some strange transformation and over the next six months ended up killing between 20 and 40 million people worldwide. Nothing had changed in the way in which the virus was being spread. But the virus had suddenly become much more deadly.

The Dutch AIDS researcher Jaap Goudsmit argues that this same kind of dramatic transformation happened with HIV. Goudsmit's work focuses on what is known as *Pneumocystis carinii* pneumonia, or PCP. All of us carry the bacterium in our bodies, probably since birth or immediately thereafter. In most of us it is harmless. Our immune systems keep it in check easily. But if something, such as HIV, wipes out our immune system, it becomes so uncontrollable that it can cause a deadly form of pneumonia. PCP is so common among AIDS patients, in fact, that it has come to be seen as an almost certain indication of the presence of the virus. What Goudsmit did was go back in the medical literature and look for cases of PCP, and what he found is quite chilling. Just after World War II, beginning in the Baltic port city of Danzig and spreading through central Europe, there was an epidemic of PCP that claimed the lives of thousands of small children.

Goudsmit has analyzed one of the towns hit hardest by the PCP epidemic, the mining town of Heerlen in the Dutch province of Limburg. Heerlen had a training hospital for midwives called the Kweekschool voor Vroedvrouwen, a single unit of which—the so-called Swedish barrack—was used in the 1950s as a special ward for underweight or premature infants. Between June 1955 and July 1958, 81 infants in the Swedish barrack came down with PCP and 24 died. Goudsmit thinks that this was an early HIV epidemic, and that somehow the virus got into the hospital, and was spread from child to child by the then, apparently common, practice of using the same needles over and over again for blood transfusions or injections of antibiotics. He writes:

> Most likely at least one adult—probably a coal miner from Poland, Czechoslovakia, or Italy—brought the virus to Limburg. This one adult could have died from AIDS with little notice…He could have transmitted the virus to his wife and offspring. His infected wife (or girlfriend) could have given birth in a Swedish barrack to a child who was HIV infected but seemingly healthy. Unsterilized needles and syringes could have spread the virus from child to child.

The truly strange thing about this story, of course, is that not all of the children died. Only a third did. The others did what today would seem almost impossible. They defeated HIV, purged it from their bodies, and went on to live healthy lives. In other words, the strains of HIV that were circulating back in the 1950s were a lot different from the strains of HIV that circulate today. They were every bit as contagious, but they were weak enough that most people—even small children— were able to fight them off and survive them. The HIV epidemic tipped in the early 1980s, in short, not just because of the enormous changes in sexual behavior in the gay communities that made it possible for the virus to spread rapidly. It also tipped because HIV itself changed. For one reason or another, the virus became a lot deadlier. Once it infected you, you stayed infected. It stuck.

This idea of the importance of stickiness in tipping has enormous implications for the way we regard social epidemics as well. We tend to spend a lot of time thinking about how to make messages more contagious—how to reach as many people as possible with our prod- ucts or ideas. But the hard part of communication is often figuring out how to make sure a message doesn't go in one ear and out the other. Stickiness means that a message makes an impact. You can't get it out of your head. It sticks in your memory. When Winston filter-tip ciga- rettes were introduced in the spring of 1954, for example, the com- pany came up with the slogan "Winston tastes good like a cigarette should." At the time, the ungrammatical and somehow provocative use of "like" instead of "as" created a minor sensation. It was the kind of phrase that people talked about, like the famous Wendy's tag line from 1984 "Where's the beef?" In his history of the cigarette industry, Richard Kruger writes that the marketers at R. J. Reynolds, which sells Winston, were "delighted with the attention" and "made the offending slogan the lyric of a bouncy little jingle on television and radio, and wryly defended their syntax as a colloquialism rather than bad grammar." Within months of its introduction, on the strength of that catchy phrase, Winston tipped, racing past Parliament, Kent, and L&M into second place, behind Viceroy, in the American cigarette market. Within a few years, it was the best-selling brand in the country. To this day, if you say to most Americans "Winston tastes good," they can finish the phrase, "like a cigarette should." That's a classically sticky advertising line, and stickiness is a critical component in tipping. Unless you remember what I tell you, why would you ever change your behavior or buy my product or go to see my movie?

The Stickiness Factor says that there are specific ways of making a contagious message memorable; there are relatively simple changes in the presentation and structuring of information that can make a big difference in how much of an impact it makes.

3.

Every time someone in Baltimore comes to a public clinic for treatment of syphilis or gonorrhea, John Zenilman plugs his or her address into his computer, so that the case shows up as a little black star on a map of the city. It's rather like a medical version of the maps police departments put up on their walls, with pins marking where crimes have occurred. On Zenilman's map, the neighborhoods of East and West Baltimore, on either side of the downtown core, tend to be thick with black stars. From those two spots, the cases radiate outward along the two central roadways that happen to cut through both neighborhoods. In the summer, where the incidence of sexually transmitted disease is highest, the clusters of black stars on the roads leading out of East and West Baltimore become thick with cases. The disease is on the move. But in the winter months, the map changes. When the weather turns cold, and the people of East and West Baltimore are much more likely to stay at home, away from the bars and clubs and street corners where sexual transactions are made, the stars in each neighborhood fade away.

The seasonal effect on the number of cases is so strong that it is not hard to imagine that a long, hard winter in Baltimore could be enough to slow or lessen substantially—at least for the season—the growth of the syphilis epidemic.

Epidemics, Zenilman's map demonstrates, are strongly influenced by their situation—by the circumstances and conditions and particulars of the environments in which they operate. This much is obvious.

What is interesting, though, is how far this principle can be extended. It isn't just prosaic factors like the weather that influence behavior. Even the smallest and subtlest and most unexpected of factors can affect the way we act. One of the most infamous incidents in New York City history, for example, was the 1964 stabbing death of a young Queens woman by the name of Kitty Genovese. Genovese was chased by her assailant and attacked three times on the street, over the course of half an hour, as thirty-eight of her neighbors watched from their windows. During that time, however, none of the thirty-eight witnesses called the police. The case provoked rounds of self-recrimination. It became symbolic of the cold and dehumanizing effects of urban life. Abe Rosenthal, who would later become editor of the *New York Times*, wrote in a book about the case:

> *Nobody can say why the thirty-eight did not lift the phone while Miss Genovese was being attacked, since they cannot say themselves. It can be assumed, however, that their apathy was indeed one of the big-city variety. It is almost a matter of psychological survival, if one is surrounded and pressed by millions of people, to prevent them from constantly impinging on you, and the only way to do this is to ignore them as often as possible. Indifference to one's neighbor and his troubles is a conditioned reflex in life in New York as it is in other big cities.*

This is the kind of environmental explanation that makes intuitive sense to us. The anonymity and alienation of big-city life makes people hard and unfeeling. The truth about Genovese, however, turns out to be a little more complicated—and more interesting. Two New York City psychologists—Bibb Latane of Columbia University and John Darley of New York University—subsequently conducted a series of studies to try to understand what they dubbed the "bystander prob-lem." They staged emergencies of one kind or another in different situations in order to see who would come and help. What they found, surprisingly, was that the one factor above all else that predicted help-ing behavior was how many witnesses there were to the event.

In one experiment, for example, Latane and Darley had a student alone in a room stage an epileptic fit. When there was just one person next door, listening, that person rushed to the student's aid 85 percent of the time. But when subjects thought that there were four others also overhearing the seizure, they came to the student's aid only 31 percent of the time. In another experiment, people who saw smoke seeping out from under a doorway would report it 75 percent of the time when they were on their own, but the incident would be reported only 38 percent of the time when they were in a group. When people are in a group, in other words, responsibility for acting is diffused. They assume that someone else will make the call, or they assume that because no one else is acting, the apparent problem—the seizure-like sounds from the other room, the smoke from the door—isn't really a problem. In the case of Kitty Genovese, then, social psychologists like Latane and Darley argue, the lesson is not that no one called despite the fact that thirty-eight people heard her scream; it's that no one called *because* thirty-eight people heard her scream. Ironically, had she been attacked on a lonely street with just one witness, she might have lived.

The key to getting people to change their behavior, in other words, to care about their neighbor in distress, sometimes lies with the smallest details of their immediate situation. The Power of Context says that human beings are a lot more sensitive to their environment than they may seem.

4.

The three rules of the Tipping Point—the Law of the Few, the Stickiness Factor, the Power of Context—offer a way of making sense of epidemics. They provide us with direction for how to go about reaching a Tipping Point. The balance of this book will take these ideas and apply them to other puzzling situations and epidemics from the world around us. How do these three rules help us understand teenage smoking, for example, or the phenomenon of word of mouth, or crime, or the rise of a bestseller? The answers may surprise you.

POSSIBILITIES FOR WRITING

1. Write a summary of Gladwell's essay. Be sure to include the three types of reasons he offers for an event or situation to "tip" over into an epidemic: the "Law of the Few," the "Stickiness Factor," and the "Power of Context." Include an example of each in your summary.
2. Write an essay in which you explain the different types of causes of a social phenomenon, such as the rise of teenage smoking; the popularity of a best-selling book (the Harry Potter series, for example) or movie (*The Lord of the Rings* series, for example); or the success of a current fashion trend (low-riding jeans or body piercing, for example).
3. Do some research on the topic of Internet dating or reality TV. Then write an essay that accounts for different kinds of reasons why Internet dating or reality TV has become popular (or why it is declining in popularity)—or both.

Ellen Goodman (*b. 1941*) *is a native of Newton, Massachusetts, and a graduate of Radcliffe College. After working as a reporter for several news organizations, she joined the Boston Globe in 1967 and has been on the staff there ever since. She writes an editorial column titled "At Large" that mixes the personal with the political in a way that has achieved broad appeal among readers; it is currently syndicated in more than 250 newspapers nationwide. These columns have been collected in several volumes, including* Paper Trail: Common Sense in Uncommon Times *(2004). Goodman won the Pulitzer Prize for commentary in 1980.*

ELLEN GOODMAN

The Company Man

In "The Company Man," Ellen Goodman presents a sketch of a character who sacrifices everything for his work. He gives up all pretension to a social life and becomes disconnected from his wife and family, while keeping his focus entirely on his job as a corporate vice president. Describing him as a "type A" workaholic who lives for his work on the job, Goodman simplifies the man and the choices he makes. What she loses in presenting Phil as a complete and complex human being, she gains in making a point about what matters, or should matter, most in our lives.

He worked himself to death, finally and precisely, at 3:00 A.M. Sunday morning.

The obituary didn't say that, of course. It said that he died of a coronary thrombosis—I think that was it—but everyone among his friends and acquaintances knew it instantly. He was a perfect Type A, a workaholic, a classic, they said to each other and shook their heads— and thought for five or ten minutes about the way they lived.

This man who worked himself to death finally and precisely at 3:00 A.M. Sunday morning—on his day off—was fifty-one years old and a vice-president. He was, however, one of six vice-presidents, and one of three who might conceivably—if the president died or retired soon enough—have moved to the top spot. Phil knew that.

He worked six days a week, five of them until eight or nine at night, during a time when his own company had begun the four-day week for everyone but the executives. He worked like the Important People. He had no outside "extracurricular interests," unless, of course, you think about a monthly golf game that way. To Phil, it was work. He always ate egg salad sandwiches at his desk. He was, of course, overweight, by 20 or 25 pounds. He thought it was okay, though, because he didn't smoke.

On Saturdays, Phil wore a sports jacket to the office instead of a suit, because it was the weekend.

He had a lot of people working for him, maybe sixty, and most of them liked him most of the time. Three of them will be seriously considered for his job. The obituary didn't mention that.

But it did list his "survivors" quite accurately. He is survived by his wife, Helen, forty-eight years old, a good woman of no particular marketable skills, who worked in an office before marrying and mothering. She had, according to her daughter, given up trying to compete with his work years ago, when the children were small. A company friend said, "I know how much you will miss him." And she answered, "I already have."

"Missing him all these years," she must have given up part of herself which had cared too much for the man. She would be "well taken care of."

His "dearly beloved" eldest of the "dearly beloved" children is a hardworking executive in a manufacturing firm down South. In the day and a half before the funeral, he went around the neighborhood researching his father, asking the neighbors what he was like. They were embarrassed.

His second child is a girl, who is twenty-four and newly married. She lives near her mother and they are close, but whenever she was alone with her father, in a car driving somewhere, they had nothing to say to each other.

The youngest is twenty, a boy, a high-school graduate who has spent the last couple of years, like a lot of his friends, doing enough odd jobs to stay in grass and food. He was the one who tried to grab at his father, and tried to mean enough to him to keep the man at home. He was his father's favorite. Over the last two years, Phil stayed up nights worrying about the boy.

The boy once said, "My father and I only board here."

At the funeral, the sixty-year-old company president told the forty-eight-year-old widow that the fifty-one-year-old deceased had meant much to the company and would be missed and would be hard to replace. The widow didn't look him in the eye. She was afraid he would read her bitterness and, after all, she would need him to straighten out the finances—the stock options and all that.

Phil was overweight and nervous and worked too hard. If he wasn't at the office, he was worried about it. Phil was a Type A, a heart-attack natural. You could have picked him out in a minute from a lineup.

So when he finally worked himself to death, at precisely 3:00 A.M. Sunday morning, no one was really surprised.

By 5:00 P.M. the afternoon of the funeral, the company president had begun, discreetly of course, with care and taste, to make inquiries about his replacement. One of three men. He asked around: "Who's been working the hardest?"

POSSIBILITIES FOR WRITING

1. Goodman's essay is marked by irony throughout. Analyze the use of irony here—in language, in juxtapositions of images, and within scenes. Do you find the level of irony appropriate, or does it ever strike you as heavy-handed?

2. Goodman wrote this essay in the early 1970s. What values and social constructs does it suggest were common at the time? Using evidence from your own experience, would you say that things today are different or pretty much the same?

3. Using Goodman as a model, write an ironic portrait of a personality type you know well. You may base your portrait on a real person or on a composite of different people. If appropriate to your subject, you may wish to focus more on humorous aspects of this personality type.

Michael Hogan (b. 1943) was born in Newport, Rhode Island. He is the author of fourteen books of fiction, poetry, and nonfiction, including Teaching from the Heart *(2003), a collection of his essays and speeches, and* The Irish Soldiers of Mexico, *a seminar work on the Mexican War of 1846–1848. His poetry and prose have been published in such literary magazines as the* Paris Review, *the* Harvard Review, *the* Iowa Review, *and the* American Poetry Review. *He is the recipient of numerous awards, including the NEA Creative Writing Fellowship and two Puschcart Prizes. He lives in Guadalajara, Mexico, with the well-known textile artist Lucinda Mayo. More recent publications include a memoir,* Newport: A Writer's Beginnings *(2012);* A Death in Newport *(2011), a novel; and* Winter Solstice: Selected Poems 1975–2012 *(2012).*

MICHAEL HOGAN

The Colonel

In "The Colonel," Michael Hogan describes his experiences in watching, learning, and playing tennis from his boyhood years into late middle age. Hogan's essay focuses on an army colonel, whose war stories induced the twelve-year-old Hogan to give up the pleasures of baseball, football, and basketball for the rigors of tennis. Colonel Flack taught the young Hogan not only the rudiments of the game, but also important lessons about sportsmanship, competitiveness, courage, and grace.

Tennis is so popular these days and so much a part of the average teenager's sports experience, that it is difficult for most of them to imagine a time when it was not. Yet, in the post-war period and the Fifties of my childhood, tennis was considered more a rich man's sport played at country clubs and exclusive resorts. Competitive singles was largely a sport of the male sex and, although women had been competing for years at Wimbledon and other international venues, most were amateurs and the few professionals who did compete got paid so little it was laughable. It wasn't until Billie Jean King's assertiveness in 1967 and the Virginia Slim tournaments of the 1970s that the sport opened up for generations of Chris Everts and Steffi Grafs, and finally grew to include million-dollar players like Venus Williams who changed the sport forever making it the dream of every athletic boy and girl.

The courts in my hometown of Newport, RI, were mostly off-limits to working class kids like me. The excellent grass center courts and the red clay courts of the private Newport Casino where the National Doubles Championships were held, were open only to wealthy members who paid a hefty annual fee. The courts at the Newport Country

Club were restricted to those few rich families who were members, as were those at the even more exclusive Bailey's Beach. At the Brenton Village navy facility inside Fort Adams there were courts for officers and their dependents but these were not accessible to locals. Both composition and clay courts were available at Salve Regina College but only for registered students and faculty. So that left two casually-maintained asphalt courts at the city park on Carroll Avenue where during the summer, students home from college would bang away in lusty volleys and dominate the courts in rugged comradery.

A twelve-year-old working at a summer job, I had little interest in tennis. To me, pickup games of basketball and football were more fun and interesting. I played both at the Carroll Street Park and at the YMCA, and in the prolonged light of New England summer evenings practicing shots alone in the backyard with a hoop hung from the front of the garage. As fall approached and football season began, I'd play touch games with my friends and rougher tackle games with boys from uptown in the same park that abutted the tennis area. On occasion we might glance over at the courts if a particular cute coed was playing doubles. Sometimes we would head over to the water fountains close by to get a drink and watch a game or two. "Love-fifteen. Love-thirty. Deuce." We had no idea what this absurd scoring method could signify. It was remote from our experience, as were the crisp white shorts, the spotless tennis shoes, and the white sports shirts which were *de rigueur* in those days. We were ragamuffins, I suppose; heady youth, and tennis seemed effete, subtle, complex and sophisticated—more like an elaborate dance than a sport, a dance to which we would never be invited.

So, it came as a surprise to me when an Army colonel who lived up the street from us began talking about tennis one day with my Dad. "Does the boy play?" I heard him ask. "No," my Dad said, "but he loves sports and plays basketball, baseball, football." "Well," replied the Colonel, "if he ever wants a lesson, tell him to stop by. I was an Army champion in my day."

Later my Dad would mention it, and when I replied that I thought it was a sissy game, he would begin to tell me of some of the great players of the day: Poncho Gonzalez, Jack Kramer, Ken Rosewall, but the names meant little to me. But I did like the old Colonel who had great stories to tell about the War which was not too distant in memory. My father's brother Harry had died in the forests of Belgium in 1944 during the last German push. A Little League baseball field in our neighborhood carried his name. War games in the local hills were still very much a part of our youthful pastimes. So, on a Saturday afternoon, home from a half day's labor at my summer job with a landscape company, I stopped by to talk to the Colonel. When the subject turned to tennis, his eyes lit up as he described the competition he faced in college and in the service. He regaled me with stories of tournaments, matches with famous players, games played at officer clubs in remote parts of the world. He said, "Tennis is the one game that, once you learn it, you will be able to play for the rest of your life. When your knees go out and you can't play football, when there is no gang of boys around for the pickup game of basketball or baseball, you can always find someone to play tennis with." So he convinced me. Or, perhaps it was his enthusiasm, my love for his stories and respect for his retired rank, his war experiences, or his genial personality and his enthusiasm, that I just felt I didn't want to disappoint. However it was, we agreed.

He loaned me one of his wooden rackets in its complicated screw-down press and the following day, right after early mass on a Sunday morning, he began teaching me the basics. In between suggestions about how to hold the racket and how to volley, he lectured me on the history of the sport, taught me how to score, how to adjust the net, how to anticipate the ball, how to refrain from cussing or displaying untoward emotional behavior. I think he probably bought me my first set of tennis whites that summer as well, although the first few games I'm sure I played in T-shirt and Levi cutoffs much to his distaste. That July was my thirteenth birthday and my father bought me my own racket, a Bancroft wood—expensive, highly polished and tightly strung with catgut and protected in a standard wooden press with butterfly screwdowns. The racket would be re-strung many times over the four years that I owned it. I would play with it in local matches, city tournaments, and even one memorable morning at the Newport Casino, where I got to volley with Poncho Gonzalez on the grass center court, courtesy of my father who owned a business next door and had persuaded the famous champion to trade a few strokes with his son.

The Colonel was, I suppose, in his mid-sixties, which seemed ancient to me then. I could not imagine, as I improved in my tennis skills, and learned to volley deep, hit cross-court passing shots and top-spin lobs, that he would be able to keep up with me. Surely, the student would outplay the master any day now. But it never happened. Colonel Flack had a whole repertoire of moves: drop shots, slices, topspin backhands, corkscrew serves, and high-bouncing serves which just cut the end of the line. He knew the angles and limits of the court and, comfortable with these absorbed geometries, kept his young opponent racing from the net to the baseline, ragged and breathless.

As the summer passed, I improved: the muscles on my right forearm grew oversized, my lung capacity deepened, and my strokes improved from the gradual anticipation of the slides and twists that the ball would take as it came off the Colonel's racket. My service improved as well, so that I sometimes caught him wrong-footed and could come to the net quickly and put the ball away. I still didn't win a set, but the games were closer and I noticed the Colonel was flushed and winded more and more often.

We played less the following year as I found new and younger competition among military dependents, boys from De La Salle Academy, and returning college players. I was often on the courts for hours each evening and on the weekends. With only two courts to play on, you had to win to keep the court and I was often a winner. Sometimes I would generously concede to play mixed doubles with couples who were waiting patiently on the sidelines.

Then one afternoon, shortly after my fourteenth birthday, all of that changed. A new boy appeared on the block; redheaded, cocky, with an easy confidence and grace and a powerful serve that could knock a poorly-gripped racket clear out of your hand. Tommy Gallagher was a compact, good-looking Irish boy who appeared from nowhere and had all the natural moves of a champion. I was blown off the court again and again in swift, blurred games of intense ferocity. I began to learn the difference between a "club player" as opposed to a "show player" or competitive athlete. Tommy played like he was born to it. There was nothing you could hit to him that he could not return. When I tried to play his game he beat me ruthlessly, contemptuously, as if I were wasting his time.

On one of those occasions, the semifinals of a citywide tournament, Colonel Flack was in the audience. Shamed by the 6–1, 6–0 defeat, I did not look him in the eye as I retreated back to the bench. "I'm not going to try and console you, Mike," he said. "You got sent to hell and back by that lad. And if you play him again, he'll beat you again. He's one of these kids who's a natural. But don't let him take away your pleasure in the game; don't let him do that to you. You're a club player and a decent one. Play your own game, take the shots you can, don't get caught up in his game. And don't be intimidated."

I was to play Tommy Gallagher several times over the next two years. He beat me, as he beat most of his competitors, but he won less easily as time went by, and never with the contemptuous indifference I had felt in that one semifinal. More importantly, losing to him did not take away from me the love of the game or my sense of myself as a player. Partly this was true because Colonel Flack and I returned to our early morning volleys interspersed with lessons. But now the lessons had more to do with eliminating distractions, watching the ball, and feeling the sun, the sweat on my skin, the slight breeze from the ocean, hearing the thwock of the perfectly hit ball coming off the strings. He taught me to be totally present in the moment, totally aware, totally focused.

He also trained me to go after every ball regardless of whether it seemed returnable or not. He taught me to play according to my skill level, placing shots carefully, not overhitting because of a desire to put it away like a pro, but stroking with the steady grace and pressure of a good club player who often tires out his more ambitious, more aggressive opponent.

Finally, he taught me that graciousness is what saves the game from savagery and ugliness. He instructed me not to give in to the temptation to call a ball out when it was in, to always give the opponent the benefit of the doubt, and that it was better to lose than to win unfairly. He reminded me to hold my temper in check, to always be polite, to return the balls in a single bounce to the server when there was no one to fetch balls.

But what he couldn't teach me and what I learned for myself over the years was that all of this was a gift. Tennis would change with the Australian 100 mph serves of Rod Laver, the aluminum and then titanium rackets, the oversized head rackets, with Wilson and Adidas logos covering every piece of equipment and raiment. Bad boys like John McEnroe would cuss out line judges and umpires, as aggressiveness had its day and then subsided ... though never completely. Competitive tennis would be enshrined in every high school and university; tennis camps would groom a new generation of players like Pete Sampras and Andre Agassi intent on making millions as they made their mark in the sport. Still, I would go right on playing my 3.5 club-level game. I would play tennis in the dry heat of the Sonoran deserts of Tucson and on the mile-high courts of Denver. I would play in Argentina and Panama. I would play after clearing the debris off a hurricane-littered court in Florida; I would hit the low-bounce ball while bundled in a jacket in up-state New York after sweeping off the snow-covered court, and—year after year—I would sweat through grueling sets in the tropical heat of May in Guadalajara. I would play through days of political unrest and assassination in my twenties, through the bitter, rancorous divorce in my thirties, through the crushing death of a beloved child in my forties, then through uncertain days of financial disasters and overseas currency devaluations in my fifties.

Now here I am in my sixties, approaching inexorably the age of my mentor, Colonel Flack, who on a summer morning took a skinny twelve-year-old out to the concrete courts of a seaside town to give him the gift of lifelong victory. It is a way of maintaining both physical and psychological fitness, but also a way of moving through life with a focus, with grace and a sure sense of gratitude. One of those ineffable spiritual gifts which continue to give again and again when I walk on to a sun-speckled court, go over to measure the net with my "stick" (a Wilson H-26 titanium racket), and all the world narrows down to the clear geometries of the white lines, to the sound of the thwock as the ball hits the strings, as my muscles respond again in their dependable way to the known rhythms of the game, and everything is suddenly whole and perfect, and the world completely intelligible.

POSSIBILITIES FOR WRITING

1. Write a brief character sketch of Colonel Flack. Try to convey a sense of the colonel as a man and as a teacher.
2. Summarize the lessons Hogan learned from the colonel. To what extent do you think that these lessons are valuable for life as well as for tennis? Explain.
3. Write an essay about a sport, game, hobby, or other leisure pursuit for which you have a passion. Explain how you became involved in it and what values it holds for you.

Barbara Holland (b. 1925) is a freelance writer based in rural Virginia. She has written fiction, essays, and articles for a wide range of publications, including Cosmopolitan, Discovery, *and* Playboy. *Among her books are* Endangered Pleasures: In Defense of Naps, Bacon, Martinis, Profanity, and Other Indulgences *(1995),* Bingo Night at the Fire Halls *(1998), and* Wasn't the Grass Greener? *(1999). Her memoir* When All the World Was Young *was published in 2005.*

BARBARA HOLLAND

Naps

In "Naps," an essay from her book *Endangered Pleasures,* Barbara Holland makes a case for the importance of the daily nap. Holland notes that a nap forms part of the daily routine of people in many countries, especially throughout Europe. She notes further that human beings are naturally inclined to fall asleep in the middle of the afternoon—and do so when "deprived of daylight and their wristwatches."

In France, on a rented canal boat, my friends and I gazed in despair at the closed oaken gates of the lock. We'd come to them only seconds after the witching hour of noon, but we were too late. There was no one to open the lock for us; *l'éclusière* was at lunch, and after lunch she would lay herself down, close her eyes, and nap. At two, but not before, she would emerge refreshed from her square granite house and set the great cogs in motion.

We tied the boat up to a spindly bush beside the towpath and waited. And waited. It was high haying season, but the fields lay empty of farmers. The roads lay empty of trucks. France lunched, and then slept. So did Spain. So did much of the civilized world.

If we'd been differently nurtured we too would have taken a nap, but we were Americans, condemned from the age of four to trudge through our sleepless days. Americans are afraid of naps.

Napping is too luxurious, too sybaritic, too unproductive, and it's free; pleasures for which we don't pay make us anxious. Besides, it seems to be a natural inclination. Those who get paid to investigate such things have proved that people deprived of daylight and their wristwatches, with no notion of whether it was night or day, sink blissfully asleep in midafternoon as regular as clocks. Fighting off natural inclinations is a major Puritan virtue, and nothing that feels that good can be respectable.

They may have a point there. Certainly the process of falling asleep in the afternoon is quite different from bedtime sleep. Whether this is physiological or merely a by-product of guilt, it's a blatantly sensual experience, a voluptuous surrender, akin to the euphoric swoon of the heroine in a vampire movie. For the self-controlled, it's frightening—*how far down am I falling? will I ever climb back?* The sleep itself has a different texture. It's blacker, thicker, more intense, and works faster. Fifteen minutes later the napper pops back to the surface as from time travel, bewildered to find that it's only ten of two instead of centuries later.

Like skydiving, napping takes practice; the first few tries are scary.

The American nap is even scarier because it's unilateral. Sleeping Frenchmen are surrounded by sleeping compatriots, but Americans who lie down by day stiffen with the thought of the busy world rushing past. There we lie, visible and vulnerable on our daylit bed, ready to cut the strings and sink into the dark, swirling, almost sexual currents of the impending doze, but what will happen in our absence? Our stocks will fall; our employees will mutiny and seize the helm; our clients will tiptoe away to competitors. Even the housewife, taking advantage of the afternoon lull, knows at the deepest level of consciousness that the phone is about to ring.

And of course, for those of us with proper jobs, there's the problem of finding a bed. Some corporations, in their concern for their employees' health and fitness, provide gym rooms where we can commit strenuous exercise at lunchtime, but where are our beds? In Japan, the productivity wonder of the industrialized world, properly run companies maintain a nap room wherein the workers may refresh themselves. Even in America, rumor has it, the costly CEOs of giant corporations work sequestered in private suites, guarded by watchpersons, mainly so they can curl up unseen to sharpen their predatory powers with a quick snooze. A couple of recent presidents famous for their all-night energies kept up the pace by means of naps. Other presidents, less famous for energy, slept by day *and* night; woe to the unwary footstep that wakened Coolidge in the afternoon.

This leaves the rest of us lackeys bolt upright, toughing it out, trying to focus on the computer screen, from time to time snatching our chins up off our collarbones and glancing furtively around to see if we were noticed. The modern office isn't designed for privacy, and most of our cubicles have no doors to close, only gaps in the portable partitions. Lay our heads down on the desk at the appropriate hour and we're exposed to any passing snitch who strolls the halls enforcing alertness. It's a wonder they don't walk around ringing bells and blowing trumpets from one till three. American employers do not see the afternoon forty winks as refreshing the creative wellsprings of mere employees. They see it as goofing off.

Apparently most of us agree. Large numbers of us are, for one reason or another, home-bound, but do we indulge in the restorative nap? Mostly not. Even with no witness but ourselves, we're ashamed to. It would mean we weren't busy. We tell ourselves we have a million urgent things to do and our lives are so full and exciting we couldn't possibly lie down by daylight. Never mind that our heads are no particular use in midafternoon and half the work we do may need to be redone in the cold light of tomorrow morning. Oozing virtue and busyness, we flog ourselves on till evening.

In the evening, at least according to the cartoons, American men fall asleep on the couch, after dinner, a-flicker with light from the television screen. They are home from work, the day's toil accomplished, and they're free to doze, though if they'd napped at the biologically appointed time they wouldn't need to now, and at this hour it's not so much a nap as an awkward preview of the night's sleep, possibly leading to four-a.m. insomnia. Women, on the other hand, are never home from work unless it's someone else's home; home for them is simply different work, and naps are not an option.

It's time to rethink the nap from both the corporate and the personal viewpoint.

Those CEOs who find their own naps such an asset to productivity might consider what they'd do for the rest of us. They could hire consultants to conduct productivity studies, dividing us into teams of sleepers and wakers. When the results were in, they might even decide to mandate naps, as naps were mandated in nursery school, when we each unfolded a name-tagged blanket and spread it on the floor and lay down and shut up for a while. Granted we can't all have office suites, or even couches, and it would be unseemly to have us stacked up like firewood on the conference table, but we could use futons, stored discreetly under the desk, or folding cots, or sleeping bags. The phones could be left to their answering devices, the faxes could pile up in the hopper, and the sales reps could pound in vain on the door as they'd find themselves doing in France.

Those of us at home, with beds at hand, should take pleasure as well as productivity into account. Consider the cat. A perfectly healthy cat can nap through the entire month of February and wake feeling all the better for it. The house may be simply pattering with uncaught mice, but no twitch of guilt quivers the whiskers of the napping cat. In summer he stretches out to full length, preferably in a breezy doorway where he's rather in the way, and sometimes on his back, looking dead enough to alarm the chance visitor, and drapes his arm over his eyes. Swiftly and easily he lowers himself into sleep, sensuous, fur-lined sleep, the sleep of the untroubled conscience. Nothing tells him he ought to be rushing about his various occupations. Sleep, for a cat, is a worthy occupation in itself.

Let us consider the cat and go to bed. Bed the haven, the motherly lap, the downy nest. Bed, from which Earth with its fuss and fidget-ing shrinks to the size of Pluto, visible only by telescope. We should loosen or remove some of our clothing, close the curtains, and lie down flat, allowing the vital forces to circulate through the brain and restore its muscle tone.

Bed is *not* a shameful, shiftless place to be by day, nor is it neces-sary to run a fever of 102 to deserve it. Bed can even be productive. The effortless horizontal body and the sensory deprivation of the quiet bedroom leave the mind free, even in sleep, to focus, to roam, some-times to forge ahead. Knotty problems can unknot themselves as if by magic. Creative solutions can tiptoe across the coverlet and nestle onto the pillow of the napper, even while the black velvet paws of Morpheus lie closely over his eyes. He may wake half an hour later with the road ahead laid clear.

Creativity doesn't come a-running to those who toil and slave for her; she's as much the daughter of rest and play as of effort. Just because we're uncomfortable doesn't mean we're productive; just because we're comfortable doesn't mean we're lazy. Milton wrote *Paradise Lost* in bed. Winston Churchill, a prodigious producer, wrote all those large impor-tant histories in bed, brandy bottle at the ready. No doubt when inspira-tion flagged and his thoughts refused to marshal, he took a nip and a nap. Now, there was a man who knew a thing or two about a good day's work.

POSSIBILITIES FOR WRITING

1. What does "nap prejudice" represent for Holland? What does she see as its sources? Why does she think allowing for naps would be a good thing more generally? Do you tend to agree or disagree with her? Why?

2. What is your experience with naps, beginning in childhood and including your current life? Who in your experience is most likely to nap? Why? What does this say about naps?

3. This essay comes from a book entitled *Endangered Pleasures*. Write an essay about what you consider an "endangered pleasure"—something you see as innocently enjoyable that is looked upon negatively by other people.

Langston Hughes (1902–1967) was born in Joplin, Missouri, to a prominent
African American family. Interested in poetry from childhood, he attended
Columbia University as an engineering major but dropped out after his first year
to pursue his literary aspirations (he later graduated from Lincoln University).
Spurred by the flourishing of black artists known as the Harlem Renaissance, he
quickly found a distinctive voice that reflected the culture of everyday life, and
he published his first works before he was out of his teens. Hughes is best known
for his poetry, which often employs vernacular language and jazz-like rhythms,
but he also wrote popular works of fiction, essays, plays, books for children, and
several volumes of autobiography, including The Big Sea (1940), focusing on his
childhood and teenage years.

LANGSTON HUGHES

Salvation

In "Salvation," Hughes describes a memorable incident from his youth,
one that had a decisive impact on his view of the world. In the span
of just a few pages, Hughes tells a story of faith and doubt, of belief
and disbelief, of how he was "saved from sin" when he was going on
thirteen. "But not really saved." This paradoxical opening to "Salvation"
establishes a tension that characterizes the essay, which culminates in
an ironic reversal of expectations for the reader and a life-altering
realization for Hughes.

I was saved from sin when I was going on thirteen. But not really
saved. It happened like this. There was a big revival at my Auntie
Reed's church. Every night for weeks there had been much preaching,
singing, praying, and shouting, and some very hardened sinners had
been brought to Christ, and the membership of the church had grown
by leaps and bounds. Then just before the revival ended, they held a
special meeting for children, "to bring the young lambs to the fold."
My aunt spoke of it for days ahead. That night I was escorted to the
front row and placed on the mourners' bench with all the other young
sinners, who had not yet been brought to Jesus.

My aunt told me that when you were saved you saw a light, and
something happened to you inside! And Jesus came into your life! And
God was with you from then on! She said you could see and hear and
feel Jesus in your soul. I believed her. I had heard a great many old
people say the same thing and it seemed to me they ought to know.
So I sat there calmly in the hot, crowded church, waiting for Jesus to
come to me.

The preacher preached a wonderful rhythmical sermon, all moans and shouts and lonely cries and dire pictures of hell, and then he sang a song about the ninety and nine safe in the fold, but one little lamb was left out in the cold. Then he said: "Won't you come? Won't you come to Jesus? Young lambs, won't you come?" And he held out his arms to all us young sinners there on the mourners' bench. And the little girls cried. And some of them jumped up and went to Jesus right away. But most of us just sat there.

A great many old people came and knelt around us and prayed, old women with jet-black faces and braided hair, old men with work-gnarled hands. And the church sang a song about the lower lights are burning, some poor sinners to be saved. And the whole building rocked with prayer and song.

Still I kept waiting to *see* Jesus.

Finally all the young people had gone to the altar and were saved, but one boy and me. He was a rounder's son named Westley. Westley and I were surrounded by sisters and deacons praying. It was very hot in the church, and getting late now. Finally Westley said to me in a whisper: "God damn! I'm tired o' sitting here. Let's get up and be saved." So he got up and was saved.

Then I was left all alone on the mourners' bench. My aunt came and knelt at my knees and cried, while prayers and songs swirled all around me in the little church. The whole congregation prayed for me alone, in a mighty wail of moans and voices. And I kept waiting serenely for Jesus, waiting, waiting—but he didn't come. I wanted to see him, but nothing happened to me. Nothing! I wanted something to happen to me, but nothing happened.

I heard the songs and the minister saying: "Why don't you come? My dear child, why don't you come to Jesus? Jesus is waiting for you. He wants you. Why don't you come? Sister Reed, what is this child's name?"

"Langston," my aunt sobbed.

"Langston, why don't you come? Why don't you come and be saved? Oh, Lamb of God! Why don't you come?"

Now it was really getting late. I began to be ashamed of myself, holding everything up so long. I began to wonder what God thought about Westley, who certainly hadn't seen Jesus either, but who was now sitting proudly on the platform, swinging his knickerbockered legs and grinning down at me, surrounded by deacons and old women on their knees praying. God had not struck Westley dead for taking his name in vain or for lying in the temple. So I decided that maybe to save further trouble, I'd better lie, too, and say that Jesus had come, and get up and be saved.

So I got up.

Suddenly the whole room broke into a sea of shouting, as they saw me rise. Waves of rejoicing swept the place. Women leaped in the air. My aunt threw her arms around me. The minister took me by the hand and led me to the platform.

When things quieted down, in a hushed silence, punctuated by a few ecstatic "Amens," all the new young lambs were blessed in the name of God. Then joyous singing filled the room.

That night, for the last time in my life but one—for I was a big boy twelve years old—I cried. I cried, in bed alone, and couldn't stop. I buried my head under the quilts, but my aunt heard me. She woke up and told my uncle I was crying because the Holy Ghost had come into my life, and because I had seen Jesus. But I was really crying because I couldn't bear to tell her that I had lied, that I had deceived everybody in the church, and I hadn't seen Jesus, and that now I didn't believe there was a Jesus any more, since he didn't come to help me.

POSSIBILITIES FOR WRITING

1. Recall a time when, like Hughes, you did something you didn't really believe in because you found it easier to go along with the crowd. In an essay, narrate the experience, focusing on the situation, the other people involved, your feelings at the time, and the aftermath of the incident.

2. In this brief narration, Hughes does a great deal to re-create his experience vividly and concretely. Analyze Hughes's use of language—specific nouns, verbs, and adjectives—as well as his use of dialogue and repetition to add punch to his story.

3. Hughes ends his narration on a note of disillusionment: "now I didn't believe there was a Jesus any more, since he didn't come to help me." Have you ever been disillusioned about a deeply held and cherished belief? In an essay, explore that experience and its consequences in detail. How did you eventually cope with your disappointment?

Zora Neale Hurston (1891–1960) was born in Eatonville, Florida, where she spent her early years. She attended Howard University and in 1925 went to New York City, becoming involved in cultural activities in Harlem. There she met Langston Hughes, who, like Hurston, was interested in the folk elements of African American culture, particularly as reflected in Southern life. From 1925 through 1927 she attended Barnard College, studying anthropology with Dr. Franz Boas. She later did field research recording the folklore and ways of African Americans, first in Harlem, then throughout the rural South. The fruits of this work appeared in her Mules and Men *(1935). Hurston's best known works are* Their Eyes Were Watching God *(1937) and the autobiographical* Dust Tracks on a Road *(1942). These and other works were rediscovered as a result of the women's movement and in conjunction with an upsurge in the study of African American literature, especially that of the Harlem Renaissance.*

ZORA NEALE HURSTON

How It Feels To Be Colored Me

In "How It Feels To Be Colored Me," Hurston discusses her blackness as an aspect of race and of her cultural, social, and personal identity. The essay's tone is confident and upbeat, as Hurston celebrates herself as a modern African American woman who knows her worth even when others do not.

I am colored but I offer nothing in the way of extenuating circumstances except the fact that I am the only Negro in the United States whose grandfather on the mother's side was *not* an Indian chief.

I

I remember the very day that I became colored. Up to my thirteenth year I lived in the little Negro town of Eatonville, Florida. It is exclusively a colored town. The only white people I knew passed through the town going to or coming from Orlando. The native whites rode dusty horses, the Northern tourists chugged down the sandy village road in automobiles. The town knew the Southerners and never stopped cane chewing when they passed. But the Northerners were something else again. They were peered at cautiously from behind curtains by the timid. The more venture-some would come out on the porch to watch them go past and got just as much pleasure out of the tourists as the tourists got out of the village.

The front porch might seem a daring place for the rest of the town, but it was a gallery seat to me. My favorite place was atop the gate-post.

Proscenium box for a born first-nighter. Not only did I enjoy the show, but I didn't mind the actors knowing that I liked it. I usually spoke to them in passing. I'd wave at them and when they returned my salute, I would say something like this: "Howdy-do-well-I-thank-you-where-you-goin'?" Usually automobile or the horse paused at this, and after a queer exchange of compliments, I would probably "go a piece of the way" with them, as we say in farthest Florida. If one of my family happened to come to the front in time to see me, of course negotiations would be rudely broken off. But even so, it is clear that I was the first "welcome-to-our-state" Floridian, and I hope the Miami Chamber of Commerce will please take notice.

During this period, white people differed from colored to me only in that they rode through town and never lived there. They liked to hear me "speak pieces" and sing and wanted to see me dance the parse-me-la, and gave me generously of their small silver for doing these things, which seemed strange to me for I wanted to do them so much that I needed bribing to stop. Only they didn't know it. The colored people gave no dimes. They deplored any joyful tendencies in me, but I was their Zora nevertheless. I belonged to them, to the nearby hotels, to the county—everybody's Zora.

But changes came in the family when I was thirteen, and I was sent to school in Jacksonville. I left Eatonville, the town of the oleanders, as Zora. When I disembarked from the river-boat at Jacksonville, she was no more. It seemed that I had suffered a sea change. I was not Zora of Orange County any more, I was now a little colored girl. I found it out in certain ways. In my heart as well as in the mirror, I became a fast brown—warranted not to rub nor run.

II

But I am not tragically colored. There is no great sorrow dammed up in my soul, nor lurking behind my eyes. I do not mind at all. I do not belong to the sobbing school of Negrohood who hold that nature somehow has given them a lowdown dirty deal and whose feelings are all hurt about it. Even in the helter-skelter skirmish that is my life, I have seen that the world is to the strong regardless of a little pigmentation more or less. No, I do not weep at the world—I am too busy sharpening my oyster knife.

Someone is always at my elbow reminding me that I am the grand-daughter of slaves. It fails to register depression with me. Slavery is sixty years in the past. The operation was successful and the patient is doing well, thank you. The terrible struggle that made me an American out of a potential slave said "On the line!" The Reconstruction said "Get set!"; and the generation before said "Go!" I am off to a flying start and I must not halt in the stretch to look behind and weep. Slavery is the price I paid for civilization, and the choice was not with me. It is a Bully adventure and worth all that I have paid through my ancestors for it. No one on earth ever had a greater chance for glory. The world to be won and nothing to be lost. It is thrilling to think—to know that for any act of mine, I shall get twice as much praise or twice as much blame. It is quite exciting to hold the center of the national stage, with the spectators not knowing whether to laugh or to weep.

The position of my white neighbor is much more difficult. No brown specter pulls up a chair beside me when I sit down to eat. No dark ghost thrusts its leg against mine in bed. The game of keeping what one has is never so exciting as the game of getting.

I do not always feel colored. Even now I often achieve the unconscious Zora of Eatonville before the Hegira. I feel most colored when I am thrown against a sharp white background.

For instance at Barnard. "Beside the waters of the Hudson" I feel my race. Among the thousand white persons, I am a dark rock surged upon, overswept by a creamy sea. I am surged upon and overswept, but through it all, I remain myself. When covered by the waters, I am; and the ebb but reveals me again.

III

Sometimes it is the other way around. A white person is set down in our midst, but the contrast is just as sharp for me. For instance, when I sit in the drafty basement that is The New World Cabaret with a white person, my color comes. We enter chatting about any little nothing that we have in common and are seated by the jazz waiters. In the abrupt way that jazz orchestras have, this one plunges into a number. It loses no time in circumlocutions, but gets right down to business. It constricts the thorax and splits the heart with its tempo and narcotic harmonies. This orchestra grows rambunctious, rears on its hind legs and attacks the tonal veil with primitive fury, rending it, clawing it until it breaks through to the jungle beyond. I follow those heathen—follow them exultingly. I dance wildly inside myself; I yell within, I whoop; I shake my assegai above my head,

I hurl it true to the mark *yeeeeooww!* I am in the jungle and living in the jungle way. My face is painted red and yellow and my body is painted blue. My pulse is throbbing like a war drum. I want to slaughter something—give pain, give death to what, I do not know. But the piece ends. The men of the orchestra wipe their lips and rest their fingers. I creep back slowly to the veneer we call civilization with the last tone and find the white friend sitting motionless in his seat, smoking calmly.

"Good music they have here," he remarks, drumming the table with his fingertips.

Music! The great blobs of purple and red emotion have not touched him. He has only heard what I felt. He is far away and I see him but dimly across the ocean and the continent that have fallen between us. He is so pale with his whiteness then and I am so colored.

IV

At certain times I have no race, I am *me*. When I set my hat at a certain angle and saunter down Seventh Avenue, Harlem City, feeling as snooty as the lions in front of the Forty-Second Street Library, for instance. So far as my feelings are concerned, Peggy Hopkins Joyce on the Boule Mich with her gorgeous raiment, stately carriage, knees knocking together in a most aristocratic manner, has nothing on me. The cosmic Zora emerges. I belong to no race nor time. I am the eternal feminine with its string of beads.

I have no separate feeling about being an American citizen and colored. I am merely a fragment of the Great Soul that surges within the boundaries. My country, right or wrong.

Sometimes, I feel discriminated against, but it does not make me angry. It merely astonishes me. How *can* any deny themselves the pleasure of my company! It's beyond me.

But in the main, I feel like a brown bag of miscellany propped against a wall. Against a wall in company with other bags, white, red and yellow. Pour out the contents, and there is discovered a jumble of small things priceless and worthless. A first-water diamond, an empty spool, bits of broken glass, lengths of string, a key to a door long since crumbled away, a rusty knife-blade, old shoes saved for a road that never was and never will be, a nail bent under the weight of things too heavy for any nail, a dried flower or two still a little fragrant. In your hand is the brown bag. On the ground before you is the jumble it held—so much like the jumble in the bags, could they be emptied, that all might be dumped in a single heap and the bags refilled without altering the content of any greatly. A bit of colored glass more or less would not matter. Perhaps that is how the Great Stuffer of Bags filled them in the first place—who knows?

POSSIBILITIES FOR WRITING

1. Hurston presents herself as happy with who she is, especially with her race. Do you think her experience and attitude are characteristic of most people? Why or why not? What does Hurston see as the advantages for her of being "colored"? Consider Hurston's presentation of herself from the standpoint of race. How does Hurston use her race to define herself, and how does she use race to convey her attitudes toward both others and toward herself?

2. Write an analysis of Hurston's essay. Consider its organization into four parts. Identify the focus and point of each part and the connections among the four parts leading to the essay's main idea. Identify and explain the key images Hurston uses to convey her main idea.

3. Write an essay in which you explore your identity in terms of gender, race, class, or ethnicity. Try to account for times when you feel especially acutely this aspect of your identity, and times when it seems to disappear or fade into near insignificance.

Stephen King (b. 1947) grew up with his mother and brother in Portland, Maine. At an early age he began writing stories, with a particular interest in and fascination for science fiction and horror stories. Following his graduation from the University of Maine, as an English major, he began sending manuscripts to publishers. His novel Carrie *was published in 1974, the first of more than thirty novels, including such successes as* The Shining *(1977) and* The Green Mile *(1996). King has also produced numerous collections of short stories, many screenplays, and various works of nonfiction, including a book on writing. He recently edited* The Best American Short Stories 2007. *More recent works of fiction include* 11/22/63 *(2012), a novel about the time of JFK's assassination, and* The Wind through the Keyhole *(2012).*

STEPHEN KING

Why We Crave Horror Movies

In "Why We Crave Horror Movies," Stephen King analyzes the causes of people's fascination with the bizarre, the strange, and the macabre. He touches on a variety of factors, from a wish to have fun to psychic release to a desire to watch people maimed and killed. And he considers the extravagant gestures of horror films and the crazy characters who inhabit them in light of normal human behavior and emotions. King provides a number of examples in his essay, not only of horror films but also of popular culture and of historical horrors, such as the murders committed by Jack the Ripper. He reminds us that in addition to the "brotherhood of man," we also share an "insanity of man," with our interest in horror films reminding us of the worst, not the best of which we are capable.

I think that we're all mentally ill; those of us outside the asylums only hide it a little better—and maybe not all that much better, after all. We've all known people who talk to themselves, people who some-times squinch their faces into horrible grimaces when they believe no one is watching, people who have some hysterical fear—of snakes, the dark, the tight place, the long drop...and, of course, those final worms and grubs that are waiting so patiently underground.

When we pay our four or five bucks and seat ourselves at tenth-row center in a theater showing a horror movie, we are daring the nightmare.

Why? Some of the reasons are simple and obvious. To show that we can, that we are not afraid, that we can ride this roller coaster. Which is not to say that a really good horror movie may not surprise a scream out of us at some point, the way we may scream when the roller coaster twists through a complete 360 or plows through a lake at the bottom of the drop. And horror movies, like roller coasters, have always been the special province of the young; by the time one turns 40 or 50, one's appetite for double twists or 360-degree loops may be considerably depleted.

We also go to re-establish our feelings of essential normality; the horror movie is innately conservative, even reactionary. Freda Jackson as the horrible melting woman in *Die, Monster, Die!* confirms for us that no matter how far we may be removed from the beauty of a Robert Redford or a Diana Ross, we are still light-years from true ugliness.

And we go to have fun.

Ah, but this is where the ground starts to slope away, isn't it? Because this is a very peculiar sort of fun indeed. The fun comes from seeing others menaced—sometimes killed. One critic has suggested that if pro football has become the voyeur's version of combat, then the horror film has become the modern version of the public lynching.

It is true that the mythic, "fairytale" horror film intends to take away the shades of gray.... It urges us to put away our more civilized and adult penchant for analysis and to become children again, seeing things in pure blacks and whites. It may be that horror movies provide psychic relief on this level because this invitation to lapse into simplicity, irrationality and even outright madness is extended so rarely. We are told we may allow our emotions a free rein...or no rein at all.

If we are all insane, then sanity becomes a matter of degree. If your insanity leads you to carve up women like Jack the Ripper or the Cleveland Torso Murderer, we clap you away in the funny farm (but neither of those two amateur-night surgeons was ever caught, heh-heh-heh); if, on the other hand, your insanity leads you only to talk to yourself when you're under stress or to pick your nose on your morning bus, then you are left alone to go about your business...though it is doubtful that you will ever be invited to the best parties.

The potential lyncher is in almost all of us (excluding saints, past and present; but then, most saints have been crazy in their own ways), and every now and then, he had to be let loose to scream and roll around in the grass. Our emotions and our fears form their own body, and we recognize that it demands its own exercise to maintain proper muscle tone. Certain of these emotional muscles are accepted—even exalted—in civilized society; they are, of course, the emotions that tend to maintain the status quo of civilization itself. Love, friendship, loyalty, kindness—these are all the emotions that we applaud, emotions that have been immortalized in the couplets of Hallmark cards and in the verses (I don't dare call it poetry) of Leonard Nimoy.

When we exhibit these emotions, society showers us with positive reinforcement; we learn this even before we get out of diapers. When, as children, we hug our rotten little puke of a sister and give her a kiss, all the aunts and uncles smile and twit and cry, "Isn't he the sweetest little thing?" Such coveted treats as chocolate-covered graham crackers often follow. But if we deliberately slam the rotten little puke of a sister's fingers in the door, sanctions follow—angry remonstrance from parents, aunts and uncles; instead of a chocolate-covered graham cracker, a spanking.

But anticivilization emotions don't go away, and they demand periodic exercise. We have such "sick" jokes as, "What's the difference between a truckload of bowling balls and a truckload of dead babies? (You can't unload a truckload of bowling balls with a pitchfork... a joke, by the way, that I heard originally from a ten-year-old.) Such a joke may surprise a laugh or a grin out of us even as we recoil, a possibility that confirms the thesis: If we share a brotherhood of man, then we also share an insanity of man. None of which is intended as a defense of either the sick joke or insanity but merely as an explanation of why the best horror films, like the best fairy tales, manage to be reactionary, anarchistic, and revolutionary all at the same time.

The mythic horror movie, like the sick joke, has a dirty job to do. It deliberately appeals to all that is worst in us. It is morbidity unchained, our most base instincts let free, our nastiest fantasies realized... and it all happens, fittingly enough, in the dark. For those reasons, good liberals often shy away from horror films. For myself, I like to see the most aggressive of them—DAWN OF THE DEAD, for instance—as lifting a trap door in the civilized forebrain and throwing a basket of raw meat to the hungry alligators swimming around in that subterranean river beneath.

Why bother? Because it keeps them from getting out, man. It keeps them down there and me up here. It was Lennon and McCartney who said that all you need is love, and I would agree with that.

As long as you keep the gators fed.

POSSIBILITIES FOR WRITING

1. Identify the reasons King advances for our interest in and fascination with horror films. Which do you find the most unsettling? Which the most convincing? Why?

2. What has been your own experience watching horror films? Are they one of your favorite film genres, or do you avoid horror films? Identify one horror film and explain your response to it.

3. How does King begin and end his essay? How effective are this opening and closing? What comparisons and analogies does King make in the essay? Select one such comparison and explain what King says or shows through its use.

Barbara Kingsolver (b. 1955) *was born in Maryland and grew up in rural Kentucky. Educated at DePauw University and the University of Arizona, she has a background in biology, and is both a naturalist and a writer. Novelist, poet, and essayist, Kingsolver is the author of a short story collection,* Homeland (1989), *as well as the novels* The Bean Trees (1988), Animal Dreams (1990), Pigs in Heaven (1993), *and* The Poisonwood Bible (1998). *More recent work includes a novel,* The Lacuna (2009), *and a nonfiction book,* Animal, Vegetable, Miracle (2007). *She has worked as a biologist and as a human rights activist, and has played keyboards with a rock band. She makes her home in Arizona with a second home in Appalachia.*

BARBARA KINGSOLVER

Stone Soup

In "Stone Soup," which first appeared in a 1995 issue of *Parenting* magazine, Barbara Kingsolver takes up the issue of families, inviting her readers to reconsider their definition of "family," adjusting their understanding of the range and variety of what might count as viable family options. Kingsolver puts forth the question: "Why are our names for home so slow to catch up to the truth of where we live?" She uses this question as a springboard to undertake what amounts to an argument for a greater social and communal commitment to children, to seeing their "families" as far wider and far larger than is commonly imagined.

In the catalog of family values, where do we rank an occasion like this? A curly-haired boy who wanted to run before he walked, age seven now, a soccer player scoring a winning goal. He turns to the bleachers with his fists in the air and a smile wide as a gap-toothed galaxy. His own cheering section of grown-ups and kids all leap to their feet and hug each other, delirious with love for this boy. He's Andy, my best friend's son. The cheering section includes his mother and her friends, his brother, his father and stepmother, a stepbrother and stepsister, and a grandparent. Lucky is the child with this many relatives on hand to hail a proud accomplishment. I'm there too, witnessing a family fortune. But in spite of myself, defensive words take shape in my head. I am thinking: I dare *anybody* to call this a broken home.

Families change, and remain the same. Why are our names for home so slow to catch up the truth of where we live?

When I was a child, I had two parents who loved me without cease. One of them attended every excuse for attention I ever contrived, and the other made it to the ones with higher production values, like piano recitals and appendicitis. So I was a lucky child too. I played with a set of paper dolls called "The Family of Dolls," four in number, who came with the factory-assigned names of Dad, Mom, Sis, and Junior. I think you know what they looked like, at least before I loved them to death and their heads fell off.

Now I've replaced the dolls with a life. I knit my days around my daughter's survival and happiness, and am proud to say her head is still on. But we aren't the Family of Dolls. Maybe you're not, either. And if not, even though you are statistically no oddity, it's probably been suggested to you in a hundred ways that yours isn't exactly a real family, but an impostor family, a harbinger of cultural ruin, a slapdash substitute—something like counterfeit money. Here at the tail end of our century, most of us are up to our ears in the noisy business of trying to support and love a thing called family. But there's a current in the air with ferocious moral force that finds its way even into political campaigns, claiming there is only one right way to do it, the Way It Has Always Been.

In the face of a thriving, particolored world, this narrow view is so pickled and absurd I'm astonished that it gets airplay. And I'm astonished that it still stings.

Every parent has endured the arrogance of a child-unfriendly grump sitting in judgment, explaining what those kids of ours really need (for example, "a good licking"). If we're polite, we move our crew to another bench in the park. If we're forthright (as I am in my mind, only, for the rest of the day), we fix them with a sweet imperious stare and say, "Come back and let's talk about it after you've changed a thousand diapers."

But it's harder somehow to shrug off the Family-of-Dolls Family Values crew when they judge (from their safe distance) that divorced people, blended families, gay families, and single parents are failures, that our children are at risk, and the whole arrangement is messy and embarrassing. A marriage that ends is not called "finished," it's called *failed*. The children of this family may have been born to a happy union, but now they are called *the children of divorce*.

I had no idea how thoroughly these assumptions overlaid my culture until I went through divorce myself. I wrote to a friend: "This might be worse than being widowed. Overnight I've suffered the same losses—companionship, financial and practical support, my identity as a wife and partner, the future I'd taken for granted. I am lonely, grieving, and hard-pressed to take care of my household alone. But instead of bringing casseroles, people are acting like I had a fit and broke up the family china."

Once upon a time I held these beliefs about divorce: that everyone who does it could have chosen not to do it. That it's a lazy way out of marital problems. That it selfishly puts personal happiness ahead of family integrity. Now I tremble for my ignorance. It's easy, in fortunate times, to forget about the ambush that could leave your head reeling: serious mental or physical illness, death in the family, abandonment, financial calamity, humiliation, violence, despair.

I started out like any child, intent on being the Family of Dolls. I set upon young womanhood believing in most of the doctrines of my generation: I wore my skirts four inches above the knee. I had that Barbie with her zebra-striped swimsuit and a figure unlike anything found in nature. And I understood the Prince Charming Theory of Marriage, a quest for Mr. Right that ends smack dab where you find him. I did not completely understand that another whole story *begins* there, and no fairy tale prepared me for the combination of bad luck and persistent hope that would interrupt my dream and lead me to other arrangements. Like a cancer diagnosis, a dying marriage is a thing to fight, to deny, and finally, when there's no choice left, to dig in and survive. Casseroles would help. Likewise, I imagine it must be a painful reckoning in adolescence (or later on) to realize one's own true love will never look like the soft-focus fragrance ads because Prince Charming (surprise!) is a princess. Or vice versa. Or has skin the color your parents didn't want you messing with, except in the Crayola box.

It's awfully easy to hold in contempt the straw-broken home, and that mythical category of persons who toss away nuclear family for the sheer fun of it. Even the legal terms we use have a suggestion of caprice. I resent the phrase "irreconcilable differences," which suggests a stubborn refusal to accept a spouse's little quirks. This is specious. Every happily married couple I know has loads of irreconcilable differences. Negotiating where to set the thermostat is not the point. A nonfunctioning marriage is a slow asphyxiation. It is waking up despised each morning, listening to the pulse of your own loneliness before the radio begins to blare its raucous gospel that you're nothing if you aren't loved. It is sharing your airless house with the threat of suicide or other kinds of violence, while the ghost that whispers, "Leave here and destroy your children," has passed over every door and nailed it shut. Disassembling a marriage in these circumstances is as much *fun* as amputating your own gangrenous leg. You do it, if you can, to save a life—or two, or more.

I know of no one who really went looking to hoe the harder row, especially the daunting one of single parenthood. Yet it seems to be the most American of customs to blame the burdened for their destiny. We'd like so desperately to believe in freedom and justice for all, we can hardly name that rogue bad luck, even when he's a close enough snake to bite us. In the wake of my divorce, some friends (even a few close ones) chose to vanish, rather than linger within striking distance of misfortune.

But most stuck around, bless their hearts, and if I'm any the wiser for my trials, it's from having learned the worth of steadfast friendship. And also, what not to say. The least helpful question is: "Did you want the divorce, or didn't you?" Did I want to keep that gangrenous leg, or not? How to explain, in a culture that venerates choice: two terrifying options are much worse than none at all. Give me any day the quick hand of cruel fate that will leave me scarred but blameless. As it was, I kept thinking of that wicked third-grade joke in which some boy comes up behind you and grabs your ear, starts in with a prolonged tug, and asks, "Do you want this ear any longer?"

Still, the friend who holds your hand and says the wrong thing is made of dearer stuff than the one who stays away. And generally, through all of it, you live. My favorite fictional character, Kate Vaiden (in the novel by Reynolds Price), advises: "Strength just comes in one brand—you stand up at sunrise and meet what they send you and keep your hair combed."

Once you've weathered the straits, you get to cross the tricky juncture from casualty to survivor. If you're on your feet at the end of a year or two, and have begun putting together a happy new existence, those friends who were kind enough to feel sorry for you when you needed it must now accept you back to the ranks of the living. If you're truly blessed, they will dance at your second wedding. Everybody else, for heavens sake, should stop throwing stones.

Arguing about whether nontraditional families deserve pity or tolerance is a little like the medieval debate about left-handedness as a mark of the devil. Divorce, remarriage, single parenthood, gay parents, and blended families simply are. They're facts of our time. Some of the reasons listed by sociologists for these family reconstructions are: the idea of marriage as a romantic partnership rather than a pragmatic one; a shift in women's expectations, from servility to self-respect and independence; and longevity (prior to antibiotics no marriage was expected to last many decades—in Colonial days the average couple lived to be married less than twelve years). Add to all this, our growing sense of entitlement to happiness and safety from abuse. Most would agree these are all good things. Yet their result—a culture in which serial monogamy and the consequent reshaping of families are the norm—gets diagnosed as "failing."

For many of us, once we have put ourselves Humpty-Dumpty-wise back together again, the main problem with our reorganized family is that other people think we have a problem. My daughter tells me the only time she's uncomfortable about being the child of divorced parents is when her friends say they feel sorry for her. It's a bizarre sympathy, given that half the kids in her school and nation are in the same boat, pursuing childish happiness with the same energy as their married-parent peers. When anyone asks how she feels about it, she spontaneously lists the benefits: our house is in the country and we have a dog, but she can go to her dad's neighborhood for the urban thrills of a pool and sidewalks for roller-skating. What's more, she has three sets of grandparents!

Why is it surprising that a child would revel in a widened family and the right to feel at home in more than one house? Isn't it the opposite that should worry us—a child with no home at all, or too few resources to feel safe? The child at risk is the one whose parents are too immature themselves to guide wisely; too diminished by poverty to nurture; too far from opportunity to offer hope. The number of children in the U.S. living in poverty at this moment is almost unfathomably large: twenty percent. There are families among us that need help all right, and by no means are they new on the landscape. The rate at which teenage girls had babies in 1957 (ninety-six per thousand) was twice what it is now. That remarkable statistic is ignored by the religious right—probably because the teen birth rate was cut in half mainly by legalized abortion. In fact, the policy gatekeepers who coined the phrase "family values" have steadfastly ignored the desperation of too-small families, and since 1979 have steadily reduced the amount of financial support available to a single parent. But, this camp's most outspoken attacks seem aimed at the notion of families getting too complex, with add-ons and extras such as a gay parent's partner, or a remarried mother's new husband and his children.

To judge a family's value by its tidy symmetry is to purchase a book for its cover. There's no moral authority there. The famous family comprised by Dad, Mom, Sis, and Junior living as an isolated economic unit is not built on historical bedrock. In *The Way We Never Were,* Stephanie Coontz writes, "Whenever people propose that we go back to the traditional family, I always suggest that they pick a ballpark date for the family they have in mind." Colonial families were tidily disciplined, but their members (meaning everyone but infants) labored incessantly and died young. Then the Victorian family adopted a new division of labor, in which women's role was domestic and children were allowed time for study and play, but this was an upper-class construct supported by myriad slaves. Coontz writes, "For every nineteenth-century middle-class family that protected its wife and child within the family circle, there was an Irish or German girl scrubbing floors…A Welsh boy mining coal to keep the homebaked goodies warm, a black girl doing the family laundry, a black mother and child picking cotton to be made into clothes for the family, and a Jewish or an Italian daughter in a sweatshop making 'ladies' dresses or artificial flowers for the family to purchase."

The abolition of slavery brought slightly more democratic arrangements, in which extended families were harnessed together in cottage industries; at the turn of the century came a steep rise in child labor in mines and sweat-shops. Twenty percent of American children lived in orphanages at the time; their parents were not necessarily dead, but couldn't afford to keep them.

During the Depression and up to the end of World War II, many millions of U.S. households were more multigenerational than nuclear. Women my grandmother's age were likely to live with a fluid assortment of elderly relatives, inlaws, siblings, and children. In many cases they spent virtually every waking hour working in the company of other women—a companionable scenario in which it would be easier, I imagine, to tolerate an estranged or difficult spouse. I'm reluctant to idealize a life of so much hard work and so little spousal intimacy, but its advantage may have been resilience. A family so large and varied would not easily be brought down by a single blow: it could absorb a death, long illness, an abandonment here or there, and any number of irreconcilable differences.

The Family of Dolls came along midcentury as a great American experiment. A booming economy required a mobile labor force and demanded that women surrender jobs to returning soldiers. Families came to be defined by a single breadwinner. They struck out for single-family homes at an earlier age than ever before, and in unprecedented numbers they raised children in suburban isolation. The nuclear family was launched to sink or swim.

More than a few sank. Social historians corroborate that the suburban family of the postwar economic boom, which we have recently selected as our definition of "traditional," was no panacea. Twenty-five percent of Americans were poor in the mid-1950s, and as yet there were no food stamps. Sixty percent of the elderly lived on less than $1,000 a year, and most had no medical insurance. In the sequestered suburbs, alcoholism and sexual abuse of children were far more widespread than anyone imagined.

Expectations soared, and the economy sagged. It's hard to depend on one other adult for everything, come what may. In the last three decades, that amorphous, adaptable structure we call "family" has been reshaped once more by economic tides. Compared with fifties families, mothers are far more likely now to be employed. We are statistically more likely to divorce, and to live in blended families or other extra-nuclear arrangements. We are also more likely to plan and space our children, and to rate our marriages as "happy." We are less likely to suffer abuse without recourse, or to stare out at our lives through a glaze of prescription tranquilizers. Our aged parents are less likely to be destitute, and we're half as likely to have a teenage daughter turn up a mother herself. All in all, I would say that if "intact" in modern family-values jargon means living quietly desperate in the bell jar, then hip-hip-hooray for "broken." A neat family model constructed to service the Baby Boom economy seems to be returning gradually to a grand, lumpy shape that human families apparently have tended toward since they first took root in the Olduvai Gorge. We're social animals, deeply fond of companionship, and children love best to run in packs. If there is a *normal* for humans, at all, I expect it looks like two or three Families of Dolls, connected variously by kinship and passion, shuffled like cards and strewn over several shoeboxes.

The sooner we can let go the fairy tale of families function-ing perfectly in isolation, the better we might embrace the relief of community. Even the admirable parents who've stayed married through thick and thin are very likely, at present, to incorporate other adults into their families—household help and baby-sitters if they can afford them or neighbors and grandparents if they can't. For single parents, this support is the rock-bottom definition of family. And most parents who have split apart, however painfully, still manage to maintain family continuity for their children, creating in many cases a boisterous phenomenon that Constance Ahrons in her book *The Good Divorce* calls the "binuclear family." Call it what you will—when ex-spouses beat swords into plowshares and jump up and down at a soccer game together, it makes for happy kids.

Cinderella, look, who needs her? All those evil stepsisters? That story always seemed like too much cotton-picking fuss over clothes. A childhood tale that fascinated me more was the one called "Stone Soup," and the gist of it is this: Once upon a time, a pair of beleaguered soldiers straggled home to a village empty-handed, in a land ruined by war. They were famished, but the villagers had so little they shouted evil words and slammed their doors. So the soldiers dragged out a big kettle, filled it with water, and put it on a fire to boil. They rolled a clean round stone into the pot, while the villagers peered through their curtains in amazement.

"What kind of soup is that?" they hooted.

"Stone soup," the soldiers replied. "Everybody can have some when it's done."

"Well, thanks," one matron grumbled, coming out with a shriveled carrot. "But it'd be better if you threw this in."

And so on, of course, a vegetable at a time, until the whole suspicious village managed to feed itself grandly.

Any family is a big empty pot, save for what gets thrown in. Each stew turns out different. Generosity, a resolve to turn bad luck into good, and respect for variety—these things will nourish a nation of children. Name-calling and suspicion will not. My soup contains a rock or two of hard times, and maybe yours does too. I expect it's a heck of a bouillabaisse.

POSSIBILITIES FOR WRITING

1. Consider the various types of families Kingsolver identifies. Select two of these family types and discuss the merits and the drawbacks each type of family provides.
2. Discuss the way Kingsolver uses personal experience and anecdote in her essay. Identify at least three instances of the personal that Kingsolver brings to bear as evidence to support her ideas about divorce or about families. Evaluate the extent to which you find her use of personal experience effective.
3. Write an essay about your own experience of family. You may wish to describe not only the type of family you are presently part of, but variations, if any, your family may have undergone. You may also wish to consider the advantages and disadvantages of the kind of family life you have experienced.

August Kleinzahler (b. 1949) *was born in Jersey City, New Jersey, and has lived much of his later life in San Francisco. Kleinzahler has been a taxi driver, a locksmith, a logger, and a building manager. He has been poet-in-residence at Brown University, has been named poet laureate of his hometown of Fort Lee, New Jersey, and has taught creative writing at the Iowa Writers' Workshop, at the University of California at Berkeley, and also to homeless veterans in the San Francisco Bay area. He is the author of seven books of poetry and is the recipient of numerous awards, including a National Book Critics Circle Award for Poetry and an Academy Award in Literature from the American Academy of Arts and Letters. His collection of new and selected poems,* Sleeping It Off in Rapid City, *was published in 2008. In 2004, he published a collection of essays and meditations,* Cutty, One Rock, *from which "The Dog, The Family: A Household Tale" has been taken.*

AUGUST KLEINZAHLER

The Dog, The Family: A Household Tale

In "The Dog, The Family: A Household Tale," August Kleinzahler describes the importance of his dog, called both Granny and Grand, in his life as a boy. Kleinzahler identifies the dog as a member of the household, one that was more influential in his upbringing, more important, and better looking than some other members of his family. Kleinzahler writes about Grand as if the dog were human, and he presents their relationship in fully human terms.

It was the dog who raised me. Oh, the others came and went with their nurturing gestures and concerns, but it was the dog on whose ear I teethed and who watched me through countless hours with the sagacity and bearing of a Ugandan tribal chief.

You can see him straining at the collar as my mother, dressed to the nines, first introduced him to me, freshly home from the hospital, lying across the nurse's lap, almost afloat, like an early Renaissance Christ child. You can see the muscles in his shoulders and neck. Perhaps he would have eaten me right then had I not been smelling of Mother, who I must say looks very pretty there in profile, probably about to head off to her Shakespeare club or into the city to see Paul Scofield in *Lear*, or something along those lines. Mother was very keen on Shakespeare, you see.

Going through the old photo albums you will find pictures of me in various stages of growing up, surrounded by the family: father, mother, sister, brother. But please notice, it is the dog at my side, seated upright, proudly displaying the musculature of his thick chest and the flame of white fur that ornamented it. I am his charge, the rest of them bit players. Not so much a Romulus-and-Remus situation as my having a guardian, a sort of dog uncle, rearing me in lieu of parents.

Actually, the dog looked very human, rather more so than one or two other members of the family. I had forgotten just how extreme was his facial resemblance to a human being until recently, when I showed my ladylove, Tarischa, an old photograph of the dog and me on the front stoop. Her eyes grew very large, then she began gagging.

We called him Granny or Grand, shortened from Twenty Grand, the famous racehorse after whom he was named. Father bought him on sale. He bought everything on sale. Grand was a boxer, purebred, but one of his ears was wrong; it didn't set up properly. And his right eye dripped. He also had a skin condition, something like mange but untreatable. Father got him for peanuts, really: a treasure, if you looked past certain cosmetic flaws.

Granny was a killer, but only when off the leash out of doors. He killed the chihuahua next door and Ernie Middelhauser's dog, Jo-Jo. He seldom attacked humans, only dogs, male dogs. Female dogs brought out his romantic side. You see, if you weren't careful when you opened the front or back door, he would shoot by you or between your legs and be gone for days. Eventually, he'd turn up hungry, looking a bit haggard. Father would kick him for a while until he tired of the exercise, and Granny would take it stoically, without growling or baring his teeth, only looking back at Father now and then with an ugly sneer.

I did miss him when he was off on one of his adventures, left alone with my toy soldiers and the cartoon shows of television's infancy. I recall one where a clown—I seem to remember his name was Cocoa—jumped out of an inkwell and made some difficulty for his creator. Cocoa was animated, the creator not: this provoked my imagination. After some difficulty, the creator always succeeded in getting Cocoa back in the bottle. There are certainly metaphors and allegories aplenty here if you go in for such things. Regardless, the dog would eventually return and we would pick up where we left off, no questions asked, no pouting or recriminations.

It's not as if the rest of the family weren't around. Father was at work, quite naturally, and Mother shopping, or perhaps at her Shakespeare club, which met on alternate Tuesdays. My brother would have been in the basement, at work on a model airplane, getting himself stoned senseless on glue fumes. Or if not in the basement, then in the apple tree, seeing how far he could get out on a limb before it snapped.

My sister lived in the attic. It was not such a bad thing to have her always up there, as she had Father's unpredictable disposition. Well, not always; she would occasionally come down to gnaw the meat off the steak bone we were ordered to save for her. Oh, and there were the suitors. My sister had an hourglass figure and a pixie hairdo. She favored very stupid boys with dodgy backgrounds and convertibles.

Otherwise, she read her Latin in the attic or, when saturated with Ovid, would play her rock-and-roll seventy-eights on her portable. She played "The Naughty Lady of Shady Lane" repeatedly, hundreds of times, for months on end. She would dance to this and other tunes: *thump, thump, thump.* No one in the family was particularly graceful, excepting the dog and, to a certain extent, me, having modeled my own movements on the dog's. My brother was not graceful but had a primitive athleticism, as I imagine the young Tecumseh or Cochise must have had, an athleticism given almost wholly over to mayhem. My brother was not unlike the dog in the behavior he evinced out of the house. Nor did Father receive my brother much differently from the dog when he'd stagger home at last with his assorted wounds and bills incurred.

My sister spent so much time in the attic with her Latin that she broke the record for A pluses at the local high school and went off to Smith College after her junior year to study Latin in the Big Leagues of American Higher Education. Such intellectual prowess was unheard of at this particular high school and my sister became a legend there, her name synonymous with braininess. The only other equivalent celebrity from that high school during that time was the fellow who wrote the hit song "Flying Purple People Eater," and there might even have been some challenge as to the song's *real* authorship.

Mother didn't like children, least of all her own, and me least among them. I was unplanned, an accident, a misfortune. You see, Mother and Father had taken the Fishblatts, their friends from around the corner, out to dinner, and everybody got quite drunk. That had been my parents' plan: to get the Fishblatts drunk. It seems the Fishblatts were making ready for a divorce, which signaled no more impromptu get-togethers only a hop, skip, and jump away. I suppose the plan was that when the appropriate level of drunkenness was achieved, there would be a series of ribald and stoical jokes about the imperfect union of marriage, hoots of exasperation, and unbridled guffaws, and the Fishblatts would stagger home, enjoy an amorous reconciliation of robust proportion, and resign themselves to being stuck with one another for the duration, a circumstance relieved from time to time by visits with my parents.

Well, now, it didn't turn out like that at all. The Fishblatts sobered up straightaway and got divorced. Mother became pregnant with me, years after she'd convinced herself she'd beaten that particular rap.

My appearance on the scene was unwelcome enough, but it turned out that I looked like the dog. I am not suggesting that Mother had been impregnated by Granny, not at all. You see, if Mother had only listened to her own mother and averted her eyes from the dog during the term of her pregnancy, it was said, this unhappy result might have been avoided. Nanny Farbisseneh, a tiny, dour creature originally from a bog outside of Kiev, who, when she spoke at all, issued terse commands in a broken English that drifted erratically into a goulash of Russian, Ukrainian, and Yiddish, held powerful, almost frightening influence over her three daughters, of whom Mother was the youngest. In the presence of Nanny, Mother and my two aunts were like zombified servant girls, oblivious of their own wants and those of their respective families.

Nanny Farbisseneh disapproved of dogs, and held a dim view of males of any species, so you see, a male dog, especially one with Granny's imperfections, could succeed only in eliciting her unalloyed revulsion. But despite Nanny Far's injunctions, Mother not only continued to look at the dog but gazed lovingly into his eyes (the right one caked with discharge) for hours on end. Mother, it turns out, loved four-legged creatures, both cloven and hoofed, and, without exception, even the most vicious and recalcitrant, they adored her, not least of all Grand. True, Mother fed the dog and saw to the removal of his feces, but Granny's love for Mother went far beyond this natural bond: the dog was in love with Mother, a situation that did not go unnoticed by Father, who routinely attacked the dog, either with his right foot or a rolled-up copy of *The Atlantic Monthly* brought down sharply on the dog's black, concertinaed snout.

So Mother, who seldom, if ever, disobeyed Nanny Far, in this instance made an egregious exception, one that she would rue and suffer to be daily reminded of for years and years. In fact, so considerable was her distress at having been delivered of this curious whelp that not a week after my birth both my parents disappeared to Guatemala for a fortnight, presumably to console one another, divert themselves with Mayan figurines, rain forests, cloudy fermented beverages made from tubers—whatever one does in such places. But in truth, knowing Father, Guatemala was probably that season's cheapest ticket. And Mother really, really wanted to get the hell out of Dodge.

My resemblance to the dog was not my only embarrassment to the family. I had a thick Czech accent as well, at least until the age of seven or so, when Father let our housekeeper, Christine, go. If memory serves, because she asked for a small raise after many years of devoted service.

Christine was a round, bosomy, gray-haired Czech woman, grandmotherly, if you will, but in the nice movie-and-storybook way as opposed to the Nanny Far way. Christine smelled of dough and fresh laundry. She loved me and had me entirely convinced I was the singular joy in her life, although I knew she had a son of her own. In the evenings, Christine would cook deep-fried potatoes, the smell of which was an enchantment. The memory of those potatoes stirs me to this day. It was an aroma of such pleasurable intensity that it seemed of another world and time, perhaps a subterranean wood-paneled beer hall–cum–restaurant somewhere in Bratislava, where officers, business leaders, and ladies of fashion would congregate a century earlier, taking refuge from the harsh elements and sustenance in the hearty, blissfully aromatic fare.

Then, after Christine had cleaned up, she would go home to her no-good, delinquent son, her three-room, cabbagey shithole, and watch *The Joe Franklin Show*, or some trash of that sort, like the ignorant bohunk she was. But to me, Christine was maternal beneficence, pleasure and abundance, my anti-Mother. Years later, as an adult, I would live with a young Czech woman, Canadian-Czech, and suck my thumb till it was raw as I watched her cook pierogi, chicken paprikash, her special Bohemian cookies. Then, when we were done eating, I'd lick her breasts while we copulated for hours, all the time thinking of Christine's tattersall apron and the smell of her fried potatoes from across the years.

When Christine had left, Mother took it into her head to take a more active role in the rearing of her youngest child, me. The dog was sent whimpering to the den. It was just Mother and me at the kitchen table. I remember the moment very well, to this day. She clearly had plans for me, and her appraising, contemptuous look augured nothing good, at least insofar as I was concerned.

"It's back to the good ol' U.S. of A. for you, babykins," she said to me. "Let's lose the Kafka accent. It's giving your father and me the creeps, and your brother and sister are too embarrassed to bring home any of their friends. You're going to speak like an American child and act like an American child. And while you're at it, wipe the *schmutz* off your chin."

Had I forgotten what I told Mother at that particular point, her tittering rendition of it over the years would have been more than adequate in refreshing my memory: "I vont you should take a valk in dee voods and a beeg, bad volf eat you all whup!" That one really cracked her pits. "You really are the limit," she said mirthlessly, shaking her head in dismay. I could hear the dog whining piteously from behind the closed parlor doors.

Mother explained to me that if I didn't come around, and in a hurry, she'd make me take a job in Uncle Ja-Ja's factory, blocking hats. Uncle Ja-Ja was Nanny Far's little brother, although he, too, was ancient. He resembled an engorged frog with thick, black-rimmed glasses, and smelled of gherkins. Ja-Ja was always looking for cheap labor—child, adult, no matter—and surely would have jumped at the idea, but it was Great-Aunt Duhnny, the final authority among the Kiev bog contingent, who put her foot down. "Dog-boy go to school like ordinary child," she said, and that was that.

Father worked and read the paper. Children and child rearing, in his view, belonged to the realm of the female, and in my case the dog. The children were Mother's bailiwick. His job was to make money, then lose it, make it again, and so on, except when he was reading the paper, which was filled with information on how to make money, along with insights into the perils of how it might be lost.

Money and the record of its activity was not Father's only interest. He had a fascination with what he called "antiquities," or at least what they cost. In particular, he liked bodhisattvas, religious statuary from the Orient of sacred figures like Avalokitesvara, Manjusri, Kshitigarbha. Why a man of almost no formal education (having been repeatedly thrown out of school for antisocial behavior) should cotton to these small sculptures of holy beings who seek Buddhahood through the practice of perfect virtues, well…Regardless, the house looked like a Chinese souvenir shop, which was a terrible cross for Mother to bear. A frightful snob about such things, Mother, who cherished a Todd Haynes look in domestic interiors, would sit there on the living-room sofa, smoking her Salems, and, regarding the clutter of sacred figures, say, "Just look at all that shit," shaking her head disconsolately.

Fortunately, or unfortunately, for Mother, Father, like those primeval forests that spontaneously autocombust every century or two to get rid of old growth and make room for new, every few months would go berserk and destroy everything in the house, invariably heading first for the bodhisattvas. I can only speculate in hindsight how many dozens of Avalokitesvaras (the bodhisattva of compassion, known as Kuan-yin in China) Father cracked over the mantelpiece.

As for the rest of us during these episodes, led by Mother, and with the dog bringing up the rear, we would retreat to the upstairs bathroom and lock ourselves in until it was evident the storm had blown itself out. It was not unpleasant to be in that small room with the rest of them for the fifteen or twenty minutes it took Father to "clear the brush out" downstairs. I seldom got to visit with my older siblings at such close quarters, and Mother seemed a veritable font of drolleries on these occasions. The dog was in good humor as well and relieved not to be on the other side of the door. When the crashing, grunts, and gargled imprecations subsided, we would proceed single file, in the exact order we had retreated, downstairs, where, inevitably, we'd find Father seated there in the living room, staring rather pensively at the rubble.

Years later, my psychologist girlfriend Clarissa would say to me, "Dog, has anyone ever suggested to you that you're rather, um, labile?"

Fucking bitch…But turns out she didn't mean what I thought.

The years passed. One day Father looked up from his paper and asked Mother where their two older children had gone; he hadn't seen them in a while. "They've been away at college for years, darling," she told him. The dog was getting on as well. I'd try to engage him in our customary frolic, but he'd only look up at me miserably, his dark jowls spread across the carpet.

In fact, Granny didn't age at all gracefully. He had never been what one would think of as a good-smelling creature, given as he was to flatulence and halitosis, along with an indefinable but distinctly unwholesome smell emanating from his diseased skin. It was not at all uncommon for the dog to puke up something he'd gotten into, and the house really was beginning to smell like a doggie vomitorium. Other than that, he slept, occasionally breaking wind or struggling to his feet to pee at the base of this chair or that. Toward the very end, he'd even gone off his horsemeat.

One day I came home from school to find Mother weeping at the foot of the hall stairs. It was a startling spectacle. I'd have been no less astonished if she'd taken wing and commenced doing the loop-the-loops over the house; or had I encountered Grand up on his hind legs singing "Que Sera, Sera" in a tremulous countertenor. Uh-oh, where was the dog? Even at this advanced stage in his decline he would probably have roused himself and staggered over. The dog would have found Mother's weeping no less peculiar and alarming than I.

So it was, staring at Mother with the curiosity and skepticism of an art historian or scientist dispatched by a museum to check out the phenomenon of "the weeping Madonna" in a dank little Italian church buried among the cypresses of some hill town, that I realized the dog was gone. Kaput. And with that realization came another: still a child, I was alone in the world; but far worse, alone with Mother and Father.

POSSIBILITIES FOR WRITING

1. What is the effect of Kleinzahler's opening sentence? Of his opening paragraph? How effective are these gambits as part of his four-paragraph introduction? Explain what this introduction accomplishes.
2. Identify the sources of humor in Kleinzahler's essay. To what extent did you find the essay funny? Compare Kleinzahler's humor with that of David Sedaris in "Me Talk Pretty One Day".
3. Write an essay about an animal, perhaps a pet, that has been a part of your life. Or write an essay about why animals have not been a part of your life.

Abraham Lincoln (1809–1865) was born in virtual poverty in rural Kentucky and spent most of his childhood in what is now Spencer County, Indiana. In 1827 he settled in New Salem, Illinois, where he worked in a general store and managed a mill. Almost completely self-educated, he spent much of his spare time during these years studying law and was elected to the state legislature in 1834, serving four terms. While in private practice as a lawyer, he ran unsuccessfully for national office several times, most notably a campaign for the Senate in which he emerged as a forceful opponent of the extension of slavery. Based on this, he was nominated for the presidency by the Republican Party in 1860, winning with less than a majority of the popular vote. Commander in chief of the Northern forces during the Civil War, Lincoln was assassinated in its final year. His speeches are among the classics of American literature.

ABRAHAM LINCOLN

The Gettysburg Address

Abraham Lincoln's "Gettysburg Address," a little over two minutes long, was occasioned by the battle of Gettysburg, which took place the first three days of July 1863, during the American Civil War. At the battle of Gettysburg, Union soldiers were victorious over their Confederate opponents. But both sides suffered heavy losses of life. Lincoln memorializes the soldiers who died at Gettysburg with language that is elevated, formal, and ceremonial. Each of Lincoln's sentences is carefully structured, with word balancing word, phrase balancing phrase, and clause balancing clause. Using contrast and repetition as well as balanced phrasing, Lincoln created a speech that is as memorable as it is beautiful.

Four score and seven years ago our fathers brought forth on this continent, a new nation, conceived in Liberty, and dedicated to the proposition that all men are created equal.

Now we are engaged in a great civil war, testing whether that nation, or any nation so conceived and so dedicated, can long endure. We are met on a great battle-field of that war. We have come to dedicate a portion of that field, as a final resting place for those who here gave their lives that that nation might live. It is altogether fitting and proper that we should do this.

But, in a larger sense, we can not dedicate—we can not consecrate—we can not hallow—this ground. The brave men, living and dead, who struggled here, have consecrated it, far above our poor power to add or detract. The world will little note, nor long remember what we say here, but it can never forget what they did here. It is for us the living, rather, to be dedicated here to the unfinished work which they who fought here have thus far so nobly advanced. It is rather for us to be here dedicated to the great task remaining before us—that from these honored dead we take increased devotion to that cause for which they gave the last full measure of devotion—that we here highly resolve that these dead shall not have died in vain—that this nation, under God, shall have a new birth of freedom—and that government of the people, by the people, for the people, shall not perish from the earth.

POSSIBILITIES FOR WRITING

1. The Gettysburg Address was composed for a very specific occasion, yet it has come to be considered one of the most profound statements in American political history. What in the speech gives it weight beyond simply honoring those who were killed during the battle of Gettysburg? In what ways does it capture elements essential to the American ideal?
2. Analyze Lincoln's use of repetition, contrast, and balanced phrasing in the Gettysburg Address. Using examples of each from the text, explore their contributions to the overall effect of the speech.
3. Do some research about the composition of the Gettysburg Address, initial public response to it, and how it was popularized. In an essay, report on the history of this document. You might wish to consult Gary Wills's book *Lincoln at Gettysburg*.

JOHN MCPHEE

Silk Parachute

In "Silk Parachute," John McPhee uses a little silk parachute to serve as the central image of his mother's devotion in a miniature memoir of her. McPhee invites his readers to consider the extent to which events he includes in his memoir are true, partly true, or in fact, fabrications. He uses wit and humor to characterize his mother, claiming that in her 99 years hardly anything could be said against her—and what might be considered less than savory is mostly inaccurate. It's an elegant tribute to his mom, charming, graceful, and appreciative.

When your mother is ninety-nine years old, you have so many memories of her that they tend to overlap, intermingle, and blur. It is extremely difficult to single out one or two, impossible to remember any that exemplify the whole.

It has been alleged that when I was in college she heard that I had stayed up all night playing poker and wrote me a letter that used the word "shame" forty-two times. I do not recall this.

I do not recall being pulled out of my college room and into the church next door.

It has been alleged that on December 24, 1936, when I was five years old, she sent me to my room at or close to 7 p.m. for using four-letter words while trimming the Christmas tree. I do not recall that.

The assertion is absolutely false that when I came home from high school with an A-minus she demanded an explanation for the minus.

It has been alleged that she spoiled me with protectionism, because I was the youngest child and therefore the most vulnerable to attack from overhead—an assertion that I cannot confirm or confute, except to say that facts don't lie.

We lived only a few blocks from the elementary school and routinely ate lunch at home. It is reported that the following dialogue and ensuing action occurred on January 22, 1941:

"Eat your sandwich."

"I don't want to eat my sandwich."

"I made that sandwich, and you are going to eat it, Mister Man. You filled yourself up on penny candy on the way home, and now you're not hungry."

"I'm late. I have to go. I'll eat the sandwich on the way back to school."

"Promise?"

"Promise."

Allegedly, I went up the street with sandwich in my hand and buried it in a snowbank in front of Dr. Wright's house. My mother, holding back the curtain in the window of the side door, was watching. She came out in the bitter cold, wearing only a light dress, ran to the snowbank, dug out the sandwich, chased me up Nassau Street,[1] and rammed the sandwich down my throat, snow and all. I do not recall any detail of that story. I believe it to be a total fabrication.

There was the case of 'the missing Cracker Jack at Lindel's corner store. Flimsy evidence pointed to Mrs. McPhee's smallest child. It has been averred that she laid the guilt on with the following words: "'Like mother, like son' is a saying so true, the world will judge largely of mother by you." It has been asserted that she immediately repeated that proverb three times, and also recited it on other occasions too numerous to count. I have absolutely no recollection of her saying that about the Cracker Jack or any other controlled substance.

We have now covered every thing even faintly unsavory that has been reported about this person in ninety-nine years, and even those items are a collection of rumors, half-truths, prevarications, false allegations, inaccuracies, innuendos, and canards.

This is the mother who—when Alfred Knopf[2] wrote her twenty-two-year-old son a letter saying, "The readers' report in the case of

[1]**Nassau Street:** Princeton's main street.
[2]**Alfred Knopf:** founder of the prominent New York publishing house that bears his name; the "K" is sounded. —Ed.

your manuscript would not be very helpful, and I think might discourage you completely"—said, "Don't listen to Alfred Knopf. Who does Alfred Knopf think he is, anyway? Someone should go in there and knock his block off." To the best of my recollection, that is what she said.

I also recall her taking me on or about March 8, my birthday, to the theater in New York every year, beginning in childhood. I remember those journeys as if they were today. I remember *A Connecticut Yankee.* Wednesday, March 8, 1944. Evidently, my father had written for the tickets, because she and I sat in the last row of the second balcony. Mother knew what to do about that. She gave me for my birthday an elegant spyglass, sufficient in power to bring the Connecticut Yankee back from Vermont. I sat there watching the play through my telescope, drawing as many guffaws from the surrounding audience as the comedy on the stage.

On one of those theater days—when I was eleven or twelve— I asked her if we could start for the city early and go out to La Guardia Field to see the comings and goings of airplanes. The temperature was well below the freeze point and the March winds were so blustery that the wind-chill factor was forty below zero. Or seemed to be. My mother figured out how to take the subway to a stop in Jackson Heights and a bus from there—a feat I am unable to duplicate to this day. At La Guardia, she accompanied me to the observation deck and stood there in the icy wind for at least an hour, maybe two, while I, spellbound, watched the DC-3s coming in on final, their wings flapping in the gusts. When we at last left the observation deck, we went downstairs into the terminal, where she bought me what appeared to be a black rubber ball but on closer inspection was a pair of hollow hemispheres hinged on one side and folded together. They contained a silk parachute. Opposite the hinge, each hemisphere had a small nib. A piece of string wrapped round and round the two nibs kept the ball closed. If you threw it high into the air, the string unwound and the parachute blossomed. If you sent it up with a tennis racket, you could put it into the clouds. Not until the development of the ten-megabyte hard disk would the world ever know such a fabulous toy. Folded just so, the parachute never failed. Always, it floated back to you—silkily, beautifully—to start over and float back again. Even if you abused it, whacked it really hard—gracefully, lightly, it floated back to you.

POSSIBILITIES FOR WRITING

1. How would you characterize the tone of this piece? How does McPhee achieve that tone?

2. What image of his mother does McPhee create through his memories— both those he claims are true and those allegations of others that he insists are not true? Write a paragraph in which you support your claim about McPhee's view of his mother.

3. Write your own miniature memoir of someone familiar to you—perhaps a family member, perhaps a relative or friend. Construct your little memoir of a series of short references to events. Try to find an image that you can use near the end to symbolize your attitude toward or to acknowledge something essential about the person you choose to write about.

Herman Melville (1819–1891) was born in New York City and attended Columbia Preparatory Academy until circumstances forced his family to move to Albany, New York. During his years in Albany, Melville studied the classics at The Albany Academy. Melville's novels grew out of his experience as a sailor and adventurer. He wrote in Moby-Dick (1851) that his voyages provided his real education. "A whaling boat was my Yale College and my Harvard," he wrote. Among his novels are Typee (1846) and Omoo (1847), an account of his experience in the South Sea Islands and Polynesia, Redburn (1849), and The Confidence Man (1859). A poet and essayist as well as a novelist, Melville is also highly regarded as a writer of short fiction, most notably the story "Bartleby the Scrivener," and the novella, Billy Budd (1924).

HERMAN MELVILLE

The Advocate

"The Advocate" is a chapter from Herman Melville's classic American novel, *Moby-Dick.* In this brief chapter, Melville's speaker/narrator "advocates" for the values of whaling as a profession, enterprise, or business. He makes his arguments in support of whaling by identifying and countering a series of potential objections against the seriousness and significance of whaling.

As Queequeg and I are now fairly embarked in this business of whaling; and as this business of whaling has somehow come to be regarded among landsmen as a rather unpoetical and disreputable pursuit; therefore, I am all anxiety to convince ye, ye landsmen, of the injustice hereby done to us hunters of whales.

In the first place, it may be deemed almost superfluous to establish the fact, that among people at large, the business of whaling is not accounted on a level with what are called the liberal professions. If a stranger were introduced into any miscellaneous metropolitan society, it would but slightly advance the general opinion of his merits, were he presented to the company as a harpooneer, say; and if in emulation of the naval officers he should append the initials S.W.F. (Sperm Whale Fishery) to his visting card, such a procedure would be deemed pre-eminently presuming and ridiculous.

Doubtless one leading reason why the world declines honoring us whalemen, is this: they think that, at best, our vocation amounts to a butchering sort of business; and that when actively engaged therein, we are surrounded by all manner of defilements. Butchers we are, that is true. But butchers, also, and butchers of the bloodiest badge have been all Martial Commanders whom the world invariably delights to honor. And as for the matter of the alleged uncleanliness of our business, ye shall soon be initiated into certain facts hitherto pretty generally unknown, and which, upon the whole, will triumphantly plant the sperm whale-ship at least among the cleanliest things of this tidy earth. But even granting the charge in question to be true; what disordered slippery decks of a whale-ship are comparable to the unspeakable carrion of those battle-fields from which so many soldiers return to drink in all ladies' plaudits? And if the idea of peril so much enhances the popular conceit of the soldier's profession; let me assure ye that many a veteran who has freely marched up to a battery, would quickly recoil at the apparition of the sperm whale's vast tail, fanning into eddies the air over his head. For what are the comprehensible terrors of man compared with the interlinked terrors and wonders of God!

But, though the world scouts at us whale hunters, yet does it unwittingly pay us the profoundest homage; yea, an all-abounding adoration! for almost all the tapers, lamps, and candles that burn round the globe, burn, as before so many shrines, to our glory!

But look at this matter in other lights; weigh it in all sorts of scales; see what we whalemen are, and have been.

Why did the Dutch in De Witt's time have admirals of their whaling fleets? Why did Louis XVI of France, at his own personal expense, fit out whaling ships from Dunkirk, and politely invite to that town some score or two of families from our own island of Nantucket? Why did Britain between the years 1750 and 1788 pay to her whalemen in bounties upwards of £1,000,000? And lastly, how comes it that we whalemen of America now outnumber all the rest of the banded whalemen in the world; sail a navy of upwards of seven hundred vessels; manned by eighteen thousand men; yearly consuming 4,000,000 of dollars; the ships worth, at the time of sailing, $20,000,000! and every year importing into our harbors a well reaped harvest of $7,000,000. How comes all this, if there be not something puissant in whaling?

But this is not the half; look again.

I freely assert, that the cosmopolite philosopher cannot, for his life, point out one single peaceful influence, which within the last sixty years has operated more potentially upon the whole broad world, taken in one aggregate, than the high and mighty business of whaling. One way and another, it has begotten events so remarkable in themselves, and so continuously momentous in their sequential issues, that whaling may well be regarded as that Egyptian mother, who bore offspring themselves pregnant from her womb. It would be a hopeless, endless task to catalogue all these things. Let a handful suffice. For many years past the whale-ship has been the pioneer in ferreting out the remotest and least known parts of the earth. She has explored seas and archipelagoes which had no chart, where no Cooke or Vancouver had ever sailed. If American and European men-of-war now peacefully ride in once savage harbors, let them fire salutes to the honor and glory of the whale-ship, which originally showed them the way, and first interpreted between them and the savages. They may celebrate as they will the heroes of Exploring Expeditions, your Cookes, your Krusensterns; but I say that scores of anonymous Captains have sailed out of Nantucket, that were as great, and greater, than your Cooke and your Krusenstern. For in their succorless empty-handedness, they, in the heathenish sharked waters, and by the beaches of unrecorded, javelin islands, battled with virgin wonders and terrors that Cooke with all his marines and muskets would not have willingly dared. All that is made such a flourish of in the old South Sea Voyages, those things were but the life-time commonplaces of our heroic Nantucketers. Often, adventures which Vancouver dedicates three chapters to, these men accounted unworthy of being set down in the ship's common log. Ah, the world! Oh, the world!

Until the whale fishery rounded Cape Horn, no commerce but colonial, scarcely any intercourse but colonial, was carried on between Europe and the long line of the opulent Spanish provinces on the Pacific coast. It was the whalemen who first broke through the jealous policy of the Spanish crown, touching those colonies; and, if space permitted, it might be distinctly shown how from those whalemen at last eventuated the liberation of Peru, Chili, and Bolivia from the yoke of Old Spain, and the establishment of the eternal democracy in those parts.

That great America on the other side of the sphere, Australia, was given to the enlightened world by whaleman. After its first blunder-born discovery by a Dutchman, all other ships, long shunned those shores as pestiferously barbarous; but the whale-ship touched there. The whale-ship is the true mother of that now mighty colony. Moreover, in the infancy of the first Australian settlement, the emigrants were several times saved from starvation by the benevolent biscuit of the whale-ship luckily dropping an anchor in their waters. The uncounted isles of all Polynesia confess the same truth, and do commercial homage to the whale-ship, that cleared the way for the missionary and the merchant, and in many cases carried the primitive missionaries to their first destinations. If that double-bolted land, Japan, is ever to become hospitable, it is the whale-ship alone to whom the credit will be due; for already she is on the threshold.

But if, in the face of all this, you still declare that whaling has no aesthetically noble associations connected with it, then am I ready to shiver fifty lances with you there, and unhorse you with a split helmet every time.

The whale has no famous author, and whaling no famous chronicler, you will say.

The whale no famous author, and whaling no famous chronicler? Who wrote the first account of our Leviathan? Who but mighty Job? And who composed the first narrative of a whaling-voyage? Who, but no less a prince than Alfred the Great, who, with his own royal pen, took down the words from Other, the Norwegian whale-hunter of those times! And who pronounced our glowing eulogy in Parliament? Who, but Edmund Burke!

True enough, but then whalemen themselves are poor devils; they have no good blood in their veins.

No good blood in their veins? They have something better than royal blood there. The grandmother of Benjamin Franklin was Mary Morrel; afterwards, by marriage, Mary Folger, one of the old settlers of Nantucket, and the ancestress to a long line of Folgers and harpooneers—all kith and kin to noble Benjamin—this day darting the barbed iron from one side of the world to the other.

Good again; but then all confess that somehow whaling is not respectable.

Whaling not respectable? Whaling is imperial! By old English statutory law, the whale is declared "a royal fish."

Oh, that's only nominal! The whale himself has never figured in any grand imposing way.

The whale never figured in any grand imposing way? In one of the mighty triumphs given to a Roman general upon his entering the world's capital, the bones of a whale, brought all the way from the Syrian coast, were the most conspicuous object in the cymballed procession.

Grant it, since you cite it; but say what you will, there is no real dignity in whaling.

No dignity in whaling? The dignity of our calling the very heavens attest. Cetus is a constellation in the south! No more! Drive down your hat in presence of the Czar, and take it off to Queequeg! No more! I know a man that, in his lifetime has taken three hundred and fifty whales. I account that man more honorable than that great captain of antiquity who boasted of taking as many walled towns.

And, as for me, if, by any possibility, there be any as yet undiscovered prime thing in me; if I shall ever deserve any real repute in that small but high hushed world which I might not be unreasonably ambitious of; if hereafter I shall do anything upon the whole, a man might rather have done than to have left undone; if, at my death, my executors, or more properly my creditors, find any precious MSS in my desk, then here I prospectively ascribe all the honor and the glory to whaling; for a whale-ship was my Yale College and my Harvard.

POSSIBILITIES FOR WRITING

1. Write a paragraph in which you incorporate answers to the following questions: How would you characterize the tone of the speaker/writer as he repeats the various italicized criticisms of whaling? How do you hear these criticisms? And how would you characterize the tone of his response to each criticism? Why does the writer italicize certain portions of the text? With what effect? How does the writer's use of punctuation and question and answer help you "hear" these varied tones of voice in the passage?

2. Write a couple of paragraphs in which you consider the extent to which the writer/speaker rebuts or refutes the challenges and criticisms brought against whaling as a profession. Are you persuaded by him? Why or why not?

3. Whaling has come under critical scrutiny in modern times for different reasons than those cited by the anti-advocates of whaling whose views we hear in the excerpted passage. What are these criticisms of whaling, and how might Melville, greatest advocate of whaling, respond to them? What other current trades, professions, or businesses are under attack today and by whom? What might be said in their defense?

Laura Miller is a journalist and critic living in New York. She is a co-founder of Salon.com, where she is currently a staff writer, and she is a regular contributor to the New York Times Book Review. Her work has appeared in the New Yorker, the Los Angeles Times, Time magazine, and other publications. She has also edited The Salon.com Reader's Guide to Contemporary Authors (2000).

LAURA MILLER

Cat People vs. Dog People

In "Cat People vs. Dog People," Laura Miller contrasts the behaviors of people who own dogs with those who own cats. She explains why "dog people" and "cat people" behave differently and the extent to which their behavior is influenced by the behavior of the animals they most love. She also explains why these two categories of people don't understand or trust each other. Miller focuses her essay on three books that she summarizes and comments on—*The Feline Mystique,* which explores the relationship between women and their cats; *Dog Culture*, a collection of humorous essays about the behavior of dogs; and *Bones Would Rain from the Sky*, an exploration of the relationship between dogs and their owners.

Of the questions that perplex humanity, some are eternal (What is the meaning of life? Do we have a spiritual essence that survives our material existence?) and some are ephemeral (Where is Osama bin Laden? Why does "Sex and the City" have a reputation for featuring fabulous clothes when most of the time poor Sarah Jessica Parker is dressed up like an organ grinder's monkey?). Still others are mundane, yet persistent. To the third category—joining that perennial earth-scorcher, "Which is better, Mac or PC?"—belongs the question at hand: Who are more annoying, cat people or dog people?

Only a noncombatant can judiciously address this one, and we often seem to be a vanishing breed; according to a 2001 survey by the American Pet Products Manufacturers Association, there are 68 million "owned dogs" and 73 million "owned cats" in America. For the record, though I should add that I like both dogs and cats and have lived with both, albeit not with either for years. When pressed to take sides, I've always leaned toward cats. I like the low-maintenance aspect of felines, and the fact that they don't smell—or not much, as long as the litter box isn't allowed to fester. Plus, all things considered, they're prettier. Admittedly, these are girly preferences, but they aren't very strong ones; I'm always up for petting a friendly pooch, too.

At any rate, the cats and dogs strike me as innocent parties to the dispute; when cat people are ragging on canines, it soon becomes obvious that the true objects of their scorn are dog owners, not the dogs themselves, and vice versa. These are discussions in which neither reason nor temperance flourish, but I'll try to summarize the essential critiques of each side in an effort to get them efficiently out of the way.

Dog people profess to be baffled by the cat person's affection for an animal that provides so little active amusement: Cats will not frolic with you in the surf or fetch sticks or point with their noses at a bird for you to shoot. Because cats can't be trained to do the same sorts of tricks that dogs do, they are considered to be less intelligent, and because they are not by nature as social as dogs, they are seen as comparatively aloof or indifferent to humans. Dog people think cat people are suckers for doting on sneaky, selfish creatures that only pretend to like people in order to get food and other goodies and that will never, say, jump into a raging, flood-swollen river to rescue a small child at the risk of their own lives, as the faithful hound supposedly will.

Cat people heap contempt on dog people for actually thinking a dog's devotion counts for much. A dog's love for its owner is, cat people say, entirely instinctual, indiscriminate and often unearned by its object; you are not loved for yourself but for the position you assume in the dog's life—anyone else would do as well. Therefore, dog owners must be so desperate for love as to be nearly undeserving of it. The willingness of dogs to learn tricks is a result not of their intelligence but of their dopey eagerness to please. That cats can't be bothered to sit or heel on command is, their partisans insist, a sign that they are more clever by half. Cats are also self-cleaning, slobber-free, handy when you've got a mouse problem and don't have to be walked.

You may notice—particularly if you are neither a cat person nor a dog person—that these arguments are boring. Through no choice of your own, you have heard them far too many times. They crop up around a dinner table or at a cocktail party, and the evening goes into a precipitous decline. But, I say, you don't know the half of it—not that is, unless you are an editor.

Some people think that an editor's primary responsibility is, when needed, to correct a writer's spelling and grammar, to gently request that a neglected aspect of the writer's topic be more fully explored, to rearrange paragraphs and suggest transitions so artfully that the writer's point emerges as a gleaming and unassailable truth. All these things are so, and yet there is more. Much of our work goes unsung. I would argue, for example, that perhaps the editor's most uncelebrated task is to prevent writers from writing about their pets, or at the very least not to publish it when they do.

If this aspect of our sacred trust puzzles you, it is only because so many of us do our job so well. And so the public remains unaware of how often it's been saved from reading reams of fawning drivel about the noble doings of The Best Dog Ever or the droll antics of The World's Sweetest Kitty. Even writers of formidably austere sensibility are prone to penning this sort of piffle when the subject is their own beloved pet. As for what the sentimental ones come up with—well, you just don't wanna know. Of course, we editors don't expect citations or to be praised for holding back the tidal wave of treacle that might otherwise roll forth and engulf the world's readers. That's not what we're about.

Unfortunately, however, we do sometimes nod. Or worse. For, just as millions of people inexplicably forked out their hard-earned cash for Robert James Waller's *The Bridges of Madison County*, so are there many potential consumers of magazines and book products devoted to the slack-jawed adoration of pets. And editors need to make a living like everyone else. Hence, the three books that provide the pretext for this essay.

The first, *The Feline Mystique* by Clea Simon, purports to take as its subject the relationship between women and cats. The evidence to support this purportation consists of the usual factoids about ancient Egypt (they worshipped cats, you know) and T. S. Eliot, who was precisely the man I was thinking of when I mentioned writers of "austere sensibility" above. And then there is the inevitable reference to Colette (I read a few cat books in my preteen years, and they all go on about Colette). Mostly, though, this book concerns Simon, a journalist, her friends and various women she interviewed on the subject of their love for their cats.

If you could boil down the central message of *The Feline Mystique* to one sentence, it would read something like this: "I was a single woman with a cat and I know people say awful things about that, but I landed a man anyway, so neener neener neener." While, being single myself, I have some sympathy with Simon's frustration at finding herself part of a stigmatized group, the truth is that all this fretting over negative images and what people are probably saying about you behind your back is a mug's game. Writing a whole book to refute such notions—unless you're going to dish up some serious data along the lines of Susan Faludi's *Backlash*—strikes me as a prodigious waste of energy.

However, Simon is not one to let a grievance slide. At one point in *The Feline Mystique* she relates at some length a quarrel she had with a woman with whom she briefly shared a rental house 17 years ago. It was an argument over the proper use of the house's sewing room. Simon sees a subtext in which the dour, rigid, "unattached" roommate, tormented by "simmering jealousy" over Simon's giddy social life, lashed out at both the author and her new kitten—and furthermore, the roommate's own pet was an "extremely neurotic cat, overweight to the point of unhealthiness and unfriendly to anyone who was not her one person." This statement is tempered by a disclaimer about Simon's own "bias" in the matter (on the principle, I suppose, that it's actually charmingly forthright to be petty if you also kinda cop to it at the same time), but the real shock is that Simon even remembers this spat, let alone in such detail, let alone with the conviction that it's worth writing down.

The Feline Mystique goes on in this vein—meandering, defensive, self-regarding, affected (no one in this book lingers at a breakfast table when they can "tarry" instead, or sees a cat at the end of a hall when they can "espy" it) and wholly untroubled by any understanding of the difference between what is interesting and what is not, a discrimination that is more or less the stock in trade of good writers. There are many anecdotes and interviews with other cat-loving women, but these tend to be the kind of people who say things like, "To me, a baby would be a cat substitute," and think it witty and rather daring— along the lines of a T-shirt with "Chocoholic" printed on it. Anyone no-nonsense and intriguing, such as the tiger wrangler for the Ringling Brothers and Barnum Bailey Circus, gets a mere two pages before we're back to autobiographical stuff like "my kitty is no tiger... but he is fierce," followed by a fond story about how Simon's cat, Cyrus, once growled at the vet.

It is easier, though, to be hard on *The Feline Mystique*—and by extension, cat lovers—for its overweening tedium when you are relatively fresh to the task of pet-related reading. By the time you get through a book like *Dog Culture: Writers on the Character of Canines*, you realize that, on the topic of their cats or dogs, almost everyone tends to say the same things over and over again. Most of the contributors to this anthology (edited by Ken Foster, a Salon contributor) are talented and genuinely funny. Foster himself even has the good sense to be sheepish about the book's premise, explaining that he initially asked contributors to "write about aspects of the dog world, but to avoid writing about their own dog. The last thing I wanted was a collection of otherwise intelligent people droning on and on about how their dog was different, more special than all the rest." Fat chance, Ken; that's like inviting an alcoholic to a wine tasting and expecting him to spit it out.

Dog Culture opens with one of its strongest essays, René Steinke's matter-of-fact account of how her initial disgust over her boyfriend's dog's eating habits (Coco chowed down on, among other things, a used tampon, birthday candles and "his own orange vomit"), morphed into affection as "day after day, the work of caring for Coco made me care about him." But, like many of the pieces in the book—and much writing about pets, especially dogs —it succumbs to a pedagogical imperative; dogs, it seems, are forever dispensing Lessons. You might think that most dogs are not gainfully employed, but in fact they are continuously occupied in teaching people how to embrace appetite, live in the moment, suffer in dignity, let go. And all for the price of a bow of kibble—they really ought to think about a union, or better yet, a development position at the Lifetime Channel.

Sometimes the perimeters of the Canine Campus expand to encompass an individual's entire life. That's the case with the dog trainer Suzanne Clothier, who has written *Bones Would Rain From the Sky: Deepening Our Relationships With Dogs*. As a professional, Clothier might be expected to have absorbed more than the odd inspirational homily from her dogs (and other animals—she lives on a farm), and so she has; this book lays out her philosophy of life as it manifests in her training method. Or, at least, I think it does, for while I am in utter awe of Clothier as a moral being, as a writer she leaves something to be desired.

Clothier holds that it's possible to achieve a rapport with dogs so that their obedience can be obtained with a minimum of coercion and with no cruel or abusive treatment at all. It's an approach that requires almost infinite patience. Unfortunately, her approach to writing requires almost as much of the same, only on the part of her reader. She will take one of her admirable ideas, round up all the worst words that can be applied to it—abstraction, clichés, psychobabble, New Ageisms, managerial euphemisms—then proceed to rearrange these words in every possible configuration for pages.

The result is lots of sentences like this: "Only through what we learn in our most profound relationships can we find the completeness in ourselves." Even Clothier's anecdotes—which mostly involve confrontations with troublesome dogs and her indefatigable efforts to understand what's bothering the creatures—have a tendency to dissolve into a terminal vagueness (did the dog ever stop snapping?) that will probably frustrate anyone hoping to use the book as a guide. Alas, good writing is essentially a brutal, Darwinian enterprise, in which many tender young sentences are invited onto the page only to be coldly eliminated in the final draft. (It is no surprise that one of the profession's most hallowed maxims is "Kill your darlings.") Clothier is simply too generous, decent and kind for such ugly work.

If writing about cats is always in danger of sliding into narcissistic preciosity, the peril in dog writing is bathos. No one, it seems, can write very much about dogs without getting into man's inhumanity to animal, and while I don't doubt that all such stories (and worse) are true and I am as horrified by cruelty as the next person, there's something creepy about the retailing of such anecdotes and the voluptuous outrage they provoke. To her credit, Clothier seldom stoops to such melodrama. She is forever reminding her readers not to sentimentalize or idealize dogs, to remember that "this is not an end point, a place to rest in safety, free from the complications and grief that may attend our human relationships." All through *Bones Would Rain From the Sky*, despite bouts of exasperation at the author's leaden prose, I was unfailingly impressed with Clothier's humility and her tireless determination to use her authority over these creatures wisely, to recognize their devotion as a responsibility and not just a gift.

I doubt that any cat book has a chapter on "leadership," as *Bones Would Rain From the Sky* does. Like us, dogs are fundamentally social animals and hard-wired for hierarchy. Cats, by contrast, are solitary by nature, and therefore, as Stephen Budiansky pointed out in the June 2002 issue of the *Atlantic Monthly,* all of their social behavior is learned. I suspect this is why, while most human-dog bonds are fairly similar, there seems to be so much variety in cat owners' relationships to their pets—every cat is a custom job. A cat may develop a personality that complements its owner's, but every dog speaks to every human being's need to be part of a pack; like us, they're political. Perhaps it's inevitable that anyone who spends a lifetime contemplating her relationships with dogs, as Clothier does, will keep returning to the same scouring quandaries that characterize our relationships to each other: how to listen, how to use the power we have justly, what we have a right to ask from others. Of course, most dog people don't seem to bother with this and are content instead to dote and regress. Still, the potential is there and so, I think the canine contingent has the edge. Just don't make me read about it ever again.

POSSIBILITIES FOR WRITING

1. Explain the characteristics of "cat people" and of "dog people" as Miller describes them. To what extent do you agree with what Miller says about them? Explain.

2. What characteristics of dogs and cats, and of the people who have them as pets, would you add to Miller's list? To what extent would you describe yourself as a dog or cat person? Do either of her characters apply to you? Why or why not?

3. Write your own essay in which you compare two different kinds of people by something they do or something they enjoy. For example: football fans and baseball fans (or basketball fans); soccer fans and tennis fans (or hockey fans); bird watchers and whale watchers; sitcom fans and reality TV fans—and so on.

Horace Miner (1912–1993), an anthropologist and teacher, was born in Saint Paul, Minnesota, and earned a B.A. from the University of Kentucky and an M.A. and Ph.D. from the University of Chicago. Miner taught sociology and anthropology at Wayne State University in Detroit and at the University of Michigan, where he was also a researcher for the Museum of Anthropology. He published numerous articles and a number of books, including Personality and Change *(1960) and* The City in Modern Africa *(1967).*

HORACE MINER

Body Ritual Among the Nacirema

"Body Ritual Among the Nacirema" first appeared in the journal *American Anthropologist* in 1956. In his essay, Miner deploys his expertise as an anthropologist to study the behavior of a group of people that is simultaneously familiar and strange. The essay is something of an ethnographic study, as it looks closely at the customs of a familiar North American culture.

The anthropologist has become so familiar with the diversity of ways in which different peoples behave in similar situations that he is not apt to be surprised by even the most exotic customs. In fact, if all of the logically possible combinations of behavior have not been found somewhere in the world, he is apt to suspect that they must be present in some yet undescribed tribe. This point has, in fact, been expressed with respect to clan organization by Murdock.[1] In this light, the magical beliefs and practices of the Nacirema present such unusual aspects that it seems desirable to describe them as an example of the extremes to which human behavior can go.

Professor Linton first brought the ritual of the Nacirema to the attention of anthropologists twenty years ago, but the culture of this people is still very poorly understood. They are a North American group living in the territory between the Canadian Cree, the Yaqui and Tarahumare of Mexico, and the Carib and Arawak of the Antilles. Little is known of their origin, although tradition states that they came from the east. . . .

Nacirema culture is characterized by a highly developed market economy which has evolved in a rich natural habitat. While much of

[1]George Peter Murdock (1897–1985) was an anthropologist who identified and classified world cultures.—Eds.

the people's time is devoted to economic pursuits, a large part of the fruits of these labors and a considerable portion of the day are spent in ritual activity. The focus of this activity is the human body, the appearance and health of which loom as a dominant concern in the ethos of the people. While such a concern is certainly not unusual, its ceremonial aspects and associated philosophy are unique.

The fundamental belief underlying the whole system appears to be that the human body is ugly and that its natural tendency is to debility and disease. Incarcerated in such a body, man's only hope is to avert these characteristics through the use of the powerful influences of ritual and ceremony. Every household has one or more shrines devoted to this purpose. The more powerful individuals in the society have several shrines in their houses and, in fact, the opulence of a house is often referred to in terms of the number of such ritual centers it possesses. Most houses are of wattle and daub construction, but the shrine rooms of the more wealthy are walled with stone. Poorer families imitate the rich by applying pottery plaques to their shrine walls.

While each family has at least one such shrine, the rituals associated with it are not family ceremonies but are private and secret. The rites are normally only discussed with children, and then only during the period when they are being initiated into these mysteries. I was able, however, to establish sufficient rapport with the natives to examine these shrines and to have the rituals described to me.

The focal point of the shrine is a box or chest which is built into the wall. In this chest are kept the many charms and magical potions without which no native believes he could live. These preparations are secured from a variety of specialized practitioners. The most powerful of these are the medicine men, whose assistance must be rewarded with substantial gifts. However, the medicine men do not provide the curative potions for their clients, but decide what the ingredients should be and then write them down in an ancient and secret language. This writing is understood only by the medicine men and by the herbalists who, for another gift, provide the required charm.

The charm is not disposed of after it has served its purpose, but is placed in the charm-box of the household shrine. As these magical materials are specific for certain ills, and the real or imagined maladies of the people are many, the charm-box is usually full to overflowing. The magical packets are so numerous that people forget what their purposes were and fear to use them again. While the natives are very vague on this point, we can only assume that the idea in retaining all the old magical materials is that their presence in the charm-box, before which the body rituals are conducted, will in some way protect the worshipper.

Beneath the charm-box is a small font. Each day every member of the family, in succession, enters the shrine room, bows his head before the charm-box, mingles different sorts of holy water in the font, and proceeds with a brief rite of ablution. The holy waters are secured from the Water Temple of the community, where the priests conduct elaborate ceremonies to make the liquid ritually pure.

In the hierarchy of magical practitioners, and below the medicine men in prestige, are specialists whose designation is best translated "holy-mouth-men." The Nacirema have an almost pathological horror of and fascination with the mouth, the condition of which is believed to have a supernatural influence on all social relationships. Were it not for the rituals of the mouth, they believe that their teeth would fall out, their gums bleed, their jaws shrink, their friends desert them, and their lovers reject them. They also believe that a strong relationship exists between oral and moral characteristics. For example, there is a ritual ablution of the mouth for children which is supposed to improve their moral fiber.

The daily body ritual performed by everyone includes a mouth-rite. Despite the fact that these people are so punctilious about care of the mouth, this rite involves a practice which strikes the uninitiated stranger as revolting. It was reported to me that the ritual consists of inserting a small bundle of hog hairs into the mouth, along with certain magical powders, and then moving the bundle in a highly formalized series of gestures.

In addition to the private mouth-rite, the people seek out a holy-mouth-man once or twice a year. These practitioners have an impressive set of paraphernalia, consisting of a variety of augers, awls, probes, and prods. The use of these objects in the exorcism of the evils of the mouth involves almost unbelievable ritual torture of the client. The holy-mouth-man opens the client's mouth and, using the above mentioned tools, enlarges any holes which decay may have created in the teeth. Magical materials are put into these holes. If there are not naturally occurring holes in the teeth, large sections of one or more teeth are gouged out so that the supernatural substance can be applied. In the client's view, the purpose of these ministrations is to arrest decay and to draw friends. The extremely sacred and traditional character of the rite is evident in the fact that the natives return to the holy-mouth-men year after year, despite the fact that their teeth continue to decay.

It is to be hoped that, when a thorough study of the Nacirema is made, there will be careful inquiry into the personality structure of these people. One has but to watch the gleam in the eye of a holy-mouth-man, as he jabs an awl into an exposed nerve, to suspect that a certain amount of sadism is involved. If this can be established, a very interesting pattern emerges, for most of the population shows definite masochistic tendencies. It was to these that Professor Linton referred in discussing a distinctive part of the daily body ritual which is per-formed only by men. This part of the rite involves scraping and lacer-ating the surface of the face with a sharp instrument. Special women's rites are performed only four times during each lunar month, but what they lack in frequency is made up in barbarity. As part of this cer-emony, women bake their heads in small ovens for about an hour. The theoretically interesting point is that what seems to be a preponder-antly masochistic people have developed sadistic specialists.

The medicine men have an imposing temple, or *latipso*, in every community of any size. The more elaborate ceremonies required to treat very sick patients can only be performed at this temple. These ceremonies involve not only the thaumaturge but a permanent group of vestal maidens who move sedately about the temple chambers in distinctive costume and headdress.

The *latipso* ceremonies are so harsh that it is phenomenal that a fair proportion of the really sick natives who enter the temple ever recover. Small children whose indoctrination is still incomplete have been known to resist attempts to take them to the temple because "that is where you go to die." Despite this fact, sick adults are not only will-ing but eager to undergo the protracted ritual purification, if they can afford to do so. No matter how ill the supplicant or how grave the emergency, the guardians of many temples will not admit a client if he cannot give a rich gift to the custodian. Even after one has gained admission and survived the ceremonies, the guardians will not permit the neophyte to leave until he makes still another gift.

The supplicant entering the temple is first stripped of all his or her clothes. In everyday life the Nacirema avoids exposure of his body and its natural functions. Bathing and excretory acts are performed only in the secrecy of the household shrine, where they are ritualized as part of the body-rites. Psychological shock results from the fact that body secrecy is suddenly lost upon entry into the *latipso*. A man, whose own wife has never seen him in an excretory act, suddenly finds himself naked and assisted by a vestal maiden while he performs his natural functions into a sacred vessel. This sort of ceremonial treatment is necessitated by the fact that the excreta are used by a diviner to ascertain the course and nature of the client's sickness. Female clients, on the other hand, find their naked bodies are subjected to the scrutiny, manipulation and prodding of the medicine men.

Few supplicants in the temple are well enough to do anything but lie on their hard beds. The daily ceremonies, like the rites of the holy-mouth-man involve discomfort and torture. With ritual precision, the vestals awaken their miserable charges each dawn and roll them about on their beds of pain while performing ablutions, in the formal movements of which the maidens are highly trained. At other times they insert magic wands in the supplicant's mouth or force him to eat substances which are supposed to be healing. From time to time the medicine men come to their clients and jab magically treated needles into their flesh. The fact that these temple ceremonies may not cure, and may even kill the neophyte, in no way decreases the people's faith in the medicine men.

There remains one other kind of practitioner, known as a "listener." This witchdoctor has the power to exorcise the devils that lodge in the heads of people who have been bewitched. The Nacirema believe that parents bewitch their own children. Mothers are particularly suspected of putting a curse on children while teaching them the secret body rituals. The counter-magic of the witchdoctor is unusual in its lack of ritual. The patient simply tells the "listener" all his troubles and fears, beginning with the earliest difficulties he can remember. The memory displayed by the Nacirema in these exorcism sessions is truly remarkable. It is not uncommon for the patient to bemoan the rejection he felt upon being weaned as a babe, and a few individuals even see their troubles going back to the traumatic effects of their own birth.

In conclusion, mention must be made of certain practices which have their base in native esthetics but which depend upon the pervasive aversion to the natural body and its functions. There are ritual fasts to make fat people thin and ceremonial feasts to make thin people fat. Still other rites are used to make women's breasts larger if they are small, and smaller if they are large. General dissatisfaction with breast shape is symbolized in the fact that the ideal form is virtually outside the range of human variation. A few women afflicted with almost inhuman hyper-mammary development are so idolized that they make a handsome living by simply going from village to village and permitting the natives to stare at them for a fee.

Reference has already been made to the fact that excretory functions are ritualized, routinized, and relegated to secrecy. Natural reproductive functions are similarly distorted. Intercourse is taboo as a topic and scheduled as an act. Efforts are made to avoid pregnancy by the use of magical materials or by limiting intercourse to certain phases of the moon. Conception is actually very infrequent. When pregnant, women dress so as to hide their condition. Parturition takes place in secret, without friends or relatives to assist, and the majority of women do not nurse their infants.

Our review of the ritual life of the Nacirema has certainly shown them to be a magic-ridden people. It is hard to understand how they have managed to exist so long under the burdens which they have imposed upon themselves. But even such exotic customs as these take on real meaning when they are viewed with the insight provided by Malinowski[2] when he wrote:

> Looking from far and above, from our high places of safety in the developed civilization, it is easy to see all the crudity and irrelevance of magic. But without its power and guidance early man could not have mastered his practical difficulties as he has done, nor could man have advanced to the higher stages of civilization.

POSSIBILITIES FOR WRITING

1. At what point did you realize what Miner is up to in this piece? When did you discover just who the "Nacirema" are? Why do you think he describes the Nacirema as being a "magic-ridden" people? Do you agree with him? Why or why not?

2. Identify three social practices that Miner describes and explain how he satirizes each. What do the practices or behaviors have in common? How and why does Miner get us to view them in a fresh manner?

3. Try your hand at writing an essay that describes some familiar contemporary customs from the standpoint of an anthropologist, perhaps an anthropologist from another culture or world. You may wish to write about physical behavior and customs; social customs such as weddings; musical events such as rock concerts; or athletic contests such as the Super Bowl, the World Series, or the World Cup.

[2]Bronislaw Malinowski (1884–1942) was a Polish-born British anthropologist.

N. Scott Momaday (b. 1934) was born in Lawton, Oklahoma, of Kiowa ancestry and grew up on a reservation in New Mexico. A graduate of the University of New Mexico and of Stanford University, he won a Pulitzer Prize for his first novel, House Made of Dawn *(1968). Author of many genres in addition to fiction, Momaday has published volumes of poetry, including* The Gourd Dancer *(1976), and the memoirs* The Way to Rainy Mountain *(1969) and* The Names *(1976), as well as children's books, essay collections, and plays. He is also an artist whose work has been widely exhibited. For many years a professor at the University of Arizona, Momaday often takes as his subject the history and culture of Native Americans and, in particular, their relationship with the physical environment. His most recent book is* In the Bear's House *(1999).*

N. SCOTT MOMADAY

The Way to Rainy Mountain

In his autobiographical memoir *The Way to Rainy Mountain*, N. Scott Momaday celebrates his Kiowa Native American heritage. Momaday describes both a place and a person in this essay from his memoir. He describes Rainy Mountain as a place saturated in the history of the Kiowa people. It is a place every aspect of which bears significance. He also memorializes his grandmother, who is, herself, a repository of Kiowa history and culture. Momaday captures her dignity and nobility as an individual and as a representative of her vanishing Kiowa world.

A single knoll rises out of the plain in Oklahoma, north and west of the Wichita Range. For my people, the Kiowas, it is an old landmark, and they gave it the name Rainy Mountain. The hardest weather in the world is there. Winter brings blizzards, hot tornadic winds arise in the spring, and in summer the prairie is an anvil's edge. The grass turns brittle and brown, and it cracks beneath your feet. There are green belts along the rivers and creeks, linear groves of hickory and pecan, willow and witch hazel. At a distance in July or August the steaming foliage seems almost to writhe in fire. Great green and yellow grasshoppers are everywhere in the tall grass, popping up like corn to sting the flesh, and tortoises crawl about on the red earth, going nowhere in the plenty of time. Loneliness is an aspect of the land. All things in the plain are isolate; there is no confusion of objects in the eye, but *one* hill or *one* tree or *one* man. To look upon that landscape in the early morning, with the sun at your back, is to lose the sense of proportion. Your imagination comes to life, and this, you think, is where Creation was begun.

I returned to Rainy Mountain in July. My grandmother had died in the spring, and I wanted to be at her grave. She had lived to be very old and at last infirm. Her only living daughter was with her when she died, and I was told that in death her face was that of a child.

I like to think of her as a child. When she was born, the Kiowas were living the last great moment of their history. For more than a hundred years they had controlled the open range from the Smoky Hill River to the Red, from the headwaters of the Canadian to the fork of the Arkansas and Cimarron. In alliance with the Comanches, they had ruled the whole of the southern Plains. War was their sacred business, and they were among the finest horsemen the world has ever known. But warfare for the Kiowas was preeminently a matter of disposition rather than of survival, and they never understood the grim, unrelenting advance of the U.S. Cavalry. When at last, divided and ill-provisioned, they were driven onto the Staked Plains in the cold rains of autumn, they fell into panic. In Palo Duro Canyon they abandoned their crucial stores to pillage and had nothing then but their lives. In order to save themselves, they surrendered to the soldiers at Fort Sill and were imprisoned in the old stone corral that now stands as a military museum. My grandmother was spared the humiliation of those high gray walls by eight or ten years, but she must have known from birth the affliction of defeat, the dark brooding of old warriors.

Her name was Aho, and she belonged to the last culture to evolve in North America. Her forebears came down from the high country in western Montana nearly three centuries ago. They were a mountain people, a mysterious tribe of hunters whose language has never been positively classified in any major group. In the late seventeenth century they began a long migration to the south and east. It was a journey toward the dawn, and it led to a golden age. Along the way the Kiowas were befriended by the Crows, who gave them the culture and religion of the Plains. They acquired horses, and their ancient nomadic spirit was suddenly free of the ground. They acquired Tai-me, the sacred Sun Dance doll, from that moment the object and symbol of their worship, and so shared in the divinity of the sun. Not least, they acquired the sense of destiny, therefore courage and pride. When they entered upon the southern Plains they had been transformed. No longer were they slaves to the simple necessity of survival; they were a lordly and dangerous society of fighters and thieves, hunters and priests of the sun. According to their origin myth, they entered the world through a hollow log. From one point of view, their migration was the fruit of an old prophecy, for indeed they emerged from a sunless world.

Although my grandmother lived out her long life in the shadow of Rainy Mountain, the immense landscape of the continental interior lay like memory in her blood. She could tell of the Crows, whom she had never seen, and of the Black Hills, where she had never been. I wanted to see in reality what she had seen more perfectly in the mind's eye, and traveled fifteen hundred miles to begin my pilgrimage.

Yellowstone, it seemed to me, was the top of the world, a region of deep lakes and dark timber, canyons and waterfalls. But, beautiful as it is, one might have the sense of confinement there. The skyline in all directions is close at hand, the high wall of the woods and deep cleavages of shade. There is a perfect freedom in the mountains, but it belongs to the eagle and the elk, the badger and the bear. The Kiowas reckoned their stature by the distance they could see, and they were bent and blind in the wilderness.

Descending eastward, the highland meadows are a stairway to the plain. In July the inland slope of the Rockies is luxuriant with flax and buckwheat, stonecrop and larkspur. The earth unfolds and the limit of the land recedes. Clusters of trees, and animals grazing far in the distance, cause the vision to reach away and wonder to build upon the mind. The sun follows a longer course in the day, and the sky is immense beyond all comparison. The great billowing clouds that sail upon it are the shadows that move upon the grain like water, dividing light. Farther down, in the land of the Crows and Blackfeet, the plain is yellow. Sweet clover takes hold of the hills and bends upon itself to cover and seal the soil. There the Kiowas paused on their way; they had come to the place where they must change their lives. The sun is at home on the plains. Precisely there does it have the certain character of a god. When the Kiowas came to the land of the Crows, they could see the dark lees of the hills at dawn across the Bighorn River, the profusion of light on the grain shelves, the oldest deity ranging after the solstices. Not yet would they veer southward to the caldron of the land that lay below; they must wean their blood from the northern winter and hold the mountains a while longer in their view. They bore Tai-me in procession to the east.

A dark mist lay over the Black Hills, and the land was like iron. At the top of a ridge I caught sight of Devil's Tower upthrust against the gray sky as if in the birth of time the core of the earth had broken through its crust and the motion of the world was begun. There are things in nature that engender an awful quiet in the heart of man; Devil's Tower is one of them. Two centuries ago, because they could not do otherwise, the Kiowas made a legend at the base of the rock. My grandmother said:

> *Eight children were there at play, seven sisters and their brother. Suddenly the boy was struck dumb; he trembled and began to run upon his hands and feet. His fingers became claws, and his body was covered with fur. Directly there was a bear where the boy had been. The sisters were terrified; they ran, and the bear after them. They came to the stump of a great tree, and the tree spoke to them. It bade them climb upon it, and as they did so it began to rise into the air. The bear came to kill them, but they were just beyond its reach. It reared against the tree and scored the bark all around with its claws. The seven sisters were borne into the sky, and they became the stars of the Big Dipper.*

From that moment, and so long as the legend lives, the Kiowas have kinsmen in the night sky. Whatever they were in the mountains, they could be no more. However tenuous their well-being, however much they had suffered and would suffer again, they had found a way out of the wilderness.

My grandmother had a reverence for the sun, a holy regard that now is all but gone out of mankind. There was a wariness in her, and an ancient awe. She was a Christian in her later years, but she had come a long way about, and she never forgot her birthright. As a child she had been to the Sun Dances; she had taken part in those annual rites, and by them she had learned the restoration of her people in the presence of Tai-me. She was about seven when the last Kiowa Sun Dance was held in 1887 on the Washita River above Rainy Mountain Creek. The buffalo were gone. In order to consummate the ancient sacrifice—to impale the head of a buffalo bull upon the medicine tree—a delegation of old men journeyed into Texas, there to beg and barter for an animal from the Goodnight herd. She was ten when the Kiowas came together for the last time as a living Sun Dance culture. They could find no buffalo; they had to hang an old hide from the sacred tree. Before the dance could begin, a company of soldiers rode out from Fort Sill under orders to disperse the tribe. Forbidden without cause the essential act of their faith, having seen the wild herds slaughtered and left to rot upon the ground, the Kiowas backed away forever from the medicine tree. That was July 20, 1890, at the great bend of the Washita. My grandmother was there. Without bitterness, and for as long as she lived, she bore a vision of deicide.

Now that I can have her only in memory, I see my grandmother in the several postures that were peculiar to her: standing at the wood stove on a winter morning and turning meat in a great iron skillet; sitting at the south window, bent above her beadwork, and afterwards, when her vision failed, looking down for a long time into the fold of her hands; going out upon a cane, very slowly as she did when the weight of age came upon her; praying. I remember her most often at prayer. She made long, rambling prayers out of suffering and hope, having seen many things. I was never sure that I had the right to hear, so exclusive were they of all mere custom and company. The last time I saw her she prayed standing by the side of her bed at night, naked to the waist, the light of a kerosene lamp moving upon her dark skin. Her long, black hair, always drawn and braided in the day, lay upon her shoulders and against her breasts like a shawl. I do not speak Kiowa, and I never understood her prayers, but there was something inherently sad in the sound, some merest hesitation upon the syllables of sorrow. She began in a high and descending pitch, exhausting her breath to silence; then again and again—and always the same intensity of effort, of something that is, and is not, like urgency in the human voice. Transported so in the dancing light among the shadows of her room, she seemed beyond the reach of time. But that was illusion; I think I knew then that I should not see her again.

Houses are like sentinels in the plain, old keepers of the weather watch. There, in a very little while, wood takes on the appearance of great age. All colors wear soon away in the wind and rain, and then the wood is burned gray and the grain appears and the nails turn red with rust. The windowpanes are black and opaque; you imagine there is nothing within, and indeed there are many ghosts, bones given up to the land. They stand here and there against the sky, and you approach them for a longer time than you expect. They belong in the distance; it is their domain.

Once there was a lot of sound in my grandmother's house, a lot of coming and going, feasting and talk. The summers there were full of excitement and reunion. The Kiowas are a summer people; they abide the cold and keep to themselves, but when the season turns and the land becomes warm and vital they cannot hold still; an old love of going returns upon them. The aged visitors who came to my grandmother's house when I was a child were made of lean and leather, and they bore themselves upright. They wore great black hats and bright ample shirts that shook in the wind. They rubbed fat upon their hair and wound their braids with strips of colored cloth. Some of them painted their faces and carried the scars of old and cherished enmities. They were an old council of warlords, come to remind and be reminded of who they were. Their wives and daughters served them well. The women might indulge themselves; gossip was at once the mark and compensation of their servitude. They made loud and elaborate talk among themselves, full of jest and gesture, fright and false alarm. They went abroad in fringed and flowered shawls, bright beadwork and German silver. They were at home in the kitchen, and they prepared meals that were banquets.

There were frequent prayer meetings, and great nocturnal feasts. When I was a child I played with my cousins outside, where the lamplight fell upon the ground and the singing of the old people rose up around us and carried away into the darkness. There were a lot of good things to eat, a lot of laughter and surprise. And afterwards, when the quiet returned, I lay down with my grandmother and could hear the frogs away by the river and feel the motion of the air.

Now there is a funeral silence in the rooms, the endless wake of some final word. The walls have closed in upon my grandmother's house. When I returned to it in mourning, I saw for the first time in my life how small it was. It was late at night, and there was a white moon, nearly full. I sat for a long time on the stone steps by the kitchen door. From there I could see out across the land; I could see the long row of trees by the creek, the low light upon the rolling plains, and the stars of the Big Dipper. Once I looked at the moon and caught sight of a strange thing. A cricket had perched upon the handrail, only a few inches away from me. My line of vision was such that the creature filled the moon like a fossil. It had gone there, I thought, to live and die, for there, of all places, was its small definition made whole and eternal. A warm wind rose up and purled like the longing within me.

The next morning I awoke at dawn and went out on the dirt road to Rainy Mountain. It was already hot, and the grasshoppers began to fill the air. Still, it was early in the morning, and the birds sang out of the shadows. The long yellow grass on the mountain shone in the bright light, and a scissortail hied above the land. There, where it ought to be, at the end of a long and legendary way, was my grandmother's grave. Here and there on the dark stones were ancestral names. Looking back once, I saw the mountain and came away.

POSSIBILITIES FOR WRITING

1. Momaday traces the migration of the Kiowa from Montana to the Great Plains in terms of both physical landscape and of spiritual development. For him, how are the two related in the rise and fall of Kiowa history and culture? What is the significance of his ending the story of his journey at his grandmother's grave?

2. What does his grandmother represent for Momaday? Why, for example, does he begin his pilgrimage to her grave from Yellowstone, fifteen hundred miles away? How do his memories of her, as he describes them, help develop this image?

3. Explore the ways in which a grandparent or other older relative provides you with ties to your history and culture. Like Momaday, you may wish to develop the influence of a particular place associated with that person as well.

Michel de Montaigne (1533–1592), *the father of the modern essay, was born in Perigord, France, to a family of wealthy landowners. He studied law at the University of Guyenne in Bordeaux and during his career served as a local magistrate and later as mayor of Bordeaux. In 1580 he published the first of his collected* Essais, *which were revised and added to in 1588. These "attempts" or "trials," as he termed them, dealt with a wide range of subjects and were intended as personal, but at the same time universal, reflections on the human condition. Intensely intellectual, the* Essais *are nonetheless written in concrete, everyday language and marked by a great deal of humor. His works were highly influential throughout Europe, not only in terms of their subject matter but also as exemplars of this unique literary form.*

MICHEL DE MONTAIGNE

Of Smells

Michel de Montaigne originated a unique style that is at once both personal and reflective. Montaigne's "Of Smells," though one of his shortest essays, exemplifies his characteristic method. It begins with a few general thoughts on the nature of odors that human beings give off. It moves quickly to a series of quotations from Montaigne's reading in classic writers from the past. And it includes a number of observations based on Montaigne's experience—his autobiographical perspective on what he himself has noticed about the way people smell, including the way he himself smells.

It is said of some, as of Alexander the Great, that their sweat emitted a sweet odor, owing to some rare and extraordinary constitution of theirs, of which Plutarch and others seek the cause. But the common make-up of bodies is the opposite, and the best condition they may have is to be free of smell. The sweetness even of the purest breath has nothing more excellent about it than to be without any odor that offends us, as is that of very healthy children. That is why, says Plautus,

> A woman smells good when she does not smell.

The most perfect smell for a woman is to smell of nothing, as they say that her actions smell best when they are imperceptible and mute. And perfumes are rightly considered suspicious in those who use them, and thought to be used to cover up some natural defect in that quarter. Whence arise these nice sayings of the ancient poets: To smell good is to stink:

> You laugh at us because we do not smell.
> I'd rather smell of nothing than smell sweet.
>
> MARTIAL

And elsewhere:

> Men who smell always sweet, Posthumus, don't smell good.
>
> MARTIAL

However, I like very much to be surrounded with good smells, and I hate bad ones beyond measure, and detect them from further off than anyone else:

> My scent will sooner be aware
> Where goat-smells, Polypus, in hairy arm-pits lurk,
> Than keen hounds scent a wild boar's lair.
>
> HORACE

The simplest and most natural smells seem to me the most agreeable. And this concern chiefly affects the ladies. Amid the densest barbarism, the Scythian women, after washing, powder and plaster their whole body and face with a certain odoriferous drug that is native to their soil; and having removed this paint to approach the men, they find themselves both sleek and perfumed.

Whatever the odor is, it is a marvel how it clings to me and how apt my skin is to imbibe it. He who complains of nature that she has left man without an instrument to convey smells to his nose is wrong, for they convey themselves. But in my particular case my mustache, which is thick, performs that service. If I bring my gloves or my handkerchief near it, the smell will stay there a whole day. It betrays the place I come from. The close kisses of youth, savory, greedy, and sticky, once used to adhere to it and stay there for several hours after. And yet, for all that, I find myself little subject to epidemics, which are caught by communication and bred by the contagion of the air; and I have escaped those of my time, of which there have been many sorts in our cities and our armies. We read of Socrates that though he never left Athens during many recurrences of the plague which so many times tormented that city, he alone never found himself the worse for it.

The doctors might, I believe, derive more use from odors than they do; for I have often noticed that they make a change in me and work upon my spirits according to their properties; which makes me approve of the idea that the use of incense and perfumes in churches, so ancient and widespread in all nations and religions, was intended to delight us and arouse and purify our senses to make us more fit for contemplation.

I should like, in order to judge of it, to have shared the art of those cooks who know how to add a seasoning of foreign odors to the savor of foods, as was particularly remarked in the service of the king of Tunis, who in our time landed at Naples to confer with the Emperor Charles. They stuffed his foods with aromatic substances, so sumptuously that one peacock and two pheasants came to a hundred ducats to dress them in that manner; and when they were carved, they filled not only the dining hall but all the rooms in his palace, and even the neighboring houses, with sweet fumes which did not vanish for some time.

The principal care I take in my lodgings is to avoid heavy, stinking air. Those beautiful cities Venice and Paris weaken my fondness for them by the acrid smell of the marshes of the one and of the mud of the other.

POSSIBILITIES FOR WRITING

1. Trace closely the arc of this brief essay, exploring the sequence of thoughts from beginning to end. Do you find a coherent pattern here? If so, explain the pattern you find. If not, how does this fact affect your reading of the essay?

2. Write an essay of your own titled "Of Smells." Focus on your personal responses to the odors you encounter at home, in public, and in man-made and natural settings, as well as on how our culture seems to define good and bad smells. Don't be afraid to be whimsical.

3. Using Montaigne as a model, write an impressionistic essay on a topic that is common to everyone's experience but that would not normally be thought of as the subject of an essay: hands or feet, say, or tears, or refrigerators, or dust. Use your imagination. Incorporate quotations as you may find them.

George Orwell (1903–1950) was born Eric Blair in Bengal, India, where his father was a minor functionary in the British colonial government. Schooled in England, he chose not to attend university and instead joined the Indian Imperial Police in Burma. After five years, however, he became disillusioned with the whole notion of colonial rule and returned to England to pursue a career as a writer. His first book, Down and Out in Paris and London *(1933), chronicled his experiences living a self-imposed hand-to-mouth existence among the poor of the two cities and established what would become one of his principle themes: the exploitation of the working classes and the injustice inherent in modern societies and governments. In addition to his many works of nonfiction, Orwell is known for his scathing political novels* Animal Farm *(1945) and* 1984 *(1949).*

GEORGE ORWELL

Some Thoughts on the Common Toad

In "Some Thoughts on the Common Toad," George Orwell presents a defense of the toad as a harbinger of spring and as an example of the need for human beings to enjoy its pleasures, whether or not they prefer flowers and birds to amphibians. As Orwell notes, "The pleasures of spring are available to everybody, and cost nothing." Just past the midpoint of his essay, however, Orwell shifts gears and asks a question: "Is it wicked to take a pleasure in spring, and other seasonal changes?" He invites us to consider whether we should allow ourselves to enjoy spring pleasures in a world filled with political, social, and other serious problems.

Before the swallow, before the daffodil, and not much later than the snowdrop, the common toad salutes the coming of spring after his own fashion, which is to emerge from a hole in the ground, where he has lain buried since the previous autumn, and crawl as rapidly as possible towards the nearest suitable patch of water. Something—some kind of shudder in the earth, or perhaps merely a rise of a few degrees in the temperature—has told him that it is time to wake up: though a few toads appear to sleep the clock round and miss out a year from time to time—at any rate, I have more than once dug them up, alive and apparently well, in the middle of the summer.

At this period, after his long fast, the toad has a very spiritual look, like a strict Anglo-Catholic toward the end of Lent. His movements are languid but purposeful, his body is shrunken, and by contrast his eyes look abnormally large. This allows one to notice, what one might not at another time, that a toad has about the most beautiful eye of any living creature. It is like gold, or more exactly it is like the golden-colored semi-precious stone which one sometimes sees in signet rings, and which I think is called a chrysoberyl.

For a few days after getting into the water the toad concentrates on building up his strength by eating small insects. Presently he has swollen to his normal size again, and then he goes through a phase of intense sexiness. All he knows, at least if he is a male toad, is that he wants to get his arms round something, and if you offer him a stick, or even your finger, he will cling to it with surprising strength and take a long time to discover that it is not a female toad. Frequently one comes upon shapeless masses of ten or twenty toads rolling over and over in the water, one clinging to another without distinction of sex. By degrees, however, they sort themselves out into couples, with the male duly sitting on the female's back. You can now distinguish males from females, because the male is smaller, darker and sits on top, with his arms tightly clasped round the female's neck. After a day or two the spawn is laid in long strings which wind themselves in and out of the reeds and soon become invisible. A few more weeks, and the water is alive with masses of tiny tadpoles which rapidly grow larger, sprout hind legs, then forelegs, then shed their tails: and finally, about the middle of the summer, the new generation of toads, smaller than one's thumbnail but perfect in every particular, crawl out of the water to begin the game anew.

I mention the spawning of the toads because it is one of the phenomena of spring which most deeply appeal to me, and because the toad, unlike the skylark and the primrose, has never had much of a boost from the poets. But I am aware that many people do not like reptiles or amphibians, and I am not suggesting that in order to enjoy the spring you have to take an interest in toads. There are also the crocus, the missel thrush, the cuckoo, the blackthorn, etc. The point is that the pleasures of spring are available to everybody, and cost nothing. Even in the most sordid street the coming of spring will register itself by some sign or other, if it is only a brighter blue between the chimney pots or the vivid green of an elder sprouting on a blitzed site. Indeed it is remarkable how Nature goes on existing unofficially, as it were, in the very heart of London. I have seen a kestrel flying over the Deptford gasworks, and I have heard a first-rate performance by a black bird in the Euston Road. There must be some hundreds of thousands, if not millions, of birds living inside the four-mile radius, and it is rather a pleasing thought that none of them pays a halfpenny of rent.

As for spring, not even the narrow and gloomy streets round the Bank of England are quite able to exclude it. It comes seeping in everywhere, like one of those new poison gases which pass through all filters. The spring is commonly referred to as "a miracle," and during the past five or six years this worn-out figure of speech has taken on a new lease of life. After the sort of winters we have had to endure recently, the spring does seem miraculous, because it has become gradually harder and harder to believe that it is actually going to happen. Every February since 1940 I have found myself thinking that this time winter is going to be permanent. But Persephone, like the toads, always rises from the dead at about the same moment. Suddenly, toward the end of March, the miracle happens and the decaying slum in which I live is transfigured. Down in the square the sooty privets have turned bright green, the leaves are thickening on the chestnut trees, the daffodils are out, the wallflowers are budding, the policeman's tunic looks positively a pleasant shade of blue, the fish-monger greets his customers with a smile, and even the sparrows are quite a different color, having felt the balminess of the air and nerved themselves to take a bath, their first since last September.

Is it wicked to take a pleasure in spring, and other seasonal changes? To put it more precisely, is it politically reprehensible, while we are all groaning, under the shackles of the capitalist system, to point out that life is frequently more worth living because of a blackbird's song, a yellow elm tree in October, or some other natural phenomenon which does not cost money and does not have what the editors of the left-wing newspapers call a class angle? There is no doubt that many people think so. I know by experience that a favorable reference to "Nature" in one of my articles is liable to bring me abusive letters, and though the keyword in these letters is usually "sentimental," two ideas seem to be mixed up in them. One is that any pleasure in the actual process of life encourages a sort of political quietism. People, so the thought runs, ought to be discontented, and it is our job to multiply our wants and not simply to increase our enjoyment of the things we have already. The other idea is that this is the age of machines and that to dislike the machine, or even to want to limit its domination, is backward-looking, reactionary, and slightly ridiculous. This is often backed up by the statement that a love of Nature is a foible of urbanized people who have no notion what Nature is really like. Those who really have to deal with the soil, so it is argued, do not love the soil, and do not take the faintest interest in birds or flowers, except from a strictly utilitarian point of view. To love the country one must live in the town, merely taking an occasional week-end ramble at the warmer times of year.

This last idea is demonstrably false. Medieval literature, for instance, including the popular ballads, is full of an almost Georgian enthusiasm for Nature, and the art of agricultural peoples such as the Chinese and Japanese centers always round trees, birds, flowers, rivers, mountains. The other idea seems to me to be wrong in a subtler way. Certainly we ought to be discontented, we ought not simply to find out ways of making the best of a bad job, and yet if we kill all pleasure in the actual process of life, what sort of future are we preparing for ourselves? If a man cannot enjoy the return of spring, why should he be happy in a labor-saving Utopia? What will he do with the leisure that the machine will give him? I have always suspected that if our economic and political problems are ever really solved, life will become simpler instead of more complex, and that the sort of pleasure one gets from finding the first primrose will loom larger than the sort of pleasure one gets from eating an ice to the tune of a Wurlitzer. I think that by retaining one's childhood love of such things as trees, fishes, butterflies, and—to return to my first instance—toads, one makes a peaceful and decent future a little more probable, and that by preaching the doctrine that nothing is to be admired except steel and concrete, one merely makes it a little surer that human beings will have no outlet for their surplus energy except in hatred and leader-worship.

At any rate, spring is here, even in London, N. 1, and they can't stop you enjoying it. This is a satisfying reflection. How many a time have I stood watching the toads mating, or a pair of hares having a boxing match in the young corn, and thought of all the important persons who would stop me enjoying this if they could. But luckily they can't. So long as you are not actually ill, hungry, frightened, or immured in a prison or a holiday camp, spring is still spring. The atom bombs are piling up in the factories, the police are prowling through the cities, the lies are streaming from the loudspeakers, but the earth is still going round the sun, and neither the dictators nor the bureaucrats, deeply as they disapprove of the process, are able to prevent it.

POSSIBILITIES FOR WRITING

1. Analyze the structure of Orwell's essay. Identify the major concern of each section of his essay and the significance of each section. Explain the overall point and purpose of the essay.

2. Support, refute, or qualify Orwell's argument. Use your experience, your reading, and your observations to support your viewpoint and idea.

3. Write an essay in which you explore your thoughts and feelings about some aspect of the natural world.

Scott Russell Sanders (b. 1945) was born into a working-class family in Memphis and received scholarships to Brown and to Cambridge University in England. He has published books in many genres: novels, poetry, children's stories, science fiction, nature writing, and personal essays. These essays, noted for their sincerity and subtle grace, have been collected in The Paradise of Bombs *(1988),* Secrets of Universe *(1991), and* Writing from the Center *(1995), among others. More recent work includes* A Private History of Awe *(2006) and* The Conservationist Manifesto *(2009).*

SCOTT RUSSELL SANDERS

The Men We Carry in Our Minds

In "The Men We Carry in Our Minds," Scott Russell Sanders suggests that the lives of most men are not nearly as glamorous and exciting as some women may think. Sanders invites us to consider a conversation he includes with a woman friend and some questions that arise from that conversation, including whether women might not appreciate his views. He also confesses to an envy of women's lives, which revolve more often around things that he himself loves.

"This must be a hard time for women," I say to my friend Anneke. "They have so many paths to choose from, and so many voices calling them."

"I think it's a lot harder for men," she replies.

"How do you figure that?"

"The women I know feel excited, innocent, like crusaders in a just cause. The men I know are eaten up with guilt."

We are sitting at the kitchen table drinking sassafras tea, our hands wrapped around the mugs because this April morning is cool and drizzly. "Like a Dutch morning," Anneke told me earlier. She is Dutch herself, a writer and midwife and peacemaker, with the round face and sad eyes of a woman in a Vermeer painting who might be waiting for the rain to stop, for a door to open. She leans over to sniff a sprig of lilac, pale lavender, that rises from a vase of cobalt blue.

"Women feel such pressure to be everything, do everything," I say. "Career, kids, art, politics. Have their babies and get back to the office a week later. It's as if they're trying to overcome a million years' worth of evolution in one lifetime."

"But we help one another. We don't try to lumber on alone, like so many wounded grizzly bears, the way men do." Anneke sips her tea. I gave her the mug with owls on it, for wisdom. "And we have this deep-down sense that we're in the *right*—we've been held back, passed

SCOTT RUSSELL SANDERS

208

over, used—while men feel they're in the wrong. Men are the ones who've been discredited, who have to search their souls."

I search my soul, I discover guilty feelings aplenty—toward the poor, the Vietnamese, Native Americans, the whales, an endless list of debts—a guilt in each case that is as bright and unambiguous as a neon sign. But toward women I feel something more confused, a snarl of shame, envy, wary tenderness, and amazement. This muddle troubles me. To hide my unease I say, "You're right, it's tough being a man these days."

"Don't laugh," Anneke frowns at me, mournful-eyed, through the sassafras steam. "I wouldn't be a man for anything. It's much easier being the victim. All the victim has to do is break free. The persecutor has to live with his past."

How deep is that past? I find myself wondering after Anneke has left. How much of an inheritance do I have to throw off? Is it just the beliefs I breathed in as a child? Do I have to scour memory back through father and grandfather? Through St. Paul? Beyond Stonehenge and into the twilit caves? I'm convinced the past we must contend with is deeper even than speech. When I think back on my childhood, on how I learned to see men and women, I have a sense of ancient, dizzying depths. The back roads of Tennessee and Ohio where I grew up were probably closer, in their sexual patterns, to the campsites of Stone Age hunters than to the genderless cities of the future into which we are rushing.

The first men, besides my father, I remember seeing were black convicts and white guards, in the cottonfield across the road from our farm on the outskirts of Memphis. I must have been three or four. The prisoners wore dingy gray and black zebra suits, heavy as canvas, sodden with sweat. Hatless, stooped, they chopped weeds in the fierce heat, row after row, breathing the acrid dust of boll-weevil poison. The overseers wore dazzling white shirts and broad shadowy hats. The oiled barrels of their shotguns flashed in the sunlight. Their faces in memory are utterly blank. Of course those men, white and black, have become for me an emblem of racial hatred. But they have also come to stand for the twin poles of my early vision of manhood—the brute toiling animal and the boss.

When I was a boy, the men I knew labored with their bodies. They were marginal farmers, just scraping by, or welders, steelworkers, carpenters; they swept floors, dug ditches, mined coal, or drove trucks, their forearms ropy with muscle. They trained horses, stoked furnaces, built tires, stood on assembly lines wrestling parts onto cars and refrigerators. They got up before light, worked all day long whatever the weather, and when they came home at night they looked as though somebody had been whipping them. In the evenings and on weekends they worked on their own places, tilling gardens that were lumpy with clay, fixing broken-down cars, hammering on houses that were always too drafty, too leaky, too small.

The bodies of the men I knew were twisted and maimed in ways visible and invisible. The nails of their hands were black and split, the hands tattooed with scars. Some had lost fingers. Heavy lifting had given many of them finicky backs and guts weak from hernias. Racing against conveyor belts had given them ulcers. Their ankles and knees ached from years of standing on concrete. Anyone who had worked for long around machines was hard of hearing. They squinted, and the skin of their faces was creased like the leather of old work gloves. There were times, studying them, when I dreaded growing up. Most of them coughed, from dust or cigarettes, and most of them drank cheap wine or whiskey, so their eyes looked bloodshot and bruised. The fathers of my friends always seemed older than the mothers. Men wore out sooner. Only women lived into old age.

As a boy I also knew another sort of men, who did not sweat and break down like mules. They were soldiers, and so far as I could tell they scarcely worked at all. During my early school years we lived on a military base, an arsenal in Ohio, and every day I saw GIs in the guardshacks, on the stoops of barracks, at the wheels of olive drab Chevrolets. The chief fact of their lives was boredom. Long after I left the Arsenal I came to recognize the sour smell the soldiers gave off as that of souls in limbo. They were all waiting—for wars, for transfers, for leaves, for promotions, for the end of their hitch—like so many braves waiting for the hunt to begin. Unlike the warriors of older tribes, however, they would have no say about when the battle would start or how it would be waged. Their waiting was broken only when they practiced for war. They fired guns at targets, drove tanks across the churned-up fields of the military reservation, set off bombs in the wrecks of old fighter planes. I knew this was all play. But I also felt certain that when the hour for killing arrived, they would kill. When the real shooting started, many of them would die. This was what soldiers were *for,* just as a hammer was for driving nails.

Warriors and toilers: those seemed, in my boyhood vision, to be the chief destinies for men. They weren't the only destinies, as I learned from having a few male teachers, from reading books, and from watching television. But the men on television—the politicians, the astronauts, the generals, the savvy lawyers, the philosophical doctors, the bosses who gave orders to both soldiers and laborers—seemed as remote and unreal to me as the figures in tapestries. I could no more imagine growing up to become one of these cool, potent creatures than I could imagine becoming a prince.

A nearer and more hopeful example was that of my father, who had escaped from a red dirt farm to a tire factory, and from the assembly line to the front office. Eventually he dressed in a white shirt and tie. He carried himself as if he had been born to work with his mind. But his body, remembering the earlier years of slogging work, began to give out on him in his fifties, and it quit on him entirely before he turned sixty-five. Even such a partial escape from man's fate as he had accomplished did not seem possible for most of the boys I knew. They joined the Army, stood in line for jobs in the smoky plants, helped build highways. They were bound to work as their fathers had worked, killing themselves or preparing to kill others.

A scholarship enabled me not only to attend college, a rare enough feat in my circle, but even to study in a university meant for the children of the rich. Here I met for the first time young men who had assumed from birth that they would lead lives of comfort and power. And for the first time I met women who told me that men were guilty of having kept all the joys and privileges of the earth for themselves. I was baffled. What privileges? What joys? I thought about the maimed, dismal lives of most of the men back home. What had they stolen from their wives and daughters? The right to go five days a week, twelve months a year, for thirty or forty years to a steel mill or a coal mine? The right to drop bombs and die in war? The right to feel every leak in the roof, every gap in the fence, every cough in the engine, as a wound they must mend? The right to feel, when the lay-off comes or the plant shuts down, not only afraid but ashamed?

I was slow to understand the deep grievances of women. This was because, as a boy, I had envied them. Before college, the only people I had ever known who were interested in art or music or literature, the only ones who read books, the only ones who ever seemed to enjoy a sense of ease and grace were the mothers and daughters. Like the menfolk, they fretted about money, they scrimped and made-do. But, when the pay stopped coming in, they were not the ones who had failed. Nor did they have to go to war, and that seemed to me a blessed fact. By comparison with the narrow, ironclad days of fathers, there was an expansiveness, I thought, in the days of mothers. They went to see neighbors, to shop in town, to run errands at school, at the library, at church. No doubt, had I looked harder at their lives, I would have envied them less. It was not my fate to become a woman, so it was easier for me to see the graces. Few of them held jobs outside the home, and those who did filled thankless roles as clerks and waitresses. I didn't see, then, what a prison a house could be, since houses seemed to me brighter, handsomer places than any factory. I did not realize—because such things were never spoken of—how often women suffered from men's bullying. I did learn about the wretchedness of abandoned wives, single mothers, widows; but I also learned about the wretchedness of lone men. Even then I could see how exhausting it was for a mother to cater all day to the needs of young children. But if I had been asked, as a boy, to choose between tending a baby and tending a machine, I think I would have chosen the baby. (Having now tended both, I know I would choose the baby.)

So I was baffled when the women at college accused me and my sex of having cornered the world's pleasures. I think something like my bafflement has been felt by other boys (and by girls as well) who grew up in dirt-poor farm country, in mining country, in black ghettos, in Hispanic barrios, in the shadows of factories, in Third World nations—any place where the fate of men is as grim and bleak as the fate of women. Toilers and warriors. I realize now how ancient these identities are, how deep the tug they exert on men, the undertow of a thousand generations. The miseries I saw, as a boy, in the lives of nearly all men I continue to see in the lives of many—the body-breaking toil, the tedium, the call to be tough, the humiliating powerlessness, the battle for a living and for territory.

When the women I met at college thought about the joys and privileges of men, they did not carry in their minds the sort of men I had known in my childhood. They thought of their fathers, who were bankers, physicians, architects, stockbrokers, the big wheels of the big cities. These fathers rode the train to work or drove cars that cost more than any of my childhood houses. They were attended from morning to night by female helpers, wives and nurses and secretaries. They were never laid off, never short of cash at month's end, never lined up for welfare. These fathers made decisions that mattered. They ran the world.

The daughters of such men wanted to share in this power, this glory. So did I. They yearned for a say over their future, for jobs worthy of their abilities, for the right to live at peace, unmolested, whole. Yes, I thought, yes yes. The difference between me and these daughters was that they saw me, because of my sex, as destined from birth to become like their fathers, and therefore as an enemy to their desires. But I knew better. I wasn't an enemy, in fact or in feeling. I was an ally. If I had known, then, how to tell them so, would they have believed me? Would they now?

POSSIBILITIES FOR WRITING

1. Tell a story of your own that compares with something Sanders describes in his essay. Perhaps you can include a conversation you had with a member of the opposite sex.
2. Analyze the way Sanders organizes his essay. Identify its basic parts; explain what he accomplishes in each part; and relate the parts to each other. Consider his use of dialogues in the beginning and his inclusions of questions and his use of contrast.
3. Support or dispute Sanders' claims about men. Use evidence from your reading and experience to substantiate your assertions.

David Sedaris (b. 1956) was born in Johnson City, New York, and raised
in Raleigh, North Carolina. Sedaris launched his career as a humorist on the
National Public Radio show "Morning Edition." His plays, one of which won
an Obie Award, have been produced at La Mama and at Lincoln Center, among
other theatrical venues. A number of his books, collections of essays, and stories
have been best-sellers, including Barrel Fever (1994), Naked (1997), Holidays
on Ice (1997), Me Talk Pretty One Day (2000), Dress Your Family in
Corduroy and Denim (2004), and When You are Engulfed in Flames (2008).
An essayist whose work appears regularly in the New Yorker and Esquire,
Sedaris was named Humorist of the Year by Time magazine in 2001, when he
also received the Thurber Prize for American Humor.

DAVID SEDARIS

Me Talk Pretty One Day

In "Me Talk Pretty One Day," David Sedaris describes his experience
learning French at the age of forty-one. With his title serving as a clue to
the difficulties he encounters, Sedaris conveys with wit and insight what it
is like to begin learning a foreign language. He also conveys what it's like
to suffer at the hands of a harsh teacher, though Sedaris exaggerates the
teacher's harshness to achieve his comic purpose.

At the age of forty-one, I am returning to school and have to think
of myself as what my French textbook calls "a true debutant." After
paying my tuition, I was issued a student ID, which allows me a dis-
counted entry fee at movie theaters, puppet shows, and Festyland, a
far-flung amusement park that advertises with billboards picturing a
cartoon stegosaurus sitting in a canoe and eating what appears to be
a ham sandwich.

I've moved to Paris with hopes of learning the language. My school
is an easy ten-minute walk from my apartment, and on the first day of
class I arrived early, watching as the returning students greeted one
another in the school lobby. Vacations were recounted, and questions were raised concerning mutual friends with names like Kang
and Vlatnya. Regardless of their nationalities, everyone spoke in what
sounded to me like excellent French. Some accents were better than
others, but the students exhibited an ease and confidence I found in-
timidating. As an added discomfort, they were all young, attractive,
and well dressed, causing me to feel not unlike Pa Kettle trapped back-
stage after a fashion show.

The first day of class was nerve-racking because I knew I'd be
expected to perform. That's the way they do it here—it's everybody

into the language pool, sink or swim. The teacher marched in, deeply tanned from a recent vacation, and proceeded to rattle off a series of administrative announcements. I've spent quite a few summers in Normandy, and I took a monthlong French class before leaving New York. I'm not completely in the dark, yet I understood only half of what this woman was saying.

"If you have not *meimslsxp* or *lgpdmurct* by this time, then you should not be in this room. Has everyone *apzkiubjxow*? Everyone? Good, we shall begin." She spread out her lesson plan and sighed, saying, "All right, then, who knows the alphabet?"

It was startling because (a) I hadn't been asked that question in a while and (b) I realized, while laughing, that I myself did *not* know the alphabet. They're the same letters, but in France they're pronounced differently. I know the shape of the alphabet but had no idea what it actually sounded like.

"Ahh." The teacher went to the board and sketched the letter *a*. "Do we have anyone in the room whose first name commences with an *ahh*?"

Two Polish Annas raised their hands, and the teacher instructed them to present themselves by stating their names, nationalities, occupations, and a brief list of things they liked and disliked in this world. The first Anna hailed from an industrial town outside of Warsaw and had front teeth the size of tombstones. She worked as a seamstress, enjoyed quiet times with friends, and hated the mosquito.

"Oh, really," the teacher said. "How very interesting. I thought that everyone loved the mosquito, but here, in front of all the world, you claim to detest him. How is it that we've been blessed with someone as unique and original as you? Tell us, please."

The seamstress did not understand what was being said but knew that this was an occasion for shame. Her rabbity mouth huffed for breath, and she stared down at her lap as though the appropriate comeback were stitched somewhere alongside the zipper of her slacks.

The second Anna learned from the first and claimed to love sunshine and detest lies. It sounded like a translation of one of those Playmate of the Month data sheets, the answers always written in the same loopy handwriting: "Turn-ons: Mom's famous five-alarm chili! Turnoffs: insecurity and guys who come on too strong!!!!"

The two Polish Annas surely had clear notions of what they loved and hated, but like the rest of us, they were limited in terms of vocabulary, and this made them appear less than sophisticated. The teacher forged on, and we learned that Carlos, the Argentine bandoneón player, loved wine, music, and, in his words, "making sex with the womens of the world." Next came a beautiful young Yugoslav who identified herself as an optimist, saying that she loved everything that life had to offer.

The teacher licked her lips, revealing a hint of the saucebox we would later come to know. She crouched low for her attack, placed her hands on the young woman's desk, and leaned close, saying, "Oh yeah? And do you love your little war?"

While the optimist struggled to defend herself, I scrambled to think of an answer to what had obviously become a trick question. How often is one asked what he loves in this world? More to the point, how often is one asked and then publicly ridiculed for his answer? I recalled my mother, flushed with wine, pounding the tabletop late one night, saying, "Love? I love a good steak cooked rare. I love my cat, and I love..." My sisters and I leaned forward, waiting to hear our names. "Tums," our mother said. "I love Tums."

The teacher killed some time accusing the Yugoslavian girl of masterminding a program of genocide, and I jotted frantic notes in the margins of my pad. While I can honestly say that I love leafing through medical textbooks devoted to severe dermatological conditions, the hobby is beyond the reach of my French vocabulary, and acting it out would only have invited controversy.

When called upon, I delivered an effortless list of things that I detest: blood sausage, intestinal pâtés, brain pudding. I'd learned these words the hard way. Having given it some thought, I then declared my love for IBM typewriters, the French word for *bruise*, and my electric floor waxer. It was a short list, but still I managed to mispronounce *IBM* and assign the wrong gender to both the floor waxer and the typewriter. The teacher's reaction led me to believe that these mistakes were capital crimes in the country of France.

"Were you always this *palicmkrexis*?" she asked. "Even a *fiuscrzsa ticiwelmun* knows that a typewriter is feminine."

I absorbed as much of her abuse as I could understand, thinking—but not saying—that I find it ridiculous to assign a gender to an inanimate object incapable of disrobing and making an occasional fool of itself. Why refer to Lady Crack Pipe or Good Sir Dishrag when these things could never live up to all that their sex implied?

The teacher proceeded to belittle everyone from German Eva, who hated laziness, to Japanese Yukari, who loved paintbrushes and soap. Italian, Thai, Dutch, Korean, and Chinese—we all left class foolishly believing that the worst was over. She'd shaken us up a little, but surely that was just an act designed to weed out the dead-weight. We didn't know it then, but the coming months would teach us what it was like to spend time in the presence of a wild animal, something completely unpredictable. Her temperament was not based on a series of good and bad days but, rather, good and bad moments. We soon learned to dodge chalk and protect our heads and stomachs whenever she approached us with a question. She hadn't yet punched anyone, but it seemed wise to protect ourselves against the inevitable.

Though we were forbidden to speak anything but French, the teacher would occasionally use us to practice any of her five fluent languages.

"I hate you," she said to me one afternoon. Her English was flaw-less. "I really, really hate you." Call me sensitive, but I couldn't help but take it personally.

After being singled out as a lazy *kfdtinvfm*, I took to spending four hours a night on my homework, putting in even more time whenever we were assigned an essay. I suppose I could have gotten by with less, but I was determined to create some sort of identity for myself: David the hard worker, David the cut-up. We'd have one of those "complete this sentence" exercises, and I'd fool with the thing for hours, invariably settling on something like "A quick run around the lake? I'd love to! Just give me a moment while I strap on my wooden leg." The teacher, through word and action, conveyed the message that if this was my idea of an identity, she wanted nothing to do with it.

My fear and discomfort crept beyond the borders of the classroom and accompanied me out onto the wide boulevards. Stopping for a coffee, asking directions, depositing money in my bank account: these things were out of the question, as they involved having to speak. Before beginning school, there'd been no shutting me up, but now I was convinced that everything I said was wrong. When the phone rang, I ignored it. If someone asked me a question, I pretended to be deaf. I knew my fear was getting the best of me when I started wonder-ing why they don't sell cuts of meat in vending machines.

My only comfort was the knowledge that I was not alone. Huddled in the hallways and making the most of our pathetic French, my fellow students and I engaged in the sort of conversation commonly over-heard in refugee camps.

"Sometime me cry alone at night."

"That be common for I, also, but be more strong, you. Much work and someday you talk pretty. People start love you soon. Maybe tomorrow, okay."

Unlike the French class I had taken in New York, here there was no sense of competition. When the teacher poked a shy Korean in the eyelid with a freshly sharpened pencil, we took no comfort in the fact that, unlike Hyeyoon Cho, we all knew the irregular past tense of the verb *to defeat*. In all fairness, the teacher hadn't meant to stab the girl, but neither did she spend much time apologizing, saying only, "Well, you should have been *vkkdyo* more *kdeynfulh*."

Over time it became impossible to believe that any of us would ever improve. Fall arrived and it rained every day, meaning we would now be scolded for the water dripping from our coats and umbrellas. It was mid-October when the teacher singled me out, saying, "Every day spent with you is like having a cesarean section." And it struck me that, for the first time since arriving in France, I could understand every word that someone was saying.

Understanding doesn't mean that you can suddenly speak the language. Far from it. It's a small step, nothing more, yet its rewards are intoxicating and deceptive. The teacher continued her diatribe and I settled back, bathing in the subtle beauty of each new curse and insult.

"You exhaust me with your foolishness and reward my efforts with nothing but pain, do you understand me?"

The world opened up, and it was with great joy that I responded, "I know the thing that you speak exact now. Talk me more, you, plus, please, plus."

POSSIBILITIES FOR WRITING

1. To what extent do you think Sedaris captures the experience of trying to learn a foreign language? To what extent do you think he exaggerates what happens in a foreign language classroom?
2. To what extent did you find the essay funny? Explain how Sedaris achieves his humorous effects. What is the purpose of the many nonsense words Sedaris includes?
3. Write an essay about your own experience learning or attempting to learn a foreign language. You may wish to compare or contrast your experience with Sedaris's. Or you may wish to compare learning a foreign language with learning another subject or learning another skill, such as playing a musical instrument, or learning computer skills.

Lee Siegel (b. 1957) was born and raised in the Bronx, New York, and received his B.A., M.A., and M.Phil. from Columbia University. He worked as an editor at the New Leader *and* ARTnews *before turning to writing full-time in 1998. In 2002, Siegel received the National Magazine Award for Reviews and Criticism. Siegel has written several essays for art catalogues and several introductions to reprinted classics, and has authored several books, including:* Falling Upwards: Essays in Defense of the Imagination *(2006),* Not Remotely Controlled: Notes on Television *(2007), and* Against the Machine: How the Web Is Reshaping Culture and Commerce—and Why It Matters *(2008), a polemic that offers a perspective on the Internet that explores a range of its consequences, good and bad.*

LEE SIEGEL

The World Is All That Is the Case

In "The World Is All That Is the Case," Lee Siegel identifies a number of ways the Internet shapes the way people live today. In a spirit of critical inquiry, he asks some basic questions about the consequences of the Internet's reshaping of culture, particularly how people behave and interact socially. Among his concerns is the way the Internet universe is driven by and saturated in economic matters, "assimilating human existence to an economic model," and thereby "embed[ding] human life in an economic model."

I go to Starbucks, sit down, open my laptop, and turn it on. In the old days—ten years ago—I would be sitting with a pen and notebook, partly concentrating on my writing and partly aware of the people in the room around me. Back in that prehistoric time, my attention faced outward. I might see someone I know, or someone I'd like to know. I might passively enjoy trying to figure out why that couple in the middle of the room are speaking so intensely—are they moving closer together to relish their intimacy or because there is a crisis in their intimacy? And who is that guy with the fedora—and why the red sneakers? Is he an original, or the copy of an original? I might be watching everyone, but some people might be watching me, too. My situation is just as permeable as theirs. A stranger could come over to my table at any minute, his sudden physical presence before me unexpected, incalculable, absolutely enigmatic in the seconds before he becomes one kind of situation or another.

But here I am, sitting in the future—I mean the present—in front of my laptop. Just about everyone around me has a laptop open also. The small mass of barely variegated gray panels looks like a scene out of Fritz Lang's *Metropolis*, but with modems and Danishes. I can hardly see anyone else's face behind the screens, and no one seems to be doing anything socially or psychologically that might be fun to try to figure out. They are bent into their screens and toward their self-interest. My attention, too, is turned toward my ego. But I am paying attention in a different way from what I do when I read a book or a newspaper. I am opening e-mail sent to me, writing e-mail expressing one or another desire that belongs to me, clicking on Google looking for information to be used by me. Ten years ago, the space in a coffeehouse abounded in experience. Now that social space has been contracted into isolated points of wanting, all locked into separate phases of inwardness.

The new situation doesn't represent the "lack of community" suddenly produced by the Internet. That is the hackneyed complaint made, again and again, by people who don't seem to have thought through the unlovely aspects of "community"—its smug provincialism and punitive conventionalism, its stasis and xenophobia—which was in any case jeopardized and transformed by the advent of modernity two hundred years ago. The simple fact is that sometimes you don't want the quiet conformities induced by "community"; sometimes you simply want to be alone, yet together with other people at the same time. The old-fashioned café provided a way to both share and abandon solitude, a fluid, intermediary experience that humans are always trying to create and perfect. The Internet could have been its fulfillment. But sitting absorbed in your screenworld is a whole other story. You are socially and psychologically cut off from your fellow caffeine addicts, but mentally beset by e-mails, commercial "pop-ups," and a million temptations that may enchant in the moment—aimed as they are at your specific and immediate interests and desires—but in retrospect are time-wasting ephemera. It's not community that the laptopization of the coffeehouse has dispelled. It's the concrete, undeniable, immutable fact of our being in the world.

Before our screens, experience is collapsed into gratifying our desires on the one hand, and on the other either satisfying or refusing to satisfy the soliciting desires of other people—or entities. As the Viennese philosopher Ludwig Wittgenstein famously said, "The world is all that is the case." We have been flung into the world whether we like it or not. But the Internet creates a vast illusion that the physical, social world of interacting minds and hearts does not exist. In this new situation, the screen is all that is the case, along with the illusion that the screen projects a world tamed, digested, abbreviated, rationalized, and ordered into a trillion connected units, called sites. This new world turns the most consequential fact of human life—other people—into seemingly manipulable half presences wholly available to our fantasies. It's a world controlled by our wrist and finger.

Yet the untamed, undigested, unrationalized, uncontrolled world is still there. People as thinking, feeling beings still exist. What form, then, do we take, in a world where there is—how else can I put it?— no world at all? To put it another way: What kind of idea do we have of the world when, day after day, we sit in front of our screens and enter further and further into the illusion that we ourselves are actually creating our own external reality out of our own internal desires? We become impatient with realities that don't gratify our impulses or satisfy our picture of reality. We find it harder to accept the immutable limitations imposed by identity, talent, personality. We start to behave in public as if we were acting in private, and we begin to fill our private world with gargantuan public appetites. In other words, we find it hard to bear simply being human.

This situation is not a crisis of technology. Rather, it is a social development that has been embodied in the new technology of the Internet, but not created by the Internet. The sudden onset of Web culture is really a dramatic turn in the timeless question of what it means to be a human being. What a shame that transformative new technologies usually either inspire uncritical celebration or incite bouts of nostalgia for a prelapsarian age that existed before said technology—anything for an uprising against cellphones and a return to the glorious phone booths of yore! The advent of new technologies pretty quickly becomes a pitched battle between the apostles of edge and Luddites wielding alarmist sentiments like pitchforks. Because each side is a caricature of itself, no one takes what is at stake very seriously at all.

And they are caricatures, for anyone who thinks technological innovation is bad in and of itself is an unimaginative crank. (I would rather go live on Pluto than return to the days of the phone booth and the desperate search for change.) But anyone who denies that technology has the potential to damage us if it is not put to good use is either cunning or naive. In the case of the Internet, the question is whether we let this remarkably promising opportunity—which, as we'll see, has until now largely been developed in service to commerce and capital— shape us to its needs or put it in the service of our own. Do we keep acquiescing in the myopic glibness and carelessness that characterize how so many of us are using the Internet? Do we keep surrendering to the highly purposeful way vested interests are foisting it upon us?

Comfortable Upheaval

The future, we were once told, shocked. Well, the future is here. But no one is shocked.

The sensational evidence of upheaval is everywhere. You can read about it in the newspaper or see it on the news by the hour. A lonely middle-aged carpenter in Arizona meets a Brazilian woman online, visits her in Rio de Janeiro twice, and then, on his third encounter with her, is murdered by his new girlfriend, her real boyfriend, and a hired assassin. A sting operation sweeps up hundreds of pedophiles luring their prey in Internet chat rooms. Computer hackers use the Internet to nearly bring down the government of Estonia. An anonymous Web site reveals the identities of federally protected witnesses in capital cases. Social-networking sites like MySpace and the video-blog site called YouTube turn the most graphic inhumanity—a Texas policeman puts up photos of a dismembered woman; anonymous users post footage of American soldiers in Iraq being gunned down—into numbing new forms of entertainment.

The Internet's most consequential changes in our lives, however, are the ones woven into our everyday routines. Maybe your teenage son—or daughter—spends hours every day and night corresponding with dozens of new "friends" on MySpace or Facebook; perhaps he's uploading a forty-minute-long video of himself dancing naked, alone in his room, onto YouTube, one of the world's most highly trafficked sites. Maybe your officemate is addicted to political blogs like Little Green Footballs, or Instapundit, or Firedoglake, in which dozens, sometimes hundreds, of people, argue with each other passionately, sometimes abusively, on interminable threads of commenters. Or your other officemate spends all of his time buying merchandise on eBay, or your boss, a high-powered attorney, closes her door on her lunch hour and logs on to JDate, a Jewish dating service, where she fields inquiries from dozens of men.

Perhaps your husband is, at this very moment, shut away in his office somewhere in your home, carrying on several torrid online affairs at the same time under his various aliases: "Caliente," "Curious," "ActionMan." When he emerges from his sequestered lair, red-faced and agitated, is it because he has been arguing for moderation with "KillBush46" on the political blog Daily Kos, has failed in his bid to purchase genuine military-issue infrared night goggles on eBay, or has been masturbating while instant-messaging "Prehistorical2"?

Then again, maybe your husband died four years ago from a rare disease, and thanks to information you discovered on the Web, you were able to find a drug that kept him alive for twice as long as he would have lived without it. An Internet grief support group helped get you through the pain of your loss and introduced you to people who are now trusted friends. They led you, in turn, to an online dating service where you met your second husband, and began a new life.

Like all significant technologies, the Internet is a blessing and a curse. Or, rather, it is obviously a blessing and obscurely a curse. It would be tedious to recite the Internet's wonders as a tool for research and a medium for connectivity in detail here—in any case, those wonders have been touted far and wide for the last decade by an all-too-willing media. But the transformations are real. For the first time in human history, a person can have romance, friendship, and sex (sort of); be fed, clothed, and entertained; receive medical, legal, and just about every other type of advice; collect all sorts of information, from historical facts to secrets about other people—all without leaving home. For the first time in human history, a technology exists that allows a person to lead as many secret lives, under a pseudonym, as he is able to manage. For the first time in human history, a person can broadcast his opinions, beliefs, and most intimate thoughts—not to mention his face, or any other part of his body—to tens of millions of other people.

The simple fact is that more and more people are able to live in a more comfortable and complete self-enclosure than ever before.

The Big Lie

Since the rise of the Internet just ten years ago, the often irrational boosterism behind it has been for the most part met by criticism that is timid, defensive, and unfocused. The Internet is possibly the most radical transformation of private and public life in the history of humankind, but from the way it is publicly discussed, you would think that this gigantic jolt to the status quo had all the consequences of buying a new car. "The Internet," the New York Times casually reports, represents "a revolution in politics and human consciousness." Online sex is "changing the lives of billions" in Asia, writes Time magazine with a shrug, and follows that astounding headline with what amounts to a lifestyle article ("A continent of 3 billion human beings is getting sexy and kicking the guilt... say a sincere hosanna to the Internet, which not only allows wired Asians to hook up but also to find out about whatever may titillate or tantalize them"). Everyone agrees the Internet has the same "epochal" significance that the printing press once did. But after the printing press made its appearance in Europe, three hundred years had to go by before the "revolutionary" new invention began to seep down from the scholar's cloister into everyday life. Even the telephone and television, the most transformative technologies of modern times, took decades to reshape "human consciousness," to borrow the *Times*'s grandiose tone. The Internet has radically changed almost every level of human experience, throughout most of the world, in just a few years. So why can't people be honest about the downside as well as the upside of what's happening to us?

Of course no one wants to stand athwart the future shaking a finger, mocking and scowling and scolding. No one wants to be a wet blanket at the party. Americans don't like naysayers, and we don't like backward lookers. Ours has got to be the only culture in the world where saying that someone belongs to "history" is a fatal insult. So what you usually get by way of criticism are sunny, facile gestures toward criticism. A typical example is the Pew Internet & American Life Project. Its September 2006 report on the current state and future of Internet culture has been widely used by anxious or self-interested journalists to forecast, among other things, the death of newspapers and print magazines. According to the Pew Project, "Internet users have become more likely to note big improvements in their ability to shop and the way they pursue their hobbies and interests. A majority of Internet users also consistently report that the internet helps them to do their job and improves the way they get information about health care." Pew also notes "addiction problems" for many Web visitors, but quickly concludes that for many respondents to the survey, " 'addiction' is an inappropriate notion to attach to people's interest in virtual environments." The report then adds this creepy glance into the future: "Tech 'refuseniks' will emerge as a cultural group characterized by their choice to live off the network. Some will do this as a benign way to limit information overload, while others will commit acts of violence and terror against technology-inspired change."

To my mind, it could well be that one reason why the Pew report is so upbeat about its subject is that eight of the twelve people on the advisory board of the Pew Internet & American Life Project, at the time the report was written, had a financial or professional stake in Internet companies. Pew asserts that its staff is independent of the advisory board. Be that as it may, the authors of the Pew report view any opposition to the Internet's darker effects as resistance to "technology-inspired change" rather than skepticism that embraces technology but recoils at some of its effects. Naturally, in their eyes, much of the opposition could not possibly be rational. It would have to come in the form of "violence and terror."

Along with Web boosters like the authors of the Pew study is another type of potent promoter: the utopian technophile. We will meet several different varieties of these along our way. One of the most energetic and persuasive is Kevin Kelly, Internet guru, co-founder of *Wired* magazine, and the author of two hugely influential books on Internet culture—*Out of Control: The New Biology of Machines, Social Systems, and the Economic World* and *New Rules for the New Economy: 10 Radical Strategies for a Connected World*. While the Pew report covered general patterns of usage, Kelly has a vision of social and cultural transformation:

> *What will entertainment technology look like in 20 years? Let's listen to what technology says. First, technology has no preference between real and simulations—(so) neither will our stories. The current distinction between biological actors and virtual actors will cease, just as the distinction between real locations and virtual locations has almost gone. The choice will simply come down to what is less expensive. The blur between real and simulated will continue to blur the line between documentary and fiction. As straight documentaries continue to surge in popularity in the next 20 years, so will hybrids between fiction and non-fiction. We'll see more reality shows that are scripted, scripted shows that run out of control, documentaries that use actors, actors that are robotic creations, news that is staged, stories that become news and the total collision and marriage between fantasy and the found.*

Now, Kelly may well be right. Yet in his feverish devotion to "technology," he sees nothing wrong with fake documentaries, deceitful "reality" shows, and "news that is staged." If technology decides that truth and falsehood shall be blurred, then for Kelly their "total collision and marriage"—whatever that means, exactly—is as historically determined, inevitable, and necessary as the Marxist belief in the dictatorship of the proletariat.

Despite the fact that Kelly cheerily predicts the imminent extinction of "old" media, nearly the entire journalistic establishment has embraced, in various degrees, his exuberant view of a dystopic future. For it is dystopic. What sane person wants a culture in which the border between truthfulness and lying is constantly being eroded? Nothing affects our values and perceptions, our thoughts and feelings, like the shows we watch, the movies we see, the books we read—and we watch far more than we read; Americans spend a large amount, if not a majority, of their leisure time being entertained. Kelly sees the engine of the Internet driving these cataclysmic changes in the culture. But journalists and other commentators are so afraid of appearing behind the times, or of being left behind, that the role the Internet plays in the disappearing borders of truth rarely gets talked about in public.

We know where we stand on a politician's lies; we know how to respond when we feel, for example, that the government's deceptions and lies led us into the Iraq war. But no one is making a cogent connection between the rise of the Internet and the accelerating blur of truth and falsity in culture—even though culture's subtle effects on our minds are a lot more profound in the long run than a politician's lies, which usually get discovered and exposed sooner or later. Instead of crying out against the manipulation of truth by "entertainment technology," as Kelly chillingly calls what used to be described as "having fun," we watch the general mendacity get turned into a joke—the comedian Stephen Colbert's celebrated quip about "truthiness"—and turn back to our various screens with a laugh.

People like the Pew group and Kevin Kelly are in a mad rush to keep the Web entrepreneurially viable or to push a fervent idealism. But in their blinkered eagerness to sell their outlooks—to focus our attention on what they are selling as an inevitable future—they rush right past the most obvious questions: How will the Internet affect the boundaries between people? As "information" consists more and more of reports from people's psyches, how will we be able to express intimate thoughts and feelings without sounding hackneyed and banal? As increasing numbers of people become dependent on the Internet, and the Internet is driven more and more by commerce—the sensational stock prices and sales of Google, MySpace, and YouTube, for example—how do we keep an obsession with the bottom line from overwhelming our lives? How do we carve out a space for a life apart from the Internet, and apart from economics?

Upgrade and Be Happy

Anyway, who wants to glower at the Internet when it brings such a cornucopia of wonders? Bill Gates describes what he considers the full potential of the Internet's developments:

> They will enable equal access to information and instantaneous
> communication with anyone in the world. They will open up vast
> markets and opportunities to businesses of any size. They will

*transcend national borders, making possible a frictionless global
economy. They will allow workers to be even more efficient and
productive, and will have the potential to make jobs more stimulating
and fulfilling. They will give developing nations the ability to leapfrog
the industrial era and move straight into the information age. They
will help people and businesses in countries with large, dispersed
populations to stay in touch, and help the smallest nations participate
as equals in the global economy.*

Gates says he is not blind to the Internet's pitfalls, either:

*As more and more people store personal information on the Internet,
how will we ensure that information is kept secure? As our economy
becomes more dependent on bits than on atoms, how will we protect
these resources from being damaged or devalued by hackers? As the
barriers to information come down, how will we protect our children
from negative and predatory influences? And as the Internet dissolves
national borders, how will we help indigenous cultures coexist with an
increasingly homogenous global culture?*

Gates's radiant view of the future and his predictions of the problems that might obstruct the Internet's promise are reiterated throughout the media. They are the standard description of the Internet's
bright side and its dark side. But there is something dark about Gates's
sunniness; there is something rosy about his premonition of difficulties along the way. Consider the bad news first. Are the problems
Gates foresees really problems at all? They have a red-herringish quality about them; they are by no means insoluble. Indeed, Gates frames
these dilemmas produced by new technology in such a way that their
resolution lies exclusively in the invention of newer technology.

For the way to keep information secure is to develop software that
will do so. We can protect against hackers by constructing systems
that thwart them. Advanced computer programs will shield our children from the dangers unleashed as "the barriers to information come
down." (Notice how Gates makes even sexual predators seem like the
necessary consequence of an unmitigated good: How could more information ever be anything but a marvelous beneficence? And who
would use "negative and predatory influences" on children as an argument against opening the floodgates of information?)

As for the disruptions that the Internet might bring to impoverished, illiterate populations, Gates formulates this conflict as a cultural, not a social, clash. The answer, he implies, is simply to introduce

the "indigenous" cultures to the techniques that are making the world "increasingly homogenous." Rather than honestly face the strange new perils the Internet has created, Gates's "realism" strengthens the impression of the Internet's power, permanence, and necessity. For Gates, the only answer to the Internet's dark side is the Internet itself.

One of the striking characteristics of conversation about the Internet is this circular, hermetic quality. The "key words and phrases," as the search engines like to say, in Gates's rosy picture of the future give you a sense of how he would answer the dilemmas posed by new technology: "access," "markets," "businesses," "economy," "efficient," "productive," "leapfrog the industrial era." Gates doesn't worry that the Internet will upset deep, irrational human needs and desires. For him, deep, irrational human needs and desires don't exist outside the super-rationally ordered universe of the Internet. And since economics is the simplest means of rationalizing human life, Gates believes that being human can be defined strictly in economic terms.

Microsoft, however, had a long arrival. Over thirty years ago, in *The Coming of Post-Industrial Society*, the sociologist Daniel Bell predicted Bill Gates. Decades before Gates made the computer the means of assimilating human existence to an economic model, Bell saw how the computer would eventually embed everyday life in an economic framework.

POSSIBILITIES FOR WRITING

1. What is the main point Siegel makes in the essay? Where is it most clearly stated? Summarize Siegel's argument in one paragraph.

2. To what extent do you think Siegel is fair and balanced in his discussion of the values and dangers of the Internet? Identify one passage in which he demonstrates a balanced approach and explain how successfully he offers a balanced view. What evidence can you find that suggests he may favor one side or the other—the positive or negative impact the Internet has had on our lives?

3. Write an essay in which you explore what you see as the virtues and vices—the values and dangers of the Internet. You may use some of Siegel's examples, if you wish. However, if you do, be sure to include them among others that he does not mention.

Leslie Marmon Silko (b. 1948), who is of native Laguna, Mexican, and Anglo-American ancestry, was born in Albuquerque, New Mexico, and raised on the nearby Laguna Pueblo Reservation. After earning a degree from the University of New Mexico, she taught at a community college, then began her career as a writer with the poetry collection Laguna Woman *(1974). Her first novel,* Ceremony, *appeared in 1977, followed by* Almanac of the Dead *(1991) and, most recently,* Gardens in the Dunes *(1999). Her short stories are collected in* Storyteller *(1981);* Yellow Woman and a Beauty of the Spirit *(1996) is a collection of essays. Silko is a recipient of the prestigious MacArthur Foundation Prize.*

LESLIE MARMON SILKO

Landscape, History, and the Pueblo Imagination

The focus of Leslie Marmon Silko's "Landscape, History, and the Pueblo Imagination" is landscape less as aesthetic object or private property than as something alive and to be appreciated, even revered. Silko describes the cycle of life and death in nature, stressing how the remains of things that have died nourish those still alive. For Silko and for the Native American tradition she reflects, all things should be celebrated, whether living or dead, because they possess spirit or being.

You see that after a thing is dead, it dries up. It might take weeks or years, but eventually if you touch the thing, it crumbles under your fingers. It goes back to dust. The soul of the thing has long since departed. With the plants and wild game the soul may have already been borne back into bones and blood or thick green stalk and leaves. Nothing is wasted. What cannot be eaten by people or in some way used must then be left where other living creatures may benefit. What domestic animals or wild scavengers can't eat will be fed to the plants. The plants feed on the dust of these few remains.

The ancient Pueblo people buried the dead in vacant rooms or partially collapsed rooms adjacent to the main living quarters. Sand and clay used to construct the roof make layers many inches deep once the roof has collapsed. The layers of sand and clay make for easy gravedigging. The vacant room fills with cast-off objects and debris. When a vacant room has filled deep enough, a shallow but adequate grave can be scooped in a far corner. Archaeologists have remarked over formal burials complete with elaborate funerary objects excavated in trash middens of abandoned rooms. But the rocks and adobe mortar of collapsed walls were valued by the ancient people. Because each rock had been carefully selected for size and shape, then chiseled to an even face. Even the pink clay adobe melting with each rainstorm had to be prayed over, then dug and carried some distance. Corn cobs and husks, the rinds and stalks and animal bones were not regarded by the ancient people as filth or garbage. The remains were merely resting at a midpoint in their journey back to dust. Human remains are not so different. They should rest with the bones and rinds where they all may benefit living creatures—small rodents and insects—until their return is completed. The remains of things—animals and plants, the clay and the stones—were treated with respect. Because for the ancient people all these things had spirit and being.

The antelope merely consents to return home with the hunter. All phases of the hunt are conducted with love. The love the hunter and the people have for the Antelope People. And the love of the antelope who agree to give up their meat and blood so that human beings will not starve. Waste of meat or even the thoughtless handling of bones cooked bare will offend the antelope spirits. Next year the hunters will vainly search the dry plains for antelope. Thus it is necessary to return carefully the bones and hair, and the stalks and leaves to the earth who first created them. The spirits remain close by. They do not leave us.

The dead become dust, and in this becoming they are once more joined with the Mother. The ancient Pueblo people called the earth the Mother Creator of all things in this world. Her sister, the Corn Mother, occasionally merges with her because all succulent green life rises out of the depths of the earth.

Rocks and clay are part of the Mother. They emerge in various forms, but at some time before, they were smaller particles or great boulders. At a later time they may again become what they once were. Dust.

A rock shares this fate with us and with animals and plants as well. A rock has being or spirit, although we may not understand it. The spirit may differ from the spirit we know in animals or plants or in ourselves. In the end we all originate from the depths of the earth. Perhaps this is how all beings share in the spirit of the Creator. We do not know.

From the Emergence Place

Pueblo potters, the creators of petroglyphs and oral narratives, never conceived of removing themselves from the earth and sky. So long as the human consciousness remains *within* the hills, canyons, cliffs, and the plants, clouds, and sky, the term *landscape,* as it has entered the English language, is misleading. "A portion of territory the eye can comprehend in a single view" does not correctly describe the relationship between the human being and his or her surroundings. This assumes the viewer is somehow *outside* or *separate from* the territory he or she surveys. Viewers are as much a part of the landscape as the boulders they stand on. There is no high mesa edge or mountain peak where one can stand and not immediately be part of all that surrounds. Human identity is linked with all the elements of Creation through the clan: you might belong to the Sun Clan or the Lizard Clan or the Corn Clan or the Clay Clan. Standing deep within the natural world, the ancient Pueblo understood the thing as it was—the squash blossom, grasshopper, or rabbit itself could never be created by the human hand. Ancient Pueblos took the modest view that the thing itself (the landscape) could not be improved upon. The ancients did not presume to tamper with what had already been created. Thus *realism,* as we now recognize it in painting and sculpture, did not catch the imaginations of Pueblo people until recently.

The squash blossom itself is *one thing:* itself. So the ancient Pueblo potter abstracted what she saw to be the key elements of the squash blossom—the four symmetrical petals, with four symmetrical stamens in the center. These key elements, while suggesting the squash flower, also link it with the four cardinal directions. By representing only its intrinsic form, the squash flower is released from a limited meaning or restricted identity. Even in the most sophisticated abstract form, a squash flower or a cloud or a lightning bolt became intricately connected with a complex system of relationships which the ancient Pueblo people maintained with each other, and with the populous natural world they lived within. A bolt of lightning is itself, but at the same time it may mean much more. It may be a messenger of good fortune when summer rains are needed. It may deliver death, perhaps the result of manipulations by the Gunnadeyahs, destructive necromancers. Lightning may strike down an evil-doer. Or lightning may strike a person of good will. If the person survives, lightning endows him or her with heightened power.

Pictographs and petroglyphs of constellations or elk or antelope draw their magic in part from the process wherein the focus of all prayer and concentration is upon the thing itself, which, in its turn, guides the hunter's hand. Connection with the spirit dimensions requires a figure or form which is all-inclusive. A "lifelike" rendering of an elk is too restrictive. Only the elk is itself. A *realistic* rendering of an elk would be only one particular elk anyway. The purpose of the hunt rituals and magic is to make contact with *all* the spirits of the Elk.

The land, the sky, and all that is within them—the landscape—includes human beings. Interrelationships in the Pueblo landscape are complex and fragile. The unpredictability of the weather, the aridity and harshness of much of the terrain in the high plateau country explain in large part the relentless attention the ancient Pueblo people gave the sky and the earth around them. Survival depended upon harmony and cooperation not only among human beings, but among all things—the animate and the less animate, since rocks and mountains were known to move, to travel occasionally.

The ancient Pueblos believed the Earth and the Sky were sisters (or sister and brother in the post-Christian version). As long as good family relations are maintained, then the Sky will continue to bless her sister, the Earth, with rain, and the Earth's children will continue to survive. But the old stories recall incidents in which troublesome spirits or beings threaten the earth. In one story, a malicious ka'tsina, called the Gambler, seizes the Shiwana, or Rainclouds, the Sun's beloved children. The Shiwana are snared in magical power late one afternoon on a high mountain top. The Gambler takes the Rainclouds to his mountain stronghold where he locks them in the north room of his house. What was his idea? The Shiwana were beyond value. They brought life to all things on earth. The Gambler wanted a big stake to wager in his games of chance. But such greed, even on the part of only one being, had the effect of threatening the survival of all life on earth. Sun Youth, aided by old Grandmother Spider, outsmarts the Gambler and the rigged game, and the Rainclouds are set free. The drought ends, and once more life thrives on earth.

Through the Stories We Hear Who We Are

All summer the people watch the west horizon, scanning the sky from south to north for rain clouds. Corn must have moisture at the time the tassels form. Otherwise pollination will be incomplete, and the ears will be stunted and shriveled. An inadequate harvest may bring disaster. Stories told at Hopi, Zuni, and at Acoma and Laguna describe drought and starvation as recently as 1900. Precipitation in west-central New Mexico averages fourteen inches annually. The western pueblos are located at altitudes over 5,600 feet above sea level, where winter temperatures at night fall below freezing. Yet evidence of their presence in the high desert plateau country goes back ten thousand years. The ancient Pueblo people not only survived in this environment, but many years they thrived. In A.D. 1100 the people at Chaco Canyon had built cities with apartment buildings of stone five stories high. Their sophistication as sky-watchers was surpassed only by Mayan and Inca astronomers. Yet this vast complex of knowledge and belief, amassed for thousands of years, was never recorded in writing.

Instead, the ancient Pueblo people depended upon collective memory through successive generations to maintain and transmit an entire culture, a world view complete with proven strategies for survival. The oral narrative, or "story," became the medium in which the complex of Pueblo knowledge and belief was maintained. Whatever the event or the subject, the ancient people perceived the world and themselves within that world as part of an ancient continuous story composed of innumerable bundles of other stories.

The ancient Pueblo vision of the world was inclusive. The impulse was to leave nothing out. Pueblo oral tradition necessarily embraced all levels of human experience. Otherwise, the collective knowledge and beliefs comprising ancient Pueblo culture would have been incomplete. Thus stories about the Creation and Emergence of human beings and animals into this World continue to be retold each year for four days and four nights during the winter solstice. The "humma-hah" stories related events from the time long ago when human beings were still able to communicate with animals and other living things. But, beyond these two preceding categories, the Pueblo oral tradition knew no boundaries. Accounts of the appearance of the first Europeans in Pueblo country or of the tragic encounters between Pueblo people and Apache raiders were no more and no less important than stories about the biggest mule deer ever taken or adulterous couples surprised in cornfields and chicken coops. Whatever happened, the ancient people instinctively sorted events and details into a loose narrative structure. Everything became a story.

Traditionally everyone, from the youngest child to the oldest person, was expected to listen and to be able to recall or tell a portion, if only a small detail, from a narrative account or story. Thus the remembering and retelling were a communal process. Even if a key figure, an elder who knew much more than others, were to die unexpectedly, the system would remain intact. Through the efforts of a great many people, the community was able to piece together valuable accounts and crucial information that might otherwise have died with an individual.

Communal storytelling was a self-correcting process in which listeners were encouraged to speak up if they noted an important fact or detail omitted. The people were happy to listen to two or three different versions of the same event or the same humma-hah story. Even conflicting versions of an incident were welcomed for the entertainment they provided. Defenders of each version might joke and tease one another, but seldom were there any direct confrontations. Implicit in the Pueblo oral tradition was the awareness that loyalties, grudges, and kinship must always influence the narrator's choices as she emphasizes to listeners this is the way *she* has always heard the story told. The ancient Pueblo people sought a communal truth, not an absolute. For them this truth lived somewhere within the web of differing versions, disputes over minor points, outright contradictions tangling with old feuds and village rivalries.

A dinner-table conversation, recalling a deer hunt forty years ago when the largest mule deer ever was taken, inevitably stimulates similar memories in listeners. But hunting stories were not merely after-dinner entertainment. These accounts contained information of critical importance about behavior and migration patterns of mule deer. Hunting stories carefully described key landmarks and locations of fresh water. Thus a deer-hunt story might also serve as a "map." Lost travelers, and lost piñon-nut gatherers, have been saved by sighting a rock formation they recognize only because they once heard a hunting story describing this rock formation.

The importance of cliff formations and water holes does not end with hunting stories. As offspring of the Mother Earth, the ancient Pueblo people could not conceive of themselves within a specific landscape. Location, or "place," nearly always plays a central role in the Pueblo oral narratives. Indeed, stories are most frequently recalled as people are passing by a specific geographical feature or the exact place where a story takes place. The precise date of the incident often is less important than the place or location of the happening. "Long, long ago," "a long time ago," "not too long ago," and "recently" are usually how stories are classified in terms of time. But the places where the stories occur are precisely located, and prominent geographical details recalled, even if the landscape is well-known to listeners. Often because the turning point in the narrative involved a peculiarity or special quality of a rock or tree or plant found only at that place. Thus, in the case of many of the Pueblo narratives, it is impossible to determine which came first: the incident or the geographical feature which begs to be brought alive in a story that features some unusual aspect of this location.

There is a giant sandstone boulder about a mile north of Old Laguna, on the road to Paguate. It is ten feet tall and twenty feet in circumference. When I was a child, and we would pass this boulder driving to Paguate village, someone usually made reference to the story about Kochininako, Yellow Woman, and the Estrucuyo, a monstrous giant who nearly ate her. The Twin Hero Brothers saved Kochininako, who had been out hunting rabbits to take home to feed her mother and sisters. The Hero Brothers had heard her cries just in time. The Estrucuyo had cornered her in a cave too small to fit its monstrous head. Kochininako had already thrown to the Estrucuyo all her rabbits, as well as her moccasins and most of her clothing. Still the creature had not been satisfied. After killing the Estrucuyo with their bows and arrows, the Twin Hero Brothers slit open the Estrucuyo and cut out its heart. They threw the heart as far as they could. The monster's heart landed there, beside the old trail to Paguate village, where the sandstone boulder rests now.

It may be argued that the existence of the boulder precipitated the creation of a story to explain it. But sandstone boulders and sandstone formations of strange shapes abound in the Laguna Pueblo area. Yet most of them do not have stories. Often the crucial element in a narrative is the terrain—some specific detail of the setting.

A high dark mesa rises dramatically from a grassy plain fifteen miles southeast of Laguna, in an area known as Swanee. On the grassy plain one hundred and forty years ago, my great-grandmother's uncle and his brother-in-law were grazing their herd of sheep. Because visibility on the plain extends for over twenty miles, it wasn't until the two sheepherders came near the high dark mesa that the Apaches were able to stalk them. Using the mesa to obscure their approach, the raiders swept around from both ends of the mesa. My great-grandmother's relatives were killed, and the herd lost. The high dark mesa played a critical role: the mesa had compromised the safety which the openness of the plains had seemed to assure. Pueblo and Apache alike relied upon the terrain, the very earth herself, to give them protection and aid. Human activities or needs were maneuvered to fit the existing surroundings and conditions. I imagine the last afternoon of my distant ancestors as warm and sunny for late September. They might have been traveling slowly, bringing the sheep closer to Laguna in preparation for the approach of colder weather. The grass was tall and only beginning to change from green to a yellow which matched the late-afternoon sun shining off it. There might have been comfort in the warmth and the sight of the sheep fattening on good pasture which lulled my ancestors into their fatal inattention. They might have had a rifle whereas the Apaches had only bows and arrows. But there would have been four or five Apache raiders, and the surprise attack would have canceled any advantage the rifles gave them.

Survival in any landscape comes down to making the best use of all available resources. On that particular September afternoon, the raiders made better use of the Swanee terrain than my poor ancestors did. Thus the high dark mesa and the story of the two lost Laguna herders became inextricably linked. The memory of them and their story resides in part with the high black mesa. For as long as the mesa stands, people within the family and clan will be reminded of the story of that afternoon long ago. Thus the continuity and accuracy of the oral narratives are reinforced by the landscape—and the Pueblo interpretation of that landscape is *maintained.*

POSSIBILITIES FOR WRITING

1. Consider Silko's final story about the slaughter of her own ancestors. In what ways does this story explain, elaborate on, and summarize the central points she makes throughout the essay?
2. Compare Silko's observations with those of N. Scott Momaday in "The Way to Rainy Mountain" (pages 411–417). Based on these two essays, what are some similarities and differences between the two writers' native cultures?
3. Write an essay about a landscape that has significant meaning for you. How similar and different is it for you to attempt to view the landscape as Silko describes here?

Susan Sontag (1933–2004) *was one of America's most prominent intellectuals, having been involved with the world of ideas all her life. After studying at the University of California at Berkeley, she earned a B.A. in philosophy from the University of Chicago at the age of eighteen, after which she studied religion at the Union Theological Seminary in New York, then philosophy and literature at Harvard, receiving master's degrees in both fields. Sontag also studied at Oxford and the Sorbonne. From the other side of the desk, she taught and lectured extensively at universities around the world, but for many years she made her academic home at Columbia and Rutgers universities. Sontag's books range widely, and include a collection of stories,* I, etcetera (1978); *a play,* Alice in Bed (1993); *and six volumes of essays, including* Against Interpretation (1966), Illness as Metaphor (1978), *and* On Photography (1977). *Among her four novels are* The Volcano Lover (1992), *which was a best-seller, and* In America (2000), *which won the National Book Critics Circle Award. In addition, Sontag wrote and directed four feature-length films and was a human rights activist for more than two decades. She was also a MacArthur Fellow.*

SUSAN SONTAG

A Woman's Beauty: Put-Down or Power Source?

In "A Woman's Beauty: Put-Down or Power Source?" Susan Sontag displays her historical interest as well as her interest in current attitudes toward gender roles. In arguing against the dangerous and limiting ideals to which women have subjected themselves (and been subjected by men), Sontag brings to bear a brisk analysis of Greek and Christian perspectives, implicating both in their consequences for contemporary women's obsessive and compulsive efforts to make themselves beautiful.

For the Greeks, beauty was a virtue: a kind of excellence. Persons then were assumed to be what we now have to call—lamely, enviously—*whole* persons. If it did occur to the Greeks to distinguish between a person's "inside" and "outside," they still expected that inner beauty would be matched by beauty of the other kind. The well-born young Athenians who gathered around Socrates found it quite paradoxical that their hero was so intelligent, so brave, so honorable, so seductive—and so ugly. One of Socrates' main pedagogical acts was to be ugly—and teach those innocent, no doubt splendid-looking disciples of his how full of paradoxes life really was.

They may have resisted Socrates' lesson. We do not. Several thousand years later, we are more wary of the enchantments of beauty. We not only split off—with the greatest facility—the "inside" (character, intellect) from the "outside" (looks); but we are actually surprised when someone who is beautiful is also intelligent, talented, good.

It was principally the influence of Christianity that deprived beauty of the central place it had in classical ideals of human excellence. By limiting excellence (*virtus* in Latin) to *moral* virtue only, Christianity set beauty adrift—as an alienated, arbitrary, superficial enchantment. And beauty has continued to lose prestige. For close to two centuries it has become a convention to attribute beauty to only one of the two sexes: the sex which, however Fair, is always Second. Associating beauty with women has put beauty even further on the defensive, morally.

A beautiful woman, we say in English. But a handsome man. "Handsome" is the masculine equivalent of—and refusal of—a compliment which has accumulated certain demeaning overtones, by being reserved for women only. That one can call a man "beautiful" in French and in Italian suggests that Catholic countries—unlike those countries shaped by the Protestant version of Christianity—still retain some vestiges of the pagan admiration for beauty. But the difference, if one exists, is of degree only. In every modern country that is Christian or post-Christian, women *are* the beautiful sex—to the detriment of the notion of beauty as well as of women.

To be called beautiful is thought to name something essential to women's character and concerns. (In contrast to men—whose essence is to be strong, or effective, or competent.) It does not take someone in the throes of advanced feminist awareness to perceive that the way women are taught to be involved with beauty encourages narcissism, reinforces dependence and immaturity. Everybody (women and men) knows that. For it is "everybody," a whole society, that has identified being feminine with caring about how one *looks*. (In contrast to being masculine—which is identified with caring about what one *is* and *does* and only secondarily, if at all, about how one looks.) Given these stereotypes, it is no wonder that beauty enjoys, at best, a rather mixed reputation.

It is not, of course, the desire to be beautiful that is wrong but the obligation to be—or to try. What is accepted by most women as a flattering idealization of their sex is a way of making women feel inferior to what they actually are—or normally grow to be. For the ideal of beauty is administered as a form of self-oppression. Women are taught to see their bodies in *parts*, and to evaluate each part separately. Breasts, feet, hips, waistline, neck, eyes, nose, complexion, hair, and so on—each in turn is submitted to an anxious, fretful, often despairing scrutiny. Even if some pass muster, some will always be found wanting. Nothing less than perfection will do.

In men, good looks is a whole, something taken in at a glance. It does not need to be confirmed by giving measurements of different regions of the body; nobody encourages a man to dissect his appearance, feature by feature. As for perfection, that is considered trivial—almost unmanly. Indeed, in the ideally good-looking man a small imperfection or blemish is considered positively desirable. According to one movie critic (a woman) who is a declared Robert Redford fan, it is having that cluster of skin-colored moles on one cheek that saves Redford from being merely a "pretty face." Think of the depreciation of women—as well as of beauty—that is implied in that judgment.

"The privileges of beauty are immense," said Cocteau. To be sure, beauty is a form of power. And deservedly so. What is lamentable is that it is the only form of power that most women are encouraged to seek. This power is always conceived in relation to men; it is not the power to do but the power to attract. It is a power that negates itself. For this power is not one that can be chosen freely—at least, not by women—or renounced without social censure.

To preen, for a woman, can never be just a pleasure. It is also a duty. It is her work. If a woman does real work—and even if she has clambered up to a leading position in politics, law, medicine, business, or whatever—she is always under pressure to confess that she still works at being attractive. But in so far as she is keeping up as one of the Fair Sex, she brings under suspicion her very capacity to be objective, professional, authoritative, thoughtful. Damned if they do—women are. And damned if they don't.

One could hardly ask for more important evidence of the dangers of considering persons as split between what is "inside" and what is "outside" than that interminable half-comic half-tragic tale, the oppression of women. How easy it is to start off by defining women as caretakers of their surfaces, and then to disparage them (or find them adorable) for being "superficial." It is a crude trap, and it has worked for too long. But to get out of the trap requires that women get some critical distance from that excellence and privilege which is beauty, enough distance to see how much beauty itself has been abridged in order to prop up the mythology of the "feminine." There should be a way of saving beauty *from* women—and *for* them.

POSSIBILITIES FOR WRITING

1. Consider the extent to which you agree (or disagree) with Sontag regarding what she says about the plight of contemporary women with respect to beauty. To what extent are men responsible for women's obsession with beauty? To what extent are women themselves responsible? Explain.

2. Sontag makes a brief historical excursion to consider the place of beauty in classical Greek culture and in early Christian times. How effective is this excursion into history? How important is it for Sontag's argument? And how persuasive is Sontag's use of these references?

3. Do your own little study of women's attitudes to beauty by surveying women you know in varying age groups. Consider both what they say and what they do with regard to the use of beauty products. Write up your findings and your analysis of the significance of beauty for women today.

Elizabeth Cady Stanton (1815–1902), an important leader of the early women's movement, was born in Johnstown, New York, and received a rigorous education for a woman of her day at the Troy Female Seminary. After attending a congress of abolitionists during which women were barred from participating, she was inspired to promote greater equality for women. She helped organize the first women's rights convention in Seneca Falls, New York, in 1848, and she continued to be a strong leader in the movement to gain women the right to vote, to liberalize divorce laws, and to help women achieve parity with men in terms of education, employment, and legal status. The mother of seven children, she was nevertheless a tireless organizer, lecturer, and writer for the cause as president of major women's suffrage associations from 1869 until her death.

ELIZABETH CADY STANTON

Declaration of Sentiments and Resolutions

Elizabeth Cady Stanton's "Declaration of Sentiments and Resolutions" was created at the Seneca Falls Convention, at which women gathered in Seneca Falls, New York, to assert their rights and demand equal respect as full U.S. citizens. In the "Declaration," Stanton makes clear and purposeful reference to the U.S. Declaration of Independence. At certain points, Stanton uses the exact wording of the American Declaration. But she adds "women" to the equation.

When, in the course of human events, it becomes necessary for one portion of the family of man to assume among the people of the earth a position different from that which they have hitherto occupied, but one to which the laws of nature and of nature's God entitle them, a decent respect to the opinions of mankind requires that they should declare the causes that impel them to such a course.

We hold these truths to be self-evident: that all men and women are created equal; that they are endowed by their Creator with certain inalienable rights; that among these are life, liberty, and the pursuit of happiness; that to secure these rights governments are instituted, deriving their just powers from the consent of the governed. Whenever any form of government becomes destructive of these ends, it is the right of those who suffer from it to refuse allegiance to it, and to insist upon the institution of a new government, laying its foundation on such principles, and organizing its powers in such form, as to them shall seem most likely to effect their safety and happiness. Prudence, indeed, will dictate that governments long established should not be changed for light and transient causes; and accordingly all experience hath shown that mankind are more disposed to suffer, while evils are sufferable, than to right themselves by abolishing the forms to which they were accustomed. But when a long train of abuses and usurpations, pursuing invariably the same object, evinces a design to reduce them under absolute despotism, it is their duty to throw off such government, and to provide new guards for their future security. Such has been the patient sufferance of the women under this government, and such is now the necessity which constrains them to demand the equal station to which they are entitled.

The history of mankind is a history of repeated injuries and usurpations on the part of man toward woman, having in direct object the establishment of an absolute tyranny over her. To prove this, let facts be submitted to a candid world.

He has never permitted her to exercise her inalienable right to the elective franchise.

He has compelled her to submit to laws, in the formation of which she had no voice.

He has withheld from her rights which are given to the most ignorant and degraded men—both natives and foreigners.

Having deprived her of this first right of a citizen, the elective franchise, thereby leaving her without representation in the halls of legislation, he has oppressed her on all sides.

He has made her, if married, in the eye of the law, civilly dead.

He has taken from her all right in property, even to the wages she earns.

He has made her, morally, an irresponsible being, as she can commit many crimes with impunity, provided they be done in the presence of her husband. In the covenant of marriage, she is compelled to promise obedience to her husband, he becoming, to all intents and purposes, her master—the law giving him power to deprive her of her liberty, and to administer chastisement.

He has so framed the laws of divorce, as to what shall be the proper causes, and in case of separation, to whom the guardianship of the children shall be given, as to be wholly regardless of the happiness of women—the law, in all cases, going upon a false supposition of the supremacy of man, and giving all power into his hands.

After depriving her of all rights as a married woman, if single, and the owner of property, he has taxed her to support a government which recognizes her only when her property can be made profitable to it.

He has monopolized nearly all the profitable employments, and from those she is permitted to follow, she receives but a scanty remuneration. He closes against her all the avenues to wealth and distinction which he considers most honorable to himself. As a teacher of theology, medicine, or law, she is not known.

He has denied her the facilities for obtaining a thorough education, all colleges being closed against her.

He allows her in Church, as well as State, but a subordinate position, claiming Apostolic authority for her exclusion from the ministry, and, with some exceptions, from any public participation in the affairs of the Church.

He has created a false public sentiment by giving to the world a different code of morals for men and women, by which moral delinquencies which exclude women from society, are not only tolerated, but deemed of little account in man.

He has usurped the prerogative of Jehovah himself, claiming it as his right to assign for her a sphere of action, when that belongs to her conscience and to her God.

He has endeavored, in every way that he could, to destroy her confidence in her own powers, to lessen her self-respect, and to make her willing to lead a dependent and abject life.

Now, in view of this entire disfranchisement of one-half the people of this country, their social and religious degradation—in view of the unjust laws above mentioned, and because women do feel themselves aggrieved, oppressed, and fraudulently deprived of their most sacred rights, we insist that they have immediate admission to all the rights and privileges which belong to them as citizens of the United States.

In entering upon the great work before us, we anticipate no small amount of misconception, misrepresentation, and ridicule; but we shall use every instrumentality within our power to effect our object. We shall employ agents, circulate tracts, petition the State and National legislatures, and endeavor to enlist the pulpit and the press in our behalf. We hope this Convention will be followed by a series of Conventions embracing every part of the country.

POSSIBILITIES FOR WRITING

1. Analyze the list of grievances Stanton enumerates. In particular, consider the extent to which these follow a logical sequence, building one upon another. Do you find that they lead successfully to her larger conclusion? Why or why not?

2. Based on your reading of Stanton's Declaration, how were women viewed in 1848, when the document was drafted and delivered—that is, what arguments *against* Stanton's position seem to have prevailed at the time? For example, how might denying women any right to vote, the most controversial grievance listed in the document, have been justified? You might do some research in responding to this question.

3. Draft your own Declaration based on Jefferson's (pages 280–288) and Stanton's. Cast yourself as a member of an aggrieved party, explain your grievances, and end with a call to action. Your effort may be serious, or you may focus on more light-hearted grievances (those of first-year college students, for example).

Jonathan Swift (1667–1745) was born to English parents in Dublin, Ireland, and received a degree from Trinity College there. Unable to obtain a living in Ireland, he worked for some years as a secretary to a nobleman in Surrey, England, during which time he became acquainted with some of the most important literary figures of his day. He eventually returned to Ireland to assume a clerical post but still spent much of his time among the literary set in London. Swift published several volumes of romantic poetry and a wide variety of literary lampoons and political broadsides, but he is best known today for Gulliver's Travels (1726), a sharp satire of human foibles. Appointed Dean of Dublin's St. Patrick's Cathedral in 1713, Swift was a tireless defender of the Irish in their struggle against England's harsh, sometimes unbearable rule.

JONATHAN SWIFT

A Modest Proposal

Jonathan Swift's "A Modest Proposal" is among the most famous satires in English. In it Swift—or rather the persona or speaker he creates to make the modest proposal—recommends killing Irish babies at one year of age. The speaker makes this proposal as a way to solve a severe economic problem that occasions great human suffering: the overpopulation of the Irish people, particularly among Irish Catholics.

It is a melancholy object to those who walk through this great town or travel in the country, when they see the streets, the roads, and cabin doors, crowded with beggars of the female sex, followed by three, four, or six children, all in rags and importuning every passenger for an alms. These mothers, instead of being able to work for their honest livelihood, are forced to employ all their time in strolling to beg sustenance for their helpless infants, who, as they grow up, either turn thieves for want of work, or leave their dear native country to fight for the Pretender in Spain, or sell themselves to the Barbadoes.

I think it is agreed by all parties that this prodigious number of children in the arms, or on the backs, or at the heels of their mothers, and frequently of their fathers, is in the present deplorable state of the kingdom a very great additional grievance; and therefore whoever could find out a fair, cheap, and easy method of making these children sound, useful members of the commonwealth would deserve so well of the public as to have his statue set up for a preserver of the nation.

But my intention is very far from being confined to provide only for the children of professed beggars; it is of a much greater extent, and shall take in the whole number of infants at a certain age who are born of parents in effect as little able to support them as those who demand our charity in the streets.

As to my own part, having turned my thoughts for many years upon this important subject, and maturely weighed the several schemes of other projectors, I have always found them grossly mistaken in their computation. It is true, a child just dropped from its dam may be supported by her milk for a solar year, with little other nourishment; at most not above the value of two shillings, which the mother may certainly get, or the value in scraps, by her lawful occupation of begging; and it is exactly at one year old that I propose to provide for them in such a manner as instead of being a charge upon their parents or the parish, or wanting food and raiment for the rest of their lives, they shall on the contrary contribute to the feeding, and partly to the clothing, of many thousands.

There is likewise another great advantage in my scheme, that it will prevent those voluntary abortions, and that horrid practice of women murdering their bastard children, alas, too frequent among us, sacrificing the poor innocent babes, I doubt, more to avoid the expense than the shame, which would move tears and pity in the most savage and inhuman breast.

The number of souls in this kingdom being usually reckoned one million and a half, of these I calculate there may be about two hundred thousand couples whose wives are breeders; from which number I subtract thirty thousand couples who are able to maintain their own children, although I apprehend there cannot be so many under the present distresses of the kingdom; but this being granted, there will remain an hundred and seventy thousand breeders. I again subtract fifty thousand for those women who miscarry, or whose children die by accident or disease within the year. There only remain an hundred and twenty thousand children of poor parents annually born. The question therefore is, how this number shall be reared and provided for, which, as I have already said, under the present situation of affairs, is utterly impossible by all the methods hitherto proposed. For we can neither employ them in handicraft or agriculture; we neither build houses (I mean in the country) nor cultivate land. They can very seldom pick up a livelihood by stealing till they arrive at six years old, except where they are of towardly parts; although I confess they learn the rudiments much earlier, during which time they can however be looked upon only as probationers, as I have been informed by a principal gentleman in the county of Cavan, who protested to me that he never knew above one or two instances under the age of six, even in a part of the kingdom so renowned for the quickest proficiency in that art.

I am assured by our merchants that a boy or a girl before twelve years old is no salable commodity; and even when they come to this age they will not yield above three pounds, or three pounds and half a crown at most on the Exchange; which cannot turn to account either to the parents or the kingdom, the charge of nutriment and rags having been at least four times that value.

I shall now therefore humbly propose my own thoughts, which I hope will not be liable to the least objection.

I have been assured by a very knowing American of my acquaintance in London, that a young healthy child well nursed is at a year old a most delicious, nourishing, and wholesome food, whether stewed, roasted, baked, or boiled; and I make no doubt that it will equally serve in a fricassee or a ragout.

I do therefore humbly offer it to public consideration that of the hundred and twenty thousand children already computed, twenty thousand may be reserved for breed, whereof only one fourth part to be males, which is more than we allow to sheep, black cattle, or swine; and my reason is that these children are seldom the fruits of marriage, a circumstance not much regarded by our savages, therefore one male will be sufficient to serve four females. That the remaining hundred thousand may at a year old be offered in sale to the persons of quality and fortune through the kingdom, always advising the mother to let them suck plentifully in the last month, so as to render them plump and fat for a good table. A child will make two dishes at an entertainment for friends; and when the family dines alone, the fore or hind quarter will make a reasonable dish, and seasoned with a little pepper or salt will be very good boiled on the fourth day, especially in winter.

I have reckoned upon a medium that a child just born will weigh twelve pounds, and in a solar year, if tolerably nursed, increaseth to twenty-eight pounds.

I grant this food will be somewhat dear, and therefore very proper for landlords, who, as they have already devoured most of the parents, seem to have the best title to the children.

Infant's flesh will be in season throughout the year, but more plentiful in March, and a little before and after. For we are told by a grave author, an eminent French physician, that fish being a prolific diet, there are more children born in Roman Catholic countries about nine months after Lent than at any other season; therefore, reckoning a year after Lent, the markets will be more glutted than usual, because the number of popish infants is at least three to one in this kingdom; and therefore it will have one other collateral advantage, by lessening the number of Papists among us.

I have already computed the charge of nursing a beggar's child (in which list I reckon all cottagers, laborers, and four fifths of the farmers) to be about two shillings per annum, rags included; and I believe no gentleman would repine to give ten shillings for the carcass of a good fat child, which, as I have said, will make four dishes of excellent nutritive meat, when he hath only some particular friend or his own family to dine with him. Thus the squire will learn to be a good landlord, and grow popular among the tenants; the mother will have eight shillings net profit, and be fit for work till she produces another child.

Those who are more thrifty (as I must confess the times require) may flay the carcass; the skin of which artificially dressed will make admirable gloves for ladies, and summer boots for fine gentlemen.

As to our city of Dublin, shambles may be appointed for this purpose in the most convenient parts of it, and butchers we may be assured will not be wanting; although I rather recommend buying the children alive, and dressing them hot from the knife as we do roasting pigs.

A very worthy person, a true lover of his country, and whose virtues I highly esteem, was lately pleased in discoursing on this matter to offer a refinement upon my scheme. He said that many gentlemen of this kingdom, having of late destroyed their deer, he conceived that the want of venison might be well supplied by the bodies of young lads and maidens, not exceeding fourteen years of age nor under twelve, so great a number of both sexes in every county being now ready to starve for want of work and service; and these to be disposed of by their parents, if alive, or otherwise by their nearest relations. But with due deference to so excellent a friend and so deserving a patriot, I cannot be altogether in his sentiments; for as to the males, my American acquaintance assured me from frequent experience that their flesh was generally tough and lean, like that of our schoolboys, by continual exercise, and their taste disagreeable; and to fatten them would not answer the charge. Then as to the females, it would, I think with humble submission, be a loss to the public, because they soon would become breeders themselves: and besides, it is not improbable that some scrupulous people might be apt to censure such a practice (although indeed very unjustly) as a little bordering upon cruelty; which, I confess, hath always been with me the strongest objection against any project, how well soever intended.

But in order to justify my friend, he confessed that this expedient was put into his head by the famous Psalmanazar, a native of the island Formosa, who came from thence to London above twenty years ago, and in conversation told my friend that in his country when any young person happened to be put to death, the executioner sold the carcass to persons of quality as a prime dainty; and that in his time the body of a plump girl of fifteen, who was crucified for an attempt to poison the emperor, was sold to his Imperial Majesty's prime minister of state, and other great mandarins of the court, in joints from the gibbet, at four hundred crowns. Neither indeed can I deny that if the same use were made of several plump young girls in this town, who without one single groat to their fortunes cannot stir abroad without a chair, and appear at the playhouse and assemblies in foreign fineries which they never will pay for, the kingdom would not be the worse.

Some persons of a desponding spirit are in great concern about that vast number of poor people who are aged, diseased, or maimed, and I have been desired to employ my thoughts what course may be taken to ease the nation of so grievous an encumbrance. But I am not in the least pain upon that matter, because it is very well known that they are every day dying and rotting by cold and famine, and filth and vermin, as fast as can be reasonably expected. And as to the younger laborers, they are now in almost as hopeful a condition. They cannot get work, and consequently pine away for want of nourishment to a degree that if at any time they are accidentally hired to common labor, they have not strength to perform it; and thus the country and themselves are happily delivered from the evils to come.

I have too long digressed, and therefore shall return to my subject. I think the advantages by the proposal which I have made are obvious and many, as well as of the highest importance.

For first, as I have already observed, it would greatly lessen the number of Papists, with whom we are yearly overrun, being the principal breeders of the nation as well as our most dangerous enemies; and who stay at home on purpose to deliver the kingdom to the Pretender, hoping to take their advantage by the absence of so many good Protestants, who have chosen rather to leave their country than to stay at home and pay tithes against their conscience to an Episcopal curate.

Secondly, the poorer tenants will have something valuable of their own, which by law may be made liable to distress, and help to pay their landlord's rent, their corn and cattle being already seized and money a thing unknown.

Thirdly, whereas the maintenance of an hundred thousand children, from two years old and upwards, cannot be computed at less than ten shillings a piece per annum, the nation's stock will be thereby increased fifty thousand pounds per annum, besides the profit of a new dish introduced to the tables of all gentlemen of fortune in the kingdom who have any refinement in taste. And the money will circulate among ourselves, the goods being entirely of our own growth and manufacture.

Fourthly, the constant breeders, besides the gain of eight shillings sterling per annum by the sale of their children, will be rid of the charge of maintaining them after the first year.

Fifthly, this food would likewise bring great custom to taverns, where the vintners will certainly be so prudent as to procure the best receipts for dressing it to perfection, and consequently have their houses frequented by all the fine gentlemen, who justly value themselves upon their knowledge in good eating; and a skillful cook, who understands how to oblige his guests, will contrive to make it as expensive as they please.

Sixthly, this would be a great inducement to marriage, which all wise nations have either encouraged by rewards or enforced by laws and penalties. It would increase the care and tenderness of mothers toward their children, when they were sure of a settlement for life to the poor babes, provided in some sort by the public, to their annual profit instead of expense. We should see an honest emulation among the married women, which of them could bring the fattest child to the market. Men would become as fond of their wives during the time of their pregnancy as they are now of their mares in foal, their cows in calf, or sows when they are ready to farrow; nor offer to beat or kick them (as is too frequent a practice) for fear of a miscarriage.

Many other advantages might be enumerated. For instance, the addition of some thousand carcasses in our exportation of barreled beef, the propagation of swine's flesh, and improvement in the art of making good bacon, so much wanted among us by the great destruction of pigs, too frequent at our tables, which are no way comparable in taste or magnificence to a well-grown, fat, yearling child, which roasted whole will make a considerable figure at a lord mayor's feast or any other public entertainment. But this and many others I omit, being studious of brevity.

Supposing that one thousand families in this city would be constant customers for infants' flesh, besides others who might have it at merry meetings, particularly weddings and christenings, I compute that Dublin would take off annually about twenty thousand carcasses, and the rest of the kingdom (where probably they will be sold some-what cheaper) the remaining eighty thousand.

I can think of no one objection that will possibly be raised against this proposal, unless it should be urged that the number of people will be thereby much lessened in the kingdom. This I freely own, and it was indeed one principal design in offering it to the world. I desire the reader will observe, that I calculate my remedy for this one individual kingdom of Ireland and for no other that ever was, is, or I think ever can be upon earth. Therefore let no man talk to me of other expedients: of taxing our absentees at five shillings a pound: of using neither clothes nor household furniture except what is of our own growth and manufacture: of utterly rejecting the materials and instruments that promote foreign luxury: of curing the expensiveness of pride, vanity, idleness, and gaming in our women: of introducing a vein of parsimony, prudence, and temperance: of learning to love our country, in the want of which we differ even from Laplanders and the inhabitants of Topinamboo: of quitting our animosities and factions, nor acting any longer like the Jews, who were murdering one another at the very moment their city was taken: of being a little cautious not to sell our country and conscience for nothing: of teaching landlords to have at least one degree of mercy toward their tenants: lastly, of putting a spirit of honesty, industry, and skill into our shopkeepers; who, if a resolution could now be taken to buy only our native goods, would immediately unite to cheat and exact upon us in the price, the measure, and the goodness, nor could ever yet be brought to make one fair proposal of just dealing, though often and earnestly invited to it.

Therefore I repeat, let no man talk to me of these and the like expedients, till he hath at least some glimpse of hope that there will ever be some hearty and sincere attempt to put them in practice.

But as to myself, having been wearied out for many years with offering vain, idle, visionary thoughts, and at length utterly despairing of success, I fortunately fell upon this proposal, which, as it is wholly new, so it hath something solid and real, of no expense and little trouble, full in our own power, and whereby we can incur no danger in disobliging England. For this kind of commodity will not bear exportation, the flesh being of too tender a consistence to admit a long continuance in salt, although perhaps I could name a country which would be glad to eat up our whole nation without it.

After all, I am not so violently bent upon my own opinion as to reject any offer proposed by wise men, which shall be found equally innocent, cheap, easy, and effectual. But before something of that kind shall be advanced in contradiction to my scheme, and offering a better, I desire the author or authors will be pleased maturely to consider two points. First, as things now stand, how they will be able to find food and raiment for an hundred thousand useless mouths and backs. And secondly, there being a round million of creatures in human figure throughout this kingdom, whose sole subsistence put into a common stock would leave them in debt two millions of pounds sterling, adding those who are beggars by profession to the bulk of farmers, cottagers, and laborers, with their wives and children who are beggars in effect; I desire those politicians who dislike my overture, and may perhaps be so bold to attempt an answer, that they will first ask the parents of these mortals whether they would not at this day think it a great happiness to have been sold for food at a year old in the manner I prescribe, and thereby have avoided such a perpetual scene of misfortunes as they have since gone through by the oppression of landlords, the impossibility of paying rent without money or trade, the want of common sustenance, with neither house nor clothes to cover them from the inclemencies of the weather, and the most inevitable prospect of entailing the like or greater miseries upon their breed forever.

I profess, in the sincerity of my heart, that I have not the least personal interest in endeavoring to promote this necessary work, having no other motive than the public good of my country, by advancing our trade, providing for infants, relieving the poor, and giving some pleasure to the rich. I have no children by which I can propose to get a single penny; the youngest being nine years old, and my wife past childbearing.

POSSIBILITIES FOR WRITING

1. Throughout "A Modest Proposal," Swift uses language that dehumanizes the Irish people. Point out examples of such language, and explain their effect both in terms of Swift's satire and his underlying purpose.

2. Though Swift never fully drops his mask, he does make a number of veiled appeals toward sympathy for the Irish and legitimate suggestions for alleviating their predicament. Citing the text, examine when and where he does so. How can you recognize his seriousness?

3. Write a "modest proposal" of your own in which you offer an outrageous solution to alleviate some social problem. Make sure that readers understand that your proposal is satirical and that they recognize your real purpose in writing.

Paul Theroux (b. 1941) *is a novelist and travel writer. Born in Medford, Massachusetts, Theroux was educated there and at the University of Maine and the University of Massachusetts, from which he graduated with a B.A. in English. He joined the Peace Corps, from which he was later expelled for political activity in Malawi. Among his books are the nonfiction travel work* The Great Railway Bazaar *(1975) and the novel* The Mosquito Coast *(1981). More recent works in each genre, respectively, are* The Tao of Travel *(2011) and* The Lower River *(2012).*

PAUL THEROUX

Being a Man

In "Being a Man," Paul Theroux expresses his dissatisfaction with being expected to live up to an image of manhood that he detests. In the course of complaining about various aspects of the male mystique, Theroux raises questions about what it means to be a man in America today. Throughout his essay, Theroux makes a number of comments about women—largely to clarify his views about masculinity.

There is a pathetic sentence in the chapter "Fetishism" in Dr. Norman Cameron's book *Personality Development and Psychopathology*. It goes, "Fetishists are nearly always men; and their commonest fetish is a woman's shoe." I cannot read that sentence without thinking that it is just one more awful thing about being a man—and perhaps it is an important thing to know about us.

I have always disliked being a man. The whole idea of manhood in America is pitiful, in my opinion. This version of masculinity is a little like having to wear an ill-fitting coat for one's entire life (by contrast, I imagine femininity to be an oppressive sense of nakedness). Even the expression "Be a man!" strikes me as insulting and abusive. It means: Be stupid, be unfeeling, obedient, soldierly, and stop thinking. Man means "manly"—how can one think about men without considering the terrible ambition of manliness? And yet it is part of every man's life. It is a hideous and crippling lie; it not only insists on difference and connives at superiority, it is also by its very nature destructive—emotionally damaging and socially harmful.

The youth who is subverted, as most are, into believing in the masculine ideal is effectively separated from women and he spends the rest of his life finding women a riddle and a nuisance. Of course, there is a female version of this male affliction. It begins with mothers encouraging little girls to say (to other adults) "Do you like my new dress?"

In a sense, little girls are traditionally urged to please adults with a kind of coquettishness, while boys are enjoined to behave like monkeys towards each other. The nine-year-old coquette proceeds to become womanish in a subtle power game in which she learns to be sexually indispensable, socially decorative, and always alert to a man's sense of inadequacy.

Femininity—being ladylike—implies needing a man as witness and seducer; but masculinity celebrates the exclusive company of men. That is why it is so grotesque; and that is also why there is no manliness without inadequacy—because it denies men the natural friendship of women.

It is very hard to imagine any concept of manliness that does not belittle women, and it begins very early. At an age when I wanted to meet girls—let's say the treacherous years of thirteen to sixteen—I was told to take up a sport, get more fresh air, join the Boy Scouts, and I was urged not to read so much. It was the 1950s and if you asked too many questions about sex you were sent to camp—boy's camp, of course: the nightmare. Nothing is more unnatural or prisonlike than a boy's camp, but if it were not for them we would have no Elks' Lodges, no pool rooms, no boxing matches, no Marines.

And perhaps no sports as we know them. Everyone is aware of how few in number are the athletes who behave like gentlemen. Just as high school basketball teaches you how to be a poor loser, the manly attitude towards sports seems to be little more than a recipe for creating bad marriages, social misfits, moral degenerates, sadists, latent rapists, and just plain louts. I regard high school sports as a drug far worse than marijuana, and it is the reason that the average tennis champion, say, is a pathetic oaf.

Any objective study would find the quest for manliness essentially right-wing, puritanical, cowardly, neurotic, and fueled largely by a fear of women. It is also certainly philistine. There is no book-hater like a Little League coach. But indeed all the creative arts are obnoxious to the manly ideal, because at their best the arts are pursued by uncompetitive and essentially solitary people. It makes it very hard for a creative youngster, for any boy who expresses the desire to be alone seems to be saying that there is something wrong with him.

It ought to be clear by now that I have something of an objection to the way we turn boys into men. It does not surprise me that when the President of the United States has his customary weekend off he dresses like a cowboy—it is both a measure of his insecurity and his willingness to please. In many ways, American culture does little more for a man than prepare him for modeling clothes in the L. L. Bean catalogue. I take this as a personal insult because for many years I found it impossible to admit to myself that I wanted to be a writer. It was my guilty secret, because being a writer was incompatible with being a man.

There are people who might deny this, but that is because the American writer, typically, has been so at pains to prove his manliness that we have come to see literariness and manliness as mingled qualities. But first there was a fear that writing was not a manly profession—indeed, not a profession at all. (The paradox in American letters is that it has always been easier for a woman to write and for a man to be published.) Growing up, I had thought of sports as wasteful and humiliating, and the idea of manliness was a bore. My wanting to become a writer was not a flight from that oppressive role-playing, but I quickly saw that it was at odds with it. Everything in stereotyped manliness goes against the life of the mind. The Hemingway personality is too tedious to go into here, and in any case his exertions are well known, but certainly it was not until this aberrant behavior was examined by feminists in the 1960s that any male writer dared question the pugnacity in Hemingway's fiction. All the bullfighting and arm wrestling and elephant shooting diminished Hemingway as a writer, but it is consistent with a prevailing attitude in American writing: one cannot be a male writer without first proving that one is a man.

It is normal in America for a man to be dismissive or even somewhat apologetic about being a writer. Various factors make it easier. There is a heartiness about journalism that makes it acceptable—journalism is the manliest form of American writing and, therefore, the profession the most independent-minded women seek (yes, it is an illusion, but that is my point). Fiction-writing is equated with a kind of dispirited failure and is only manly when it produces wealth—money is masculinity. So is drinking. Being a drunkard is another assertion, if misplaced, of manliness. The American male writer is traditionally proud of his heavy drinking. But we are also a very literal-minded people. A man proves his manhood in America in old-fashioned ways. He kills lions, like Hemingway; or he hunts ducks, like Nathanael West; or he makes pronouncements like, "A man should carry enough knife to defend himself with," as James Jones once said to a *Life* interviewer. Or he says he can drink you under the table. But even tiny drunken William Faulkner loved to mount a horse and go fox hunting, and Jack Kerouac roistered up and down Manhattan in a lumberjack shirt (and spent every night of *The Subterraneans* with his mother in Queens).

And we are familiar with the lengths to which Norman Mailer is prepared, in his endearing way, to prove that he is just as much a monster as the next man.

When the novelist John Irving was revealed as a wrestler, people took him to be a very serious writer, and even a bubble reputation like Eric (*Love Story*) Segal's was enhanced by the news that he ran the marathon in a respectable time. How surprised we would be if Joyce Carol Oates were revealed as a Sumo wrestler or Joan Didion active in pumping iron. "Lives in New York City with her three children" is the typical woman writer's biographical note, for just as the male writer must prove he has achieved a sort of muscular manhood, the woman writer—or rather her publicists—must prove her motherhood.

There would be no point in saying any of this if it were not generally accepted that to be a man is somehow—even now in feminist-influenced America—a privilege. It is on the contrary an unmerciful and punishing burden. Being a man is bad enough; being manly is appalling (in this sense, women's lib has done much more for men than for women). It is the sinister silliness of men's fashions and a clubby attitude in the arts. It is the subversion of good students. It is the so-called Dress Code of the Ritz-Carlton Hotel in Boston, and it is the institutionalized cheating in college sports. It is the most primitive insecurity.

And this is also why men often object to feminism, but are afraid to explain why: of course women have a justified grievance, but most men believe—and with reason—that their lives are just as bad.

POSSIBILITIES FOR WRITING

1. Analyze Theroux's essay in terms of his complaints about cultural expectations of manhood. What does he object to and why in terms of these expectations about masculinity?
2. Analyze the humor in Theroux's essay. Explain what his humor contributes to his essay's tone and how humor helps him develop his argument.
3. Write an essay in which you explore the concept of masculinity or "manliness." Or of femininity, if you prefer. Identify the central aspects of masculinity or femininity and illustrate them with examples. Include personal experience if you like.

Lewis Thomas (1913–1993) was born in Flushing, New York, the son of a family doctor. He also became a physician, graduating from Princeton University and Harvard Medical School, and he spent most of his career on the faculty at Yale University's medical school. He also served as president of the Sloan-Kettering Memorial Cancer Center. In the early 1970s, he began contributing a monthly essay to the New England Journal of Medicine. *Personal and informal in nature, these short pieces achieved immediate popularity that spread well beyond the medical community. Thomas published his first collection,* The Lives of a Cell, *in 1974; it won the National Book Award. Four other collections followed, including* Late Night Thoughts on Listening to Mahler's Ninth Symphony *(1984) and* The Fragile Species *(1992), all praised for their insight and grace.*

LEWIS THOMAS

Crickets, Cats, Bats, and Chaos

In "Crickets, Cats, Bats, and Chaos," Lewis Thomas invites us to consider our relationships to other animals, namely the crickets, cats, and bats of his title. He encourages us to consider the extent to which such creatures can be said to "think," and the relationship between their forms of thinking and ours, particularly in how thinking aids survival. In the process, Thomas explores the concept of mind and awareness and what it might mean to become aware of our own awareness.

I am not sure where to classify the mind of my cat Jeoffry. He is a small Abyssinian cat, a creature of elegance, grace, and poise, a piece of moving sculpture, and a total mystery. We named him Jeoffry after the eighteenth-century cat celebrated by the unpredictable poet Christopher Smart in a poem titled "Jubilate Agno," one section of which begins, "For I will consider my cat Jeoffry." The following lines are selected more or less at random:

> For he counteracts the powers of darkness by
> his electrical skin and glaring eyes.
> For he counteracts the Devil, who is death, by
> brisking about the life . . .
> For he is of the tribe of Tiger . . .
> For he purrs in thankfulness, when God tells
> him he's a god Cat . . .
> For he is an instrument for the children to
> learn benevolence upon . . .
> For he is a mixture of gravity and waggery . . .

For there is nothing sweeter than his peace
when at rest.
For there is nothing brisker than his life when
in motion.

I have not the slightest notion what goes on in the mind of my cat Jeoffry, beyond the conviction that it is a genuine mind, with genuine thoughts and a strong tendency to chaos, but in all other respects a mind totally unlike mine. I have a hunch, based on long moments of observing him stretched on the rug in sunlight, that his mind has more periods of geometric order, and a better facility for switching itself almost, but not quite, entirely off, and accordingly an easier access to pure pleasure. Just as he is able to hear sounds that I cannot hear, and smell important things of which I am unaware, and suddenly leap like a crazed gymnast from chair to chair, upstairs and downstairs through the house, flawless in every movement and searching for something he never finds, he has periods of meditation on matters I know nothing about.

While thinking about what nonhumans think is, in most biological quarters, an outlandish question, even an impermissible one, to which the quick and easy answer is nothing, or almost nothing, or certainly nothing like *thought* as we use the word, I still think about it. For while none of them may have real thoughts, foresee the future, regret the past, or be self-aware, most of us up here at the peak of evolution cannot manage the awareness of our own awareness, a state of mind only achieved when the mind succeeds in emptying itself of all other information and switches off all messages, interior and exterior. This is the state of mind for which the Chinese Taoists long ago used a term meaning, literally, no-knowledge. With no-knowledge, it is said, you get a different look at the world, an illumination.

Falling short of this, as I do, and dispossessed of anything I could call illumination, it has become my lesser satisfaction to learn second-hand whatever I can, and then to think, firsthand, about the behavior of other kinds of animals.

I think of crickets, for instance, and the thought of their unique, very small thoughts—principally about mating and bats—but also about the state of cricket society. The cricket seems to me an eminently suitable animal for sorting out some of the emotional issues bound to arise in any consideration of animal awareness. Nobody, so far as I know, not even an eighteenth-century minor poet, could imagine any connection between events in the mind of a cricket and those in the mind of a human. If there was ever a creature in nature meriting the dismissive description of a living machine, mindless and thought-less, the cricket qualifies. So in talking about what crickets are up to when they communicate with each other, as they unmistakably do, by species-unique runs and rhythms of chirps and trills, there can be no question of *anthropomorphization*, that most awful of all terms for the deepest error a modern biologist can fall into.

If you reduce the temperature of a male cricket, the rate of his emission of chirping signals is correspondingly reduced. Indeed, some of the earlier naturalists used the technical term "thermometer crickets" because of the observation that you can make a close guess at the air temperature in a field by counting the rate of chirps of familiar crickets.

This is curious, but there is a much more curious thing going on when the weather changes. The female crickets in the same field, ge-netically coded to respond specifically to the chirp rhythm of their species, adjust their recognition mechanism to the same tempera-ture change and the same new, slower rate of chirps. That is, as John Doherty and Ronald Hoy wrote on observing the phenomenon, "warm females responded best to the songs of warm males, and cold females responded best to the songs of cold males." The same phenomenon, known as temperature coupling, has been encountered in grasshop-pers and tree frogs, and also in fireflies, with their flash communica-tion system. The receiving mind of the female cricket, if you are willing to call it that, adjusts itself immediately to match the sending mind of the male. This has always struck me as one of the neatest examples of animals adjusting to a change in their environment.

But I started thinking about crickets with something quite differ-ent in mind, namely bats. It has long been known that bats feed vo-raciously on the nocturnal flights of crickets and moths, which they detect on the wing by their fantastically accurate ultrasound mecha-nism. What should have been guessed at, considering the ingenuity of nature, is that certain cricket species, green lacewings, and certain moths have ears that can detect the ultrasound emissions of a bat, and can analyze the distance and direction from which the ultrasound is coming. These insects can employ two separate and quite distinct de-fensive maneuvers for evading the bat's keen sonar.

The first is simply swerving away. This is useful behavior when the bat signal is coming from a safe distance, twenty to thirty meters away. At this range the insect can detect the bat, but the bat is too far off to receive the bounced ultrasound back to its own ears. So the cricket or moth needs to do nothing more, at least for the moment, than swing out of earshot. But when the bat is nearby, three meters or less, the insect is in immediate and mortal danger, for now the bat's sonar provides an accurate localization. It is too late for swerving or veering; because of its superior speed, the bat can easily track such simple evasions. What to do? The answer has been provided by Kenneth Roeder, who designed a marvelous laboratory model for field studies, including instruments to imitate the intensity and direction of bat signals.

The answer, for a cricket or moth or lacewing who hears a bat homing in close by, is *chaos*. Instead of swerving away, the insect launches into wild, totally erratic, random flight patterns, as unpredictable as possible. This kind of response tends to confuse the bat and results in escape for the insect frequently, enough to have been selected by evolution as the final, stereotyped, "last chance" response to the threat. It has the look of a very smart move, whether thought out or not.

So chaos is part of the useful, everyday mental equipment of a cricket or a moth, and that, I submit, is something new to think about. I don't wish to push the matter beyond its possible significance, but it seems to me to justify a modest nudge. The long debate over the problem of animal awareness is not touched by the observation, but it does bring up the opposite side of that argument, the opposite of anthropomorphization. It is this: Leaving aside the deep question as to whether the lower animals have anything going on in their mind that we might accept as conscious thought, are there important events occurring in our human minds that are matched by habits of the animal mind?

Surely chaos is a capacious area of common ground. I am convinced that my own mind spends much of its waking hours, not to mention its sleeping time, in a state of chaos directly analogous to that of the cricket hearing the sound of the nearby bat. But there is a big difference. My chaos is not induced by a bat; it is not suddenly switched on in order to facilitate escape; it is not an evasive tactic set off by any new danger. It is, I think, the normal state of affairs, and not just for my brain in particular but for human brains in general. The chaos that is my natural state of being is rather like the concept of chaos that has emerged in higher mathematical circles in recent years.

As I understand it, and I am quick to say that I understand it only quite superficially, chaos occurs when any complex, dynamic system is perturbed by a small uncertainty in one or another of its subunits. The inevitable result is an amplification of the disturbance and then the spread of unpredictable, random behavior throughout the whole system. It is the total unpredictability and randomness that makes the word "chaos" applicable as a technical term, but it is not true that the behavior of the system becomes disorderly. Indeed, as James P. Crutchfield and his associates have written, "There is order in chaos: underlying chaotic behavior there are elegant geometric forms that create randomness in the same way as a card dealer shuffles a deck of cards or a blender mixes cake batter." The random behavior of a turbulent stream of water, or of the weather, or of Brownian movement, or of the central nervous system of a cricket in flight from a bat, are all determined by the same mathematical rules. Behavior of this sort has been encountered in computer models of large cities: When a small change was made in one small part of the city model, the amplification of the change resulted in enormous upheavals, none of them predictable, in the municipal behavior at remote sites in the models.

I suggest that a moth or a cricket has a small enough nervous system to *seem* predictable and orderly most of the time. There are not all that many neurons, and the circuitry contains what seem to be mostly simple reflex pathways. Laboratory experiments suggest that in a normal day, one thing—the sound of a bat at a safe distance, say—leads to another, predictable thing—a swerving off to one side in flight. It is only when something immensely new and important happens—the bat sound at three meters away—that the system is thrown into chaos.

I suggest that the difference with us is that chaos is the norm. Predictable, small-scale, orderly, cause-and-effect sequences are hard to come by and don't last long when they do turn up. Something else almost always turns up at the same time, and then another sequential thought intervenes alongside, and there come turbulence and chaos again. When we are lucky, and the system operates at its random best, something astonishing may suddenly turn up, beyond predicting or imagining. Events like these we recognize as good ideas.

My cat Jeoffry's brain is vastly larger and more commodious than that of a cricket, but I wonder if it is qualitatively all that different. The cricket lives with his two great ideas in mind, mating and predators, and his world is a world of particular, specified sounds. He is a tiny machine, I suppose, depending on what you mean by "machine," but it is his occasional moments of randomness and unpredictability that entitle him to be called aware. In order to achieve that feat of wild chaotic flight, and thus escape, he has to make use, literally, of his brain. When Int-1, an auditory interneuron, is activated by the sound of a bat closing in, the message is transmitted by an axon connected straight to the insect's brain, and it is here, and only here, that the swerving is generated. This I consider to be a thought, a very small thought, but still a thought. Without knowing what to count as a thought, I figure that Jeoffry, with his kind of brain, has a trillion thoughts of about the same size in any waking moment. As for me, and my sort of brain, I can't think where to begin.

We like to think of our minds as containing trains of thought, or streams of consciousness, as though they were orderly arrangements of linear events, one notion leading in a cause-and-effect way to the next notion. Logic is the way to go; we set a high price on logic, unlike E. M. Forster's elderly lady in *Aspects of the Novel*, who, when accused of being illogical, replied, "Logic? Good gracious! What rubbish! How can I tell what I think till I see what I say?"

But with regard to our own awareness of nature, I believe we've lost sight of, lost track of, lost touch with, and to some measurable degree lost respect for, the chaotic and natural in recent years—and during the very period of history when we humans have been learning more about the detailed workings of nature than in all our previous millennia. The more we learn, the more we seem to distance ourselves from the rest of life, as though we were separate creatures, so different from other occupants of the biosphere as to have arrived from another galaxy. We seek too much to explain, we assert a duty to run the place, to dominate the planet, to govern its life, but at the same time we ourselves seem to be less a part of it than ever before.

We leave it whenever we can, we crowd ourselves from open green countrysides onto the concrete surfaces of massive cities, as far removed from the earth as we can get, staring at it from behind insulated glass, or by way of half-hour television clips.

At the same time, we talk a great game of concern. We shout at each other in high virtue, now more than ever before, about the befoulment of our nest and about whom to blame. We have mechanized our lives so extensively that most of us live with the illusion that our only connection with nature is the nagging fear that it may one day turn on us and do us in. Polluting our farmlands and streams, even the seas, worries us because of what it may be doing to the food and water supplies necessary for human beings. Raising the level of CO_2, methane, and hydro-fluorocarbons in the atmosphere troubles us because of the projected effects of climate upheaval on human habitats.

These anxieties do not extend, really, to nature at large. They are not the result of any new awareness.

Nature itself, that vast incomprehensible meditative being, has come to mean for most of us nothing much more than odd walks in the nearby woods, or flowers in the rooftop garden, or the soap opera stories of the last giant panda or whooping crane, or curiosities like the northward approach, from Florida, of the Asiatic flying cockroach.

I will begin to feel better about us, and about our future, when we finally start learning about some of the things that are still mystifications. Start with the events in the mind of a cricket, I'd say, and then go on from there. Comprehend my cat Jeoffry and we'll be on our way. Nowhere near home, but off and dancing, getting within a few millennia of understanding why the music of Bach is what it is, ready at last for open outer space. Give us time, I'd say, the kind of endless time we mean when we talk about the real world.

POSSIBILITIES FOR WRITING

1. Outline the organization or structure of Thomas's essay. How does it begin and end? What does Thomas accomplish with the middle of his essay? Divide that middle into parts and provide a title for each of those parts. Explain their relationship to one another.

2. In a paragraph or two, explain Thomas's idea about how chaos informs and affects thinking—both human thinking and animal thinking. Consider the example, especially, of the bat that Thomas discusses. Clarify the distinction Thomas makes between what chaos means for bats and what it means for us. Then in an additional paragraph, explain your idea about what Thomas says about chaos.

3. Write your own essay about what you think about the way animals might think. You will have to do at least a bit of research on this topic. A few places to begin are with a famous essay about "the dance of the bees," which describes a dance honeybees enact to share information with the hive about where to find nectar; and some ideas about the differences between signs and symbols in the writings of the philosopher Suzanne Langer. You can also rely, of course, on your observation, experience, and other reading to develop your essay.

Henry David Thoreau (1817–1862) was born in Concord, Massachusetts, where he spent most of his life. A graduate of Harvard, he was an early protégé of Ralph Waldo Emerson, whom he served for several years as an assistant and under whose tutelage he began to write for publication. Thoreau was philosophically a strict individualist and antimaterialist, and in 1845 he retired for two years to an isolated cabin on Walden Pond, near Concord, where he lived in comparative solitude, studying the natural world, reading, and keeping a journal that would become the basis for Walden *(1854), a lyrical but deeply reasoned account of his experiences there and what they meant to him, as well as four later volumes. His work has influenced generations of writers, thinkers, and even political movements in terms of determining what constitutes true human and natural value.*

HENRY DAVID THOREAU

Why I Went to the Woods

In this excerpt from the second chapter of *Walden,* Thoreau explains why he "went to the woods," that is, why he took a sabbatical from civilization to get away from it all for a while. Essentially, Thoreau wanted time to read, write, and think. He wanted to make time for nature. And he wanted to test himself, to see just how much he could simplify his life, to determine how much time he could save to do what he really wanted to do with every minute of every day.

I went to the woods because I wished to live deliberately, to front only the essential facts of life, and see if I could not learn what it had to teach, and not, when I came to die, discover that I had not lived. I did not wish to live what was not life, living is so dear; nor did I wish to practice resignation, unless it was quite necessary. I wanted to live deep and suck out all the marrow of life, to live so sturdily and Spartan-like as to put to rout all that was not life, to cut a broad swath and shave close, to drive life into a corner, and reduce it to its lowest terms, and, if it proved to be mean, why then to get the whole and genuine meanness of it, and publish its meanness to the world; or if it were sublime, to know it by experience, and be able to give a true account of it in my next excursion. For most men, it appears to me, are in a strange uncertainty about it, whether it is of the devil or of God, and have *somewhat hastily* concluded that it is the chief end of man here to "glorify God and enjoy him forever."

Still we live meanly, like ants; though the fable tells us that we were long ago changed into men; like pygmies we fight with cranes; it is error upon error, and clout upon clout, and our best virtue has for its occasion a superfluous and evitable wretchedness. Our life is frittered away by detail. An honest man has hardly need to count more than his ten fingers, or in extreme cases he may add his ten toes, and lump the rest. Simplicity, simplicity, simplicity! I say, let your affairs be as two or three, and not a hundred or a thousand; instead of a million count half a dozen, and keep your accounts on your thumb-nail. In the midst of this chopping sea of civilized life, such are the clouds and storms and quicksands and thousand-and-one items to be allowed for, that a man has to live, if he would not founder and go to the bottom and not make his port at all, by dead reckoning, and he must be a great calculator indeed who succeeds. Simplify, simplify. Instead of three meals a day, if it be necessary eat but one; instead of a hundred dishes, five; and reduce other things in proportion. Our life is like a German Confederacy, made of up petty states, with its boundary forever fluctuating, so that even a German cannot tell you how it is bounded at any moment. The nation itself, with all its so-called internal improvements, which, by the way are all external and superficial, is just such an unwieldy and overgrown establishment, cluttered with furniture and tripped up by its own traps, ruined by luxury and heedless expense, by want of calculation and a worthy aim, as the million households in the lands; and the only cure for it, as for them, is in a rigid economy, a stern and more than Spartan simplicity of life and elevation of purpose. It lives too fast. Men think that it is essential that the *Nation* have commerce, and export ice, and talk through a telegraph, and ride thirty miles an hour, without a doubt, whether *they* do or not; but whether we should live like baboons or like men, is a little uncertain. If we do not get our sleepers, and forge rails, and devote days and nights to the work, but go to tinkering upon our *lives* to improve *them,* who will build railroads? And if railroads are not built, how shall we get to heaven in season? But if we stay at home and mind our business, who will want railroads? We do not ride on the railroad; it rides upon us. Did you ever think what those sleepers are that underlie the railroad? Each one is a man, an Irishman, or a Yankee man. The rails are laid on them, and they are covered with sand, and the cars run smoothly over them. They are sound sleepers, I assure you. And every few years a new lot is laid down and run over; so that, if some have the pleasure of riding on a rail, others have the misfortune to be ridden upon. And when they run over a man that is walking in his sleep, a supernumerary sleeper in the wrong position, and wake him up, they suddenly stop the cars, and make a hue and cry about it, as if this were an exception. I am glad to know that it takes a gang of men for every five miles to keep the sleepers down and level in their beds as it is, for this is a sign that they may sometimes get up again.

Why should we live with such hurry and waste of life? We are determined to be starved before we are hungry. Men say that a stitch in time saves nine, and so they take a thousand stitches today to save nine tomorrow. As for *work,* we haven't any of any consequence. We have the Saint Vitus' dance, and cannot possibly keep our heads still. If I should only give a few pulls at the parish bell-rope, as for a fire, that is, without setting the bell, there is hardly a man on his farm in the outskirts of Concord, notwithstanding that press of engagements which was his excuse so many times this morning, nor a boy, nor a woman, I might almost say, but would foresake all and follow that sound, not mainly to save property from the flames, but, if we will confess the truth, much more to see it burn, since burn it must, and we, be it known, did not set it on fire—or to see it put out, and have a hand in it, if that is done as handsomely; yes, even if it were the parish church itself. Hardly a man takes a half-hour's nap after dinner, but when he wakes he holds up his head and asks, "What's the news?" as if the rest of mankind had stood his sentinels. Some give directions to be waked every half-hour, doubtless for no other purpose; and then, to pay for it, they tell what they have dreamed. After a night's sleep the news is as indispensable as the breakfast. "Pray tell me anything new that has happened to a man anywhere on this globe"—and he reads it over his coffee and rolls, that a man has had his eyes gouged out this morning on the Wachito River; never dreaming the while that he lives in the dark unfathomed mammoth cave of this world, and has but the rudiment of an eye himself.

For my part, I could easily do without the post-office. I think that there are very few important communications made through it. To speak critically, I never received more than one or two letters in my life—I wrote this some years ago—that were worth the postage. The penny-post is, commonly, an institution through which you seriously offer a man that penny for his thoughts which is so often safely offered in jest. And I am sure that I never read any memorable news in a newspaper. If we read of one man robbed, or murdered, or killed by accident, or one house burned, or one vessel wrecked, or one steamboat blown up, or one cow run over on the Western Railroad, or one mad dog killed, or one lot of grasshoppers in the winter—we never need read of another. One is enough. If you are acquainted with the principle, what do you care for a myriad instances and applications? To a philosopher all *news,* as it is called, is gossip, and they who edit and read it are old women over their tea. Yet not a few are greedy after this gossip. There was such a rush, as I hear, the other day at one of the offices to learn the foreign news by the last arrival, that several large squares of plate glass belonging to the establishment were broken by the pressure—news which I seriously think a ready wit might write a twelvemonth, or twelve years, beforehand with sufficient accuracy. As for Spain, for instance, if you know how to throw in Don Carlos and the Infanta, and Don Pedro and Seville and Granada, from time to time in the right proportions—they may have changed the names a little since I saw the papers—and serve up a bullfight when other entertainments fail, it will be true to the letter, and give us as good an idea of the exact state or ruin of things in Spain as the most succinct and lucid reports under this head in the newspapers; and as for England, almost the last significant scrap of news from that quarter was the revolution of 1649; and if you have learned the history of her crops for an average year, you never need attend to that thing again, unless your speculations are of a merely pecuniary character. If one may judge who rarely looks into the newspapers, nothing new does ever happen in foreign parts, a French revolution not excepted.

What news! how much more important to know what that is which was never old! "Kieou-he-yu (great dignitary of the state of Wei) sent a man to Khoung-tseu to know his news. Khoung-tseu caused the messenger to be seated near him, and questioned him in these terms: What is your master doing? The messenger answered with respect: My master desires to diminish the number of his faults, but he cannot come to the end of them. The messenger being gone, the philosopher remarked: What a worthy messenger! What a worthy messenger!" The preacher, instead of vexing the ears of drowsy farmers on their day of rest at the end of the week—for Sunday is the fit conclusion of an ill-spent week, and not the fresh and brave beginning of a new one—with this one other draggle-tail of a sermon, should shout with thundering voice, "Pause! Avast! Why so seeming fast, but deadly slow?"

Shams and delusions are esteemed for soundest truths, while reality is fabulous. If men would steadily observe realities only, and not allow themselves to be deluded, life, to compare it with such things as we know, would be like a fairy tale and the Arabian Nights' Entertainments. If we respected only what is inevitable and has a right to be, music and poetry would resound along the streets. When we are unhurried and wise, we perceive that only great and worthy things have any permanent and absolute existence, that petty fears and petty pleasures are but the shadow of the reality. This is always exhilarating and sublime. By closing the eyes and slumbering, and consenting to be deceived by shows, men establish and confirm their daily life of routine and habit everywhere, which still is built on purely illusory foundations. Children, who play life, discern its true law and relations more clearly than men, who fail to live it worthily, but who think that they are wiser by experience, that is, by failure. I have read in a Hindoo book, that "there was a king's son, who, being expelled in infancy from his native city, was brought up by a forester, and, growing up to maturity in that state, imagined himself to belong to the barbarous race with which he lived. One of his father's ministers having discovered him, revealed to him what he was, and the misconception of his character was removed, and he knew himself to be a prince. So soul," continues the Hindoo philosopher, "from the circumstances in which it is placed, mistakes its own character, until the truth is revealed to it by some holy teacher and then it knows itself to be *Brahme*." I perceive that we inhabitants of New England live this mean life that we do because our vision does not penetrate the surface of things. We think that that *is* which *appears* to be. If a man should walk through this town and see only the reality, where, think you, would the "Mill-dam" go to? If he should give us an account of the realities he beheld there, we should not recognize the place in his description. Look at the meetinghouse, or a courthouse, or a jail, or a shop, or a dwelling-house, and say what that thing really is before a true gaze, and they would all go to pieces in your account of them. Men esteem truth remote, in the outskirts of the system, behind the farthest star, before Adam and after the last man. In eternity there is indeed something true and sublime. But all these times and places and occasions are now and here. God himself culminates in the present moment, and will never be more divine in the lapse of all the ages. And we are enabled to apprehend at all what is sublime and noble only by the perpetual instilling and drenching of the reality that surrounds us. The universe constantly and obediently answers to our conceptions; whether we travel fast or slow, the track is laid for us. Let us spend our lives in conceiving then. The poet or the artist never yet had so fair and noble a design but some of his posterity at least could accomplish it.

Let us spend one day as deliberately as Nature, and not be thrown off the track by every nutshell and mosquito's wing that falls on the rails. Let us rise early and fast, or breakfast, gently and without perturbation; let company come and let company go, let the bells ring and the children cry—determined to make a day of it. Why should we knock under and go with the stream? Let us not be upset and over-whelmed in that terrible rapid and whirlpool called a dinner, situated in the meridian shallows. Weather this danger and you are safe, for the rest of the way is downhill. With unrelaxed nerves, with morning vigor, sail by it, looking another way, tied to the mast like Ulysses. If the engine whistles, let it whistle till it is hoarse for its pains. If the bell rings, why should we run? We will consider what kind of music they are like. Let us settle ourselves and work and wedge our feet down-ward through the mud and slush of opinion, and prejudice, and tra-dition, and delusion, and appearance, that alluvion which covers the globe, through Paris and London, through New York and Boston and Concord, through Church and State, through poetry and philosophy and religion, till we come to a hard bottom and rocks in place, which we can call *reality*, and say, This is, and no mistake; and then begin, having a *point d'appui*, below freshet and frost and fire, a place where you might found a wall or a state, or set a lamp-post safely, or perhaps a gauge, not a Nilometer, but a Realometer, that future ages might know how deep a freshet of shams and appearances had gathered from time to time. If you stand right fronting and face to face to a fact, you will see the sun glimmer on both its surfaces, as if it were a cimeter, and feel its sweet edge dividing you through the heart and marrow, and so you will happily conclude your mortal career. Be it life or death, we crave only reality. If we are really dying, let us hear the rattle in our throats and feel cold in the extremities; if we are alive, let us go about our business.

Time is but the stream I go afishing in. I drink at it; but while I drink I see the sandy bottom and detect how shallow it is. Its thin current slides away but eternity remains. I would drink deeper; fish in the sky, whose bottom is pebbly with stars. I cannot count one. I know not the first letter of the alphabet. I have always been regretting that I was not as wise as the day I was born. The intellect is a cleaver; it discerns and rifts its way into the secret of things. I do not wish to be any more busy with my hands than is necessary. My head is hands and feet. I feel all my best faculties concentrated in it. My instinct tells me that my head is an organ for burrowing, as some creatures use their snout and fore paws, and with it I would mine and burrow my way through these hills. I think that the richest vein is somewhere here-abouts; so by the divining-rod and thin rising vapors, I judge; and here I will begin to mine.

POSSIBILITIES FOR WRITING

1. Analyze the recommendations that Thoreau is making here. What are his general recommendations? What are his specific recommendations? How might these recommendations be applied to life as it is lived in the twenty-first century?

2. Thoreau's writing is characterized by extensive use of metaphor. Choose several of these to analyze in detail. How well does metaphor contribute to clarifying Thoreau's ideas?

3. Throughout the essay, Thoreau includes what are for him statements of observed truth, for example, "Our life is frittered away by detail" and "I perceive that we...live this mean life that we do because our vision does not penetrate the surface of things." Choose one of these ideas that you find interesting as the basis for an essay of your own.

Sojourner Truth (c. 1797–1883) was born a slave in Ulster County, New York, with the given name Isabella. When slavery was abolished in the state, she worked for a time with a Quaker family and was caught up in the religious fervor then sweeping American Protestantism. In 1843, announcing that she had received messages from heaven, she took on the name Sojourner Truth and began a career as an itinerant preacher, advocating the abolishment of slavery and the advancement of women's rights. While basically illiterate, she was nevertheless a highly effective speaker and a powerful physical presence. After the Civil War, she counseled newly freed slaves and petitioned for a "Negro state" on public lands in the West. Her memoirs, dictated to Olive Gilbert, were published as Narratives of Sojourner Truth *(1878).*

SOJOURNER TRUTH

Ain't I a Woman?

The following speech was made by Sojourner Truth, a black female slave, when she attended a women's rights convention held in Akron, Ohio, in May of 1851. Sojourner Truth was the only black woman in attendance. On the second day of the convention she approached the podium, and addressed the audience in a deep and powerful voice. Francis D. Gage, who presided at the convention, recorded the speech. Later, it was transcribed.

Well children, where there is so much racket there must be somethin' out o'kilter. I think that 'twixt the Negroes of the North and the South and the women at the North, all talkin' 'bout rights, the white men will be in a fix pretty soon. But what's all this here talkin' 'bout?

That man over there say that women needs to be helped into carriages, and lifted over ditches, and to have the best place everywhere. Nobody ever helps me into carriages, or over mud-puddles, or give me any best place! And ain't I a woman? Look at me! Look at my arm! I have ploughed, and planted, and gathered into barns, and no man could head me! And ain't I a woman? I could work as much and eat as much as a man—when I could get it—and bear the lash as well! And ain't I a woman? I have borne thirteen children, and seen 'em mos' all sold off to slavery, and when I cried out with my mother's grief, none but Jesus heard me! And ain't I a woman?

Then they talk about this thing in the head; what's this they call it? ["Intellect," whispered someone near.] That's it honey. What's that got to do with women's rights or Negro's rights? If my cup won't hold but a pint and yours holds a quart, wouldn't you be mean not to let me have my little measure full?

Then that little man in black there, he says women can't have as much rights as men, 'cause Christ wasn't a woman! Where did your Christ come from? Where did your Christ come from? From God and a woman! Man had nothin' to do with Him.

If the first woman God ever made was strong enough to turn the world upside down all alone, these women together ought to be able to turn it back and get it right side up again; and now they is asking to do it, they better let 'em. 'Bliged to you for hearin' me, and now ole Sojourner hasn't got nothin' more to say.

POSSIBILITIES FOR WRITING

1. There are a number of striking points packed into this very brief argument—about both slavery and women's rights. Analyze each of the assertions Sojourner Truth makes, whether explicit or implied, and how she supports each assertion.

2. Read "Ain't I a Woman?" along with Elizabeth Cady Stanton's "Declaration of Sentiments and Resolutions" (pages 511–514). Although the two speeches are very different, consider in particular what they have in common. Then think about how the two women go about achieving their point.

3. "Translate" Sojourner Truth's speech into standard, more formal English. Then analyze the differences between the two texts, taking into account differences when the two are read aloud.

Mark Twain (1835–1910) was born Samuel L. Clemens in Florida, Missouri, and spent most of his childhood in the river town of Hannibal. As a young man, he worked as a printer and as a journalist, and for five years he piloted steamboats on the Mississippi River. He began his writing career in earnest when he journeyed west in the 1860s, reporting for newspapers in Virginia City, Nevada, and later in San Francisco. Initially known for his humorous "tall tales," Twain soon became a popular lecturer. After marrying and settling in Hartford, Connecticut, he produced a string of popular works, including the classic novels of adolescence The Adventures of Tom Sawyer (1876) and The Adventures of Huckleberry Finn (1884). In Life on the Mississippi (1883), he recounted his experiences as a river boat pilot. He remains one of the best loved and most widely read of American writers.

MARK TWAIN

Reading the Mississippi River

Mark Twain is best known for his classic novel, *The Adventures of Huckleberry Finn.* One of the central characters of that book is the Mississippi River, where much of the book's action occurs. Twain also wrote another book about the river, *Life on the Mississippi,* from which the following excerpt has been taken. In this selection, Twain describes his experience as an apprentice steamboat pilot, who had to learn to "read" the river to ensure the safe passage of his boat, his passengers, and his crew.

It turned out to be true. The face of the water in time became a wonderful book—a book that was a dead language to the uneducated passenger but which told its mind to me without reserve, delivering its most cherished secrets as clearly as if it uttered them with a voice. And it was not a book to be read once and thrown aside, for it had a new story to tell every day. Throughout the long twelve hundred miles there was never a page that was void of interest, never one that you could leave unread without loss, never one that you would want to skip, thinking you could find higher enjoyment in some other thing. There never was so wonderful a book written by man, never one whose interest was so absorbing, so unflagging, so sparklingly renewed with every reperusal. The passenger who could not read it was charmed with a peculiar sort of faint dimple on its surface (on the rare occasions when he did not overlook it altogether) but to the pilot, that was an italicized passage; indeed it was more than that, it was a legend of the largest capitals with a string of shouting exclamation-points at the end of it, for it meant that a wreck or a rock was buried there that could tear the life out of the strongest vessel that ever floated. It is the faintest and simplest expression the water ever makes, and the most hideous to a pilot's eye. In truth, the passenger who could not read this book saw nothing but all manner of pretty pictures in it, painted by the sun and shaded by the clouds, whereas to the trained eye these were not pictures at all, but the grimmest and most dead-earnest of reading matter.

Now when I had mastered the language of this water and had come to know every trifling feature that bordered the great river as familiarly as I knew the letters of the alphabet, I had made a valuable acquisition. But I had lost something, too. I had lost something which could never be restored to me while I lived. All the grace, the beauty, the poetry, had gone out of the majestic river! I still kept in mind a certain wonderful sunset which I witnessed when steamboating was new to me. A broad expanse of the river was turned to blood; in the middle distance the red hue brightened into gold, through which a solitary log came floating, black and conspicuous; in one place a long, slanting mark was broken by boiling, tumbling rings, that were as many-tinted as an opal; where the ruddy flush was faintest, was a smooth spot that was covered with graceful circles and radiating lines, ever so delicately traced; the shore on our left was densely wooded and the somber shadow that fell from this forest was broken in one place by a long, ruffled trail that shone like silver; and high above the forest wall a clean-stemmed dead tree waved a single leafy bough that glowed like a flame in the unobstructed splendor that was flowing from the sun. There were graceful curves, reflected images, woody heights, soft distances, and over the whole scene, far and near, the dissolving lights drifted steadily, enriching it every passing moment with new marvels of coloring.

I stood like one bewitched. I drank it in, in a speechless rapture. The world was new to me and I had never seen anything like this at home. But as I have said, a day came when I began to cease from noting the glories and the charms which the moon and the sun and the twilight wrought upon the river's face; another day came when I ceased altogether to note them. Then, if that sunset scene had been repeated, I should have looked upon it without rapture, and should have commented upon it inwardly after this fashion: "This sun means that we are going to have wind tomorrow; that floating log means that the river is rising, small thanks to it; that slanting mark on the water refers to a bluff reef which is going to kill somebody's steamboat one of these nights, if it keeps on stretching out like that; those tumbling 'boils' show a dissolving bar and a changing channel there; the lines and circles in the slick water over yonder are a warning that that troublesome place is shoaling up dangerously; that silver streak in the shadow of the forest is the 'break' from a new snag and he has located himself in the very place he could have found to fish for steamboats; that tall dead tree, with a single living branch, is not going to last long, and then how is a body ever going to get through this blind place at night without the friendly old landmark?

No, the romance and beauty were all gone from the river. All the value any feature of it had for me now was the amount of usefulness it could furnish toward compassing the safe piloting of a steamboat. Since those days, I have pitied doctors from my heart. What does the lovely flush in a beauty's cheek mean to a doctor but a "break" that ripples above some deadly disease? Are not all her visible charms sown thick with what are to him the signs and symbols of hidden decay? Does he ever see her beauty at all, or doesn't he simply view her professionally and comment upon her unwholesome condition all to himself? And doesn't he sometimes wonder whether he has gained most or lost most by learning his trade?

POSSIBILITIES FOR WRITING

1. This passage is built around three different examples of comparison and contrast in paragraphs 1, 2–3, and 4. How do each of these work to elaborate on Twain's point? How does the analogy of reading apply in each case?

2. Describe a subject of your own choosing as Twain does, from the vantage point first of a novice and then of someone more experienced with the subject. Don't ignore possibilities for humor here.

3. Try to observe a familiar setting with fresh eyes. Describe what you see there, paying special note to things you hadn't noticed before and things you had begun to take so for granted that you no longer noticed them consciously. What does such close observation suggest to you about everyday perception?

Alice Walker (b. 1944) grew up in Eatonton, Georgia, the only daughter of a sharecropping family. A gifted student, she won scholarships to attend histori- cally black Spelman College and, later, Sarah Lawrence. Walker published her first volume of poetry when she was twenty-four, and this was soon followed by a novel and a collection of short stories. Her fame increased with The Color Purple *(1982), a novel which won the Pulitzer Prize. During the 1970s and 1980s, Walker was an ongoing contributor to* Ms. *magazine, where many of the essays collected in* In Search of Our Mothers' Gardens: Womanist Prose *(1983) and* Living by the Word *(1988) originally appeared. One of the most striking African American voices of her generation, Walker more recently published the short story collection* The Way Forward Is with a Broken Heart *(2000) and* Overcoming Speechlessness *(2010).*

ALICE WALKER

Beauty: When the Other Dancer Is the Self

Alice Walker's essay about beauty grows out of a childhood experience during which she suffered an eye injury that left a psychological scar as well as a physical one. Walker shows how she learned to live with her wound, how she learned to accept her physical imperfection, and how she overcame her damaged self-regard, transforming it into a serene self-acceptance, scar and all.

It is a bright summer day in 1947. My father, a fat, funny man with beautiful eyes and a subversive wit, is trying to decide which of his eight children he will take with him to the county fair. My mother, of course, will not go. She is knocked out from getting most of us ready: I hold my neck stiff against the pressure of her knuckles as she hastily completes the braiding and then ribboning of my hair.

My father is the driver for the rich old white lady up the road. Her name is Miss Mey. She owns all the land for miles around, as well as the house in which we live. All I remember about her is that she once offered to pay my mother thirty-five cents for cleaning her house, rak- ing up piles of her magnolia leaves, and washing her family's clothes, and that my mother—she of no money, eight children, and a chronic earache—refused it. But I do not think of this in 1947. I am two and a half years old. I want to go everywhere my daddy goes. I am excited at the prospect of riding in a car. Someone has told me fairs are fun. That there is room in the car for only three of us doesn't faze me at all. Whirling happily in my starchy frock, showing off my biscuit-polished patent-leather shoes and lavender socks, tossing my head in a way that makes my ribbons bounce, I stand, hands on hips, before my father. "Take me, Daddy." I say with assurance; "I'm the prettiest!"

Later, it does not surprise me to find myself in Miss Mey's shiny black car, sharing the back seat with the other lucky ones. Does not surprise me that I thoroughly enjoy the fair. At home that night I tell the unlucky ones all I can remember about the merry-go-round, the man who eats live chickens, and the teddy bears, until they say: that's enough, baby Alice. Shut up now, and go to sleep.

It is Easter Sunday, 1950. I am dressed in a green, flocked, scalloped hem dress (handmade by my adoring sister, Ruth) that has its own smooth satin petticoat and tiny hot-pink roses tucked into each scallop. My shoes, new T-strap patent leather, again highly biscuit-polished. I am six years old and have learned one of the longest Easter speeches to be heard that day, totally unlike the speech I said when I was two: "Easter lilies/pure and white/blossom in/the morning light." When I rise to give my speech I do so on a great wave of love and pride and expectation. People in the church stop rustling their new crinolines. They seem to hold their breath. I can tell they admire my dress, but it is my spirit, bordering on sassiness (womanishness), they secretly applaud.

"That girl's a little *mess*," they whisper to each other, pleased.

Naturally I say my speech without stammer or pause, unlike those who stutter, stammer, or, worst of all, forget. This is before the word "beautiful" exists in people's vocabulary, but "Oh, isn't she the *cutest* thing!" frequently floats my way. "And got so much sense!" they gratefully add... for which thoughtful addition I thank them to this day.

It was great fun being cute. But then, one day, it ended.

I am eight years old and a tomboy. I have a cowboy hat, cowboy boots, checkered shirt and pants, all red. My playmates are my brothers, two and four years older than I. Their colors are black and green, the only difference in the way we are dressed. On Saturday nights we all go to the picture show, even my mother; Westerns are her favorite kind of movie. Back home, "on the ranch," we pretend we are Tom Mix, Hopalong Cassidy, Lash LaRue (we've even named one of our dogs Lash LaRue); we chase each other for hours rustling cattle, being outlaws, delivering damsels from distress. Then my parents decide to buy my brothers guns. These are not "real" guns. They shoot "BBs," copper pellets my brothers say will kill birds. Because I am a girl, I do not get a gun. Instantly I am relegated to the position of Indian. Now there appears a great distance between us. They shoot and shoot at everything with their new guns. I try to keep up with my bow and arrows.

One day while I am standing on top of our makeshift "garage"— pieces of tin nailed across some poles—holding my bow and arrow and looking out toward the fields, I feel an incredible blow in my right eye. I look down just in time to see my brother lower his gun.

Both brothers rush to my side. My eye stings, and I cover it with my hand. "If you tell," they say, "we will get a whipping. You don't want that to happen, do you?" I do not. "Here is a piece of wire," says the older brother, picking it up from the roof; "say you stepped on one end of it and the other flew up and hit you." The pain is beginning to start. "Yes," I say. "Yes, I will say that is what happened." If I do not say this is what happened, I know my brothers will find ways to make me wish I had. But now I will say anything that gets me to my mother.

Confronted by our parents we stick to the lie agreed upon. They place me on a bench on the porch and I close my left eye while they examine the right. There is a tree growing from underneath the porch that climbs past the railing to the roof. It is the last thing my right eye sees. I watch as its trunk, its branches, and then its leaves are blotted out by the rising blood.

I am in shock. First there is intense fever, which my father tries to break using lily leaves bound around my head. Then there are chills: my mother tires to get me to eat soup. Eventually, I do not know how, my parents learn what has happened. A week after the "accident" they take me to see a doctor. "Why did you wait so long to come?" he asks, looking into my eye and shaking his head. "Eyes are sympathetic," he says. "If one is blind, the other will likely become blind too."

This comment of the doctor's terrifies me. But it is really how I look that bothers me most. Where the BB pellet struck there is a glob of whitish scar tissue, a hideous cataract, on my eye. Now when I stare at people—a favorite pastime, up to now—they will stare back. Not at the "cute" little girl, but at her scar. For six years I do not stare at anyone, because I do not raise my head.

Years later, in the throes of a mid-life crisis, I ask my mother and sister whether I changed after the "accident." "No," they say, puzzled. "What do you mean?"

What do I mean?

I am eight, and, for the first time, doing poorly in school, where I have been something of a whiz since I was four. We have just moved to the place where the "accident" occurred. We do not know any of the people around us because this is a different county. The only time I see the friends I knew is when we go back to our old church. The new school is the former state penitentiary. It is a large stone building, cold and drafty, crammed to overflowing with boisterous, ill-disciplined children. On the third floor there is a huge circular imprint of some partition that has been torn out.

"What used to be here?" I ask a sullen girl next to me on our way past it to lunch.

"The electric chair," says she.

At night I have nightmares about the electric chair, and about all the people reputedly "fried" in it. I am afraid of the school, where all the students seem to be budding criminals.

"What's the matter with your eye?" they ask, critically.

When I don't answer (I cannot decide whether it was an "accident" or not), they shove me, insist on a fight.

My brother, the one who created the story about the wire, comes to my rescue. But then brags so much about "protecting" me, I become sick.

After months of torture at the school, my parents decide to send me back to our old community, to my old school. I live with my grandparents and the teacher they board. But there is no room for Phoebe my cat. By the time my grandparents decide there is room, and I ask for my cat, she cannot be found. Miss Yarborough, the boarding teacher, takes me under her wing, and begins to teach me to play the piano. But soon she marries an African—a "prince," she says—and is whisked away to his continent.

At my old school there is at least one teacher who loves me. She is the teacher who "knew me before I was born" and bought my first baby clothes. It is she who makes life bearable. It is her presence that finally helps me turn on the one child to the school who continually calls me "one-eyed bitch." One day I simply grab him by his coat and beat him until I am satisfied. It is my teacher who tells me my mother is ill.

My mother is lying in bed in the middle of the day, something I have never seen. She is in too much pain to speak. She has an abscess in her ear. I stand looking down on her, knowing that if she dies, I cannot live. She is being treated with warm oils and hot bricks held against her cheek. Finally a doctor comes. But I must go back to my grandparents' house.

The weeks pass but I am hardly aware of it. All I know is that my mother might die, my father is not so jolly, my brothers still have their guns, and I am the one sent away from home.

"You did not change," they say.

Did I imagine the anguish of never looking up?

I am twelve. When relatives come to visit I hide in my room. My cousin Brenda, just my age, whose father works in the post office and whose mother is a nurse, comes to find me. "Hello," she says. And then she asks, looking at my recent school picture, which I did not want taken, and on which the "glob," as I think of it, is clearly visible, "You still can't see out of that eye?"

"No," I say and flop back on the bed over my book.

That night, as I do almost every night, I abuse my eye. I rant and rave at it, in front of the mirror. I plead with it to clear up before morning. I tell it I hate and despise it. I do not pray for sight. I pray for beauty.

"You did not change." they say.

I am fourteen and baby-sitting for my brother Bill, who lives in Boston. He is my favorite brother and there is a strong bond between us. Understanding my feelings of shame and ugliness he and his wife take me to a local hospital, where the "glob" is removed by a doctor named O. Henry. There is still a small bluish crater where the scar tissue was, but the ugly white stuff is gone. Almost immediately I become a different person from the girl who does not raise her head. Or so I think. Now that I've raised my head I win the boyfriend of my dreams. Now that I've raised my head I have plenty of friends. Now that I've raised my head classwork comes from my lips as faultlessly as Easter speeches did, and I leave high school as valedictorian, most popular student, and *queen*, hardly believing my luck. Ironically, the girl who was voted most beautiful in our class (and was) was later shot twice through the chest by a male companion, using a "real" gun, while she was pregnant. But that's another story in itself. Or is it?

"You did not change," they say.

It is now thirty years since the "accident." A beautiful journalist comes to visit and to interview me. She is going to write a cover story for her magazine that focuses on my latest book. "Decide how you want to look on the cover," she says. "Glamorous, or whatever."

Never mind "glamorous," it is the "whatever" that I hear. Suddenly all I can think of is whether I will get enough sleep the night before the photography session: if I don't, my eye will be tired and wander, as blind eyes will.

At night in bed with my lover I think up reasons why I should not appear on the cover of a magazine. "My meanest critics will say I've sold out," I say. "My family will now realize I write scandalous books."

"But what's the real reason you don't want to do this?" he asks.

"Because in all probability," I say in a rush, "my eye won't be straight."

"It will be straight enough," he says. Then, "Besides, I thought you'd made your peace with that."

And I suddenly remember that I have.

I remember:

I am talking to my brother Jimmy, asking if he remembers anything unusual about the day I was shot. He does not know I consider that day the last time my father, with his sweet home remedy of cool lily leaves, chose me, and that I suffered and raged inside because of this. "Well," he says, "all I remember is standing by the side of the highway with Daddy, trying to flag down a car. A white man stopped, but when Daddy said he needed somebody to take his little girl to the doctor, he drove off."

I remember:

I am in the desert for the first time. I fall totally in love with it. I am so overwhelmed by its beauty, I confront for the first time, consciously, the meaning of the doctor's words years ago: "Eyes are sympathetic. If one is blind, the other will likely become blind too." I realize I have dashed about the world madly, looking at this looking at that, storing up images against the fading of the light. *But I might have missed seeing the desert!* The shock of that possibility—and gratitude for over twenty-five years of sight—sends me literally to my knees. Poem after poem comes—which is perhaps how poets pray.

On Sight

I am so thankful I have seen
The Desert
And the creatures in the desert
And the desert Itself.
The desert has its own moon
Which I have seen
With my own eye.
There is no flag on it.

Trees of the desert have arms
All of which are always up
That is because the moon is up
The sun is up
Also the sky
The stars
Clouds
None with flags.

If there were flags, I doubt
the trees would point.
Would you?

But mostly, I remember this:

I am twenty-seven and my baby daughter is almost three. Since her birth I have worried about her discovery that her mother's eyes are different from other people's. Will she be embarrassed? I think. What will she say? Every day she watches a television program called "Big Blue Marble." It begins with a picture of the earth as it appears from the moon. It is bluish, a little battered-looking, but full of light, with whitish clouds swirling around it. Every time I see it I weep with love, as if it is a picture of Grandma's house. One day when I am putting Rebecca down for her nap, she suddenly focuses on my eye. Something inside me cringes, gets ready to try to protect myself. All children are cruel about physical differences, I know from experience, and that they don't always mean to be is another matter. I assume Rebecca will be the same.

But no-o-o-o. She studies my face intently as we stand, her inside and me outside her crib. She even holds my face maternally between her dimpled little hands. Then, looking every bit as serious and lawyerlike as her father, she says, as if it may just possibly have slipped my attention: "Mommy, there's a *world* in your eye." (As in, "Don't be alarmed, or do anything crazy.") And then gently, but with great interest: "Mommy, where did you *get* that world in your eye?"

For the most part, the pain left then. (So what, if my brothers grew up to buy even more powerful pellet guns for their sons and to carry real guns themselves. So what, if a young "Morehouse man" once nearly fell off the steps of Trevor Arnett Library because he thought my eyes were blue.) Crying and laughing I ran to the bathroom, while Rebecca mumbled and sang herself off to sleep. Yes indeed, I realized, looking into the mirror. There *was* a world in my eye. And I saw that it was possible to love it: that in fact, for all it had taught me of shame and anger and inner vision, I *did* love it. Even to see it drifting out of orbit in boredom, or rolling up out of fatigue, not to mention floating back at attention in excitement (bearing witness, a friend has called it), deeply suitable to my personality, and even characteristic of me.

That night I dream I am dancing to Stevie Wonder's song "Always" (the name of the song is really "As," but I hear it as "Always"). As I dance, whirling and joyous, happier than I've ever been in my life, another bright-faced dancer joins me. We dance and kiss each other and hold each other through the night. The other dancer has obviously come through all right, as I have done. She is beautiful, whole and free. And she is also me.

POSSIBILITIES FOR WRITING

1. Trace Walker's image of herself from childhood onward as it is related to the disfiguring of her eye. The final image of the two dancers resolves the essay, but does it seem to you a true resolution for Walker? Why or why not?
2. Walker's picture of herself here is of someone who is highly self-absorbed, in some cases, perhaps, even vain. Do you find her generally sympathetic or not? Point to specific passages in the text that contribute to your response.
3. Like Walker as child, people can be highly self-conscious about some aspect of their appearance. In your experience—both in terms of your thoughts about your own appearance and thoughts about their appearance friends may have shared with you—is such self-consciousness generally justified or not?

David Foster Wallace (1962–2008) was born in Ithaca, New York. As a young child, Wallace and his family lived in Champaign and Urbana, Illinois. As an adolescent, Wallace was a regionally ranked junior tennis player. He attended Amherst College and majored in English and philosophy, with a focus on logic and mathematics theses in 1985. In 1987, he earned an M.F.A. in Creative Writing from the University of Arizona. Best known for his novel Infinite Jest *(1996), he won a MacArthur "genius" award in 1997 and the Aga Khan Prize for Fiction, awarded by editors of the* Paris Review. *His essays and fiction appeared in numerous magazines, including the* Paris Review, Playboy, Esquire, *the* New Yorker, *and* Science, *among many others. In 2002, he moved to Claremont, California, to become professor of creative writing and professor of English at Pomona College. After long suffering from serious depression, Wallace committed suicide on September 12, 2008. His* Fate, Time, and Language: An Essay on Free Will *(2010) was published posthumously.*

DAVID FOSTER WALLACE

Consider the Lobster

"Consider the Lobster," originally published in *Gourmet* magazine in 2004, was selected for *Best American Essays* 2005, and serves as the title essay of a 2008 collection of Wallace's nonfiction prose. The essay grew out of his visit to the Maine Lobster Festival and serves as a kind of "review" of that sprawling and popular annual event.

The enormous, pungent, and extremely well-marketed Maine Lobster Festival is held every late July in the state's midcoast region, meaning the western side of Penobscot Bay, the nerve stem of Maine's lobster industry. What's called the midcoast runs from Owl's Head and Thomaston in the south to Belfast in the north. (Actually, it might extend all the way up to Bucksport, but we were never able to get farther north than Belfast on Route 1, whose summer traffic is, as you can imagine, unimaginable.) The region's two main communities are Camden, with its very old money and yachty harbor and five-star restaurants and phenomenal B&Bs, and Rockland, a serious old fishing town that hosts the festival every summer in historic Harbor Park, right along the water.[1]

Tourism and lobster are the midcoast region's two main industries, and they're both warm-weather enterprises, and the Maine Lobster Festival represents less an intersection of the industries than a deliberate collision, joyful and lucrative and loud. The assigned subject

---

[1] There's a comprehensive native apothegm: "Camden by the sea, Rockland by the smell."

of this *Gourmet* article is the 56th Annual MLF, 30 July–3 August 2003, whose official theme this year was "Light-houses, Laughter, and Lobster." Total paid attendance was over 100,000, due partly to a national CNN spot in June during which a senior editor of *Food & Wine* magazine hailed the MLF as one of the best food-themed galas in the world. 2003 festival highlights: concerts by Lee Ann Womack and Orleans, annual Maine Sea Goddess beauty pageant, Saturday's big parade, Sunday's William G. Atwood Memorial Crate Race, annual Amateur Cooking Competition, carnival rides and midway attractions and food booths, and the MLF's Main Eating Tent, where something over 25,000 pounds of fresh-caught Maine lobster is consumed after preparation in the World's Largest Lobster Cooker near the grounds' north entrance. Also available are lobster rolls, lobster turnovers, lobster sauté, Down East lobster salad, lobster bisque, lobster ravioli, and deep-fried lobster dumplings. Lobster Thermidor is obtainable at a sit-down restaurant called the Black Pearl on Harbor Park's northwest wharf. A large all-pine booth sponsored by the Maine Lobster Promotion Council has free pamphlets with recipes, eating tips, and Lobster Fun Facts. The winner of Friday's Amateur Cooking Competition prepares Saffron Lobster Ramekins, the recipe for which is now available for public downloading at www.mainelobsterfestival .com. There are lobster T-shirts and lobster bobblehead dolls and inflatable lobster pool toys and clamp-on lobster hats with big scarlet claws that wobble on springs. Your assigned correspondent saw it all, accompanied by one girlfriend and both his own parents—one of which parents was actually born and raised in Maine, albeit in the extreme northern inland part, which is potato country and a world away from the touristic midcoast.[2]

For practical purposes, everyone knows what a lobster is. As usual, though, there's much more to know than most of us care about—it's all a matter of what your interests are. Taxonomically speaking, a lobster is a marine crustacean of the family Homaridae, characterized by five pairs of jointed legs, the first pair terminating in large pincerish claws used for subduing prey. Like many other species of benthic carnivore, lobsters are both hunters and scavengers. They have stalked eyes, gills on their legs, and antennae. There are a dozen or so different kinds worldwide, of which the relevant species here is the Maine lobster,

---

[2]N.B. All personally connected parties have made it clear from the start that they do not want to be talked about in this article.

Homarus americanus. The name "lobster" comes from the Old English *loppestre,* which is thought to be a corrupt form of the Latin word for locust combined with the Old English *loppe,* which meant spider.

Moreover, a crustacean is an aquatic arthropod of the class Crustacea, which comprises crabs, shrimp, barnacles, lobsters, and freshwater crayfish. All this is right there in the encyclopedia. And arthropods are members of the phylum Arthropoda, which phylum covers insects, spiders, crustaceans, and centipedes/millipedes, all of whose main commonality, besides the absence of a centralized brain-spine assembly, is a chitinous exoskeleton composed of segments, to which appendages are articulated in pairs.

The point is that lobsters are basically giant sea insects.[3] Like most arthropods, they date from the Jurassic period, biologically so much older than mammalia that they might as well be from another planet. And they are—particularly in their natural brown-green state, brandishing their claws like weapons and with thick antennae awhip—not nice to look at. And it's true that they are garbagemen of the sea, eaters of dead stuff,[4] although they'll also eat some live shellfish, certain kinds of injured fish, and sometimes one another.

But they are themselves good eating. Or so we think now. Up until sometime in the 1800s, though, lobster was literally low-class food, eaten only by the poor and institutionalized. Even in the harsh penal environment of early America, some colonies had laws against feeding lobsters to inmates more than once a week because it was thought to be cruel and unusual, like making people eat rats. One reason for their low status was how plentiful lobsters were in old New England. "Unbelievable abundance" is how one source describes the situation, including accounts of Plymouth Pilgrims wading out and capturing all they wanted by hand, and of early Boston's seashore being littered with lobsters after hard storms—these latter were treated as a smelly nuisance and ground up for fertilizer. There is also the fact that premodern lobster was cooked dead and then preserved, usually packed in salt or crude hermetic containers. Maine's earliest lobster industry was based around a dozen such seaside canneries in the 1840s, from which lobster was shipped as far away as California, in demand only because it was cheap and high in protein, basically chewable fuel.

---

[3]Midcoasters' native term for a lobster is, in fact, "bug," as in "Come around on Sunday and we'll cook up some bugs."
[4]Factoid: Lobster traps are usually baited with dead herring.

Now, of course, lobster is posh, a delicacy, only a step or two down from caviar. The meat is richer and more substantial than most fish, its taste subtle compared to the marine-gaminess of mussels and clams. In the US pop-food imagination, lobster is now the seafood analog to steak, with which it's so often twinned as Surf 'n' Turf on the really expensive part of the chain steakhouse menu.

In fact, one obvious project of the MLF, and of its omnipresently sponsorial Maine Lobster Promotion Council, is to counter the idea that lobster is unusually luxe or unhealthy or expensive, suitable only for effete palates or the occasional blow-the-diet treat. It is emphasized over and over in presentations and pamphlets at the festival that lobster meat has fewer calories, less cholesterol, and less saturated fat than chicken.[5] And in the Main Eating Tent, you can get a "quarter" (industry shorthand for a 1¼-pound lobster), a four-ounce cup of melted butter, a bag of chips, and a soft roll w/ butter-pat for around $12.00, which is only slightly more expensive than supper at McDonald's.

Be apprised, though, that the Maine Lobster Festival's democratization of lobster comes with all the massed inconvenience and aesthetic compromise of real democracy. See, for example, the aforementioned Main Eating Tent, for which there is a constant Disneyland-grade queue, and which turns out to be a square quarter mile of awning-shaded cafeteria lines and rows of long institutional tables at which friend and stranger alike sit cheek by jowl, cracking and chewing and dribbling. It's hot, and the sagged roof traps the steam and the smells, which latter are strong and only partly food-related. It is also loud, and a good percentage of the total noise is masticatory. The suppers come in styrofoam trays, and the soft drinks are iceless and flat, and the coffee is convenience-store coffee in more styrofoam, and the utensils are plastic (there are none of the special long skinny forks for pushing out the tail meat, though a few savvy diners bring their own). Nor do they give you near enough napkins considering how messy lobster is to eat, especially when you're squeezed onto benches alongside children of various ages and vastly different levels of fine-motor development—not to mention the people who've somehow smuggled in

---

[5]Of course, the common practice of dipping the lobster meat in melted butter torpedoes all these happy fat-specs, which none of the council's promotional stuff ever mentions, any more than potato industry PR talks about sour cream and bacon bits.

their own beer in enormous aisle-blocking coolers, or who all of a sudden produce their own plastic tablecloths and spread them over large portions of tables to try to reserve them (the tables) for their own little groups. And so on. Any one example is no more than a petty inconvenience, of course, but the MLF turns out to be full of irksome little downers like this—see for instance the Main Stage's headliner shows, where it turns out that you have to pay $20 extra for a folding chair if you want to sit down; or the North Tent's mad scramble for the Nyquil-cup-sized samples of finalists' entries handed out after the Cooking Competition; or the much-touted Maine Sea Goddess pageant finals, which turn out to be ex-cruciatingly long and to consist mainly of endless thanks and tribute to local sponsors. Let's not even talk about the grossly inadequate Port-A-San facilities or the fact that there's nowhere to wash your hands before or after eating. What the Maine Lobster Festival really is is a midlevel county fair with a culinary hook, and in this respect it's not unlike Tidewater crab festivals, Midwest corn festivals, Texas chili festivals, etc., and shares with these venues the core paradox of all teeming commercial demotic events: It's not for everyone.[6] Nothing against the euphoric senior editor of *Food & Wine,* but I'd

---

[6]In truth, there's a great deal to be said about the differences between working-class Rockland and the heavily populist flavor of its festival versus comfortable and elitist Camden with its expensive view and shops given entirely over to $200 sweaters and great rows of Victorian homes converted to upscale B&Bs. And about these differences as two sides of the great coin that is US tourism. Very little of which will be said here, except to amplify the above-mentioned paradox and to reveal your assigned correspondent's own preferences. I confess that I have never understood why so many people's idea of a fun vacation is to don flip-flops and sunglasses and crawl through maddening traffic to loud, hot, crowded tourist venues in order to sample a "local flavor" that is by definition ruined by the presence of tourists. This may (as my festival companions keep pointing out) all be a matter of personality and hardwired taste: the fact that I do not like tourist venues means that I'll never understand their appeal and so am probably not the one to talk about it (the supposed appeal). But, since this FN will almost surely not survive magazine-editing anyway, here goes:
    As I see it, it probably really is good for the soul to be a tourist, even if it's only once in a while. Not good for the soul in a refreshing or enlivening way, though, but rather in a grim, steely-eyed, let's-look-honestly-at-the-facts-and-find-some-way-to-deal-with-them way. My personal experience has not been that traveling around the country is broadening or relaxing, or that radical changes in place and context have a salutary effect, but rather that international tourism is radically constricting, and humbling in the hardest way—hostile to my fantasy of being a true individual, of living somehow outside and above it all. (Coming up is the part that my companions find especially unhappy and repellent, a sure way to spoil the fun of vacation travel:) To be a mass tourist, for me, is to become a pure late-date American: alien, ignorant, greedy for something you cannot ever have, disappointed in a way you can never admit. It is to spoil, by way of sheer ontology, the very unspoiledness you are there to experience. It is to impose yourself on places that in all non-economic ways would be better, realer, without you. It is, in lines and gridlock and transaction after transaction, to confront a dimension of yourself that is as inescapable as it is painful: As a tourist, you become economically significant but existentially loathsome, an insect on a dead thing.

be surprised if she'd ever actually been here in Harbor Park, amid crowds of people slapping canal-zone mosquitoes as they eat deep-fried Twinkies and watch Professor Paddywhack, on six-foot stilts in a raincoat with plastic lobsters protruding from all directions on springs, terrify their children.

Lobster is essentially a summer food. This is because we now prefer our lobsters fresh, which means they have to be recently caught, which for both tactical and economic reasons takes place at depths less than 25 fathoms. Lobsters tend to be hungriest and most active (i.e., most trappable) at summer water temperatures of 45–50 degrees. In the autumn, most Maine lobsters migrate out into deeper water, either for warmth or to avoid the heavy waves that pound New England's coast all winter. Some burrow into the bottom. They might hibernate; nobody's sure. Summer is also lobsters' molting season—specifically early- to mid-July. Chitinous arthropods grow by molting, rather the way people have to buy bigger clothes as they age and gain weight. Since lobsters can live to be over 100, they can also get to be quite large, as in 30 pounds or more—though truly senior lobsters are rare now because New England's waters are so heavily trapped.[7] Anyway, hence the culinary distinction between hard- and soft-shell lobsters, the latter sometimes a.k.a. shedders. A soft-shell lobster is one that has recently molted. In midcoast restaurants, the summer menu often offers both kinds, with shedders being slightly cheaper even though they're easier to dismantle and the meat is allegedly sweeter. The reason for the discount is that a molting lobster uses a layer of seawater for insulation while its new shell is hardening, so there's slightly less actual meat when you crack open a shedder, plus a redolent gout of water that gets all over everything and can sometimes jet out lemonlike and catch a tablemate right in the eye. If it's winter or you're buying lobster someplace far from New England, on the other hand, you can almost bet that the lobster is a hard-shell, which for obvious reasons travel better.

As an à la carte entrée, lobster can be baked, broiled, steamed, grilled, sautéed, stir-fried, or microwaved. The most common method, though, is boiling. If you're someone who enjoys having lobster at home, this is probably the way you do it, since boiling is so easy. You need a large kettle w/ cover, which you fill about half full with water

---

[7]Datum: In a good year, the US industry produces around 80,000,000 pounds of lobster, and Maine accounts for more than half that total.

(the standard advice is that you want 2.5 quarts of water per lobster). Seawater is optimal, or you can add two Tbsp salt per quart from the tap. It also helps to know how much your lobsters weigh. You get the water boiling, put in the lobsters one at a time, cover the kettle, and bring it back up to a boil. Then you bank the heat and let the kettle simmer—ten minutes for the first pound of lobster, then three minutes for each pound after that. (This is assuming you've got hard-shell lobsters, which, again, if you don't live between Boston and Halifax is probably what you've got. For shedders, you're supposed to subtract three minutes from the total.) The reason the kettle's lobsters turn scarlet is that boiling somehow suppresses every pigment in their chitin but one. If you want an easy test of whether the lobsters are done, you try pulling on one of their antennae—if it comes out of the head with minimal effort, you're ready to eat.

A detail so obvious that most recipes don't even bother to mention it is that each lobster is supposed to be alive when you put it in the kettle. This is part of lobster's modern appeal—it's the freshest food there is. There's no decomposition between harvesting and eating. And not only do lobsters require no cleaning or dressing or plucking, they're relatively easy for vendors to keep alive. They come up alive in the traps, are placed in containers of seawater, and can—so long as the water's aerated and the animals' claws are pegged or banded to keep them from tearing one another up under the stresses of captivity[8]—survive right up until they're boiled. Most of us have been in supermarkets or restaurants that feature tanks of live lobsters, from which you can pick out your supper while it watches you point. And part of the overall spectacle of the Maine Lobster Festival is that you can see actual lobstermen's vessels docking at the wharves along the northeast grounds and unloading fresh-caught product, which is transferred by hand or cart 150 yards to the great clear tanks stacked up around the festival's cooker—which is, as mentioned, billed as the

[8]N.B. Similar reasoning underlies the practice of what's termed "debeaking" broiler chickens and brood hens in modern factory farms. Maximum commercial efficiency requires that enormous poultry populations be confined in unnaturally close quarters, under which conditions many birds go crazy and peck one another to death. As a purely observational side-note, be apprised that debeaking is usually an automated process and that the chickens receive no anesthetic. It's not clear to me whether most *Gourmet* readers know about debeaking, or about related practices like dehorning cattle in commercial feed lots, cropping swine's tails in factory hog farms to keep psychotically bored neighbors from chewing them off, and so forth. It so happens that your assigned correspondent knew almost nothing about standard meat-industry operations before starting work on this article.

World's Largest Lobster Cooker and can process over 100 lobsters at a time for the Main Eating Tent.

So then here is a question that's all but unavoidable at the World's Largest Lobster Cooker, and may arise in kitchens across the US: Is it all right to boil a sentient creature alive just for our gustatory pleasure? A related set of concerns: Is the previous question irksomely PC or sentimental? What does "all right" even mean in this context? Is the whole thing just a matter of personal choice?

As you may or may not know, a certain well-known group called People for the Ethical Treatment of Animals thinks that the morality of lobster-boiling is not just a matter of individual conscience. In fact, one of the very first things we hear about the MLF...well, to set the scene: We're coming in by cab from the almost indescribably odd and rustic Knox County Airport[9] very late on the night before the festival opens, sharing the cab with a wealthy political consultant who lives on Vinalhaven Island in the bay half the year (he's headed for the island ferry in Rockland). The consultant and cabdriver are responding to informal journalistic probes about how people who live in the midcoast region actually view the MLF, as in is the festival just a big-dollar tourist thing or is it something local residents look forward to attending, take genuine civic pride in, etc. The cabdriver (who's in his seventies, one of apparently a whole platoon of retirees the cab company puts on to help with the summer rush, and wears a US-flag lapel pin, and drives in what can only be called a very *deliberate* way) assures us that locals do endorse and enjoy the MLF, although he himself hasn't gone in years, and now come to think of it no one he and his wife know has, either. However, the demilocal consultant's been to recent festivals a couple times (one gets the impression it was at his wife's behest), of which his most vivid impression was that "you have to line up for an ungodly long time to get your lobsters, and meanwhile there are all these ex-flower children coming up and down along the line handing out pamphlets that say the lobsters die in terrible pain and you shouldn't eat them."

And it turns out that the post-hippies of the consultant's recollection were activists from PETA. There were no PETA people in obvious

---

[9]The terminal used to be somebody's house, for example, and the lost-luggage-reporting room was clearly once a pantry.

view at the 2003 MLF,[10] but they've been conspicuous at many of the recent festivals. Since at least the mid-1990s, articles in everything from the *Camden Herald* to the *New York Times* have described PETA urging boycotts of the Maine Lobster Festival, often deploying celebrity spokesmen like Mary Tyler Moore for open letters and ads saying stuff like "Lobsters are extraordinarily sensitive" and "To me, eating a lobster is out of the question." More concrete is the oral testimony of Dick, our florid and extremely gregarious rental-car liaison,[11] to the effect that PETA's been around so much during recent years that a kind of brittlely tolerant homeostasis now obtains between the activists and the festival's locals, e.g.: "We had some incidents a couple years ago. One lady took most of her clothes off and painted herself like a lobster, almost got herself arrested. But for the most part they're let alone. [Rapid series of small ambiguous laughs, which with Dick happens a lot.] They do their thing and we do our thing."

This whole interchange takes place on Route 1, 30 July, during a four-mile, 50-minute ride from the airport[12] to the dealership to sign car-rental papers. Several irreproducible segues down the road from the PETA anecdotes, Dick—whose son-in-law happens to be a professional lobsterman and one of the Main Eating Tent's regular suppliers—explains what he and his family feel is the crucial mitigating factor in the whole morality-of-boiling-lobsters-alive issue: "There's a part of the brain in people and animals that lets us feel pain, and lobsters' brains don't have this part."

---

[10]It turned out that one Mr. William R. Rivas-Rivas, a high-ranking PETA official out of the group's Virginia headquarters, was indeed there this year, albeit solo, working the festival's main and side entrances on Saturday, 2 August, handing out pamphlets and adhesive stickers emblazoned with "Being Boiled Hurts," which is the tagline in most of PETA's published material about lobsters. I learned that he'd been there only later, when speaking with Mr. Rivas-Rivas on the phone. I'm not sure how we missed seeing him *in situ* at the festival, and I can't see much to do except apologize for the oversight—although it's also true that Saturday was the day of the big MLF parade through Rockland, which basic journalistic responsibility seemed to require going to (and which, with all due respect, meant that Saturday was maybe not the best day for PETA to work the Harbor Park grounds, especially if it was going to be just one person for one day, since a lot of diehard MLF partisans were off-site watching the parade (which, again with no offense intended, was in truth kind of cheesy and boring, consisting mostly of slow home-made floats and various midcoast people waving at one another, and with an extremely annoying man dressed as Blackbeard ranging up and down the length of the crowd saying "Arrr" over and over and brandishing a plastic sword at people, etc.; plus it rained)).
[11]By profession, Dick is actually a car salesman; the midcoast region's National Car Rental franchise operates out of a Chevy dealership in Thomaston.
[12]The short version regarding why we were back at the airport after already arriving the previous night involves lost luggage and a miscommunication about where and what the midcoast's National franchise was—Dick came out personally to the airport and got us, out of no evident motive but kindness. (He also talked nonstop the entire way, with a very distinctive speaking style that can be described only as manically laconic; the truth is that I now know more about this man than I do about some members of my own family.)

Besides the fact that it's incorrect in about nine different ways, the main reason Dick's statement is interesting is that its thesis is more or less echoed by the festival's own pronouncement on lobsters and pain, which is part of a Test Your Lobster IQ quiz that appears in the 2003 MLF program courtesy of the Maine Lobster Promotion Council:

> *The nervous system of a lobster is very simple, and is in fact most similar to the nervous system of the grasshopper. It is decentralized with no brain. There is no cerebral cortex, which in humans is the area of the brain that gives the experience of pain.*

Though it sounds more sophisticated, a lot of the neurology in this latter claim is still either false or fuzzy. The human cerebral cortex is the brain-part that deals with higher faculties like reason, metaphysical self-awareness, language, etc. Pain reception is known to be part of a much older and more primitive system of nociceptors and prostaglandins that are managed by the brain stem and thalamus.[13]

On the other hand, it is true that the cerebral cortex is involved in what's variously called suffering, distress, or the emotional experience of pain—i.e., experiencing painful stimuli as unpleasant, very unpleasant, unbearable, and so on.

Before we go any further, let's acknowledge that the questions of whether and how different kinds of animals feel pain, and of whether and why it might be justifiable to inflict pain on them in order to eat them, turn out to be extremely complex and difficult. And comparative neuroanatomy is only part of the problem. Since pain is a totally subjective mental experience, we do not have direct access to anyone or anything's pain but our own; and even just the principles by which we can infer that other human beings experience pain and have a legitimate interest in not feeling pain involve hard-core philosophy—metaphysics, epistemology, value theory, ethics. The fact that even the most highly evolved nonhuman mammal can't use language to communicate with us about their subjective mental experience is only the first layer of additional complication in trying to extend our reasoning about pain and morality to animals. And everything gets progressively more abstract and convolved as we move farther and farther out from

---

[13]To elaborate by way of example: The common experience of accidentally touching a hot stove and yanking your hand back before you're even aware that anything's going on is explained by the fact that many of the processes by which we detect and avoid painful stimuli do not involve the cortex. In the case of the hand and stove, the brain is bypassed altogether; all the important neurochemical action takes place in the spine.

the higher-type mammals into cattle and swine and dogs and cats and rodents, and then birds and fish, and finally invertebrates like lobsters.

The more important point here, though, is that the whole animal-cruelty-and-eating issue is not just complex, it's also uncomfortable. It is, at any rate, uncomfortable for me, and for just about everyone I know who enjoys a variety of foods and yet does not want to see herself as cruel or unfeeling. As far as I can tell, my own main way of dealing with this conflict has been to avoid thinking about the whole unpleasant thing. I should add that it appears to me unlikely that many readers of *Gourmet* wish to think about it, either, or to be queried about the morality of their eating habits in the pages of a culinary monthly. Since, however, the assigned subject of this article is what it was like to attend the 2003 MLF, and thus to spend several days in the midst of a great mass of Americans all eating lobster, and thus to be more or less impelled to think hard about lobster and the experience of buying and eating lobster, it turns out that there is no honest way to avoid certain moral questions.

There are several reasons for this. For one thing, it's not just that lobsters get boiled alive, it's that you do it yourself—or at least it's done specifically for you, on-site.[14] As mentioned, the World's Largest Lobster Cooker, which is highlighted as an attraction in the festival's program, is right out there on the MLF's north grounds for everyone to see. Try to imagine a Nebraska Beef Festival[15] at which part of the festivities is watching trucks pull up and the live cattle get driven down the ramp and slaughtered right there on the World's Largest Killing Floor or something—there's no way.

The intimacy of the whole thing is maximized at home, which of course is where most lobster gets prepared and eaten (although note

[14]Morality-wise, let's concede that this cuts both ways. Lobster-eating is at least not abetted by the system of corporate factory farms that produces most beef, pork, and chicken. Because, if nothing else, of the way they're marketed and packaged for sale, we eat these latter meats without having to consider that they were once conscious, sentient creatures to whom horrible things were done. (N.B. "Horrible" here meaning really, really horrible. Write off to PETA or peta.org for their free "Meet Your Meat" video, narrated by Mr. Alec Baldwin, if you want to see just about everything meat-related you don't want to see or think about. (N. B., Not that PETA's any sort of font of unspun truth. Like many partisans in complex moral disputes, the PETA people are fanatics, and a lot of their rhetoric seems simplistic and self-righteous. But this particular video, replete with actual factory-farm and corporate-slaughterhouse footage, is both credible and traumatizing.))

[15]Is it significant that "lobster," "fish," and "chicken" are our culture's words for both the animal and the meat, whereas most mammals seem to require euphemisms like "beef" and "pork" that help us separate the meat we eat from the living creature the meat once was? Is this evidence that some kind of deep unease about eating higher animals is endemic enough to show up in English usage, but that the unease diminishes as we move out of the mammalian order? (And is "lamb"/"lamb" the counterexample that sinks the whole theory, or are there special, biblico-historical reasons for that equivalence?)

already the semiconscious euphemism "prepared," which in the case of lobsters really means killing them right there in our kitchens). The basic scenario is that we come in from the store and make our little preparations like getting the kettle filled and boiling, and then we lift the lobsters out of the bag or whatever retail container they came home in...whereupon some uncomfortable things start to happen. However stuporous a lobster is from the trip home, for instance, it tends to come alarmingly to life when placed in boiling water. If you're tilting it from a container into the steaming kettle, the lobster will sometimes try to cling to the container's sides or even to hook its claws over the kettle's rim like a person trying to keep from going over the edge of a roof. And worse is when the lobster's fully immersed. Even if you cover the kettle and turn away, you can usually hear the cover rattling and clanking as the lobster tries to push it off. Or the creature's claws scraping the sides of the kettle as it thrashes around. The lobster, in other words, behaves very much as you or I would behave if we were plunged into boiling water (with the obvious exception of screaming[16]). A blunter way to say this is that the lobster acts as if it's in terrible pain, causing some cooks to leave the kitchen altogether and to take one of those little lightweight plastic oven-timers with them into another room and wait until the whole process is over.

There happen to be two main criteria that most ethicists agree on for determining whether a living creature has the capacity to suffer and so has genuine interests that it may or may not be our moral duty to consider.[17] One is how much of the neurological hardware required for pain-experience the animal comes equipped with—nociceptors, prostaglandins, neuronal opioid receptors, etc. The other criterion is whether the animal demonstrates behavior associated with pain. And it takes a lot of intellectual gymnastics and behaviorist hairsplitting

[16]There's a relevant populist myth about the high-pitched whistling sound that sometimes issues from a pot of boiling lobster. The sound is really vented steam from the layer of seawater between the lobster's flesh and its carapace (this is why shedders whistle more than hard-shells), but the pop version has it that the sound is the lobster's rabbit-like death-scream. Lobsters communicate via pheromones in their urine and don't have anything close to the vocal equipment for screaming, but the myth's very persistent—which might, once again, point to a low-level cultural unease about the boiling thing.

[17]"Interests" basically means strong and legitimate preferences, which obviously require some degree of consciousness, responsiveness to stimuli, etc. See, for instance, the utilitarian philosopher Peter Singer, whose 1974 *Animal Liberation* is more or less the bible of the modern animal-rights movement:

> It would be nonsense to say that it was not in the interests of a stone to be kicked along the road by a schoolboy. A stone does not have interests because it cannot suffer. Nothing that we can do to it could possibly make any difference to its welfare. A mouse, on the other hand, does have an interest in not being kicked along the road, because it will suffer if it is.

not to see struggling, thrashing, and lid-clattering as just such pain-behavior. According to marine zoologists, it usually takes lobsters be-tween 35 and 45 seconds to die in boiling water. (No source I could find talks about how long it takes them to die in superheated steam; one rather hopes it's faster.)

There are, of course, other ways to kill your lobster on-site and so achieve maximum freshness. Some cooks' practice is to drive a sharp heavy knife point-first into a spot just above the midpoint be-tween the lobster's eyestalks (more or less where the Third Eye is in human foreheads). This is alleged either to kill the lobster instantly or to render it insensate, and is said at least to eliminate some of the cowardice involved in throwing a creature into boiling water and then fleeing the room. As far as I can tell from talking to proponents of the knife-in-head method, the idea is that it's more violent but ultimately more merciful, plus that a willingness to exert personal agency and accept responsibility for stabbing the lobster's head honors the lobster somehow and entitles one to eat it (there's often a vague sort of Native American spirituality-of-the-hunt flavor to pro-knife arguments). But the problem with the knife method is basic biology: Lobsters' nervous systems operate off not one but several ganglia, a.k.a. nerve bundles, which are sort of wired in series and distributed all along the lobster's underside, from stem to stern. And disabling only the frontal ganglion does not normally result in quick death or unconsciousness.

Another alternative is to put the lobster in cold saltwater and then very slowly bring it up to a full boil. Cooks who advocate this method are going on the analogy to a frog, which can supposedly be kept from jumping out of a boiling pot by heating the water incrementally. In order to save a lot of research-summarizing, I'll simply assure you that the analogy between frogs and lobsters turns out not to hold—plus, if the kettle's water isn't aerated seawater, the immersed lobster suffers from slow suffocation, although usually not decisive enough suffoca-tion to keep it from still thrashing and clattering when the water gets hot enough to kill it. In fact, lobsters boiled incrementally often dis-play a whole bonus set of gruesome, convulsion-like reactions that you don't see in regular boiling.

Ultimately, the only certain virtues of the home-lobotomy and slow-heating methods are comparative, because there are even worse/crueler ways people prepare lobster. Time-thrifty cooks sometimes microwave them alive (usually after poking several vent-holes in the carapace, which is a precaution most shellfish-microwavers learn about the hard way). Live dismemberment, on the other hand, is big in Europe—some chefs cut the lobster in half before cooking; others like to tear off the claws and tail and toss only these parts into the pot.

And there's more unhappy news respecting suffering-criterion number one. Lobsters don't have much in the way of eyesight or hearing, but they do have an exquisite tactile sense, one facilitated by hundreds of thousands of tiny hairs that protrude through their carapace. "Thus it is," in the words of T. M. Prudden's industry classic *About Lobster*, "that although encased in what seems a solid, impenetrable armor, the lobster can receive stimuli and impressions from without as readily as if it possessed a soft and delicate skin." And lobsters do have nociceptors,[18] as well as invertebrate versions of the prostaglandins and major neurotransmitters via which our own brains register pain.

Lobsters do not, on the other hand, appear to have the equipment for making or absorbing natural opioids like endorphins and enkephalins, which are what more advanced nervous systems use to try to handle intense pain. From this fact, though, one could conclude either that lobsters are maybe even *more* vulnerable to pain, since they lack mammalian nervous systems' built-in analgesia, or, instead, that the absence of natural opioids implies an absence of the really intense pain-sensations that natural opioids are designed to mitigate. I for one can detect a marked upswing in mood as I contemplate this latter possibility. It could be that their lack of endorphin/enkephalin hardware means that lobsters' raw subjective experience of pain is so radically different from mammals' that it may not even deserve the term "pain." Perhaps lobsters are more like those frontal-lobotomy patients one reads about who report experiencing pain in a totally different way than you and I. These patients evidently do feel physical pain, neurologically speaking, but don't dislike it—though neither do they like it; it's more that they feel it but don't feel anything *about* it—the point being that the pain is not distressing to them or something they want to get away from. Maybe lobsters, who are also without frontal lobes, are detached from the neurological-registration-of-injury-or-hazard we call pain in just the same way. There is, after all, a difference between (1) pain as a purely neurological event, and (2) actual suffering, which seems crucially to involve an emotional component, an awareness of pain as unpleasant, as something to fear/dislike/want to avoid.

---

[18]This is the neurological term for special pain-receptors that are "sensitive to potentially damaging extremes of temperature, to mechanical forces, and to chemical substances which are released when body tissues are damaged."

Still, after all the abstract intellection, there remain the facts of the frantically clanking lid, the pathetic clinging to the edge of the pot. Standing at the stove, it is hard to deny in any meaningful way that this is a living creature experiencing pain and wishing to avoid/escape the painful experience. To my lay mind, the lobster's behavior in the kettle appears to be the expression of a *preference;* and it may well be that an ability to form preferences is the decisive criterion for real suffering.[19] The logic of this (preference → suffering) relation may be easiest to see in the negative case. If you cut certain kinds of worms in half, the halves will often keep crawling around and going about their vermiform business as if nothing had happened. When we assert, based on their post-op behavior, that these worms appear not to be suffering, what we're really saying is that there's no sign the worms know anything bad has happened or would *prefer* not to have gotten cut in half.

Lobsters, though, are known to exhibit preferences. Experiments have shown that they can detect changes of only a degree or two in water temperature; one reason for their complex migratory cycles (which can often cover 100-plus miles a year) is to pursue the temperatures they like best.[20] And, as mentioned, they're bottom-dwellers and do not like bright light—if a tank of food-lobsters is out in the sunlight or a store's fluorescence, the lobsters will always congregate in whatever part is darkest. Fairly solitary in the ocean, they also clearly dislike the crowding that's part of their captivity in tanks, since (as also mentioned) one reason why lobsters' claws are banded on capture is to keep them from attacking one another under the stress of close-quarter storage.

---

[19]"Preference" is maybe roughly synonymous with "interests," but it is a better term for our purposes because it's less abstractly philosophical—"preference" seems more personal, and it's the whole idea of a living creature's personal experience that's at issue.

[20]Of course, the most common sort of counterargument here would begin by objecting that "like best" is really just a metaphor, and a misleadingly anthropomorphic one at that. The counterarguer would posit that the lobster seeks to maintain a certain optimal ambient temperature out of nothing but unconscious instinct (with a similar explanation for the low-light affinities upcoming in the main text). The thrust of such a counterargument will be that the lobster's thrashings and clankings in the kettle express not unpreferred pain but involuntary reflexes, like your leg shooting out when the doctor hits your knee. Be advised that there are professional scientists, including many researchers who use animals in experiments, who hold to the view that nonhuman creatures have no real feelings at all, merely "behaviors." Be further advised that this view has a long history that goes all the way back to Descartes, although its modern support comes mostly from behaviorist psychology.
To these what-looks-like-pain-is-really-just-reflexes counterarguments, however, there happen to be all sorts of scientific and pro-animal rights counter-counterarguments. And then further attempted rebuttals and redirects, and so on. Suffice it to say that both the scientific and the philosophical arguments on either side of the animal-suffering issue are involved, abstruse, technical, often informed by self-interest or ideology, and in the end so totally inconclusive that as a practical matter, in the kitchen or restaurant, it all still seems to come down to individual conscience, going with (no pun) your gut.

In any event, at the MLF, standing by the bubbling tanks outside the World's Largest Lobster Cooker, watching the fresh-caught lobsters pile over one another, wave their hobbled claws impotently, huddle in the rear corners, or scrabble frantically back from the glass as you approach, it is difficult not to sense that they're unhappy, or frightened, even if it's some rudimentary version of these feelings . . . and, again, why does rudimentariness even enter into it? Why is a primitive, inarticulate form of suffering less urgent or uncomfortable for the person who's helping to inflict it by paying for the food it results in? I'm not trying to give you a PETA-like screed here—at least I don't think so. I'm trying, rather, to work out and articulate some of the troubling questions that arise amid all the laughter and saltation and community pride of the Maine Lobster Festival. The truth is that if you, the festival attendee, permit yourself to think that lobsters can suffer and would rather not, the MLF begins to take on the aspect of something like a Roman circus or medieval torture-fest.

Does that comparison seem a bit much? If so, exactly why? Or what about this one: Is it possible that future generations will regard our present agribusiness and eating practices in much the same way we now view Nero's entertainments or Mengele's experiments? My own initial reaction is that such a comparison is hysterical, extreme—and yet the reason it seems extreme to me appears to be that I believe animals are less morally important than human beings;[21] and when it comes to defending such a belief, even to myself, I have to acknowledge that (a) I have an obvious selfish interest in this belief, since I like to eat certain kinds of animals and want to be able to keep doing it, and (b) I haven't succeeded in working out any sort of personal ethical system in which the belief is truly defensible instead of just selfishly convenient.

Given this article's venue and my own lack of culinary sophistication, I'm curious about whether the reader can identify with any of these reactions and acknowledgments and discomforts. I'm also concerned not to come off as shrill or preachy when what I really am is more like confused. For those *Gourmet* readers who enjoy well-prepared and -presented meals involving beef, veal, lamb, pork, chicken, lobster, etc.: Do you think much about the (possible) moral status and

[21]Meaning *a lot* less important, apparently, since the moral comparison here is not the value of one human's life vs. the value of one animal's life, but rather the value of one animal's life vs. the value of one human's taste for a particular kind of protein. Even the most diehard carniphile will acknowledge that it's possible to live and eat well without consuming animals.

(probable) suffering of the animals involved? If you do, what ethical convictions have you worked out that permit you not just to eat but to savor and enjoy flesh-based viands (since of course refined *enjoyment,* rather than mere ingestion, is the whole point of gastronomy)? If, on the other hand, you'll have no truck with confusions or convictions and regard stuff like the previous paragraph as just so much fatuous navel-gazing, what makes it feel truly okay, inside, to just dismiss the whole thing out of hand? That is, is your refusal to think about any of this the product of actual thought, or is it just that you don't want to think about it? And if the latter, then why not? Do you ever think, even idly, about the possible reasons for your reluctance to think about it? I am not trying to bait anyone here—I'm genuinely curious. After all, isn't being extra aware and attentive and thoughtful about one's food and its overall context part of what distinguishes a real gourmet? Or is all the gourmet's extra attention and sensibility just supposed to be sensuous? Is it really all just a matter of taste and presentation?

These last few queries, though, while sincere, obviously involve much larger and more abstract questions about the connections (if any) between aesthetics and morality—about what the adjective in a phrase like "The Magazine of Good Living" is really supposed to mean—and these questions lead straightaway into such deep and treacherous waters that it's probably best to stop the public discussion right here. There are limits to what even interested persons can ask of each other.

POSSIBILITIES FOR WRITING

1. Describe your experience of reading "Consider the Lobster." To what extent did you find yourself, at various points, experiencing different feelings and thoughts? Write a letter to the publisher of Gourmet Magazine, where Wallace's essay appeared. Explain your response to reading "Consider the Lobster."

2. Using some of the details Wallace provides, write a much briefer review of the 2003 Maine Lobster Festival—five hundred words or so. Try to give an overview of the event, and decide whether to make your review strictly a factual report or to include a judgment about its quality and/or its value.

3. Taking off from the second half of Wallace's essay about the ethics of killing lobsters for food, write an essay in which you explore this issue. Explain whether you think it is or is not justified, with your reasons. You may quote from Wallace, if you wish.

Geoffrey Wolff (b. 1937) was born in Los Angeles and attended Princeton and Cambridge universities. In the course of his career he has worked as a journalist, book review editor, and visiting lecturer at a number of colleges; he is currently writer-in-residence at Brandeis University. His first novel, Bad Debts, *appeared in 1969, and later novels include* Inklings *(1977),* Providence *(1986), and* The Age of Consent *(1995). Wolff has also published two works of biography,* Black Sun: The Brief Transit and Violent Eclipse of Harry Crosby *(1976) and* The Duke of Deception: Memories of My Father *(1979), as well as an essay collection,* A Day at the Beach *(1992). More recently, Wolff has published* The Hard Way Around *(2010), a biography of Joshua Slocum.*

GEOFFREY WOLFF

The Duke of Deception

In this excerpt, the opening chapter from his biography *The Duke of Deception*, Geoffrey Wolff describes his father, whose behavior and style provide Wolff with the title for his book. Wolff's father is shown to be a liar, a cheat, and a fraud, yet the author characterizes him as witty and charming as well. Unsatisfied with his life as it was, Wolff's father invented a reality more in tune with his hopes and expectations, something that would provide him with more status and prestige than he actually possessed, and that would allow him to live in the style to which he wished to become accustomed.

I listen for my father and I hear a stammer. This was explosive and unashamed, not a choking on words but a spray of words. His speech was headlong, edgy, breathless: there was neither room in his mouth nor time in the day to contain what he burned to utter. I have a remnant of that stammer, and I wish I did not; I stammer and blush, my father would stammer and grin. He depended on a listener's good will. My father depended excessively upon people's good will.

As he spoke straight at you, so did he look at you. He could stare down anyone, though this was a gift he rarely practiced. To me, everything about him seemed outsized. Doing a school report on the Easter Islanders I found in an encyclopedia pictures of their huge sculptures, and there he was, massive head and nose, nothing subtle or delicate. He was in fact (and how diminishing those words, *in fact*, look to me now) an inch or two above six feet, full bodied, a man who lumbered from here to there with deliberation. When I was a child I noticed that people were respectful of the cubic feet my father occupied; later I understood that I had confused respect with resentment.

I recollect things, a gentleman's accessories, deceptively simple fabrications of silver and burnished nickle, of brushed Swedish stainless, of silk and soft wool and brown leather. I remember his shoes, so meticulously selected and cared for and used, thin-soled, with cracked uppers, older than I was or could ever be, shining dully and from the depths. Just a pair of shoes? No: I knew before I knew any other complicated thing that for my father there was nothing he possessed that was "just" something. His pocket watch was not "just" a timepiece, it was a miraculous instrument with a hinged front and a representation on its back of porcelain ducks rising from a birch-girt porcelain pond. It struck the hour unassertively, musically, like a silver tine touched to a crystal glass, no hurry, you might like to know it's noon.

He despised black leather, said black shoes reminded him of black attaché cases, of bankers, lawyers, look-before-you-leapers anxious not to offend their clients. He owned nothing black except his dinner jacket and his umbrella. His umbrella doubled as a shooting-stick, and one afternoon at a polo match at Brandywine he was sitting on it when a man asked him what he would do if it rained, sit wet or stand dry? I laughed. My father laughed also, but tightly, and he did not reply: nor did he ever again use this quixotic contraption. He took things, *things*, seriously.

My father, called Duke, taught me skills and manners; he taught me to shoot and to drive fast and to read respectfully and to box and to handle a boat and to distinguish between good jazz music and bad jazz music. He was patient with me, led me to understand for myself why Billie Holiday's understatements were more interesting than Ella Fitzgerald's complications. His codes were not novel, but they were rigid, the rules of decorum that Hemingway prescribed. A gentleman kept his word, and favored simplicity of sentiment; a gentleman chose his words with care, as he chose his friends. A gentleman accepted responsibility for his acts, and welcomed the liberty to act unambiguously. A gentleman was a stickler for precision and punctilio; life was no more than an inventory of small choices that together formed a man's character, entire. A gentleman was this, and not that; a *man* did, did not, said, would not say.

My father could, however, be coaxed to reveal his bona fides. He had been schooled at Groton and passed along to Yale. He was just barely prepared to intimate that he had been tapped for "Bones," and I remember his pleasure when Levi Jackson, the black captain of Yale's 1948 football team, was similarly honored by that secret society. He was proud of Skull and Bones for its hospitality toward the exotic. He did sometimes wince, however, when he pronounced Jackson's Semitic Christian name, and I sensed that his tolerance for Jews was not inclusive; but I never heard him indulge express bigotry, and the first of half a dozen times he hit me was for having called a neighbor's kid a guinea.

There was much luxury in my father's affections, and he hated what was narrow, pinched, or mean. He understood exclusion, mind you, and lived his life believing the world to be divided between a few *us's* and many *them's*, but I was to understand that aristocracy was a function of taste, courage, and generosity. About two other virtues—candor and reticence—I was confused, for my father would sometimes proselytize the one, sometimes the other.

If Duke's preoccupation with bloodlines was finite, this did not cause him to be unmindful of his ancestors. He knew whence he had come, and whither he meant me to go. I saw visible evidence of this, a gold signet ring which I wear today, a heavy bit of business inscribed arsy-turvy with lions and flora and a motto, *nulla vestigium retrorsit.* "Don't look back" I was told it meant.

After Yale—class of late nineteen-twenty something, or early nineteen-thirty something—my father batted around the country, living a high life in New York among school and college chums, flying as a test pilot, marrying my mother, the daughter of a rear admiral. I was born a year after the marriage, in 1937, and three years after that my father went to England as a fighter pilot with Eagle Squadron, a group of American volunteers in the Royal Air Force. Later he transferred to the OSS, and was in Yugoslavia with the partisans; just before the Invasion he was parachuted into Normandy, where he served as a sapper with the Resistance, which my father pronounced *ray-zee-staunce.*

His career following the war was for me mysterious in its particulars; in the service of his nation, it was understood, candor was not always possible. This much was clear: my father mattered in the world, and was satisfied that he mattered, whether or not the world understood precisely why he mattered.

A pretty history for an American clubman. Its fault is that it was not true. My father was a bullshit artist. True, there were many boarding schools, each less pleased with the little Duke than the last, but none of them was Groton. There was not Yale, and by the time he walked from a room at a mention of Skull and Bones I knew this, and he knew that I knew it. No military service would have him: his teeth were bad. So he had his teeth pulled and replaced, but the Air Corps and Navy and Army and Coast Guard still thought he was a bad idea. The ring I wear was made according to his instructions by a jeweler two blocks from Schwab's drugstore in Hollywood, and was never paid for. The motto, engraved backwards so that it would come right on a red wax seal, is dog Latin and means in fact "leave no trace behind," but my father did not believe me when I told him this.

My father was a Jew. This did not seem to him a good idea, and so it was his notion to disassemble his history, begin at zero, and re-create himself. His sustaining line of work till shortly before he died was as a confidence man. If I now find his authentic history more surprising, more interesting, than his counterfeit history, he did not. He would not make peace with his actualities, and so he was the author of his own circumstances, and indifferent to the consequences of this nervy program.

There were some awful consequences, for other people as well as for him. He was lavish with money, with others' money. He preferred to stiff institutions: jewelers, car dealers, banks, fancy hotels. He was, that is, a thoughtful buccaneer, when thoughtfulness was convenient. But people were hurt by him. Much of his mischief was casual enough. I lost a tooth when I was six, and the Tooth Fairy, "financially inconvenienced" or "temporarily out of pocket," whichever was then his locution, left under my pillow an IOU, a sight draft for two bits, or two million.

I wish he hadn't selected from among the world's possible disguises the costume and credentials of a yacht club commodore. Beginning at scratch he might have reached further, tried something a bit more bold and odd, a bit less inexorably conventional, a bit less calculated to please. But it is true, of course, that a confidence man who cannot inspire confidence in his marks is nothing at all, so perhaps his tuneup of his bloodline, educational *vita*, and war record was merely the price of doing business in a culture preoccupied with appearances.

I'm not even now certain what I wish he had made of himself: I once believed that he was most naturally a fictioneer. But for all his preoccupation with make-believe, he never tried seriously to write it. A confidence man learns early in his career that to commit himself to paper is to court trouble. The successful bunco artist does his game, and disappears himself: Who was that masked man? No one, no one at all, *nulla vestigium [sic] retrorsit [sic]*, not a trace left behind.

Well, I'm left behind. One day, writing about my father with no want of astonishment and love, it came to me that I am his creature as well as his get. I cannot now shake this conviction, that I was trained as his instrument of perpetuation, put here to put him into the record. And that my father knew this, calculated it to a degree. How else explain his eruption of rage when I once gave up what he and I called "writing" for journalism? I had taken a job as the book critic of *The Washington Post*, was proud of myself: it seemed then like a wonderful job, honorable and enriching. My father saw it otherwise: "You have failed me," he wrote, "you have sold yourself at discount" he wrote to me, his prison number stamped below his name.

He was wrong then, but he was usually right about me. He would listen to anything I wished to tell him, but would not tell me only what I wished to hear. He retained such solicitude for his clients. With me he was strict and straight, except about himself. And so I want to be strict and straight with him, and with myself. Writing to a friend about this book, I said that I would not now for anything have had my father be other than what he was, except happier, and that most of the time he was happy enough, cheered on by imaginary successes. He gave me a great deal, and not merely life, and I didn't want to bellyache; I wanted, I told my friend, to thumb my nose on his behalf at everyone who had limited him. My friend was shrewd, though, and said that he didn't believe me, that I couldn't mean such a thing, that if I followed out its implications I would be led to a kind of ripe sentimentality, and to mere piety. Perhaps, he wrote me, you would not have wished him to lie to himself, to lie about being a Jew. Perhaps you would have him fool others but not so deeply trick himself. "In writing about a father," my friend wrote me about our fathers, "one clambers up a slippery mountain, carrying the balls of another in a bloody sack, and whether to eat them or worship them or bury them decently is never cleanly decided."

So I will try here to be exact. I wish my father had done more head-long, more elegant inventing. I believe he would respect my wish, be willing to speak with me seriously about it, find some nobility in it. But now he is dead, and he had been dead two weeks when they found him. And in his tiny flat at the edge of the Pacific they found no address book, no batch of letters held with a rubber band, no photograph. Not a thing to suggest that he had ever known another human being.

POSSIBILITIES FOR WRITING

1. What is your response to Wolff's description of his father? Do the pieces seem to add up? What about Wolff's writing evokes your response?

2. What legacy does Wolff inherit from his father? What value does this legacy have for him? What is the importance for Geoffrey Wolff of writing about his father's life?

3. Wolff quotes a letter from a friend which suggests the complexity of the feelings of adult children for their parents. Try writing about a parent without platitudes and sentimentality but honestly describing both strengths and failings.

Mary Wollstonecraft (1759–1797), a radical feminist centuries before the term had been coined, was born in London to a well-off family whose fortune was squandered by her dissolute father. Forced to earn a living, she took on the only jobs open to an educated woman of the time: schoolmistress, companion, and governess. In her mid-twenties, Wollstonecraft became part of a circle of radical English thinkers and artists, and in 1790 she published A Vindication of the Rights of Man, *an impassioned defense of the French Revolution which earned her great attention both positive and negative. Even more controversial was her* A Vindication of the Rights of Woman (1792), *a revolutionary examination of the status of women in eighteenth-century society that earned her the epithet "hyena in petticoats." She died of complications related to the birth of her second child, Mary Shelley.*

MARY WOLLSTONECRAFT

A Vindication of the Rights of Woman

Mary Wollstonecraft wrote *A Vindication of the Rights of Woman* as a defense of women's rights and as an encouragement for women to believe in their strength of mind and spirit. In this excerpt, she provides a bracing antidote to the conventional image of women as frail and fragile, delicate and demure. Wollstonecraft will have none of that, as she urges women to abandon the "soft phrases," "delicacy of sentiment," and "refinement of taste," with which they are presumably comfortable and to which they are presumed to have been accustomed. Wollstonecraft dismisses that characterization of her sex as a dangerous way to subordinate women to the control of men. She presents an image of woman, not as a weaker vessel but as an equal vessel, one who should develop her character as a human being on an equal footing with a man.

My own sex, I hope, will excuse me, if I treat them like rational creatures, instead of flattering their *fascinating* graces, and viewing them as if they were in a state of perpetual childhood, unable to stand alone. I earnestly wish to point out in what true dignity and human happiness consists—I wish to persuade women to endeavor to acquire strength, both of mind and body, and to convince them that the soft phrases, susceptibility of heart, delicacy of sentiment, and refinement of taste, are almost synonymous with epithets of weakness, and that those beings who are only the objects of pity and that kind of love, which has been termed its sister, will soon become objects of contempt.

Dismissing, then, those pretty feminine phrases, which the men condescendingly use to soften our slavish dependence, and despising that weak elegancy of mind, exquisite sensibility, and sweet docility of manners, supposed to be the sexual characteristics of the weaker vessel, I wish to show that elegance is inferior to virtue, that the first object of laudable ambition is to obtain a character as a human being, regardless of the distinction of sex; and that secondary views should be brought to this simple touchstone.

This is a rough sketch of my plan; and should I express my conviction with the energetic emotions that I feel whenever I think of the subject, the dictates of experience and reflection will be felt by some of my readers. Animated by this important object, I shall disdain to cull my phrases or polish my style; I aim at being useful, and sincerity will render me unaffected; for, wishing rather to persuade by the force of my arguments, than dazzle by the elegance of my language, I shall not waste my time in rounding periods, or in fabricating the turgid bombast of artificial feelings, which, coming from the head, never reach the heart. I shall be employed about things, not words! and, anxious to render my sex more respectable members of society, I shall try to avoid that flowery diction which has slided from essays into novels, and from novels into familiar letters and conversation.

These pretty superlatives, dropping glibly from the tongue, vitiate the taste, and create a kind of sickly delicacy that runs away from simple unadorned truth; and a deluge of false sentiments and overstretched feelings, stifling the natural emotions of the heart, render the domestic pleasures insipid, that ought to sweeten the exercise of those severe duties, which educate a rational and immortal being for a nobler field of action.

The education of women has, of late, been more attended to than formerly; yet they are still reckoned a frivolous sex, and ridiculed or pitied by the writers who endeavor by satire or instruction to improve them. It is acknowledged that they spend many of the first years of their lives in acquiring a smattering of accomplishments; meanwhile strength of body and mind are sacrificed to libertine notions of beauty, to the desire of establishing themselves—the only way women can rise in the world—by marriage. And this desire making mere animals of them, when they marry they act as such children may be expected to act—they dress; they paint, and nickname God's creatures. Surely these weak beings are only fit for a seraglio!—Can they be expected to govern a family with judgment, or take care of the poor babes whom they bring into the world?

If then it can be fairly deduced from the present conduct of the sex, from the prevalent fondness for pleasure which takes the place of ambition, and those nobler passions that open and enlarge the soul; that the instruction which women have hitherto received has only tended, with the constitution of civil society, to render them insignificant objects of desire—mere propagators of fools!—if it can be proved that in aiming to accomplish them, without cultivating their understandings, they are taken out of their sphere of duties, and made ridiculous and useless when the short-lived bloom of beauty is over,[1] I presume that *rational* men will excuse me for endeavoring to persuade them to become more masculine and respectable.

Indeed the word masculine is only a bugbear: there is little reason to fear that women will acquire too much courage or fortitude; for their apparent inferiority with respect to bodily strength, must render them, in some degree, dependent on men in the various relations of life; but why should it be increased by prejudices that give a sex to virtue, and confound simple truths with sensual reveries?

Women are, in fact, so much degraded by mistaken notions of female excellence, that I do not mean to add a paradox when I assert, that this artificial weakness produces a propensity to tyrannize, and gives birth to cunning, the natural opponent of strength, which leads them to play off those contemptible infantine airs that undermine esteem even whilst they excite desire. Let men become more chaste and modest, and if women do not grow wiser in the same ratio, it will be clear that they have weaker understandings. It seems scarcely necessary to say, that I now speak of the sex in general. Many individuals have more sense than their male relatives; and, as nothing preponderates where there is a constant struggle for an equilibrium, without it has naturally more gravity, some women govern their husbands without degrading themselves, because intellect will always govern.

---

[1] A lively writer, I cannot recollect his name, asks what business women turned of forty have to do in the world?

POSSIBILITIES FOR WRITING

1. Wollstonecraft argues here that what in her day was regarded as proper conduct for women allowed men to define them as weak and frivolous. What conduct does she refer to, and what would she substitute in its place? What advice does she have for men?

2. Wollstonecraft writes that although she is encouraging women to become more masculine, "their apparent inferiority with respect to bodily strength must render them, in some degree, dependent on men in the various relations of life." In the context of her whole argument, what point is she making here? To what extent do you think this attitude still exists today? Why?

3. Would you say that women at the beginning of the twenty-first century have achieved equality with men? You may base your essay on personal observations as well as research if you wish.

Virginia Woolf (1882–1941) was born Virginia Stephen into one of London's most prominent literary families. Essentially self-educated in her father's vast library, by her early twenties Woolf was publishing reviews and critical essays in literary journals. Her first novel appeared in 1915, but it was the publication of Mrs. Dalloway *in 1925 and* To the Lighthouse *in 1927 that established her reputation as an important artistic innovator. Four more novels followed, and her criticism and essays were collected in* The Common Reader *(1925, 1932),* Three Guineas *(1938), and* The Death of the Moth and Other Essays *(1942), edited posthumously by her husband after her tragic suicide. Her* Collected Essays *(1967) numbers four volumes. Woolf is also remembered for* A Room of One's Own *(1929), an early feminist consideration of the difficulties facing women writers.*

VIRGINIA WOOLF

The Death of the Moth

In her classic essay "The Death of the Moth," Virginia Woolf writes memorably about a moth she chances to see while gazing out her window on a sunny September morning. Watching the moth fly within a small square of window pane, Woolf speculates about the life force that animates the moth and about the myriad forms of life she notices in the fields. With his seemingly unflagging energy, the moth represents, for Woolf, the pure energy of "life itself."

Moths that fly by day are not properly to be called moths; they do not excite that pleasant sense of dark autumn nights and ivy-blossom which the commonest yellow-underwing asleep in the shadow of the curtain never fails to rouse in us. They are hybrid creatures, neither gay like butterflies nor sombre like their own species. Nevertheless the present specimen, with his narrow hay-coloured wings, fringed with a tassel of the same colour, seemed to be content with life. It was a pleasant morning, mid-September, mild, benignant, yet with a keener breath than that of the summer months. The plough was already scoring the field opposite the window, and where the share had been, the earth was pressed flat and gleamed with moisture. Such vigour came rolling in from the fields and the down beyond that it was difficult to keep the eyes strictly turned upon the book. The rooks too were keeping one of their annual festivities; soaring round the tree tops until it looked as if a vast net with thousands of black knots in it had been cast up into the air; which, after a few moments sank slowly down upon the trees until every twig seemed to have a knot at the end of it. Then, suddenly, the net would be thrown into the air again in a wider circle this time, with the utmost clamour and vociferation, as though to be thrown into the air and settle slowly down upon the tree tops were a tremendously exciting experience.

The same energy which inspired the rooks, the ploughmen, the horses, and even, it seemed, the lean bare-backed downs, sent the moth fluttering from side to side of his square of the window-pane. One could not help watching him. One was, indeed, conscious of a queer feeling of pity for him. The possibilities of pleasure seemed that morning so enormous and so various that to have only a moth's part in life, and a day moth's at that, appeared a hard fate, and his zest in enjoying his meagre opportunities to the full, pathetic. He flew vigorously to one corner of his compartment, and, after waiting there a second, flew across to the other. What remained for him but to fly to a third corner and then to a fourth? That was all he could do, in spite of the size of the downs, the width of the sky, the far-off smoke of houses, and the romantic voice, now and then, of a steamer out at sea. What he could do he did. Watching him, it seemed as if a fibre, very thin but pure, of the enormous energy of the world had been thrust into his frail and diminutive body. As often as he crossed the pane, I could fancy that a thread of vital light became visible. He was little or nothing but life.

Yet, because he was so small, and so simple a form of the energy that was rolling in at the open window and driving its way through so many narrow and intricate corridors in my own brain and in those of other human beings, there was something marvellous as well as pathetic about him. It was as if someone had taken a tiny bead of pure life and decking it as lightly as possible with down and feathers, had set it dancing and zig-zagging to show us the true nature of life. Thus displayed one could not get over the strangeness of it. One is apt to forget all about life, seeing it humped and bossed and garnished and cumbered so that it has to move with the greatest circumspection and dignity. Again, the thought of all that life might have been had he been born in any other shape caused one to view his simple activities with a kind of pity.

After a time, tired by his dancing apparently, he settled on the window ledge in the sun, and, the queer spectacle being at an end, I forgot about him. Then, looking up, my eye was caught by him. He was trying to resume his dancing, but seemed either so stiff or so awkward that he could only flutter to the bottom of the window-pane;

and when he tried to fly across it he failed. Being intent on other matters I watched these futile attempts for a time without thinking, unconsciously waiting for him to resume his flight, as one waits for a machine, that has stopped momentarily, to start again without considering the reason of its failure. After perhaps a seventh attempt he slipped from the wooden ledge and fell, fluttering his wings, on to his back on the window sill. The helplessness of his attitude roused me. It flashed upon me that he was in difficulties; he could no longer raise himself; his legs struggled vainly. But, as I stretched out a pencil, meaning to help him to right himself, it came over me that the failure and awkwardness were the approach of death. I laid the pencil down again.

The legs agitated themselves once more. I looked as if for the enemy against which he struggled. I looked out of doors. What had happened there? Presumably it was midday, and work in the fields had stopped. Stillness and quiet had replaced the previous animation. The birds had taken themselves off to feed in the brooks. The horses stood still. Yet the power was there all the same, massed outside indifferent, impersonal, not attending to anything in particular. Somehow it was opposed to the little hay-coloured moth. It was useless to try to do anything. One could only watch the extraordinary efforts made by those tiny legs against an oncoming doom which could, had it chosen, have submerged an entire city, not merely a city, but masses of human beings; nothing, I knew, had any chance against death. Nevertheless after a pause of exhaustion the legs fluttered again. It was superb this last protest, and so frantic that he succeeded at last in righting himself. One's sympathies, of course, were all on the side of life. Also, when there was nobody to care or to know, this gigantic effort on the part of an insignificant little moth, against a power of such magnitude, to retain what no one else valued or desired to keep, moved one strangely. Again, somehow, one saw life, a pure bead. I lifted the pencil again, useless though I knew it to be. But even as I did so, the unmistakable tokens of death showed themselves. The body relaxed, and instantly grew stiff. The struggle was over. The insignificant little creature now knew death. As I looked at the dead moth, this minute wayside triumph of so great a force over so mean an antagonist filled me with wonder. Just as life had been strange a few minutes before, so death was now as strange. The moth having righted himself now lay most decently and uncomplainingly composed. O yes, he seemed to say, death is stronger than I am.

POSSIBILITIES FOR WRITING

1. The moth in Woolf's essay becomes a potent symbol for life and then also for death more generally. How does Woolf manage to do this? Point to specific passages in the essay that directly or by implication tie the moth to the world beyond itself.

2. For all its concreteness, this essay is quite philosophical. How would you characterize Woolf's conception of the universe, based on the ideas that this essay provokes?

3. In order to explore your feelings about an abstract concept—love, courage, greed, humility, loss, or another of your choice—construct an essay, as Woolf does, around a central symbol. Describe your symbol in primarily concrete terms so that the concept itself becomes concrete.